Brenda Fonseca
Mesa Community College

STUDY GUIDE
AND
CONCEPT NOTES
FOR
PSYCHOLOGY

SECOND EDITION

Saundra K. Ciccarelli
Gulf Coast Community College

J. Noland White
Georgia College & State University

PEARSON

Prentice
Hall

Upper Saddle River, New Jersey 07458

© 2009 by PEARSON EDUCATION, INC.
Upper Saddle River, New Jersey 07458

10 9 8 7 6 5 4 3 2 1

ISBN 10: 0-13-604127-2
ISBN 13: 978-0-13-604127-6

Contents

YOU KNOW YOU ARE READY FOR THE TEST IF YOU ARE ABLE TO...

- Define psychology and describe the goals that psychologists hope to achieve.
- Describe the history of psychology.
- Discuss the current state of psychology, including the most common perspectives and major professions in the field.
- Describe the scientific method and discuss its strengths and weaknesses.
- Explain the basic guidelines and ethical concerns of psychological research.
- Introduce the criteria for critical thinking and its application in psychology.

RAPID REVIEW

Psychology is defined as the scientific study of behavior and mental processes. The goals of psychology are to describe, explain, predict, and control the behaviors and mental process of both humans and animals. The goals of psychology can be thought of in terms of what, why, when, and how behaviors and mental processes occur.

The field of psychology is relatively new (around 125 years old) but has its origins in the much older fields of physiology and philosophy. Wilhelm Wundt formed the first psychology laboratory in Germany in 1879. Wundt used the method of introspection in an attempt to objectively study human thought processes. Because of his innovative efforts, Wundt is often referred to as the father of psychology. The reality, however, is that multiple people in multiple locations began studying psychology and promoting their particular perspective around the same time. Five historical perspectives are discussed in the text.

Edward Titchener, a student of Wundt's, expanded on Wundt's ideas and brought the method of introspection to the U.S. Titchener called his approach **structuralism** because his ultimate goal was to describe the precise structure of our mental processes. At the same time in the U.S., William James was focused on discovering how our mental processes help us to function in our daily lives and began to promote his viewpoint known as **functionalism**. The terms structuralism and functionalism are no longer used to describe specific viewpoints in the field of psychology. Meanwhile, back in Germany, the **Gestalt psychologists** were studying how sensation and perception create a whole pattern that is greater than the sum of the individual components. Max Wertheimer was a major proponent of Gestalt psychology. In neighboring Austria, Sigmund Freud developed his theory of **psychoanalysis** based on the concept of the unconscious. Freud believed the unconscious played an important role in controlling our day-to-day behaviors and thoughts. Freud's theory is also referred to as the psychodynamic perspective. On the opposite end of the spectrum, and back in the United States, was John Watson. Watson expanded the findings of Russian physiologist Ivan Pavlov, to promote the perspective of **behaviorism**. The behaviorists believed that psychology should focus on concepts that could be studied scientifically and they felt that the only area of psychology that could be approached scientifically was observable behavior.

Today there are seven major perspectives within the field of psychology. The **psychodynamic perspective** focuses on the role of the unconscious. **Behaviorism** attempts to study psychology by focusing on observable actions and events. The **humanistic perspective** emphasizes human potential and free will. **Biopsychology** focuses on the biology underlying our behavior and thoughts, while the **cognitive perspective** focuses on the thoughts or "cognitions" themselves. **Cognitive neuroscience** is a specific area of the cognitive perspective that focuses on the physical changes in the brain that occur when we think, remember, or engage in other mental processes. The **sociocultural perspective** explores the role of social and cultural factors on our behaviors and thoughts, while **evolutionary** psychologists attempt to explain behavior and thoughts in terms of their adaptive or "survival" qualities.

There are many professional opportunities within the field of psychology. **Psychiatrists** receive a medical degree (M.D.), treat serious psychological disorders, and can prescribe medication for their patients. A **psychologist** attends graduate school to obtain a doctorate degree (either a Ph.D., Ed.D. or Psy.D.) and can select one of many career options from research to counseling to consulting for a business. A **psychoanalyst** is a psychiatrist or psychologist who has received special training in Freud's method of psychoanalysis. A **psychiatric social worker** receives a Master of Social Work degree (M.S.W.) and provides counseling to patients or possibly conducts research.

Psychologists use the **scientific method** to reduce bias and error in their observations. The steps of the scientific method include asking a question, turning your question into a **hypothesis** - a statement about what you believe the actual answer is, testing your hypothesis, drawing a conclusion, and reporting your findings. Your findings can then be further strengthened if other researchers conduct a study and draw the same conclusions as you did, or in other words if other researchers **replicate** your findings. The method you use to test your hypothesis depends on which of the four goals of psychology you are attempting to achieve. If you would like to answer the question of "what" (goal = describe), you would use a descriptive method. **Naturalistic observation** provides a realistic picture of behavior but can become biased through the **observer effect** (subjects act differently when they know they are being watched) and **observer bias** (the researcher only sees what he or she wants to see). Laboratory observation is similar to naturalistic observation but the participants are observed in a laboratory setting instead of "out in nature." Sometimes a researcher will disguise herself as an actual participant in order to reduce the observer effect. This approach is called **participant observation**. A **case study** is a detailed investigation of one individual, or case, and can provide a great deal of information about that one person but is hard to generalize to a larger population. For a **survey**, researchers ask a group of subjects a series of questions. Surveys allow researchers to gather a lot of information quickly. However, with a survey there is no guarantee that the subjects will answer the questions truthfully. Also, researchers must be sure to take a **representative sample** of the **population** they are interested in. A researcher interested in discovering the relationship between two variables would use the **correlational method**. A **correlation coefficient** tells the researcher the direction and strength of the relationship. The coefficient will always be a number between -1.00 and +1.00. A correlation shows that a relationship between two variables exists, but cannot explain the cause of the relationship. In order to answer the question of "why," a researcher must conduct an experiment. Remember the example with the churches and the bars. The new churches did not cause the construction of the new bars. In an **experiment**, the researcher manipulates a variable (the **independent variable**) and measures some response from the participants (the **dependent variable**). In order to measure the dependent variable, the researcher must come up with an **operational definition** for the variable. An operational definition is a set of instructions that explains exactly how to measure the variable. For example, aggressive behavior could be operationally defined as the number of times a subject swings a toy sword in a five-minute observation period. The overall goal of the experiment is to keep everything the same except the independent variable. In order to accomplish this, the researcher usually observes two groups: an **experimental group** and a **control group**. The researcher will most likely use **random assignment** to determine which participants will go in which group. Often, the control group receives a fake treatment in order to control for the **placebo effect** in which the participant's expectations actually influence the results of the experiment. Normally, the subjects are not told which group they are in (**single-blind study**). In order to control for any expectations the experimenter might have (the **experimenter effect**) the study is often designed so that neither the participants nor the experimenter know who is in what group (**double-blind study**). All psychological research must follow the ethical guidelines specified by the American Psychological Association.

Understanding the scientific method can help you in your daily life as you apply the four principles of **critical thinking** to problems you face day to day. The four criteria are that (1) most truths need to be tested, (2) all evidence is not equal, (3) authorities are not always right, and (4) an open mind is still important.

STUDY HINTS

1. Be careful not to confuse the independent variable (i.v.) with the dependent variable (d.v.). The independent variable is the variable the researcher manipulates her or himself. If you think about it as if you were the researcher conducting the experiment, the independent variable is the one that **I** control. Another way to make sure you have correctly labeled the variables in an experiment is to insert the variable names into the following phrase and make sure it still makes sense. The test phrase is:

$$\text{How} \underline{\hspace{2cm}} \text{affects} \underline{\hspace{2cm}}.$$
$$\text{\small (i.v.)} \qquad\qquad \text{\small (d.v.)}$$

Here is an example for you to practice using the test phrase.

> *A researcher conducts a study looking at the color of different rooms and aggressiveness. She takes a group of 40 college students and randomly assigns 20 to the red room and 20 to the blue room. After the students have been in the rooms for 30 minutes, she measures each person's aggressiveness level on a scale of 1 to 10. In this experiment, which variable is the independent variable and which is the dependent? Try inserting the variable names into the phrase above.*

You can see that "How aggressiveness affects room color" does not make sense and is not what the researcher is interested in. However, "How room color affects aggressiveness" does correspond to the researchers' goals. So in this case, the room color is the independent variable and aggressiveness is the dependent variable.

Try one more example.

> *A researcher conducts an experiment to study memory skills and caffeine intake. The researcher has a total of 20 volunteer subjects. He gives 10 subjects a can of caffeinated soda and the other 10 subjects receive a can of decaffeinated soda. He then has all the subjects complete a memory task. What are his independent and dependent variables? Try inserting the variable names into the phrase above.*

Again, you can see that "How memory skills affect caffeine intake" does not make sense and is not what the researcher is interested in. However, "How caffeine intake affects memory skills" does correspond to the researcher's goals. So in this case, the caffeine intake is the independent variable and memory skill is the dependent variable.

2. The concept of operational definitions is introduced in this chapter. An operational definition can be thought of as a recipe telling a researcher precisely how to make her observations. In other words, they define the operations or procedures the researcher should go through in order to record her data. Operational definitions are based on behaviors and actions that can be observed and they are much different than the definitions given in a standard dictionary. For example, the dictionary might define fear as feeling anxious or apprehensive about a possible situation. However, that definition does not tell the researcher how to measure one individual's level of fear. On the other hand, the researcher might operationally define fear as the percent increase in heart rate from a baseline level during a two-minute observation period.

Try this example yourself.

Dictionary Definition of anger: _____

Operational Definition of anger: _____

The dictionary might define anger as a strong feeling of displeasure. However, an operational definition of anger might be something like the number of times an adult slams his or her fists on the table.

Now, try to figure out what variable is being operationally defined below.

The number of times a person laughs within a five-minute period.

Operational Definition of _____:

The score an individual receives on an IQ test.

Operational Definition of _____:

The first example is operationally defining the variable of happiness and the second example gives an operational definition for intelligence.

LEARNING OBJECTIVES

1.1   What defines psychology as a field of study, and what are psychology's four primary goals?

1.2   How did structuralism and functionalism differ, and who were the important people in those early fields?

1.3   What were the basic ideas and who were the important people behind the early approaches known as Gestalt, psychoanalysis, and behaviorism?

1.4   What are the basic ideas behind the seven modern perspectives, as well as the important contributions of Skinner, Maslow, and Rogers?

1.5   How does a psychiatrist differ from a psychologist, and what are the other types of professionals who work in the various areas of psychology?

1.6   Why is psychology considered a science, and what are the steps in using the scientific method?

1.7   How are naturalistic and laboratory settings used to describe behavior, and what are some of the advantages and disadvantages associated with these settings?

1.8   How are case studies and surveys used to describe behavior, and what are some drawbacks to each of these methods?

1.9   What is the correlational technique, and what does it tell researchers about relationships?

1.10   How are operational definitions, independent and dependent variables, experimental and control groups, and random assignment used in designing an experiment?

1.11   Why are the placebo and the experimenter effects problems for an experiment, and how can single-blind and double-blind studies control for these effects?

1.12   What are the basic elements of Amabile's creativity experiment?

1.13   What are some ethical concerns that can occur when conducting research with people and animals?

1.14   What are the basic principles of critical thinking, and how can critical thinking be useful in everyday life?

PRACTICE EXAM

For the following multiple choice questions, select the answer you feel best answers the question.

1. How is psychology different from philosophy?
    a) Psychology uses the scientific method to answer questions.
    b) Psychology is interested in questions related to human behavior.
    c) There is no difference between philosophy and psychology.
    d) The field of psychology is much older than the field of philosophy.

2. A researcher is attempting to design a program to help people stop smoking. The goal she is attempting to achieve is to
   a) describe.
   b) predict.
   c) explain.
   d) control.

3. A researcher is interested in finding out the percentage of adolescents in the U.S. who have depression. The goal he is attempting to achieve is to
   a) describe.
   b) predict.
   c) explain.
   d) control.

4. Which of the following research questions would NOT fall within the field of psychology?
   a) How can you increase the amount of time a female bird stays with its mate after the birdlings hatch?
   b) What changes occur in the brain of a rat that has been deprived of sleep?
   c) Why do students perform better on exams when the exam is given in the same room in which they learned the material?
   d) All of the questions above could be studied by a psychologist.

5. The first psychology laboratory was opened in _____ in order to study _____.
   a) 1065, psychological disorders
   b) 1946, learning
   c) 1879, introspection
   d) 1809, biopsychology

6. Which of these is the most accurate definition of the discipline of psychology?
   a) the science of behavior
   b) the science of mental processes
   c) the science of behavior and mental processes
   d) the science of human behavior and mental processes

7. The psychological perspective of structuralism focused on
   a) how the whole structure is bigger than the individual parts.
   b) understanding each individual structure of human thought.
   c) how mental thought helps us structure our daily activities.
   d) the structure of society at large.

8. The school of psychology called *structuralism* used a technique called _____, which involved reporting the contents of consciousness to study a person's experiences.
   a) intervention
   b) introspection
   c) insight inventory
   d) induction

9. William James believed that mental processes could not be studied as an isolated, static event but instead needed to be viewed in terms of how they helped people perform in their daily lives. James was a strong proponent for
   a) structuralism.
   b) functionalism.

      c)   behaviorism.

      d)   the humanistic perspective.

10.   Gestalt psychologists are associated with which of the following sayings?
      a)   The pineal gland is the seat of the human soul.
      b)   Psychology should reach into the soul of mankind.
      c)   Behavior should be broken down into its individual components.
      d)   The whole is greater than the sum of its parts.

11.   Freud said phobias were _____ whereas Watson said phobias were _____.
      a)   learned; inherited
      b)   repressed conflicts; learned
      c)   sexual; unconscious
      d)   conditioned; unconditioned

12.   Which of the following statements would Sigmund Freud have most likely been overheard saying?
      a)   "Human behavior is largely determined by our own free will."
      b)   "The only way to understand behavior is to study behavior."
      c)   "We will never understand why people do the things they do."
      d)   "The key to understanding behavior is in the unconscious."

13.   What was John Watson's biggest complaint about the field of psychology?
      a)   Psychologists were attempting to study nonobservable events using the scientific method.
      b)   Psychology was not focused enough on the free will of humans.
      c)   Psychologists were ignoring the role of the unconscious in determining behavior.
      d)   Psychologists were spending too much time doing research.

14.   A researcher who studies the chemical changes in the brains of patients with depression would be approaching psychology from which perspective?
      a)   behaviorist
      b)   psychodynamic
      c)   cognitive
      d)   biopsychological

15.   One of the reasons psychodynamic theories have persisted over the years is that they are
   _____.
      a)   supported by significant scientific research
      b)   based on facts
      c)   difficult to scientifically test and, thus, difficult to disprove
      d)   used by the majority of psychologists

16.   A humanistic psychologist would be interested in which of the following research studies?
      a)   describing a group of people who claim to have reached their full potential
      b)   understanding the role of the unconscious in a child's decision to disobey her parents
      c)   investigating the role of hormones in the mating behavior of birds
      d)   figuring out visual illusions are possible

17.   Cognitive psychologists are interested in
      a)   social interactions.
      b)   the adaptive value of particular behaviors.
      c)   mental processes.
      d)   the unconscious.

18. Taylor received her degree from a medical school and now meets with patients on a daily basis. Most of her patients have a serious psychological disorder and often Taylor will prescribe medication to treat the disorder. Taylor is a
    a) psychologist.
    b) psychiatrist.
    c) psychiatric social worker.
    d) school nurse.

19. Vido has an M.S.W. and is interested in working on the causes of poverty. What type of professional is Vido most likely to become?
    a) educational psychologist
    b) psychiatrist
    c) school psychologist
    d) psychiatric social worker

20. Why do psychologists use the scientific method?
    a) It is easier to use than other methods.
    b) All academic fields must use the scientific method.
    c) It is the only method available to answer questions.
    d) It reduces bias and error in measurement.

21. The tendency to look for information that supports one's own belief is called _____.
    a) the principle of falsifiability
    b) confirmation bias
    c) criterion validity
    d) volunteer bias

22. Deb spent the entire day at the park observing children with their parents to see whether fathers or mothers spent more time playing with their kids. Deb used the method of
    a) naturalistic observation.
    b) laboratory observation.
    c) survey.
    d) case study.

23. Which of the following topics would be best studied using the case study method?
    a) the reaction times of adults in a stressful situation
    b) the sleep pattern of adolescents
    c) the impact of club sports involvement on female adolescent self-esteem
    d) the personality characteristics of a man accused of killing five people

24. What is an advantage of the survey method?
    a) nonrepresentative samples
    b) courtesy bias
    c) large amounts of information
    d) observer bias

25. A researcher stops people at the mall and asks them questions about their attitudes toward gun control. Which research technique is being used?
    a) survey
    b) experiment
    c) case study
    d) naturalistic observation

26. A group of randomly selected subjects that matches the population on important characteristics such as age and sex is called _____.
   a) volunteer bias
   b) a representative sample
   c) the experimental group
   d) the control group

27. The word *correlation* is often used as a synonym for _____.
   a) validity
   b) reliability
   c) variable
   d) relationship

28. Which of the following correlation coefficients represents the strongest relationship between two variables?
   a) +0.62
   b) -0.98
   c) +0.01
   d) +1.24

29. A researcher finds that as the number of classes missed increases, the students' grades decrease. This is an example of a
   a) positive correlation.
   b) negative correlation.
   c) zero correlation.
   d) case study.

30. Marcy is trying to define *anxiety* in a way that can be empirically tested. She is attempting to find an appropriate _____.
   a) hypothesis
   b) operational definition
   c) double-blind study
   d) theory

31. A researcher is investigating the effects of exercise on weight. What are the independent and dependent variables in this experiment?
   a) The dependent variable is weight; the independent variable is exercise.
   b) The independent variable is calories consumed; the dependent variable is diet.
   c) The independent variable is weight; the dependent variable is calories consumed.
   d) The dependent variable is amount of exercise; the independent variable is calories consumed.

32. In a laboratory, smokers are asked to "drive" using a computerized driving simulator equipped with a stick shift and a gas pedal. The object is to maximize the distance covered by driving as fast as possible on a winding road while avoiding rear-end collisions. Some of the participants smoke a real cigarette immediately before climbing into the driver's seat. Others smoke a fake cigarette without nicotine. You are interested in comparing how many collisions the two groups have. In this study, the *cigarette without nicotine* is _____.
   a) the control group
   b) the driving simulator
   c) the experimental group
   d) the no-control group

33. A psychology professor feels that her students will do better on her exams if there is music playing while they take their exams. To test her hypothesis she divides her class in half. One half takes the exam in a room with music playing and the other half takes the exam in a similar room but without the music playing. In this case, the independent variable is
    a) the room the exam is taken in.
    b) the absence or presence of music playing.
    c) the exam.
    d) the students' scores on the exam.

34. For the experiment described in Question 33, the dependent variable is
    a) the room the exam is taken in.
    b) the absence or presence of music playing.
    c) the exam.
    d) the students' scores on the exam.

35. Twenty volunteers are brought into a sleep laboratory in the evening. Ten are allowed eight hours of sleep while the other ten are only allowed two hours of sleep. In the morning, all 20 subjects are tested for their reaction time in a driving simulation program. For this experiment, the reaction time in the simulation program is the
    a) independent variable.
    b) dependent variable.
    c) confounding variable.
    d) random variable.

36. For the experiment described in Question 35, the amount of sleep allowed is the
    a) independent variable.
    b) dependent variable.
    c) confounding variable.
    d) random variable.

37. Which of the following situations best illustrates the placebo effect?
    a) You sleep because you are tired.
    b) You throw up after eating bad meat.
    c) You have surgery to repair a defective heart valve.
    d) You drink a nonalcoholic drink and become "intoxicated" because you think it contains alcohol.

38. _____ is an experiment in which neither the participants nor the individuals running the experiment know if participants are in the experimental or the control group until after the results are tallied.
    a) The double-blind study
    b) Field research
    c) The single-blind study
    d) Correlational research

39. Dr. Teresa Amabile conducted an actual experiment in which she had two groups of girls aged 7 to 10 years create artwork in the classroom. One group was told that the girl with the best artwork would receive a prize at the end of the session, and the other group was told that prizes would be raffled off when the session was over. Amabile then measured the level of creativity for the artwork in both groups and found that the second group had higher levels of creativity. In this experiment, the dependent variable is the

a) prize.
b) level of creativity.
c) way the prize was distributed.
d) group of girls.

40. Each of the following is a common ethical guideline suggested by the American Psychological Association EXCEPT _____.
   a) participants must be informed of the nature of the research in clearly understandable language
   b) participants cannot be deceived or have information concealed from them at any time during an experiment
   c) risks, possible adverse effects, and limitations on confidentiality must be spelled out in advance
   d) informed consent must be documented

41. Which of the following is NOT one of the four principles of critical thinking?
   a) All truths need to be tested.
   b) An open mind is always important.
   c) Authorities can almost always be trusted.
   d) All evidence is not equal.

42. Which of the following questions applies the concept of critical thinking to the real world pseudo-psychology of astrology?
   a) What is my astrological sign?
   b) What does my astrological sign predict will happen to me today?
   c) How up to date are the charts used by astrologists today?
   d) Should I marry someone that is the same sign as I?

PRACTICE EXAM ANSWERS

1. a   Psychology bases its answers on observations, while philosophy answers its questions using logic and reasoning. Both fields are interested in human behavior. The field of psychology is only 125 years old, while philosophy is much older.

2. d   She is trying to change people's behaviors. This corresponds to the question of "how" (in other words, "How" do I help people to stop smoking?).

3. a   He would like to describe this particular group with regards to depression rates. He is trying to answer the question of "what." What is the current depression rate among U.S. teenagers?

4. d   All of the questions fall under the category of describing, predicting, explaining, or controlling behavior and/or mental processes of humans and animals.

5. c   Wilhelm Wundt opened his laboratory in Germany in 1879 and used the method of introspection to study the basic elements of mental processes.

6. c   Psychology deals with both behavior and mental processes and includes other animals besides humans.

7   b   Structuralists felt that mental processes had to be broken down into their most basic or elemental form in order to be understood.

8. b   Introspection was used in an attempt to self-examine the structure of the mind. Although the word "intervention" looks similar, it has a completely different meaning.

9. b   James believed we need to understand the <u>function</u> of mental processes.

10. d   Gestalt psychologists believed that you had to look at the whole picture in order to understand the larger processes of perception and sensation and that it could not be broken down into its smaller components without losing its essence.

11. b   Freud studied repressed (unconscious) conflict and Watson studied observable behavior. Watson did not believe that the unconscious could be studied scientifically.

12. d   Sigmund Freud was a major proponent of the perspective of psychoanalysis, which emphasizes the role of the unconscious on human behavior.

13. a   John Watson started the idea of behaviorism that states the only subject matter that can be scientifically studied is observable behavior.

14. d   The biopsychological perspective focuses on studying the biological changes that underlie behavior and mental processes.

15. c   Since it is very hard to scientifically test the psychodynamic theories there is little scientific data to support the theories.

16. a   The humanistic perspective focuses on the uniqueness and potential of human beings and tries to suggest ways for humans to maximize their potential.

17. d   Cognitive psychologists focus on "cognitions" or mental processes, including topics such as memory, decision making, problem solving, perception, language comprehension, creativity, and reasoning.

18. b   Psychiatrists have M.D.s, counsel patients with serious disorders, and can prescribe medications.

19. d   Psychiatric social workers typically have their Masters of Social Work (M.S.W.) and counsel patients with less severe disorders or focus on social issues such as poverty.

20. d   The scientific method is based on observations so that the influence of the researcher's bias is minimized.

21. b   The principle of falsifiability is not an actual principle in psychology.

22. a   Naturalistic observation consists of recording behaviors as they occur in their normal settings.

23. d   A case study focuses on one individual (or "case") and provides a detailed description of that individual.

24. c   A survey allows the researcher to collect a large amount of information quickly. The other three options are all potential disadvantages of the survey method.

25. a   A survey asks the same questions of many people, while naturalistic observation never involves asking questions.

26. b   A representative sample is a randomly selected group that matches the population on important characteristics. An experimental group is not necessarily representative of the population.

27. d   Correlation means relationship between two variables.

28. b   The correlation coefficient must be between +1.00 and -1.00 so option D is automatically excluded. The sign of the coefficient indicates the direction of the relationship and the absolute value of the coefficient indicates the strength; therefore, 0.98 is the largest absolute value listed between 0 and 1.

29. b   For a negative correlation, the variables move in the opposite direction. As one variable increases the other one decreases. In this case, as the number of absences increase the grade in class decreases.

30. b   An operational definition defines responses in terms that allow them to be measured, while a hypothesis is an educated guess, not a definition.

31. a   The exercise is controlled by the experimenter and is, therefore, *independent* of anything the participants do, while the participants' weight is expected to *depend* on the amount of exercise.

32. a   A control group gets either no treatment or treatment that has no effect (in this case, experimenters are controlling for the possibility that the cigarette itself, and not the nicotine, might cause people to get into collisions).

33. b   The independent variable is the variable the researcher manipulates. In this case, the instructor manipulated whether there was music playing or not.

34.   d   Recall the test phrase, "How _____(*i.v.*) affects _____ (*d.v.*). The professor is testing "How music affects student test scores." The dependent variable is the subjects' responses. The room the test is taken in and the test itself should be the same for both groups.

35.   b   The reaction time is the response observed in the subject. It is not manipulated by the experimenter.

36.   a   Recall the test phrase, "How hours slept affects driving reaction time."

37.   d   The placebo effect is brought on by expectations, and in this case you felt drunk only because you believed you were drinking alcohol.

38.   a   The double-blind study is an experiment in which neither the participants nor the individuals running the experiment know if the participants are in the experimental or control group. In a single-blind study, only the participants are "blind."

39.   b   Dr. Amabile was looking at "how method of reward affects creativity," and creativity serves as the dependent variable.

40.   b   Participants may be deceived or have information concealed from them at any time during an experiment.

41.   c   Simply because someone is an authority, does not mean they should automatically be trusted.

42.   c   Critical thinking involves making reasoned judgments and questioning the basis that others are using to make judgments, such as in response c.

CHAPTER GLOSSARY

behaviorism	the science of behavior that focuses on observable behavior only.
biopsychological perspective	perspective that attributes human and animal behavior to biological events occurring in the body, such as genetic influences, hormones, and the activity of the nervous system.
case study	study of one individual in great detail; modern perspective that focuses on memory, intelligence, perception, problem solving, and learning.
cognitive neuroscience	study of the physical changes in the brain and nervous system that occur during thinking or other mental processes.
cognitive perspective	modern perspective that focuses on memory, intelligence, perception, problem solving, and learning.
control group	subjects in an experiment that are not subjected to the independent variable and who may receive a placebo treatment.
correlation	a measure of the relationship between two variables.
correlation coefficient	a number for measuring a correlation that indicates the strength and the direction of the relationship between the two variables.
critical thinking	making reasoned judgments about claims.
dependent variable	variable in an experiment that represents the measurable response or behavior of the subjects in the experiment.
double-blind study	study in which neither the experimenter nor the subjects know if the subjects are in the experimental or control group.
evolutionary perspective	perspective that focuses on the biological bases of universal mental characteristics that all humans share.
experiment	a deliberate manipulation of a variable to see if corresponding changes in behavior result, allowing the determination of cause and effect relationships.
experimental group	subjects in an experiment that are subjected to the independent variable.

experimenter effect	tendency of the experimenter's expectations for a study to unintentionally influence the results of the study.
functionalism	early perspective in psychology associated with William James, in which the focus of study is how the mind allows people to adapt, live, work, and play.
Gestalt psychology	early perspective in psychology focusing on perception and sensation, particularly the perception of patterns and whole figures.
humanistic perspective	perspective that emphasizes human potential and the idea that people have the freedom to choose their own destiny.
hypothesis	a statement about some event that can then be tested through observation.
independent variable	variable in an experiment that is manipulated by the experimenter.
introspection	the process of examining and measuring one's own thoughts and mental activities.
naturalistic observation	study in which the researcher observes people or animals in their normal environment.
observer bias	tendency of observers to see what they expect to see.
observer effect	tendency of people or animals to behave differently from normal when they know they are being observed.
operational definition	definition of a variable of interest that allows it to be directly measured.
placebo effect	the phenomenon in which the expectations of the participants in a study can influence their behavior.
population	the entire group of people or animals that the researcher is interested in.
psychiatric social worker	a social worker with some training in therapy methods who focuses on environmental conditions that can have an impact on mental disorders, such as poverty, overcrowding, stress, and drug abuse.
psychiatrist	a medical doctor who has specialized in the diagnosis and treatment of psychological disorders.
psychoanalysis	the theory and therapy based on the work of Sigmund Freud.
psychoanalyst	either a psychiatrist or a psychologist who has special training in the theories of Sigmund Freud and his method of psychoanalysis.
psychodynamic perspective	modern version of psychoanalysis that is more focused on the development of a sense of self and the discovery of other motivations behind a person's behavior than sexual motivations.
psychologist	a professional with an academic degree and specialized training in one or more areas of psychology.
psychology	the scientific study of behavior and mental processes.
random assignment	process of assigning subjects to the experimental or control groups randomly, so that each subject has an equal chance of being in either group.
replicate	in research, repeating a study or experiment to see if the same results will be obtained in an effort to demonstrate reliability of results.
representative sample	randomly selected sample of subjects from a larger population.
scientific method	system of gathering data so that bias and error in measurement are reduced.
single-blind study	study in which the subjects do not know if they are in the experimental or the control group.
sociocultural perspective	perspective that focuses on the relationship between social behavior and culture.
structuralism	early perspective in psychology associated with Wilhelm Wundt and Edward Titchener, in which the focus of study is the structure or basic elements of the mind.
survey	study conducted by asking a series of questions to a group of people.

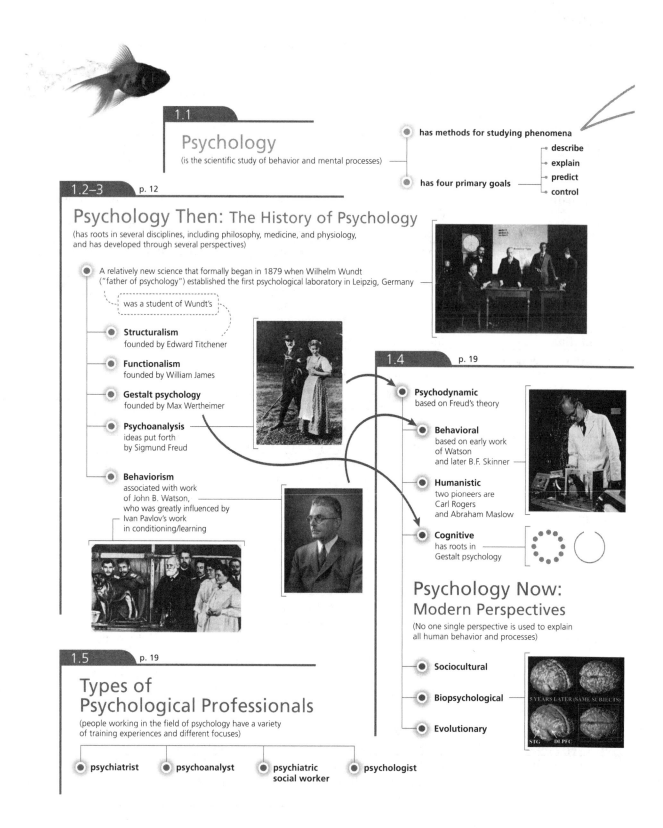

1.1

Psychology
(is the scientific study of behavior and mental processes)

- has methods for studying phenomena
  - describe
  - explain
  - predict
  - control
- has four primary goals

1.2–3   p. 12

Psychology Then: The History of Psychology
(has roots in several disciplines, including philosophy, medicine, and physiology, and has developed through several perspectives)

A relatively new science that formally began in 1879 when Wilhelm Wundt ("father of psychology") established the first psychological laboratory in Leipzig, Germany

was a student of Wundt's

Structuralism
founded by Edward Titchener

Functionalism
founded by William James

Gestalt psychology
founded by Max Wertheimer

Psychoanalysis
ideas put forth
by Sigmund Freud

Behaviorism
associated with work
of John B. Watson,
who was greatly influenced by
Ivan Pavlov's work
in conditioning/learning

1.4   p. 19

Psychodynamic
based on Freud's theory

Behavioral
based on early work
of Watson
and later B.F. Skinner

Humanistic
two pioneers are
Carl Rogers
and Abraham Maslow

Cognitive
has roots in
Gestalt psychology

Psychology Now:
Modern Perspectives
(No one single perspective is used to explain all human behavior and processes)

Sociocultural

Biopsychological

Evolutionary

1.5   p. 19

Types of Psychological Professionals
(people working in the field of psychology have a variety of training experiences and different focuses)

psychiatrist   psychoanalyst   psychiatric social worker   psychologist

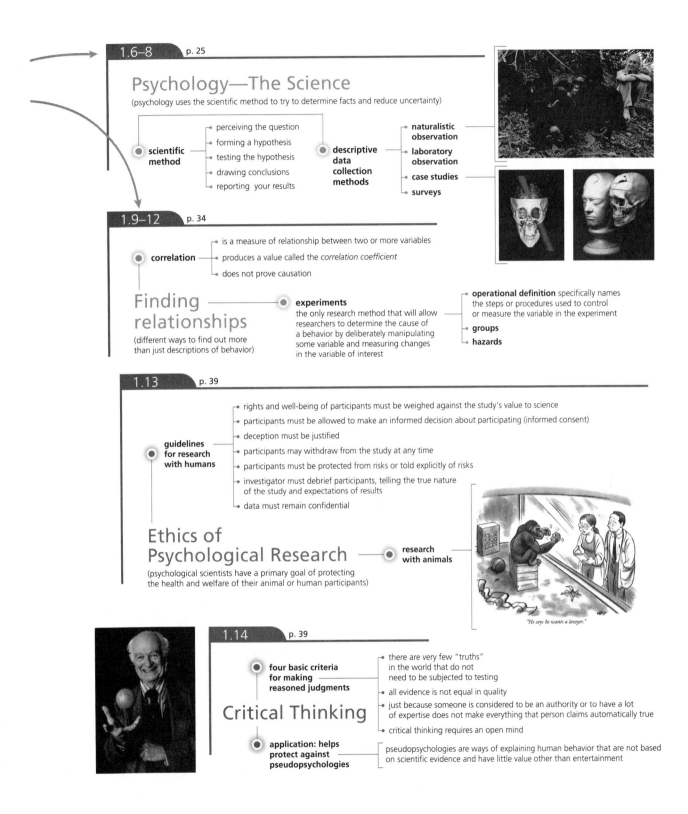

1.6–8   p. 25

Psychology—The Science

(psychology uses the scientific method to try to determine facts and reduce uncertainty)

- **scientific method**
  - perceiving the question
  - forming a hypothesis
  - testing the hypothesis
  - drawing conclusions
  - reporting your results
- **descriptive data collection methods**
  - naturalistic observation
  - laboratory observation
  - case studies
  - surveys

1.9–12   p. 34

- **correlation**
  - is a measure of relationship between two or more variables
  - produces a value called the *correlation coefficient*
  - does not prove causation

Finding relationships

(different ways to find out more than just descriptions of behavior)

- **experiments**
  the only research method that will allow researchers to determine the cause of a behavior by deliberately manipulating some variable and measuring changes in the variable of interest
  - **operational definition** specifically names the steps or procedures used to control or measure the variable in the experiment
  - **groups**
  - **hazards**

1.13   p. 39

- **guidelines for research with humans**
  - rights and well-being of participants must be weighed against the study's value to science
  - participants must be allowed to make an informed decision about participating (informed consent)
  - deception must be justified
  - participants may withdraw from the study at any time
  - participants must be protected from risks or told explicitly of risks
  - investigator must debrief participants, telling the true nature of the study and expectations of results
  - data must remain confidential

Ethics of Psychological Research

(psychological scientists have a primary goal of protecting the health and welfare of their animal or human participants)

- **research with animals**

"He says he wants a lawyer."

1.14   p. 39

- **four basic criteria for making reasoned judgments**
  - there are very few "truths" in the world that do not need to be subjected to testing
  - all evidence is not equal in quality
  - just because someone is considered to be an authority or to have a lot of expertise does not make everything that person claims automatically true
  - critical thinking requires an open mind

Critical Thinking

- **application: helps protect against pseudopsychologies**
  - pseudopsychologies are ways of explaining human behavior that are not based on scientific evidence and have little value other than entertainment

Psychology

_____
_____
_____
_____
_____
_____
_____
_____
_____

1.2–1.3 **History of Psychology**

_____
_____
_____
_____
_____
_____
_____
_____
_____
_____
_____

Figure 1.1 **A Gestalt Perception**

_____
_____
_____
_____
_____
_____
_____
_____
_____
_____
_____

1.4　Modern Perspectives

_____
_____
_____
_____
_____
_____
_____
_____
_____
_____
_____
_____
_____
_____
_____
_____
_____
_____
_____

1.5　Types of Psychological Professionals

_____
_____
_____
_____
_____
_____
_____
_____
_____
_____
_____
_____
_____
_____
_____
_____
_____
_____
_____
_____
_____

Figure 1.2 **Work Settings and Subfields of Psychology**

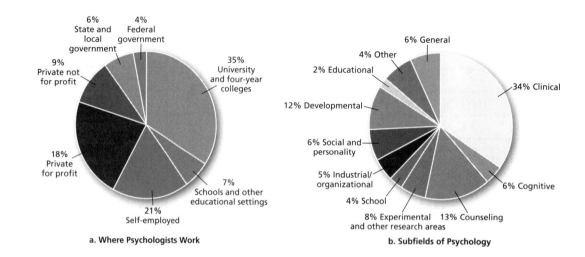

a. Where Psychologists Work

b. Subfields of Psychology

1.6–1.8 Psychology—The Science

1.9–1.12　Finding Relationships

_____

_____

_____

_____

_____

_____

_____

_____

_____

1.13　Ethics of Psychological Research

_____

_____

_____

_____

_____

_____

_____

_____

_____

_____

1.14　Critical Thinking

_____

_____

_____

_____

_____

_____

_____

_____

_____

_____

_____

NOTES

CHAPTER 2 – THE BIOLOGICAL PERSPECTIVE

YOU KNOW YOU ARE READY FOR THE TEST IF YOU ARE ABLE TO...
- Explain what neurons are and how they work to transfer and process information.
- Introduce the peripheral nervous system and describe its role in the body.
- Describe the methods used to observe the structure and activity of the brain.
- Identify the basic structures of the brain and explain their functions.
- Discuss the role of the endocrine system.

RAPID REVIEW

The **nervous system** is made up of a complex network of cells throughout your body. Since psychology is the study of behavior and mental processes, understanding how the nervous system works provides fundamental information about what is going on inside your body when you engage in a specific behavior, feel a particular emotion, or have an abstract thought. The field of study that deals with these types of questions is called **neuroscience**. The role of the nervous system is to carry information. Without your nervous system, you would not be able to think, feel, or act. The cells in the nervous system that carry information are called **neurons**. Information enters a neuron at the **dendrites**, flows through the cell body (or **soma**) and down the **axon** in order to pass the information on to the next cell. Although, neurons are the cells that carry the information, most of the nervous system consists of **glial cells**. Glial cells provide food, support, and insulation to the neuron cells. The insulation around the neuron is called **myelin** and works in a way very similar to the plastic coating of an electrical wire. Bundles of myelin-coated axons are wrapped together in cable like structures called **nerves**.

Neurons use an electrical signal to send information from one end of its cell to the other. At rest, a neuron has a negative charge inside and a positive charge outside. When a signal arrives, gates in the cell wall next to the signal open and the positive charge moves inside. The positive charge inside the cell causes the next set of gates to open and those positive charges move inside. In this way, the electrical signal makes its way down the length of the cell. The movement of the electrical signal is called an **action potential**. After the action potential is over, the positive charges get pumped back out of the cell and the neuron returns to its negatively charged state. This condition is called the **resting potential**. A neuron acts in an **all-or-none** manner. This means the neuron either has an action potential or it does not. The neuron indicates the strength of the signal by how many action potentials are produced or "fired" within a certain amount of time.

Neurons pass information on to target cells using a chemical signal. When the electrical signal travels down the axon and reaches the other end of the neuron called the **axon terminal**, it enters the very tip of the terminal called the **synaptic knob** and causes the **neurotransmitters** in the **synaptic vesicles** to be released into the fluid-filled space between the two cells. This fluid-filled space is called the **synapse** or the **synaptic gap**. The neurotransmitters are the chemical signals the neuron uses to communicate with its target cell. The neurotransmitters fit into the **receptor sites** of the target cell and create a new electrical signal that then can be transmitted down the length of the target cell.

Neurotransmitters can have two different effects on the target cell. If the neurotransmitter increases the likelihood of an action potential in the target cell, the connection is called an **excitatory synapse**. If the neurotransmitter decreases the likelihood of an action potential, the connection is called an **inhibitory synapse**. **Agonists** and **antagonists** are chemicals that are not naturally found in our body but that can fit into the receptor sites of target cells when they get into our nervous system. Agonists lead to a similar response in the target cell as the neurotransmitter itself, while antagonists block or reduce the action of the neurotransmitter on the target cell. There are at least 50-100 different types of neurotransmitters in the human body. Acetylcholine was the first to be discovered; it is an excitatory neurotransmitter that causes your muscles to contract. Gamma amino butyric acid (GABA) is an inhibitory neurotransmitter that decreases the activity level of neurons in your brain. Serotonin is both an excitatory and inhibitory neurotransmitter and has been linked with sleep, mood, and appetite. Low levels of the neurotransmitter dopamine have been found to cause Parkinson's disease and increased levels of dopamine have been linked to the psychological disorder known as schizophrenia. Endorphin is a special neurotransmitter called a neural regulator that controls the release of other neurotransmitters. When endorphin is released in the body, they neurons transmitting information about pain are not able to fire action potentials. All the different types of neurotransmitters are cleared out of the synaptic gap through the process of **reuptake**, diffusion, or by being broken apart by an enzyme.

The **central nervous system (CNS)** is made up of the brain and the **spinal cord**. The spinal cord is a long bundle of neurons that transmits messages between the brain and the body. The cell bodies or somas of the neurons are located along the inside of the spinal cord and the cell axons run along the outside of the spinal cord. **Afferent (sensory) neurons** send information from our senses to the spinal cord. For example, sensory neurons would relay information about a sharp pain in your finger. **Efferent (motor) neurons** send commands from the spinal cord to our muscles, such as a command to pull your finger back. **Interneurons** connect sensory and motor neurons and help to coordinate the signals. All three of these neurons act together in the spinal cord to form a **reflex arc**. The ability of the brain and spinal cord to change both in structure and function is referred to as **neuroplasticity**. One type of cell that facilitates these changes are **stem cells**.

The **peripheral nervous system (PNS)** is made up of all the nerves and neurons that are NOT in the brain or spinal cord. This includes all the nerves that connect to your eyes, ears, skin, mouth, and muscles. The PNS is divided into two parts, the **somatic nervous system** and the **autonomic nervous system**. The somatic nervous system consists of all the nerves coming from our sensory systems, called the **sensory pathway**, and all the nerves going to the skeletal muscles that control our voluntary movements, called the **motor pathway**. The autonomic nervous system is made up of the nerves going to and from our organs, glands, and involuntary muscles and is divided into two parts: the **sympathetic division** and the **parasympathetic division**. The sympathetic division turns on the body's fight-or-flight reactions, which include responses such as increased heart rate, increased breathing, and dilation of your pupils. The parasympathetic division controls your body when you are in a state of rest to keep the heart beating regularly, to control normal breathing, and to coordinate digestion. The parasympathetic division is active most of the time.

Researchers have used animal models to learn a great deal about the human brain. Two of the most common techniques used in animals involve either destroying a specific area of the brain (**deep lesioning**) or stimulating a specific brain area (electrical stimulation of the brain or ESB) to see the effect. In work with humans, researchers have developed several methods to observe the structure and activity of a living brain. If a researcher wants a picture of the structure of the brain, she might choose a **CT scan** or an **MRI**. Computed tomography (CT) scans use x-rays to create images of the structures within the brain. Magnetic resonance images (MRIs) use a magnetic field to "take a picture" of the brain. MRIs provide much greater detail than CT scans. On the other hand, if a researcher wanted to record the activity of the brain, he might select an **EEG**, **fMRI**, or **PET scan**. An electroencephalogram (EEG) provides a record of the electrical activity of groups of neurons just below the surface of the skull. A functional magnetic resonance image (fMRI) uses magnetic fields in the same way as an MRI, but goes a step further and pieces the pictures together to show changes over a short period of time. A positron emission tomography (PET) scan involves injecting a person with a low dose of a radioactive substance and then recording the activity of that substance in the person's brain.

The brain can be roughly divided into three sections: the brainstem, the cortex, and the structures under the cortex. The **brainstem** is the lowest part of the brain that connects to the spinal cord. The outer wrinkled covering of the brain is the **cortex**, and the structures under the cortex are essentially everything between the brainstem and the cortex. The brainstem contains four important structures. The **medulla**, controls life-sustaining functions such as heart beat, breathing, and swallowing. The **pons** influences sleep, dreaming, and coordination of movements. The **reticular formation** plays a crucial role in attention and arousal, and the **cerebellum** controls all of the movements we make without really "thinking" about it.

One main group of structures under the cortex is the **limbic system**. The limbic system includes the **thalamus**, **hypothalamus**, **hippocampus**, and **amygdala**. The thalamus receives input from your sensory systems, processes it, and then passes it on to the appropriate area of the cortex. The hypothalamus interacts with the endocrine system to regulate body temperature, thirst, hunger, sleeping, sexual activity, and mood. It appears that the hippocampus is critical for the formation of long-term memories and for memories of the locations of objects. The amygdala is a small almond-shaped structure that is involved in our response to fear.

The outer part of the brain, or **cortex**, is divided into right and left sections called **cerebral hemispheres**. The two hemispheres communicate with each other through a thick band of neurons called the **corpus callosum**. Each cerebral hemisphere can be roughly divided into four sections. These sections are called lobes. The **occipital lobes** are at the back of the brain and process visual information. The **parietal lobes** are located at the top and back half of the brain and deal with information regarding touch, temperature, body position, and possibly taste. The **temporal lobes** are just behind your temples and process auditory information. The **frontal lobes** are located at the front of your head and are responsible for higher mental functions such as planning, personality, and decision making, as well as language and motor movements. Motor movements are controlled by a band of neurons located at the back of the frontal lobe called the **motor cortex**.

Association areas are the areas within each of the lobes that are responsible for "making sense" of all the incoming information. **Broca's area** is located in the left frontal lobe in most people and is responsible for the language production. A person with damage to this area would have trouble producing the words that he or she wants to speak. This condition is referred to as **Broca's aphasia**. The comprehension of language takes place in **Wernicke's area** located in the left temporal lobe. If this area of the brain is damaged, individuals are often still able to speak fluently, but their words do not make sense. This type of language disorder is referred to as **Wernicke's aphasia**. Damage to the right parietal and occipital lobes can cause a condition known as **spatial neglect** where the individual ignores objects in their left visual field.

The **cerebrum** is made up of the two cerebral hemispheres and the structures connecting them. The **split-brain research** studies of Roger Sperry helped scientists to figure out that the two cerebral hemispheres are not identical. The left hemisphere is typically more active when a person is using language, math, and other analytical skills, while the right hemisphere shows more activity during tasks of perception, recognition, and expression of emotions. This split in the tasks of the brain is referred to as lateralization.

The **endocrine glands** represent a second communication system in the body. The endocrine glands secrete chemicals called **hormones** directly into the bloodstream. The **pituitary gland** is located in the brain and secretes the hormones that control milk production, salt levels, and the activity of other glands. The **pineal gland** is also located in the brain and regulates the sleep cycle through the secretion of melatonin. The **thyroid gland** is located in the neck and releases a hormone that regulates metabolism. The **pancreas** controls the level of blood sugar in the body, while the **gonad** sex glands – called the **ovaries** in females and the **testes** in males, regulate sexual behavior and reproduction. The **adrenal glands** play a critical role in regulating the body's response to stress.

Mirror neurons, neurons that fire when we perform an action and also when we see someone else perform that action, may explain a great deal of the social learning that takes place in humans from infancy on.

STUDY HINTS

1. You will need to know the different functions of the peripheral nervous system (PNS). Recall that the PNS is divided into two main sections: the somatic nervous system and the autonomic nervous system. The somatic nervous system deals with the senses and the skeletal muscles (all "S's") and is fairly straightforward to understand. The autonomic nervous system is slightly more complicated. First, understand that the *autonomic* nervous system deals with all the *automatic* functions of your body. What are some functions that are controlled automatically in your body? List them here:

    _____, _____, _____, _____,

You probably mentioned functions such as digestion, heart rate, pupil dilation, breathing, salivation, or perspiration, to name a few. These are the functions controlled by the autonomic system.

There are two components of the autonomic system and they serve to balance each other out. The two divisions are the sympathetic and parasympathetic divisions. Most of the time, the parasympathetic division is in control. Some people have called the parasympathetic division the rest-and-digest system because it controls the digestive processes, maintains a resting heart and breathing rate, and in general keeps your body in its normal relaxed state. The sympathetic division goes into action when your body needs to react to some type of threat. It might be helpful to associate **s**ympathetic with **s**urprise, since the sympathetic division is the part of your nervous system that responds when you are surprised. This system is often referred to as the fight-or flight system. What happens to your body when you are surprised? List some of the responses here:

_____, _____, _____, _____,

You probably mentioned responses such as your heart rate increases, you breathe faster, your pupils dilate, you begin to sweat, to name a few. All of these responses are "turned on" by the sympathetic division of your autonomic nervous system and aid in your survival by allowing you to respond quickly to a threat.

2.   Two of the brain structures most commonly confused with each other are the hippocampus and the hypothalamus. Both of the structures are located in the limbic system in the area of your brain above your brainstem and below the outer surface. The hippocampus has been found to be important in helping us form memories that last more than just a few seconds. Patients with damage to the hippocampus often cannot remember information for longer than a few seconds. Also, the hippocampus is very important in storing memories of where things are located, a spatial map. On the other hand, the hypothalamus is important in controlling many of our basic bodily functions such as sleeping, drinking, eating, and sexual activities. The structures are often confused because the two words sound so similar to each other. Can you think of any memory device or "trick" to help you keep these two brain structures separate? List your idea in the space below:

hippocampus: _____

hypothalamus: _____

One suggestion might be as follows. If you look at the word hippocampus *you can think of the last part of the word –* campus. *In order to get around on your college campus, you need to keep in mind where certain buildings and areas are located. This is exactly what your hippocampus is involved in. Without your hippo-campus, you would have a very hard time finding your way around your college campus.*

To remember the hypothalamus, first it might help to understand how the name came about. "Hypo" means under or below. For example, if someone has "hypothermia" their body temperature is under the normal amount and the person is probably feeling very cold. If someone has "hypoglycemica" they have under or lower than the normal amount of blood sugar (glycemia is referring to the sugar found in your blood). What do you think "hypothalamus" means?

_____

If you wrote "under the thalamus," then you are correct. The hypothalamus is located directly underneath the thalamus. You might also look at the name to try to remember some of the activities the hypothalamus regulates. Recall that we said the hypothalamus plays a role in hunger, sleep, thirst, and sex. If you look at the "hypo" of hypothalamus you might memorize "h" – hunger, "y" – yawning, "p" – parched (or very, very thirsty), and "o" – overly excited.

LEARNING OBJECTIVES

2.1   *What are the nervous system, neurons, and nerves, and how do they relate to one another?*

2.2   *How do neurons use neurotransmitters to communicate with each other and with the body?*

2.3   *How do the brain and spinal cord interact?*

2.4   *How do the somatic and autonomic nervous systems allow people and animals to interact with their surroundings and control the body's automatic functions?*

2.5   *How do psychologists study the brain and how it works?*

2.6   *What are the different structures of the bottom part of the brain and what do they do?*

2.7   *What are the structures of the brain that control emotion, learning, memory, and motivation?*

2.8   *What parts of the cortex control the different senses and the movement of the body?*

2.9   *What parts of the cortex are responsible for higher forms of thought, such as language?*

2.10   *How does the left side of the brain differ from the right side?*

2.11   *How do the hormones released by glands interact with the nervous system and affect behavior?*

PRACTICE EXAM

For the following multiple choice questions, select the answer you feel best answers the question.

1. The function of the _____ is to carry information to and from all parts of the body.
   a) soma
   b) synapse
   c) nervous system
   d) endorphins

2. The central nervous system is made of which two components?
   a) the somatic and autonomic systems
   b) the brain and the spinal cord
   c) the sympathetic and parasympathetic divisions
   d) neurotransmitters and hormones

3. A specialized cell that makes up the nervous system that receives and sends messages within that system is called a _____.
   a) glial cell
   b) neuron.
   c) cell body
   d) myelin sheath

4. What type of signal is used to relay a message from one end of a neuron to the other end?
   a) chemical
   b) hormonal
   c) biochemical
   d) electrical

5. A chemical found in the synaptic vesicles which, when release, has an effect on the next cell is called a_____.
    a) glial cell
    b) neurotransmitter
    c) precursor cell
    d) synapse

6. What event causes the release of chemicals into the synaptic gap?
    a) an agonist binding to the dendrites
    b) an action potential reaching the axon terminal
    c) the reuptake of neurotransmitters
    d) excitation of the glial cells

7. Sara has been experiencing a serious memory problem. An interdisciplinary team has ruled out a range of causes and believes that a neurotransmitter is involved. Which neurotransmitter is most likely involved in this problem?
    a) GABA
    b) dopamine
    c) serotonin
    d) acetylcholine

8. A neuron releases neurotransmitters into the synaptic gap that reduce the frequency of action potentials in the neighboring cell. The neuron most likely released is
    a) an inhibitory neurotransmitter.
    b) an excitatory neurotransmitter.
    c) acetylcholine.
    d) an agonist.

9. Which part of the nervous system takes the information received from the senses, makes sense out of it, makes decisions, and sends commands out to the muscles and the rest of the body?
    a) spinal cord
    b) brain
    c) reflexes
    d) interneurons

10. Every deliberate action you make, such as pedaling a bike, walking, scratching, or smelling a flower, involves neurons in the _____ nervous system.
    a) sympathetic
    b) somatic
    c) parasympathetic
    d) autonomic

11. Involuntary muscles are controlled by the _____nervous system.
    a) somatic
    b) autonomic
    c) sympathetic
    d) parasympathetic

12. Which of the following responses would occur if your sympathetic nervous system has been activated?
    a) increased heart rate
    b) pupil constriction
    c) slowed breathing
    d) increased digestion

13. Small metal disks are pasted onto Miranda's scalp and they are connected by wire to a machine that translates the electrical energy from her brain into wavy lines on a moving piece of paper. From this description, it is evident that Miranda's brain is being studied through the use of_____.
    a) a CT Scan
    b) functional magnetic resonance imaging (fMRI)
    c) a microelectrode
    d) an electroencephalograph

14. Which method would a researcher select if she wanted to determine if her patient's right hemisphere was the same size as his left hemisphere?
    a) EEG
    b) deep lesioning
    c) CT scan
    d) PET scan

15. Which of the following is responsible for the ability to selectively attend to certain kinds of information in one's surroundings and become alert to changes in information?
    a) reticular formation
    b) pons
    c) medulla
    d) cerebellum

16. When a professional baseball player swings a bat and hits a homerun, he is relying on his _____ to coordinate the practiced movements of his body.
    a) pons
    b) medulla
    c) cerebellum
    d) reticular formation

17. Eating, drinking, sexual behavior, sleeping, and temperature control are most strongly influenced by the _____.
    a) hippocampus
    b) thalamus
    c) hypothalamus
    d) amygdala

18. After a brain operation, a laboratory rat no longer displays any fear when placed into a cage with a snake. Which part of the rat's brain was most likely damaged during the operation?
    a) amygdala
    b) hypothalamus
    c) cerebellum
    d) hippocampus

19. Darla was in an automobile accident that resulted in an injury to her brain. Her sense of touch has been affected. Which part of the brain is the most likely site of the damage?
    a) frontal lobes
    b) temporal lobes
    c) occipital lobes
    d) parietal lobes

20. If a person damages their occipital lobes, which would be the most likely problem they would report to their doctor?
    a) trouble hearing
    b) problems with their vision
    c) decreased sense of taste
    d) numbness on the right side of their body

21. Damage to what area of the brain would result in an inability to comprehend language?
    a) occipital lobes
    b) Broca's area
    c) Wernicke's area
    d) parietal lobe

22. If Darren's brain is like that of most people, then language will be handled by his
    a) corpus callosum.
    b) occipital lobe.
    c) right hemisphere.
    d) left hemisphere.

23. The two hemispheres of the brain are identical copies of each other.
    a) true
    b) false

24. The hormone released by the pineal gland that reduces body temperature and prepares you for sleep is
    a) melatonin
    b) DHEA
    c) parathormone
    d) thyroxin

25. Which endocrine gland regulates your body's response to stress?
    a) pancreas
    b) thyroid gland
    c) pineal gland
    d) adrenal gland

PRACTICE EXAM ANSWERS

1. c   The nervous system is the correct answer because sending information to and from all parts of the body is the primary function of the nervous system. The soma and the synapse are both parts of an individual neuron, and endorphins are one type of neurotransmitter found in the body.

2. b   The central nervous system is composed of the nerves and neurons in the center of your body. Choices a and c are both components of the peripheral nervous system. Hormones are the chemical messengers for the endocrine system.

3. b   B is the correct answer because neurons are a specialized cell that makes up the nervous system that receives and sends messages within that system. A is incorrect because glial cells serve as a structure for neurons.

4. d   Neurons use electrical signals to communicate within their own cell. The electrical signal is called an action potential.

5. b   Neurotransmitters are stored in the synaptic vesicles. D is incorrect because the synapse is the space between the synaptic knob of one cell and the dendrites.

6. d   When the electrical signal (called an action potential) reaches the axon terminal, the synaptic vesicles release their contents into the synaptic gap.

7. d   Acetylcholine is found in a part of the brain responsible for forming new memories.

8. a   Inhibitory neurotransmitters inhibit the electrical activity of the receptor cell.

9. b   The spinal cord carries messages to and/from the body to the brain, but it is the job of the brain, to make sense of all the information.

10. b   The somatic nervous system controls voluntary muscle movement, whereas the autonomic nervous system consists of nerves that control all of the involuntary muscles, organs, and glands.

11. b   The autonomic nervous system controls involuntary muscles like the heart, stomach, and intestines.

12. a   The sympathetic division is responsible for controlling your body's fight-or-flight response which prepares your body to deal with a potential threat. The responses include increased heart rate and breathing, pupil dilation, decreased digestion, among others.

13. d   An electroencephalograph or EEG records brain wave patterns. CT scans take computer-controlled x-rays of the brain.

14. c   C is the only selection that would allow the researcher to take a picture of the structure of the brain. All other options listed would provide information about the activity of the brain.

15. b   The reticular formation plays a role in selective attention.

16. c   The cerebellum is responsible for controlling the movements that we have practiced repeatedly, the movements that we don't have to really "think about."

17. c   The hypothalamus regulates sleep, hunger, thirst, and sex.

18. a   The amygdala has been found to regulate the emotion of fear. The amygdala is found within the limbic system, a part of our brain responsible for regulating emotions and memories.

19. d   The parietal lobes contain the centers for touch, taste, and temperature.

20. b   The occipital lobes are responsible for processing visual information.

21. c   Wernicke's area is located in the temporal lobe and is important in the comprehension of language. Broca's area is located in the frontal lobe and plays a role in the production of language

22. d   For most people the left hemisphere specializes in language.

23. b   The left hemisphere is more active during language and math problems, while the right hemisphere appears to play a larger role in nonverbal and perception based tasks.

24. a   The pineal gland secretes melatonin.

25. d   The adrenal glands secrete several hormones in response to stress.

CHAPTER GLOSSARY

agonists	chemical substances that mimic or enhance the effects of a neurotransmitter on the receptor sites of the next cell, increasing or decreasing the activity of that cell.
acetylcholine	the first neurotransmitter to be discovered. Found to regulate memories in the CNS and the action of skeletal and smooth muscles in the PNS.
action potential	the release of the neural impulse consisting of a reversal of the electrical charge within the axon.
adrenal glands	endocrine glands located on top of each kidney and which secrete over thirty different hormones to deal with stress, regulate salt intake, and provide a secondary source of sex hormones affecting the sexual changes that occur during adolescence.
all-or-none	referring to the fact that a neuron either fires completely or does not fire at all.
amygdala	brain structure located near the hippocampus, responsible for fear responses and memory of fear.
antagonists	chemical substances that block or reduce a cell's response to the action of other chemicals or neurotransmitters.
association areas	areas within each lobe of the cortex responsible for the coordination and interpretation of information, as well as higher mental processing.
autonomic nervous system	division of the PNS consisting of nerves that control all of the involuntary muscles, organs, and glands.
axon	long tube-like structure that carries the neural message to other cells.
axon terminals	branches at the end of the axon.
brainstem	section of the brain that connects directly to the spinal cord and regulates vital functions such as breathing, the heart, reflexes, and level of alertness.
Broca's area	association area of the brain located in the frontal lobe that is responsible for language production and language processing.
central nervous system (CNS)	part of the nervous system consisting of the brain and spinal cord.
cerebellum	part of the lower brain located behind the pons that controls and coordinates involuntary, rapid, fine motor movement.
cerebral hemispheres	the two sections of the cortex on the left and right sides of the brain.
computed tomography (CT)	brain imaging method using computer-controlled x-rays of the brain.
corpus callosum	thick band of neurons that connects the right and left cerebral hemispheres.

cortex	outermost covering of the brain consisting of densely packed neurons, responsible for higher thought processes and interpretation of sensory input.
dendrites	branch-like structures that receive messages from other neurons.
dopamine	neurotransmitter that regulates movement, balance, and walking and is involved in the disorders of schizophrenia and Parkinson's disease.
electroencephalograph (EEG)	machine designed to record the brain wave patterns produced by electrical activity of the surface of the brain.
endocrine glands	glands that secrete chemicals called hormones directly into the bloodstream.
endorphin	neurotransmitter that is found naturally in the body and works to block pain and elevate mood. It is chemically similar to morphine and its name is short for "endogenous morphine."
excitatory neurotransmitter	neurotransmitter that causes the receiving cell to fire.
frontal lobes	areas of the cortex located in the front and top of the brain, responsible for higher mental processes and decision making as well as the production of fluent speech.
functional magnetic resonance imaging (fMRI)	a method used to observe activity in the brain, it shows which structures are active during particular mental operations using the same basic procedure as MRI.
GABA	abbreviation for gamma-aminobutyric acid, the major inhibitory neurotransmitter in the brain.
glial cells	grey fatty cells that provide support for the neurons to grow on and around, deliver nutrients to neurons, produce myelin to coat axons, and clean up waste products and dead neurons.
hippocampus	curved structure located within each temporal lobe, responsible for the formation of long-term memories and the storage of memory for location of objects.
hormones	chemicals released into the bloodstream by endocrine glands.
hypothalamus	small structure in the brain located below the thalamus and directly above the pituitary gland, responsible for motivational behavior such as sleep, hunger, thirst, and sex.
inhibitory neurotransmitter	neurotransmitter that causes the receiving cell to stop firing.
interneuron	a neuron found in the center of the spinal cord which receives information from the sensory neurons and sends commands to the muscles through the motor neurons. Interneurons also make up the bulk of the neurons in the brain.
limbic system	a group of several brain structures located under the cortex and involved in learning, emotion, memory, and motivation.
magnetic resonance imaging (MRI)	brain imaging method using radio waves and magnetic fields of the body to produce detailed images of the brain.
medulla	the first large swelling at the top of the spinal cord, forming the lowest part of the brain and which is responsible for life-sustaining functions such as breathing, swallowing, and heart rate.
motor neuron	a neuron that carries messages from the central nervous system to the muscles of the body. Also called efferent neuron.
myelin	fatty substances produced by certain glial cells that coat the axons of neurons to insulate, protect, and speed up the neural impulse.
nervous system	an extensive network of specialized cells that carry information to and from all parts of the body.

neurons	the basic cell that makes up the nervous system and which receives and sends messages within that system.
neurotransmitter	chemical found in the synaptic vesicles which, when released, has an effect on the next cell.
occipital lobes	sections of the brain located at the rear and bottom of each cerebral hemisphere, containing the visual centers of the brain.
pancreas	endocrine gland that controls the levels of sugar in the blood.
parasympathetic division	part of the autonomic system that restores the body to normal functioning after arousal and is responsible for the day-to-day functioning of the organs and glands. Sometimes referred to as the rest-and-digest system.
parietal lobes	sections of the brain located at the top and back of each cerebral hemisphere, containing the centers for touch, taste, and temperature sensations.
peripheral nervous system (PNS)	all nerves and neurons that are not contained in the brain and spinal cord but which run through the body itself.
pineal gland	endocrine gland located near the base of the cerebrum which secretes melatonin.
pituitary gland	gland located in the brain that secretes human growth hormone and influences all other hormone-secreting glands. Also known as the master gland.
pons	the larger swelling above the medulla which connects the top of the brain to the bottom, and which plays a part in sleep, dreaming, left-right body coordination, and arousal.
positron emission tomography (PET)	brain imaging method in which a radioactive sugar is injected into the subject and a computer compiles a color-coded image of the activity of the brain, with lighter colors indicating more activity
resting potential	the state of the neuron when not firing a neural impulse.
reticular formation	an area of neurons running through the middle of the medulla and the pons and slightly beyond, responsible for selective attention.
reuptake	process by which neurotransmitters are taken back into the synaptic vesicles.
sensory neuron	a neuron that carries information from the senses to the central nervous system. Also called afferent neuron.
serotonin	neurotransmitter involved in pain disorders and emotional perceptions. Is also known as 5-hydroxytryptamine (5-HT).
soma	the cell body of the neuron, responsible for maintaining the life of the cell.
somatic nervous system	division of the PNS consisting of nerves that carry information from the senses to the CNS and from the CNS to the voluntary muscles of the body.
spinal cord	a long bundle of neurons that carries messages to and from the body to the brain and that is responsible for very fast, life-saving reflexes.
sympathetic division	part of the autonomic nervous system that is responsible for reacting to stressful events and bodily arousal. Also known as the fight-or-flight system.
synaptic gap	microscopic fluid-filled space between the rounded areas on the end of the axon terminals of one cell and the dendrites or surface of the next cell.
synaptic vesicles	sack-like structures found inside the synaptic knob containing chemicals.
temporal lobes	areas of the cortex located just behind the temples, containing the neurons responsible for the sense of hearing and meaningful speech.

thalamus	part of the limbic system located in the center of the brain, this structure relays sensory information from the lower part of the brain to the proper areas of the cortex, and processes some sensory information before sending it to its proper area.
thyroid gland	endocrine gland found in the neck that regulates metabolism.
Wernicke's area	association area of the brain in the temporal lobe that has been found to be involved in the comprehension of spoken language.

Neurons and Nerves

(the brain is comprised of glial cells and neurons)

- **glial cells**
  provide physical and metabolic support to neurons

- **neurons**
  specialized cells in nervous system

  → have specialized components

→ have an electrical charge at rest—the resting potential (see Fig. 2.3, p. 52)

→ are affected by neurotransmitters (see Table 2.1, p. 56)

→ are separated by a gap called the synapse

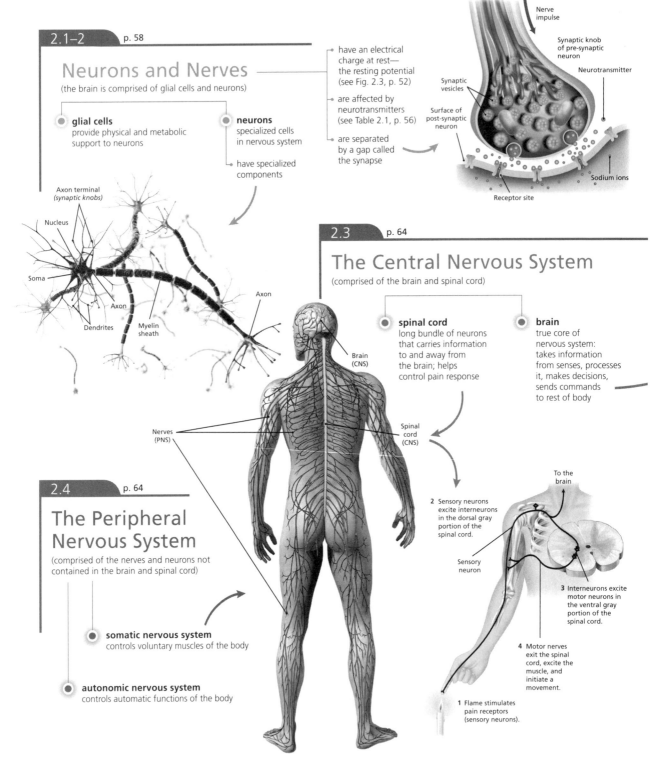

Nerve impulse

Synaptic knob of pre-synaptic neuron

Neurotransmitter

Synaptic vesicles

Surface of post-synaptic neuron

Sodium ions

Receptor site

Axon terminal (synaptic knobs)

Nucleus

Soma

Axon

Dendrites

Myelin sheath

Axon

The Central Nervous System

(comprised of the brain and spinal cord)

- **spinal cord**
  long bundle of neurons that carries information to and away from the brain; helps control pain response

- **brain**
  true core of nervous system: takes information from senses, processes it, makes decisions, sends commands to rest of body

Brain (CNS)

Nerves (PNS)

Spinal cord (CNS)

The Peripheral Nervous System

(comprised of the nerves and neurons not contained in the brain and spinal cord)

- **somatic nervous system**
  controls voluntary muscles of the body

- **autonomic nervous system**
  controls automatic functions of the body

2 Sensory neurons excite interneurons in the dorsal gray portion of the spinal cord.

To the brain

Sensory neuron

3 Interneurons excite motor neurons in the ventral gray portion of the spinal cord.

4 Motor nerves exit the spinal cord, excite the muscle, and initiate a movement.

1 Flame stimulates pain receptors (sensory neurons).

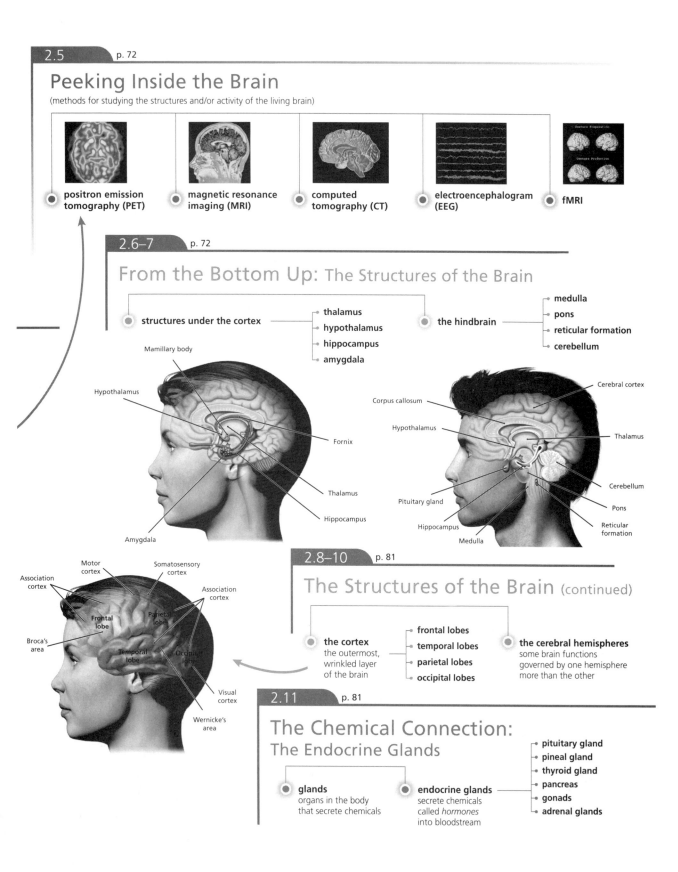

2.5 — p. 72

Peeking Inside the Brain

(methods for studying the structures and/or activity of the living brain)

- **positron emission tomography (PET)**
- **magnetic resonance imaging (MRI)**
- **computed tomography (CT)**
- **electroencephalogram (EEG)**
- **fMRI**

2.6–7 — p. 72

From the Bottom Up: The Structures of the Brain

- **structures under the cortex**
  - thalamus
  - hypothalamus
  - hippocampus
  - amygdala
- **the hindbrain**
  - medulla
  - pons
  - reticular formation
  - cerebellum

Mamillary body

Hypothalamus

Fornix

Thalamus

Hippocampus

Amygdala

Cerebral cortex

Corpus callosum

Hypothalamus

Thalamus

Pituitary gland

Cerebellum

Hippocampus

Pons

Medulla

Reticular formation

2.8–10 — p. 81

The Structures of the Brain (continued)

- **the cortex**
  the outermost, wrinkled layer of the brain
  - frontal lobes
  - temporal lobes
  - parietal lobes
  - occipital lobes
- **the cerebral hemispheres**
  some brain functions governed by one hemisphere more than the other

Motor cortex

Association cortex

Somatosensory cortex

Association cortex

Frontal lobe

Parietal lobe

Broca's area

Temporal lobe

Occipital lobe

Visual cortex

Wernicke's area

2.11 — p. 81

The Chemical Connection: The Endocrine Glands

- **glands**
  organs in the body that secrete chemicals
- **endocrine glands**
  secrete chemicals called *hormones* into bloodstream
  - pituitary gland
  - pineal gland
  - thyroid gland
  - pancreas
  - gonads
  - adrenal glands

Figure 2.1 **An Overview
of the Nervous System**

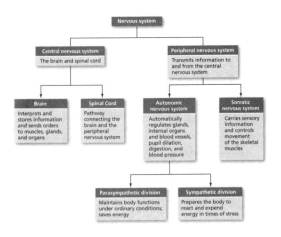

Figure 2.2 **The Structure of the Neuron**

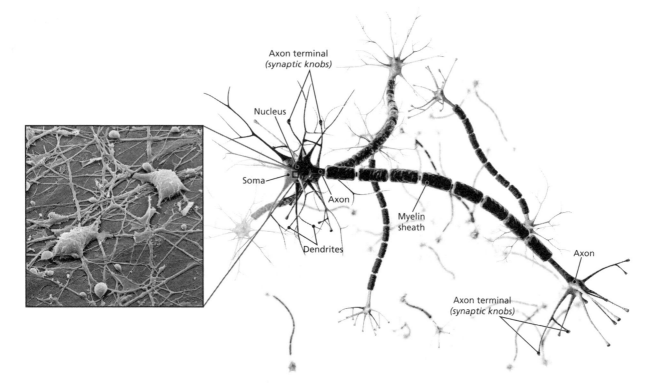

Axon terminal
(synaptic knobs)

Nucleus

Soma

Axon

Dendrites

Myelin
sheath

Axon

Axon terminal
(synaptic knobs)

Figure 2.3 **The Neural Impulse Action Potential**

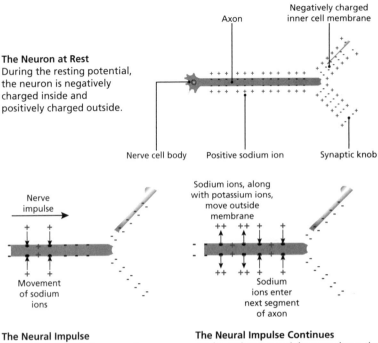

The Neuron at Rest
During the resting potential, the neuron is negatively charged inside and positively charged outside.

Axon

Negatively charged inner cell membrane

Nerve cell body

Positive sodium ion

Synaptic knob

Nerve impulse

Movement of sodium ions

Sodium ions, along with potassium ions, move outside membrane

Sodium ions enter next segment of axon

The Neural Impulse
The action potential occurs when positive sodium ions enter into the cell, causing a reversal of the electrical charge from negative to positive.

The Neural Impulse Continues
As the action potential moves down the axon toward the axon terminals, the cell areas behind the action potential return to their resting state of a negative charge as the positive sodium ions are pumped to the outside of the cell, and the positive potassium ions rapidly leave.

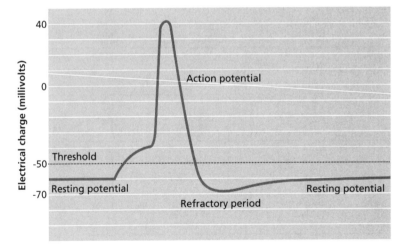

Figure 2.4 **The Synapse**

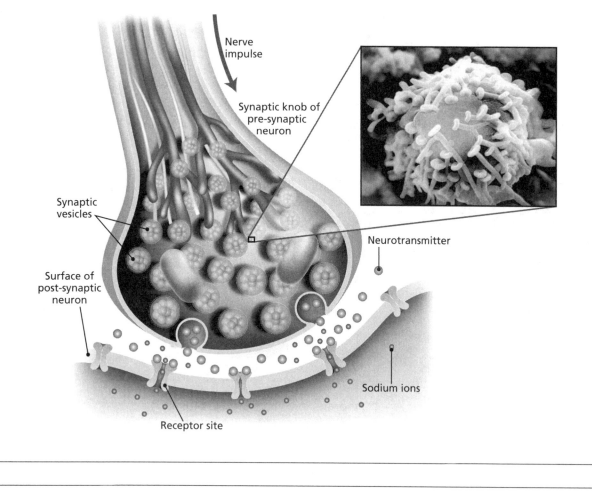

Synaptic knob of
pre-synaptic
neuron

Nerve
impulse

Synaptic
vesicles

Neurotransmitter

Surface of
post-synaptic
neuron

Sodium ions

Receptor site

Table 2.1 **Neurotransmitters and Their Functions**

Table 2.1   **Neurotransmitters and Their Functions**

NEUROTRANSMITTERS	FUNCTIONS
Acetylcholine	Excitatory or inhibitory; involved in memory and controls muscle contractions.
Serotonin	Excitatory or inhibitory; involved in mood, sleep, and appetite.
GABA (gamma-aminobutyric acid)	Major inhibitory neurotransmitter; involved in sleep and inhibits movement.
Glutamate	Major excitatory neurotransmitter; involved in learning, memory formation, and nervous system development.
Norepinephrine	Mainly excitatory; involved in arousal and mood.
Dopamine	Excitatory or inhibitory; involved in control of movement and sensations of pleasure.
Endorphins	Inhibitory neural regulators; involved in pain relief.

Figure 2.5 **Reuptake of Dopamine**

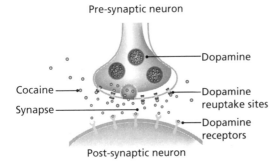

Pre-synaptic neuron
Dopamine
Cocaine
Dopamine reuptake sites
Synapse
Dopamine receptors
Post-synaptic neuron

Figure 2.6 **The Spinal Cord Reflex**

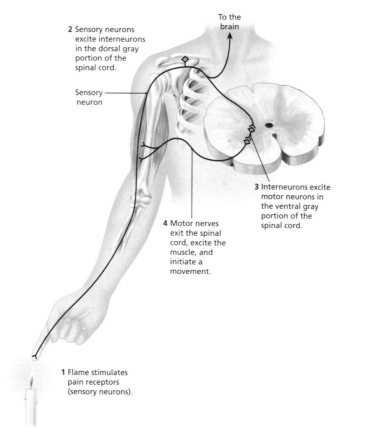

To the brain

2 Sensory neurons excite interneurons in the dorsal gray portion of the spinal cord.

Sensory neuron

3 Interneurons excite motor neurons in the ventral gray portion of the spinal cord.

4 Motor nerves exit the spinal cord, excite the muscle, and initiate a movement.

1 Flame stimulates pain receptors (sensory neurons).

Figure 2.8 **The Peripheral Nervous System**

Figure 2.9 Functions of the Parasympathetic and Sympathetic Divisions of the Nervous System

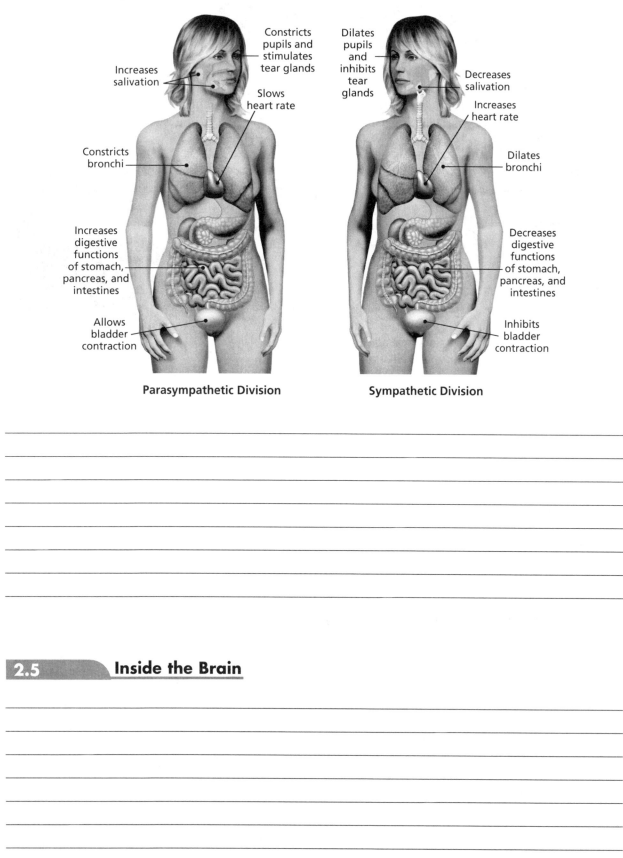

Parasympathetic Division

Sympathetic Division

Constricts pupils and stimulates tear glands

Increases salivation

Slows heart rate

Constricts bronchi

Increases digestive functions of stomach, pancreas, and intestines

Allows bladder contraction

Dilates pupils and inhibits tear glands

Decreases salivation

Increases heart rate

Dilates bronchi

Decreases digestive functions of stomach, pancreas, and intestines

Inhibits bladder contraction

_____
_____
_____
_____
_____
_____
_____
_____

2.5 Inside the Brain

_____
_____
_____
_____
_____
_____
_____
_____
_____

Figure 2.10 **Studying the Brain**

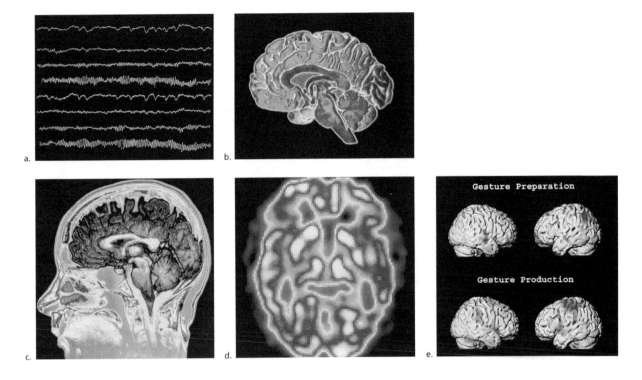

a.

b.

c.

d.

e. Gesture Preparation / Gesture Production

2.6–2.7 The Structures of the Brain

Figure 2.11 The Major Structures of the Human Brain

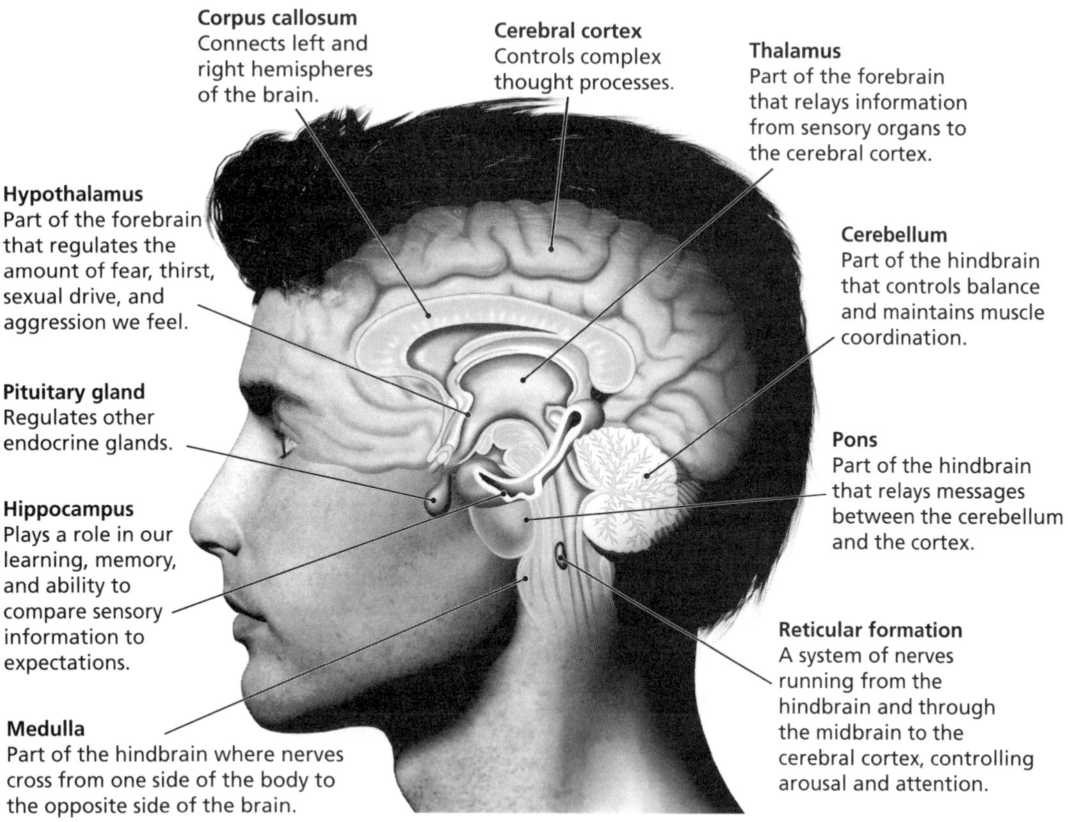

Corpus callosum
Connects left and right hemispheres of the brain.

Cerebral cortex
Controls complex thought processes.

Thalamus
Part of the forebrain that relays information from sensory organs to the cerebral cortex.

Hypothalamus
Part of the forebrain that regulates the amount of fear, thirst, sexual drive, and aggression we feel.

Cerebellum
Part of the hindbrain that controls balance and maintains muscle coordination.

Pituitary gland
Regulates other endocrine glands.

Pons
Part of the hindbrain that relays messages between the cerebellum and the cortex.

Hippocampus
Plays a role in our learning, memory, and ability to compare sensory information to expectations.

Reticular formation
A system of nerves running from the hindbrain and through the midbrain to the cerebral cortex, controlling arousal and attention.

Medulla
Part of the hindbrain where nerves cross from one side of the body to the opposite side of the brain.

Figure 2.12 **The Limbic System**

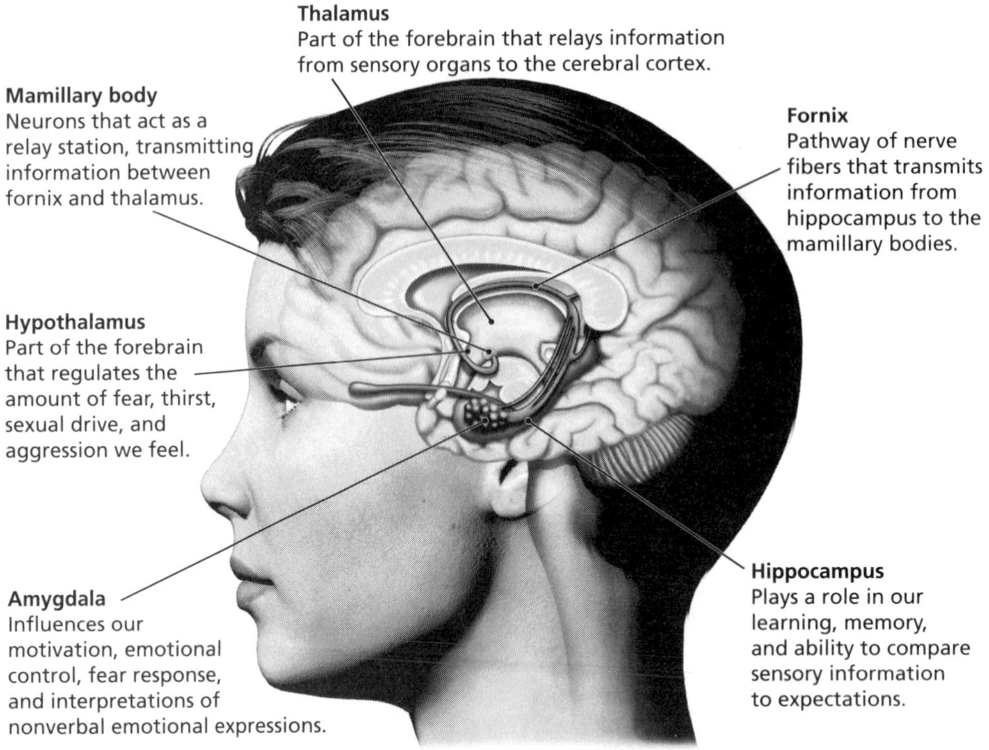

Thalamus
Part of the forebrain that relays information
from sensory organs to the cerebral cortex.

Mamillary body
Neurons that act as a
relay station, transmitting
information between
fornix and thalamus.

Fornix
Pathway of nerve
fibers that transmits
information from
hippocampus to the
mamillary bodies.

Hypothalamus
Part of the forebrain
that regulates the
amount of fear, thirst,
sexual drive, and
aggression we feel.

Amygdala
Influences our
motivation, emotional
control, fear response,
and interpretations of
nonverbal emotional expressions.

Hippocampus
Plays a role in our
learning, memory,
and ability to compare
sensory information
to expectations.

2.8–2.10 The Structures of the Brain *(continued)*

Figure 2.13 **The Lobes of the Brain: Occipital, Parietal, Temporal, and Frontal**

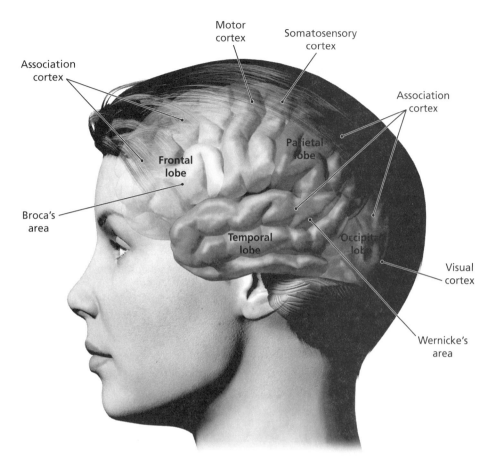

Figure 2.14 **The Motor and Somatosensory Cortex**

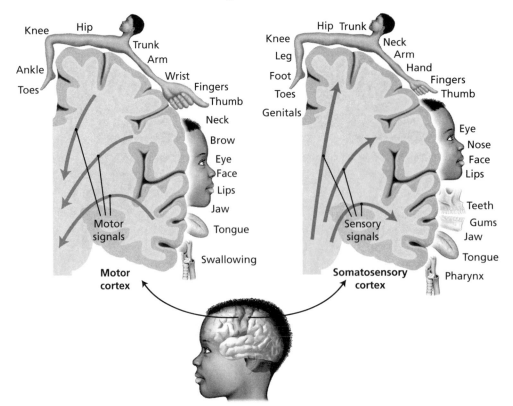

Table 2.2 **Specialization of the Two Hemispheres**

Table 2.2   **Specialization of the Two Hemispheres**

LEFT HEMISPHERE	RIGHT HEMISPHERE
Controls the right hand	Controls the left hand
Spoken language	Nonverbal
Written language	Visual-spatial perception
Mathematical calculations	Music and artistic processing
Logical thought processes	Emotional thought and recognition
Analysis of detail	Processes the whole
Reading	Pattern recognition
	Facial recognition

Figure 2.15 **The Split-Brain Experiment**

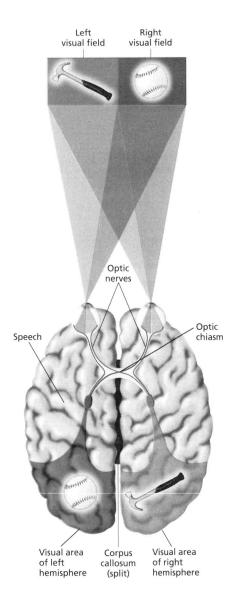

Left visual field Right visual field

Optic nerves

Speech

Optic chiasm

Visual area of left hemisphere

Corpus callosum (split)

Visual area of right hemisphere

2.11   **The Endocrine Glands**

Figure 2.16 **The Endocrine Glands**

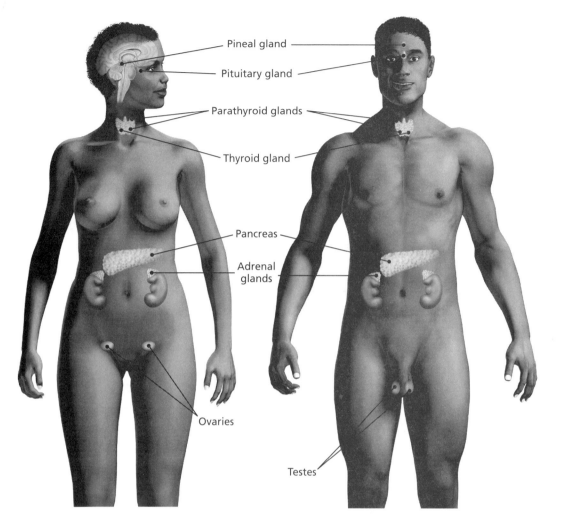

Pineal gland
Pituitary gland
Parathyroid glands
Thyroid gland
Pancreas
Adrenal glands
Ovaries
Testes

NOTES

YOU KNOW YOU ARE READY FOR THE TEST IF YOU ARE ABLE TO...

- Define sensation and introduce some of the key concepts developed by researchers in the study of sensation.
- Explain in detail how our sense of sight and our sense of hearing work and discuss some causes for impairments in these senses.
- Discuss the chemical senses of taste and smell and the lesser known somesthetic senses of touch, body position, and balance.
- Describe our experience of perception, especially in relation to visual stimuli.

RAPID REVIEW

Sensation allows us to receive information from the world around us. **Synesthesia** is the rare condition in which a person experiences more than one sensation from a single stimulus, for example the person who can hear and see a sound. Outside stimuli (such as the sound of your mother's voice) activate **sensory receptors** which convert the outside stimulus into a message that our nervous system can understand – electrical and chemical signals. The process of converting the outside stimulus into the electrical-chemical signal of the nervous system is called sensory **transduction**. The sensory receptors are specialized forms of neurons and make up part of our somatic nervous system. Ernst Weber and Gustav Fechner were two pioneers in the study of sensory thresholds. Weber studied the smallest difference between two stimuli that a person could detect 50 percent of the time. He called this difference a **just noticeable difference (jnd)** and he discovered that the jnd is always a constant. For instance, if a person needs to add 5 percent more weight to notice the difference in the heaviness of a package, then this person's jnd is 5 percent. If the initial weight of the package is 10 lbs, then 0.5 lbs would need to be added to detect a difference (5 percent of 10 lb = 0.5lb). If the initial weight is 100 lbs than 5 lbs would need to be added in order for the person to detect a difference in weight (5 percent of 100 lb = 5 lb). The fact that the jnd is always a constant is known as Weber's law. Fechner investigated the lowest level of a stimulus that a person could detect 50 percent of the time. He called this level the **absolute threshold**. **Habituation** and **sensory adaptation** are two methods our body uses to ignore unchanging information. Habituation takes place when the lower centers of the brain prevent conscious attention to a constant stimulus, such as the humming of a desktop computer. Sensory adaptation occurs in the sensory receptors themselves when the receptors stop responding to a constant stimulus, such as the feeling of your shirt on your skin.

The visual sensory system is activated by light waves. There are three psychological aspects to our experience of light. **Brightness** is determined by the height, or amplitude, of the wave. **Color**, or hue, is determined by the length of the light wave, and **saturation**, or purity, is determined by the mixture of wavelengths of varying heights and lengths. Light enters your eye through the cornea which protects your eye and helps to focus the light, and then travels through a hole in your iris, called your pupil. The iris is a group of muscles that control the size of the pupil. The light then passes through the lens which focuses the light and allows you to focus on objects that are close or far away. This process is known as **visual accommodation**. The light then travels through the vitreous humor in the middle of your eyeball to reach the **retina** at the very back of your eye. The retina is the size of a postage stamp and contains the sensory receptor neurons that convert the incoming light waves in to an electrical-chemical signal that the nervous system can understand. Your eye contains two types of sensory receptors, **rods** and **cones**. About 70 percent of the sensory receptors in your eyes are rods. Rods detect the brightness of light and send information about the levels of black, white, and shades of gray. The rods are located over the entire retina except at the very center. Rods are extremely sensitive to light but produce images with low acuity, or sharpness. Our eyes' ability to adapt to a dark room and eventually see objects is mediated by the rods in our eyes and is called **dark adaptation**. Cones make up the remaining 30 percent of the sensory receptors in your eyes and are located mainly in the center of the retina. Cones transmit information about color and produce images with very high acuity. Our ability to quickly adapt when we enter a bright room is called **light adaptation** and is accomplished by the cones. The place where the information from the rods and cones leaves the eye is called the **blind spot** because there are no visual receptors there to receive information.

The exact method the cones use to transmit information about color is still unknown. Two theories are currently proposed. The **trichromatic theory** was originally proposed by Thomas Young and later modified by Hermann Helmholtz. The theory suggests that there are three types of cones, red, green, and blue, that combine to produce sensation of color much like three spotlights would combine to produce the full spectrum of colors. The trichromatic theory most likely is an accurate description of the cones but cannot explain certain visual phenomena such as the **afterimage**. The afterimage is the image you see after staring at something and then looking away. For example, stare at something red, then look away and you see a green afterimage. A different theory of color perception known as the **opponent-process theory** was developed to explain phenomena such as the afterimage. The theory states that cones are arranged in pairs with a red-green pair and a blue-yellow pair. In one member of the pair is firing, then the other member cannot. When you stare at something red, the red member sends information and the green member is inhibited. When you look away, the green member is no longer inhibited and sends information even though you are not looking at anything green. Both the trichromatic theory and the opponent-process theory are probably correct. The trichromatic theory most likely explains the actions of cones in the retina, while the opponent-process theory explains the actions higher up in the visual system in the thalamus of the brain.

After light is converted to an electrical-chemical signal by the rods and cones, the message travels out of the eye through the optic nerve, crosses over at the optic chiasm, enters the medulla and then the thalamus. From the thalamus the signal is sent to the occipital lobes, when if you recall from the previous chapter, are responsible for processing visual information. Color blindness is caused by defective cones in the retina and can be one of three types.

Our sense of hearing, the auditory system, is activated by the vibrations of molecules in the air that surrounds us. These vibrations are called sound waves, and like light waves, we respond to three features of sound waves. **Pitch** corresponds to the frequency of the wave, **volume** is determined by the amplitude of the wave, and **timbre** relates to the purity of the wavelengths. Humans can only respond to wavelengths of a certain frequency. The average range for humans is between 20 and 20,000 **Hertz** (Hz) or waves per second. Sound waves enter our auditory system through the **pinna**, travel down the ear canal – also known as the **auditory canal,** and then vibrate the eardrum which causes the hammer, anvil, and stirrup to vibrate. The vibrations of the stirrup cause the oval window to move back and forth which causes the fluid in the **cochlea** to vibrate. The fluid causes the basilar membrane to vibrate which causes the organ of Corti to move up, and this causes the **hair cells** to bend. The hair cells are the sensory receptors of the auditory system, and the movement of the hair cells triggers an action potential in the axon. The axons travel to the brain in a bundle called the **auditory nerve**. A louder noise causes the hair cells to fire more action potentials.

There are three theories that explain how the brain receives information about pitch. **Place theory** states that pitch is determined by the place on the organ of Corti that is stimulated. The **frequency theory** suggests that the speed of vibrations of the basilar membrane determine the pitch heard by the person. The **volley principle** suggests that hair cells take turns firing in a process called volleying. All three theories are correct. Frequency theory holds true for wavelengths of 100 Hz or less, volley theory covers the wavelengths from 100 to 1000 Hz, and place theory seems to account for the wavelengths faster than 1000 Hz. Hearing impairment is the term used to describe difficulties in hearing. Conduction hearing impairment occurs from damage to the eardrum or the bones of the middle ear. Nerve hearing impairment is caused by problems in the inner ear or in the auditory pathways and cortical areas of the brain. Ordinary hearing aids are designed to assist with conduction hearing impairment, whereas **cochlear implants** can be used to restore some hearing for people with nerve hearing impairment.

The sense of taste, or **gustation**, is activated by chemicals that dissolve in the mouth. The sensory receptors are receptor cells found within the **taste buds** that are located on the little bumps on the tongue, cheek, and roof of your mouth The little bumps that you can actually see with your eye are called papillae. Five basic tastes have been proposed; they are sweet, sour, salty, bitter, and umami. Umami is the newest taste and corresponds to a "brothy" taste like the taste from chicken soup.

The sense of smell, or **olfaction**, is also a chemical sense. Humans have about 10 million olfactory receptor cells located in a 1 square inch area at the top of the nasal passage. Olfactory receptor cells send their axons directly to the **olfactory bulbs** which are located right under the frontal lobes.

The sense of touch is actually composed of several sensations and is more accurately referred to as **somesthetic senses**. The three somesthetic senses are **skin**, **kinesthetic**, and **vestibular**. The skin contains at least six different types of sensory receptors and transmits information about touch, pressure, temperature, and pain. The currently accepted theory about pain is called **gate-control theory** and suggests that pain information is regulated by a number of factors in the brain and spinal cord. Two chemicals involved with pain messages are substance P and endorphins. Substance P transmits information about pain to the brain and spinal cord, while endorphins inhibit the transmission of signals of pain. The kinesthetic sense relays information about your body's sense of position in space. The information comes from sensory receptors called **proprioceptive receptors** located in your skin, joints, muscles, and tendons. Our sense of balance, or **vestibular sense**, is regulated by receptor cells in the otolith organs and the **semicircular canals**. Both structures are located near the cochlea of the inner ear. The otolith organs contain small crystals suspended in fluid. Movement causes the crystals to move and activates the sensory receptors. The semicircular canals are three fluid-filled cavities located in three different planes.

Perception is the interpretation of sensation and seems to follow some basic principles, although individual and cultural differences in perception have been recorded. One principle is that of perceptual constancy. We tend to view objects as the same **size**, **shape**, and **brightness** even if the sensations we are receiving from our sensory systems are not constant in size, shape, or brightness. An example of perceptual constancy is our perception of the size and shape of a door as it is opened and closed. Gestalt psychologists believe that when people are presented with visual information, they interpret the information according to certain expected patterns or rules. The patterns are called the Gestalt principles of perception, and they include the following seven rules: **figure-ground relationships**, **closure**, **similarity**, **continuity**, **contiguity**, **proximity**, and common region. The principle of figure-ground relationships can be illustrated by looking at **reversible figures**, which are visual illusions in which the figure and ground seem to switch back and forth.

Visual perception of depth, called **depth perception**, appears to be present at a very early age. Visual cues for depth that require the use of one eye are referred to as **monocular cues** and include **linear perspective**, **relative size**, **overlap** or interposition, **aerial perspective**, **texture gradient**, **motion parallax**, and **accommodation**. Visual cues that use two eyes are called **binocular cues** and include **convergence** and **binocular disparity**. An **illusion** is a perception that does not correspond to reality. Some famous visual illusions include the **Müller-Lyer illusion**, the moon illusion, and illusions of motion. In addition to cultural and individual differences, perceptions can be influenced by **perceptual sets** or expectancies. One example of perceptual expectancy is **top-down processing** and occurs when a person uses pre-existing knowledge to fit individual features into an organized whole. If there is no expectancy to help organize information, a person might use **bottom-up processing** to build a complete perception by making sense of the smaller features piece by piece.

Parapsychology is the field of psychology that studies phenomenon that fall outside the normal realm of psychology such as extrasensory perception or ESP.

1. Chapter 3 presented information about seven different sensory systems. A chart can be extremely helpful in organizing these various components. See how much of the information you can fill in below and go to the textbook to find the remaining answers. The first row is filled in for you. A complete table can be found at the end of the Study Hints section.

Sensory System	External Stimulus	Sensory Organ	Sensory Receptor	Proposed Theories
visual system	light waves	eyes	rods and cones	trichromatic theory opponent-process theory

2. Many students confuse the Gestalt principles of perception with the monocular cues for depth perception. The two are listed below. The principles of perception deal with the rules we use to decide which objects should be grouped together, while the monocular depth cues are used to determine how far away objects are.

Gestalt principles of perception	Monocular depth cues
closure	linear perspective
similarity	texture gradient
contiguity	aerial position
continuity	interposition
figure-ground relationship	motion parallax
proximity	relative size

In order to help clarify the difference, use these cues to draw two separate pictures.

Use one or more of the Gestalt principles to create a picture with at least two separate groups of objects.

Use one or more of the monocular depth cues to draw a picture of a tree, house and a person. Make sure the tree is the farthest object and the person is the closest object.

Sensory System	External Stimulus	Sensory Organ	Sensory Receptor	Proposed Theories
visual system	light waves	eyes	rods and cones	trichromatic theory opponent-process theory
auditory system	sound waves	ears	hair cells in the organ of Corti	place theory frequency theory volley theory
gustatory system (taste)	soluble chemicals	tongue, cheeks, mouth	taste cells in the taste buds	
olfactory system (smell)	air-borne chemicals	nose	olfactory receptors	
skin senses	pressure, temperature, pain	skin	six different types including free nerve endings and pacinian corpuscles	gate-control theory of pain
kinesthetic	body position	skin, joints, muscles, and tendons	proprioceptive receptors	
vestibular	acceleration and tilt	semicircular canals and otolith organs	hair cells	

LEARNING OBJECTIVES

3.1   How does sensation travel through the central nervous system, and why are some sensations ignored?

3.2   What is light, and how does it travel through the various parts of the eye?

3.3   How do the eyes see, and how do the eyes see different colors?

3.4   What is sound, and how does it travel through the various parts of the ear?

3.5   Why are some people unable to hear, and how can their hearing be improved?

3.6   How do the senses of taste and smell work, and how are they alike?

3.7   What allows people to experience the sense of touch, pain, motion, and balance?

3.8   What are perception and perceptual constancies?

3.9   What are the Gestalt principles of perception?

3.10 How do infants develop perceptual abilities, including the perception of depth and its cues?

3.11 What are visual illusions, and how can they and other factors influence and alter perception?

PRACTICE EXAM

For the following multiple choice questions, select the answer you feel best answers the question.

1. The most important role of sensory receptors is to _____.
    a) coordinate communications within the body
    b) regulate the body's response to pain
    c) control skeletal muscle contractions
    d) convert an external stimulus into an electrical-chemical message the nervous system can use

2. The point at which a person can detect a stimulus 50 percent of the time it is presented is called the
    _____.
    a) absolute threshold
    b) range threshold
    c) differential threshold
    d) noticeable threshold

3. An automobile manufacturer has decided to add a little bit of horsepower to its cars. They have a device that alters horsepower one unit at a time. Suppose drivers first notice the increase on a 200 horsepower car when it reaches 220 horsepower. How much horsepower must be added to a 150 horsepower car for drivers to notice the difference?
    a) 5
    b) 10
    c) 15
    d) 25

4. If you stared at a picture for a long period of time, you might think the image of the picture would fade due to sensory adaptation. This would be the case except for the tiny vibrations of your eye called
   a) glissades.
   b) saccades.
   c) habituation movements.
   d) light wave responses.

5. Light is said to have a dual nature, meaning it can be thought of in two different ways. These two ways are
   a) particles and photons.
   b) waves and frequencies.
   c) photons and waves.
   d) dark light and daylight.

6. When light waves enter the eye, they first pass through the
   a) iris.
   b) lens.
   c) pupil.
   d) cornea.

7. Which of the following is true about cones?
   a) They are more sensitive to light than rods.
   b) They are found mainly in the center of the eye.
   c) They operate mainly at night.
   d) They respond only to black and white.

8. The existence of afterimages in complementary colors best supports the _____ theory of color vision.
   a) opponent-process
   b) place
   c) vibrational
   d) Hering trichromatic

9. Which of the following properties of sound would be the most similar to the color or hue of light?
   a) pitch
   b) loudness
   c) purity
   d) timbre

10. Vibrating molecules in the air are called
    a) light waves.
    b) sound waves.
    c) odor molecules.
    d) taste sensations.

11. The membrane stretched over the opening to the middle ear is the
    a) pinna.
    b) oval window.
    c) tympanic membrane.
    d) cochlea.

12. Which is the correct order of the three bones of the middle ear, from the outside in?
   a) anvil, hammer, stirrup
   b) hammer, anvil, stirrup
   c) stirrup, anvil, hammer
   d) stirrup, hammer, anvil

13. Which theory proposes that above 100 Hz but below 1000Hz, auditory neurons do not fire all at once but in rotation?
   a) place theory
   b) volley theory
   c) frequency theory
   d) rotational theory

14. The _____ theory explains how we hear sounds above 1,000 Hz.
   a) place
   b) frequency
   c) volley
   d) adaptive

15. Ringing or buzzing sensations in the ears may be a sign of
   a) noise-produced hearing damage.
   b) habituation of the hair cells.
   c) rigidity of the ossicles.
   d) volley theory morbidity.

16. _____ is the term used to refer to difficulties in hearing.
   a) Hearing impairment
   b) Timbre blindness
   c) Acoustic stiffness
   d) Volley involution

17. If a severe ear infection damages the bones of the middle ear, you may develop _____ hearing impairedness.
   a) nerve
   b) stimulation
   c) brain pathway
   d) conduction

18. Cochlear implants bypass the
   a) outer ear.
   b) outer and middle ear.
   c) outer, middle, and inner ear.
   d) none of the above

19. The "bumps" on the tongue that are visible to the eye are the _____.
   a) olfactory receptors
   b) taste buds
   c) papillae
   d) taste receptors

20. An olfactory stimulus travels from receptor to _____.
   a) olfactory bulb
   b) thalamus
   c) amygdala
   d) pons

21 In gate-control theory, Substance P
   a) opens the spinal gates for pain.
   b) closes the spinal gates for pain.
   c) is unrelated to pain.
   d) is similar in function to endorphins.

22. Which is the best description of the vestibular senses?
   a) having to do with touch, pressure, temperature, and pain
   b) having to do with the location of body parts in relation to the ground and to each other
   c) having to do with movement and body position
   d) having to do with your location as compared to the position of the sun

23. We know when we are moving up and down in an elevator because of the movement of tiny crystals in the
   a) outer ear.
   b) inner ear.
   c) otolith organs.
   d) middle ear.

24. Which might be the best explanation of motion sickness, according to your textbook?
   a) the conflict between vision and the vestibular organs
   b) fluid circulating in the semicircular canals
   c) human evolutionary history in that poisons make us dizzy, so when motion makes us dizzy we try to expel the poison
   d) none of these

25. The tendency to interpret an object as always being the same size, regardless of its distance from the viewer, is known as _____.
   a) size constancy
   b) shape constancy
   c) brightness constancy
   d) color constancy

26. Closure is the tendency _____
   a) to perceive objects, or figures, on some background.
   b) to complete figures that are incomplete.
   c) to perceive objects that are close to each other as part of the same grouping.
   d) to perceive things with a continuous pattern rather than with a complex, broken-up pattern.

27. Which Gestalt principle is at work in the old phrase, "birds of a feather flock together"?
   a) closure
   b) similarity
   c) expectancy
   d) continuity

28. Visual distance and depth cues that require the use of both eyes are called _____.
   a) monocular cues
   b) diocular cues
   c) binocular cues
   d) dichromatic cues

29. The Müller-Lyer illusion exists in cultures in which there are
   a) more men than women.
   b) more women than men.
   c) few buildings.
   d) buildings with lots of corners.

30. People's tendency to perceive things a certain way because their previous experiences or expectations influence them is called
   a) a perceptual set.
   b) binocular disparity.
   c) motion parallax.
   d) accommodation.

31. A recent review of studies on ESP using the ganzfeld procedure concluded that _____.
   a) no convincing evidence for psychic ability had emerged from any of the studies .
   b) no convincing evidence for psychic ability had emerged from the majority of studies.
   c) convincing evidence for psychic ability had been found in the majority of studies.
   d) convincing evidence for psychic ability had been found in virtually all studies.

PRACTICE EXAM ANSWERS

1. d   D is the correct answer. Sensory receptors are the body's "antennae" to the outside world. Each sensory receptor type is specially designed to receive a specific external signal and convert it to an electrical-chemical signal.

2. a   Gustav Fechner investigated the sensitivity of the human sensory systems and called the lowest level of a stimulus that a person could detect half of the time the absolute threshold.

3. c   According to Weber's law, the just noticeable difference (jnd) is a constant proportion. A change from 200 to 220 represents an increase of 20 units and a jnd of 20/200 or 0.10, which is 10 percent. If the company starts with 150 horsepower, they will need to increase it by 10 percent in order for the driver to notice a difference. Ten percent of 150 is 15.

4. b   Saccades are the small quick movements your eye makes in order to keep the visual stimuli changing. When our sensory receptors receive unchanging, constant stimuli, they eventually stop responding to the stimulus. This process is known as sensory adaptation.

5. c   Light can be thought of as a wave and as particles. Photons are the specific type of particles that light is composed of.

6. d   The cornea is the outermost coating of the eye. It is transparent and serves to protect the eye and to help focus the light coming in to the eye.

7. b   Cones are the sensory receptors that respond to color and send visual information of high acuity or visual sharpness. The cones are located primarily in the center of the retina. Choices a and d more accurately describe the rods.

8. a   The opponent process theory of color vision was introduced, in part, to explain the phenomenon of the afterimage.

9. a   Pitch is determined by the length of the wave just as color is determined by the length of the wave. Both brightness and loudness are determined by the height of the wave.

10. b   The outer and middle ear are designed to funnel the vibrating air molecules to the inner ear where they are translated into an electrical signal and sent to the brain.

11. c   The tympanic membrane is also known as the eardrum. Sound waves cause the tympanic membrane to vibrate when then causes the bones of the middle ear to move back and forth.

12. b   The order of the bones is hammer, anvil, stirrup which spells "has."

13. b   Volley theory describes the perception of pitch for the middle frequencies (100 – 1000 Hz). Frequency theory describes the low frequencies (100 Hz and less), and Place theory describes the fastest frequencies (1000 Hz and higher).

14. a   The idea is that at very high sound frequencies, the action potential frequency can't keep up, so pitch has to be coded by the place on the basilar membrane that is activated.

15. a   Damage to the hair cells can cause the receptors to fire action potentials even when no stimulus is present. This can cause a sensation of ringing in the ears.

16. a   Hearing impairments are usually divided into impairments of conduction and nerve.

17. d   Conduction hearing impairment is caused by damage to the outer or middle ear.

18. b   Cochlear implants use an electronic device instead of the movements of the bones in the middle ear to convert the sound wave into a signal that is then sent to the auditory nerve in the inner ear.

19. c   The bumps you can see with your eye are the papillae. The taste buds are located along the sides of the papillae. Each taste bud contains 10-20 taste receptors.

20. a   The olfactory system is the only system in which the receptors send their signal directly to the higher brain and bypass the filtering process of the lower brain.

21. d   The gate-control theory of pain suggests that there are a number of factors in the central and peripheral nervous system that can inhibit or allow pain signals to be transmitted to the brain.

22. c   The vestibular sense provides you with a sense of balance and sends your brain information about acceleration and tilt.

23. c   Although the otolith organs are located in the inner ear, choice c is a more precise answer.

24. c   Although choice a is partially correct, the conflict between the visual and vestibular systems only explains the sense of dizziness, it does not explain the sense of nausea. Probably the best explanation for that is human evolutionary theory.

25. a   Size constancy refers to the fact that our perception of the size of an object tends to remain constant.

26. b   Closure is one of the Gestalt principles of perception and refers to our tendency to "close" objects to form a complete picture.

27. b   The saying is emphasizing that objects with similar characteristics ("birds of a feather") tend to be grouped together ("flock together"). This is the principle of similarity.

28. c   The phrase "ocular" means having to do with the eyes. "Mono" refers to one and "bi" refers to two. Therefore, the term binocular means seeing depth with two eyes.

29.   d   The carpentered-world theory states that the Müller-Lyer illusion does not exist in certain "primitive" cultures because they are not surrounded by straight lines and corners.

30.   a   An individual's expectations or perceptual set often influence perception of objects.

31.   b   The majority of quality studies have found no evidence for ESP. The studies that reported positive results have been flawed.

CHAPTER GLOSSARY

absolute threshold	the smallest amount of energy needed for a person to consciously detect a stimulus 50 percent of the time it is present.
accommodation	as a monocular clue, the brain's use of information about the changing thickness of the lens of the eye in response to looking at objects that are close or far away.
aerial perspective	the haziness that surrounds objects that are farther away from the viewer, causing the distance to be perceived as greater.
afterimage	images that occur when a visual sensation persists for a brief time even after the original stimulus is removed.
audition (auditory system)	the sensation of hearing.
auditory canal	short tunnel that runs from the pinna to the eardrum.
auditory nerve	bundle of axons from the hair cells in the inner ear.
binocular cues	cues for perceiving depth based on both eyes.
binocular disparity	the difference in images between the two eyes, which is greater for objects that are close and smaller for distant objects.
blind spot	area in the retina where visual information travels to the brain and thus no visual receptors are present.
bottom-up processing	the analysis of the smaller features to build up to a complete perception.
brightness	corresponds to the amplitude (or height) of a light wave.
brightness constancy	the tendency to perceive the apparent brightness of an object as the same even when the light conditions change.
closure	the tendency to complete figures that are incomplete.
cochlea	snail-like structure of the inner ear, filled with fluid.
cochlear implants	medical device surgically implanted to bypass damage in the inner ear and directly stimulate auditory nerve endings.
color blindness	reduced ability to distinguish colors due to damage to the cones of the retina.
color or hue	determined by the frequency (or length) of a light wave.
cones	visual sensory receptor found at the back of the retina, responsible for color vision and sharpness of vision.
contiguity	the tendency to perceive two things that happen close together in time as being related.
continuity	the tendency to perceive things as simply as possible, with a continuous pattern rather than with a complex, broken-up pattern.
convergence	the rotation of the two eyes in their sockets to focus on a single object, resulting in greater convergence for closer objects and less convergence if objects are distant.

dark adaptation	the recovery of the eye's sensitivity to visual stimuli in darkness after exposure to bright lights.
depth perception	the ability to perceive the world in three dimensions.
figure-ground relationships	the tendency to perceive objects, or figures, as existing on a background.
frequency theory	states that the perceived pitch is caused by the frequency of the incoming sound wave and subsequently the frequency of firing in the auditory nerve.
gate-control theory	theory of pain that states the psychological experience of pain is controlled by a series of "gates" in the central and peripheral nervous system that can allow or block the flow of the pain information depending on a number of factors.
gustation (gustatory system)	the sensation of taste.
habituation	tendency of the brain to stop attending to constant, unchanging information.
hair cells	sensory receptors of the auditory system. Specifically, specialized neurons that convert sound into an electrical-chemical signal.
Hertz (Hz)	cycles or waves per second, a measurement of frequency.
illusion	a perception that does not correspond to reality.
interposition (overlap)	the assumption that an object that appears to be blocking part of another object is in front of the second object and closer to the viewer.
just noticeable difference (jnd)	the smallest difference between two stimuli that is detectable 50 percent of the time.
kinesthetic senses	sense of the location of body parts in relation to the ground and each other.
light adaptation	the recovery of the eye's sensitivity to visual stimuli in light after exposure to darkness.
linear perspective	the tendency for parallel lines to appear to converge on each other.
monocular cues	cues for perceiving depth based on one eye only.
motion parallax	the perception of motion of objects in which close objects appear to move more quickly than objects that are farther away.
Müller-Lyer illusion	illusion of line length that is distorted by inward-turning or outward-turning corners on the ends of the lines, causing lines of equal length to appear to be different.
olfaction (olfactory system)	the sensation of smell.
olfactory bulbs	areas of the brain located just above the sinus cavity and just below the frontal lobes that receive information from the olfactory receptor cells.
opponent-process theory	theory of color vision that proposes four primary colors with cones arranged in pairs: red and green, blue and yellow.
optic nerve	bundle of axons carrying visual information from the retina to the brain.
parapsychology	the study of ESP, ghosts, and other subjects that do not normally fall in the realm of ordinary psychology.
perception	the method by which the sensations experienced at any given moment are interpreted and organized in some meaningful fashion.
perceptual sets	the tendency to perceive things a certain way because previous experiences or expectations influence those perceptions.
pinna	the outer ear that focuses sound waves for the middle and inner ears.
pitch	psychological experience of sound that corresponds to the frequency (or length) of the sound waves; higher frequencies are perceived as higher pitches.
place theory	theory of pitch that states that different pitches are experienced by the stimulation of hair cells in different locations on the organ of Corti.

proprioceptive receptors (proprioceptors)	sensory receptors that detect pain and pressure in the organs.
proximity	the tendency to perceive objects that are close to each other as part of the same grouping.
relative size	perception that occurs when objects that a person expects to be of a certain size appear to be small and are therefore assumed to be much farther away.
retina	nerve tissue lining the inside of the back of the eye that contains sensory receptors that convert focused light into nerve impulses and transmits the information to the brain through the optic nerves.
reversible figures	visual illusions in which the figure and ground can be reversed.
rods	visual sensory receptor found at the back of the retina, responsible for non-color sensitivity to low levels of light.
saturation	relates to the degree of mixture of light waves of varying frequency.
semicircular canals	three circular tubes filled with fluid and lined with hair-like receptors that fire when the body moves in any direction.
sensation	the activation of receptors in the various sense organs.
sensory adaptation	tendency of sensory receptor cells to become less responsive to a stimulus that is unchanging.
sensory receptors	specialized neurons designed to convey information regarding external stimuli to the nervous system.
shape constancy	the tendency to interpret the shape of an object as being constant, even when its shape changes on the retina.
similarity	the tendency to perceive things that look similar to each other as being part of the same group.
size constancy	the tendency to interpret an object as always being the same actual size, regardless of its actual distance.
skin senses	the sensations of touch, pressure, temperature, and pain.
somesthetic senses	the body senses consisting of the skin senses, the kinesthetic sense, and the vestibular senses.
synesthesia	a condition in which one sensory input is perceived by more than one sensory system. For example, the individual might eat something and experience the taste sensation along with a visual sensation.
taste buds	small structures located under the papillae in the mouth that contain the sensory receptors for the gustatory system.
texture gradient	the tendency for textured surfaces to appear to become smaller and finer as distance from the viewer increases.
timbre	(pronounced TAM-br) the quality of a sound that distinguishes it from other sounds with the same pitch and volume Also referred to as sound quality, for example, thin, thick, light, dark, sharp, dull, smooth, rough, warm, cold. It is this quality which allows you to distinguish between a flute and an oboe playing the same pitch at the same volume. Corresponds to the degree of mixture of varying wavelengths.
top-down processing	the use of pre-existing knowledge to organize individual features into a unified whole.
transduction	the process of converting outside stimuli into neural activity.
trichromatic theory	theory of color vision that proposes three types of cones: red, blue, and green.
vestibular senses	the sensations of movement, balance, and body position.

volley principle	theory of pitch that states that frequencies above 100 Hz cause the hair cells (auditory neurons) to fire in a volley pattern, or taking turns in firing.
volume	sensation of the loudness of sound determined by the amplitude (or height) of a sound wave.
Weber's law	states that the size of the just noticeable difference is a constant proportion.

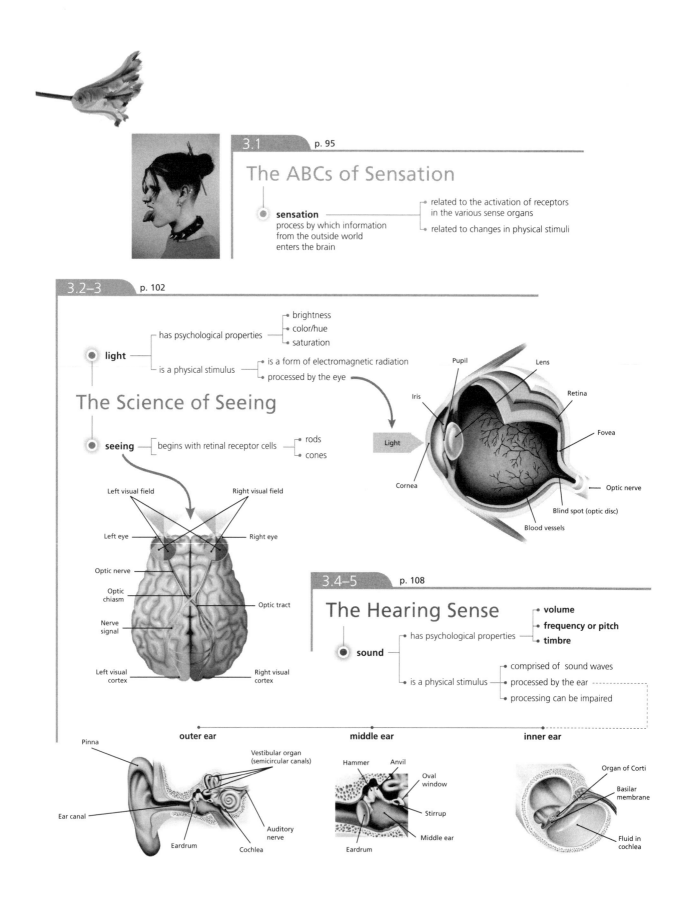

3.1   p. 95

The ABCs of Sensation

sensation — related to the activation of receptors in the various sense organs
process by which information from the outside world enters the brain — related to changes in physical stimuli

3.2–3   p. 102

light — has psychological properties — brightness
— color/hue
— saturation

is a physical stimulus — is a form of electromagnetic radiation
— processed by the eye

The Science of Seeing

seeing — begins with retinal receptor cells — rods
— cones

Pupil
Lens
Iris
Retina
Light
Fovea
Cornea
Optic nerve
Blind spot (optic disc)
Blood vessels

Left visual field
Right visual field
Left eye
Right eye
Optic nerve
Optic chiasm
Optic tract
Nerve signal
Left visual cortex
Right visual cortex

3.4–5   p. 108

The Hearing Sense

sound — has psychological properties — **volume**
— **frequency or pitch**
— **timbre**

is a physical stimulus — comprised of sound waves
— processed by the ear
— processing can be impaired

outer ear   **middle ear**   **inner ear**

Pinna
Vestibular organ (semicircular canals)
Hammer   Anvil
Oval window
Organ of Corti
Basilar membrane
Ear canal
Stirrup
Eardrum
Cochlea
Auditory nerve
Middle ear
Eardrum
Fluid in cochlea

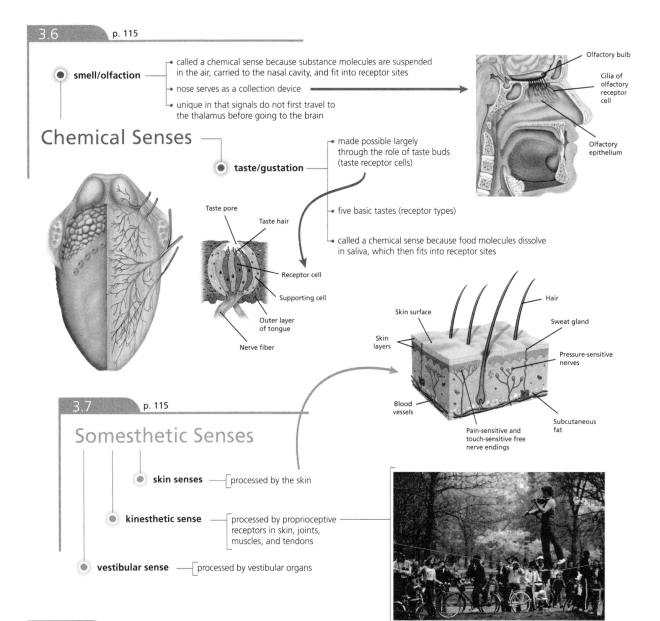

- **smell/olfaction**
  - called a chemical sense because substance molecules are suspended in the air, carried to the nasal cavity, and fit into receptor sites
  - nose serves as a collection device
  - unique in that signals do not first travel to the thalamus before going to the brain

Olfactory bulb

Cilia of olfactory receptor cell

Olfactory epithelium

Chemical Senses

- **taste/gustation**
  - made possible largely through the role of taste buds (taste receptor cells)
  - five basic tastes (receptor types)
  - called a chemical sense because food molecules dissolve in saliva, which then fits into receptor sites

Taste pore

Taste hair

Receptor cell

Supporting cell

Outer layer of tongue

Nerve fiber

Hair

Skin surface

Sweat gland

Skin layers

Pressure-sensitive nerves

Blood vessels

Pain-sensitive and touch-sensitive free nerve endings

Subcutaneous fat

Somesthetic Senses

- **skin senses** ⎯ processed by the skin
- **kinesthetic sense** ⎯ processed by proprioceptive receptors in skin, joints, muscles, and tendons
- **vestibular sense** ⎯ processed by vestibular organs

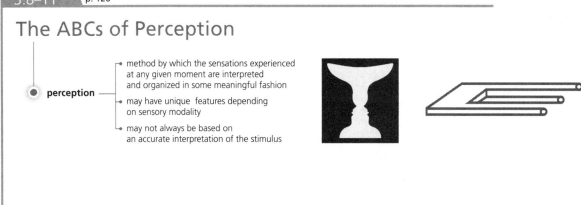

The ABCs of Perception

- **perception**
  - method by which the sensations experienced at any given moment are interpreted and organized in some meaningful fashion
  - may have unique features depending on sensory modality
  - may not always be based on an accurate interpretation of the stimulus

3.1 The ABCs of Sensation

Table 3.1 **Examples of Absolute Thresholds**

Table 3.1 **Examples of Absolute Thresholds**

SENSE	THRESHOLD
Sight	A candle flame at 30 miles on a clear, dark night
Hearing	The tick of a watch 20 feet away in a quiet room
Smell	One drop of perfume diffused throughout a three-room apartment
Taste	1 teaspoon of sugar in 2 gallons of water
Touch	A bee's wing falling on the cheek from 1 centimeter above

_____
_____
_____
_____
_____
_____
_____
_____
_____

Figure 3.1 **The Visible Spectrum**

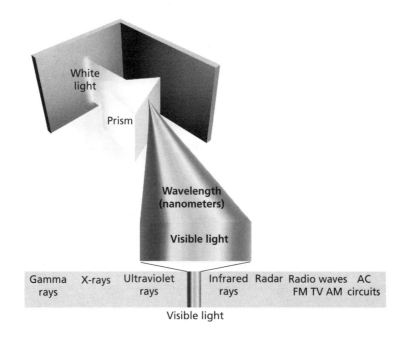

Figure 3.2 **Structure of the Eye**

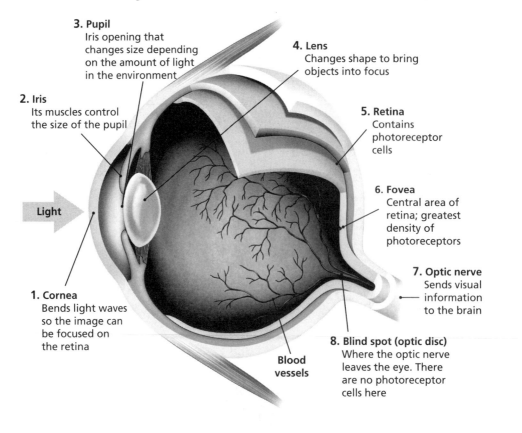

3. Pupil
Iris opening that changes size depending on the amount of light in the environment

4. Lens
Changes shape to bring objects into focus

2. Iris
Its muscles control the size of the pupil

5. Retina
Contains photoreceptor cells

Light

6. Fovea
Central area of retina; greatest density of photoreceptors

7. Optic nerve
Sends visual information to the brain

1. Cornea
Bends light waves so the image can be focused on the retina

Blood vessels

8. Blind spot (optic disc)
Where the optic nerve leaves the eye. There are no photoreceptor cells here

Figure 3.3 **Common Visual Problems: Nearsightedness and Farsightedness**

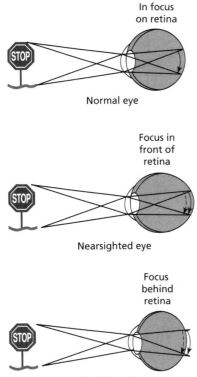

In focus
on retina

Normal eye

Focus in
front of
retina

Nearsighted eye

Focus
behind
retina

Farsighted eye

Figure 3.4 **The Parts of the Retina**

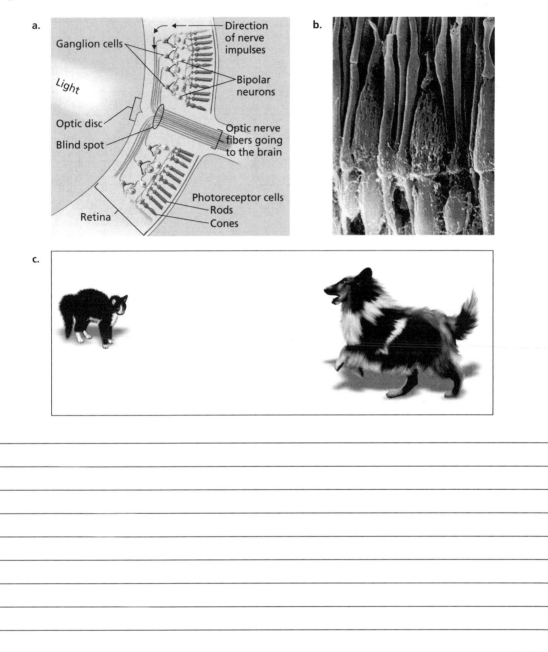

a.
Ganglion cells
Light
Optic disc
Blind spot
Retina

Direction of nerve impulses
Bipolar neurons
Optic nerve fibers going to the brain
Photoreceptor cells
Rods
Cones

b.

c.

Figure 3.5 **Crossing of the Optic Nerve**

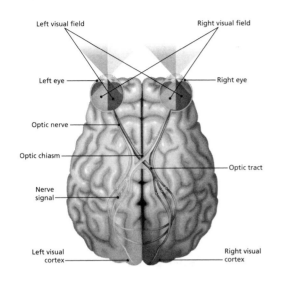

Left visual field

Right visual field

Left eye

Right eye

Optic nerve

Optic chiasm

Optic tract

Nerve signal

Left visual cortex

Right visual cortex

3.4–3.5 **The Hearing Sense**

Figure 3.8 **Sound Waves and Decibels**

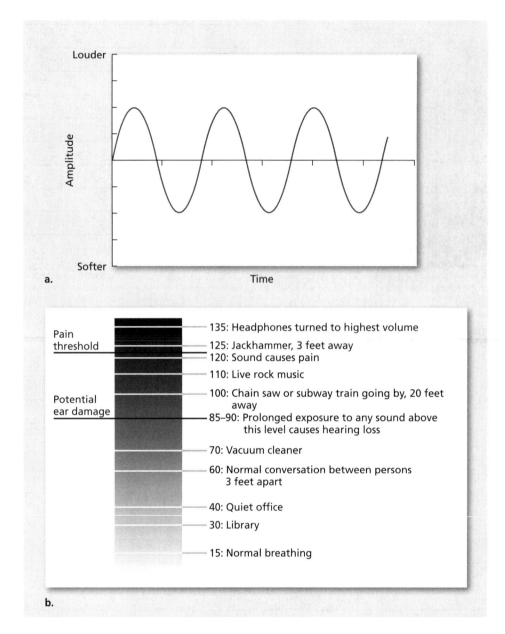

Figure 3.9 **The Structure of the Ear**

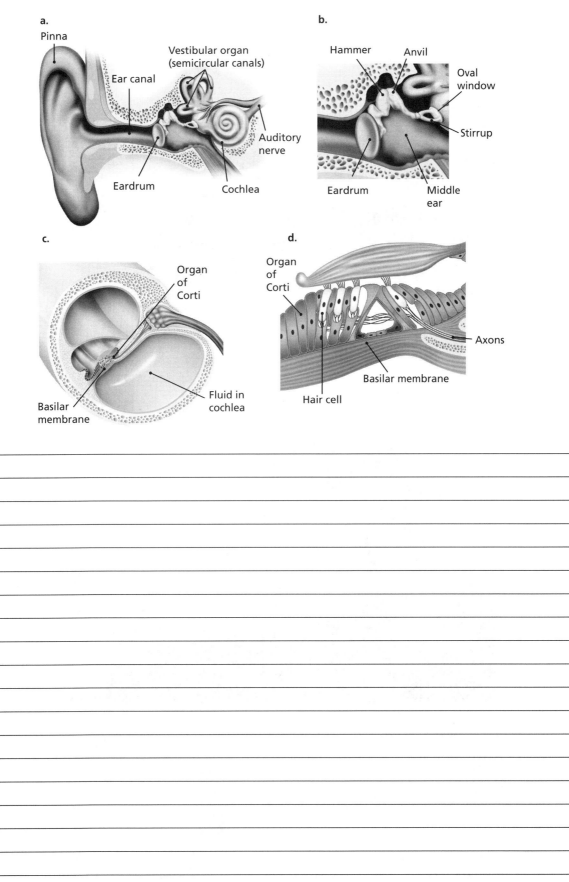

Figure 3.10 **Cochlear Implant**

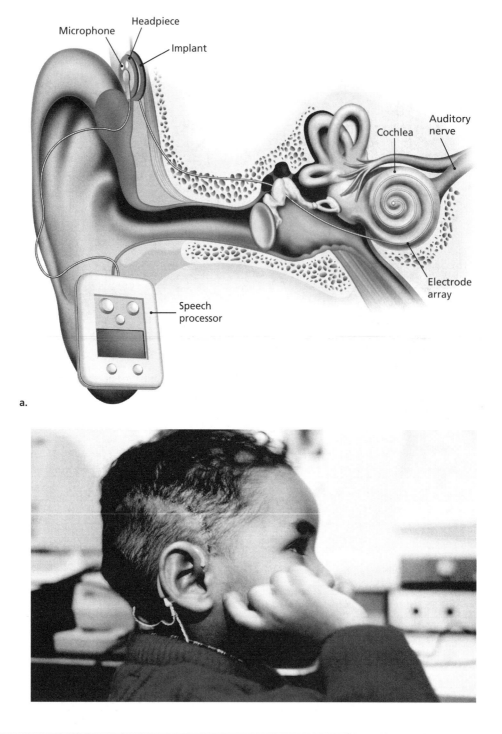

a.

_____
_____
_____
_____
_____
_____
_____
_____
_____
_____

Figure 3.11 **The Tongue and Taste Buds—A Crosscut View of the Tongue**

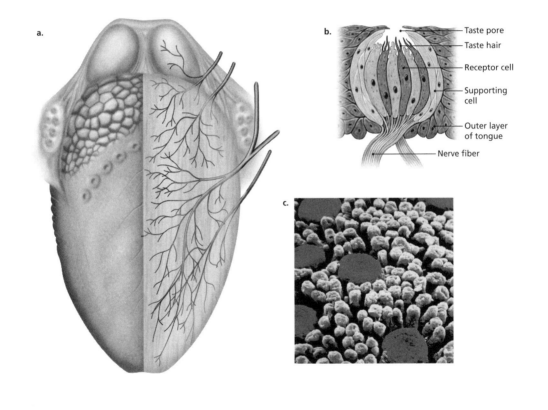

a.

b.
- Taste pore
- Taste hair
- Receptor cell
- Supporting cell
- Outer layer of tongue
- Nerve fiber

c.

_____
_____
_____
_____
_____
_____
_____

Figure 3.12 **The Olfactory Receptors**

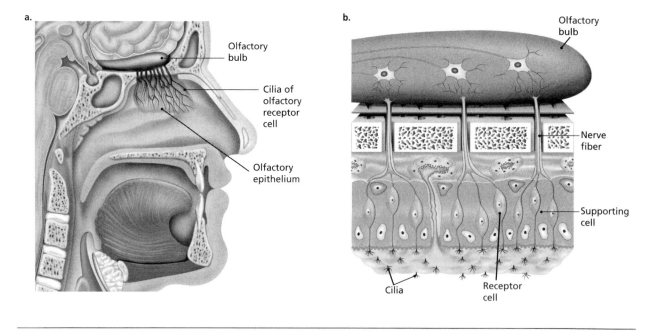

a.

Olfactory bulb

Cilia of olfactory receptor cell

Olfactory epithelium

b.

Olfactory bulb

Nerve fiber

Supporting cell

Cilia

Receptor cell

_____

_____

_____

_____

_____

_____

_____

_____

_____

_____

_____

_____

_____

3.7 **Somesthetic Senses**

_____

_____

_____

_____

_____

_____

_____

_____

_____

_____

_____

_____

Figure 3.13 **Cross Section of the Skin and Its Receptors**

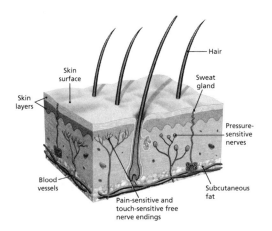

_____
_____
_____
_____
_____
_____
_____
_____
_____
_____

3.8–3.11 **The ABCs of Perception**

_____
_____
_____
_____
_____
_____
_____
_____
_____
_____

Figure 3.14 **Shape Constancy**

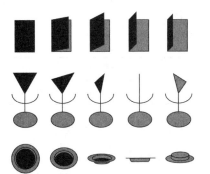

_____
_____
_____
_____
_____
_____
_____
_____
_____
_____

Figure 3.15 **The Necker Cube**

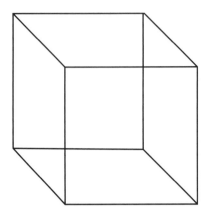

Figure 3.16 **Figure–Ground Illusion**

Figure 3.17 **Gestalt Principles of Grouping**

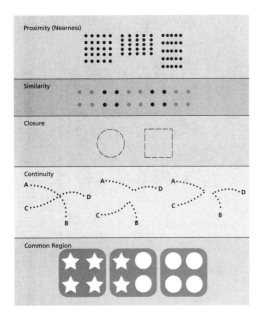

_____
_____
_____
_____
_____
_____
_____
_____
_____
_____
_____
_____
_____
_____
_____
_____
_____
_____

Figure 3.18 **The Visual Cliff Experiment**

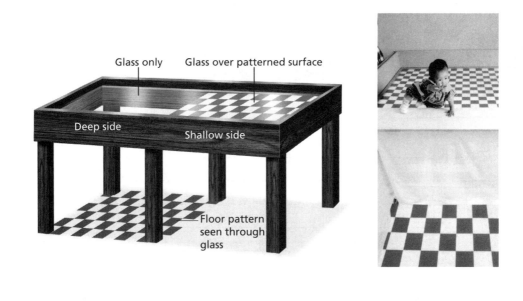

_____
_____
_____
_____
_____
_____
_____
_____

Figure 3.19 **Examples of Pictorial Depth Cues**

Figure 3.20 **Binocular Cues to Depth Perception**

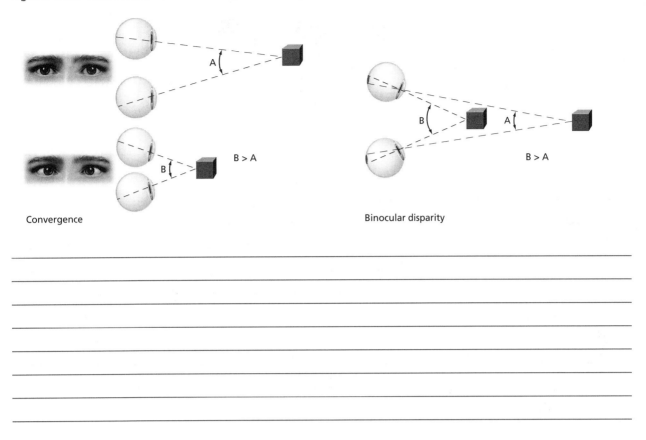

Convergence

Binocular disparity

Figure 3.21 **The Müller-Lyer Illusion**

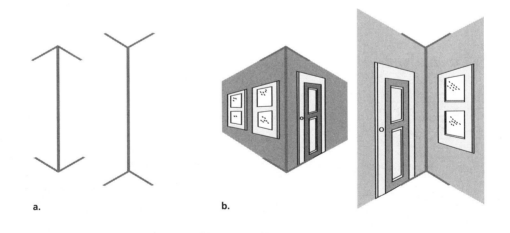

a.

b.

Figure 3.22 **Perceptual Set**

_____
_____
_____
_____
_____
_____
_____
_____
_____
_____
_____
_____
_____
_____
_____
_____

Figure 3.23 **The Devil's Trident**

NOTES

NOTES

YOU KNOW YOU ARE READY FOR THE TEST IF YOU ARE ABLE TO...

- Define consciousness and discuss the different levels of consciousness.
- Explain the factors that control sleep, theories on the purpose of sleep, the stages of sleep, and disorders of sleep.
- Discuss dreams and three theories that attempt to explain the purpose of dreams.
- Introduce the phenomenon of hypnosis and two theories suggesting the underlying mechanism.
- Describe properties and potential dangers of psychoactive drugs including stimulants, depressants, narcotics, and hallucinogens.
- Talk about the effects of sleep deprivation

RAPID REVIEW

Consciousness is defined as a person's awareness of the world around him or her. **Waking consciousness** is defined as the state of awareness where our thoughts and feelings are clear and organized. **Altered states of consciousness** describe a shift in the quality or pattern of a person's awareness. Examples of altered states of consciousness include using drugs, daydreaming, being hypnotized, or simply sleeping.

The sleep-wake cycle is a **circadian rhythm**, meaning one cycle takes about a day to complete. The cycle is regulated by the **suprachiasmatic nucleus (SCN)** located in the hypothalamus. The SCN responds to changes in daylight and regulates the release of melatonin from the pineal gland and body temperature accordingly. By the end of the day, higher melatonin levels and lower body temperature cause people to feel sleepy. In addition, high levels of serotonin are believed to produce feelings of sleepiness. The sleep-wake cycle tends to shift to a 25-hour cycle when subjects do not have access to the sun or clocks. **Sleep deprivation**, or loss of sleep, results in an increase in **microsleeps**, concentration problems, and an inability to perform simple tasks. Participants in a number of sleep deprivation studies reported that they were unaware of their impaired functioning. Two theories are currently proposed for why we sleep. The **adaptive theory** suggests that we sleep to avoid predators, while the **restorative theory** states that sleep is needed to replenish chemicals and repair cellular damage. Both theories are probably partially correct.

Based on brain wave activity recorded with the use of an EEG, sleep has been divided into two different types, **rapid eye movement (REM) sleep** and **non-REM sleep**. Non-REM sleep is a deep, restful sleep and consists of four stages. Stage 1 sleep is also called light sleep and occurs when brain activity begins to shift from **alpha** to **theta wave** activity. Many people experience a hypnic jerk in this stage when their body jerks suddenly and wakes them up. As body temperature continues to drop and heart rate slows, sleep spindles begin to appear on the EEG recording, signaling Stage 2 of non-REM sleep. Stage 3 occurs when the slow, large **delta waves** first appear; and when delta waves account for more than 50 percent of the total brain activity, the person is said to be in Stage 4, the deepest stage of sleep.

After a person cycles through Stages 1-4 and back, instead of entering Stage 1, people experience REM sleep. During this type of sleep, the brain is active and displays beta wave activity, the eye exhibits rapid movements, and the skeletal muscles of the body are temporarily paralyzed. This paralysis is referred to as **REM paralysis**. When a person is wakened from this type of sleep they often report being in a dream state. Most likely, around 90 percent of dreams take place in REM sleep, although dreams also do occur in non-REM sleep. Contrary to popular belief, people do not go crazy when deprived of REM sleep; however, they do spend longer amounts of time in REM sleep when allowed to sleep normally again. This phenomenon is known as **REM rebound**. **Nightmares** are bad dreams and typically occur in REM sleep. **REM behavior disorder** is a rare disorder in which a person's muscles are not paralyzed during REM sleep, allowing them to thrash about and even get up and act out their dreams.

There are a large number of disorders associated with sleep. **Sleepwalking**, or somnambulism, occurs in Stage 4, as well as the rare disorder of **night terrors**. Most people state that they are not aware of the actions they committed during a sleepwalking episode. The explanation of "sleepwalking" has been used as a successful defense in several trials for murder, but in these cases, the term sleepwalking is more likely referring to the condition known as REM behavior disorder. **Insomnia** is the inability to get to sleep, stay asleep, or get a good night of quality sleep. **Sleep apnea** is a disorder in which a person actually stops breathing for brief periods throughout the night. **Narcolepsy** is a genetic disorder in which a person suddenly enters REM sleep during the day. The attack can occur many times throughout the day and without warning. The attacks often occur with cataplexy, or a sudden loss of muscle tone.

Several theories have been proposed to explain why dreams occur. Sigmund Freud believed that dreams represented our unconscious thoughts and desires. He called the actual content of our dream the <u>manifest content</u> and the real meaning of the dream the <u>latent content</u>. The **activation-synthesis hypothesis** was originally proposed by Hobson and McCarley and suggests that dreams are caused by lower brain areas activating the cortex and the cortex fitting together (or synthesizing) the random input from the lower brain. The **activation-information mode model (AIM)** expands on the activation-synthesis model in an attempt to explain the meaningful, realistic, and consistent nature of many dreams. AIM proposes that the cortex uses information from the previous days as it pieces together the input coming from the lower brain. A considerable amount of information is known about the content of dreams. Most dreams tend to reflect events in everyday life as well as the "personality" of the dreamer's culture. Men tend to dream about males, weapons, tools, cars, roads; and their dreams occur in outdoor or unfamiliar settings containing more physical aggression than women's dreams. Men also report more sexual dreams. Women tend to dream about men and women equally; they also are more likely to report dreams about people they know, family, home, concerns about their appearances and dreams in which they are the victims of aggressive acts. Dreams of being naked in public appear to be common in many cultures.

Hypnosis is a state of consciousness in which a person is especially susceptive to suggestion. Hypnosis can reduce the sensation of pain, create temporary states of amnesia, and affect sensory perception; but it cannot increase physical strength, enhance memory, or regress a person back to their childhood. One theory of hypnosis proposed by Ernst Hilgard suggests that the hypnotized person is in a state of dissociation with one part of the brain unaware of the activities happening under hypnosis and another part aware and simply watching what is happening. Hilgard called the part of the conscious that was aware of the activities the hidden observer. The **social-cognitive explanation** of hypnosis states that people who are hypnotized are not in an altered state but are simply playing the role they feel is expected of them in the situation.

A **psychoactive drug** is any drug that alters a person's thinking, perception, or memory. **Physical dependence** on a drug occurs when the user's body does not function normally without the drug. Two signs of physical dependence are drug tolerance and symptoms of **withdrawal** when deprived of the drug. **Psychological dependence** occurs when a drug is needed to maintain a feeling of emotional or psychological well-being. Psychoactive drugs can be classified into major categories including stimulants, depressants, narcotics, and psychogenic drugs.

Stimulants are a class of drugs that increase the activity of the nervous system and the organs connected to it. Specifically, stimulants activate the fight-or-flight response of the sympathetic nervous system. **Amphetamines** are man-made stimulants and include drugs such as benzedrine, methedrine, and dexedrine. Large doses of amphetamines can lead to a severe mental disturbance and paranoia called amphetamine psychosis. **Cocaine** is a naturally occurring stimulant found in coca plant leaves. Cocaine produces feelings of happiness, energy, power, and pleasure and also reduces pain and suppresses appetite. Cocaine is highly addictive and can cause convulsions and death even in first-time users. Signs of cocaine abuse include compulsive use, loss of control, and disregard for the consequences of use. **Nicotine** is a mild yet toxic naturally-occurring stimulant that raises blood pressure, accelerates the heart, and provides a rush of sugar into the bloodstream. Nicotine has been found to be more addictive than heroin or alcohol and is linked to nearly 430,000 deaths in the United States each year. **Caffeine** is a third naturally occurring stimulant that increases alertness and can enhance the effectiveness of certain pain relievers.

Depressants are drugs that slow down the central nervous system and include **barbiturates**, **benzodiazepines**, and **alcohol**. Barbituates have a strong sedative, or sleep-inducing, effect and are known as the major tranquilizers. The minor tranquilizers, or benzodiazepines, have a relatively minor depressant effect and are used to lower anxiety and reduce stress. Some common benzodiazepines include Valium, Xanax, Halcion, Ativan, Librium, and Rohypnol (also known as the date rape drug). The most commonly used and abused depressant is alcohol.

Narcotics reduce the sensation of pain by binding to and activating the receptor sites for endorphins. All narcotics are derived from the plant-based substance of opium. **Opium** itself is made from the opium poppy and reduces pain as well as increases feelings of well-being. **Morphine** is made from opium and is used for the short-term relief of severe pain. Due to its highly addictive nature, the use of morphine is carefully controlled. **Heroin** is also made from opium but is not used as a medicine due to the fact that it is more addictive than morphine or opium. Narcotics are thought to be so addictive because they mimic the action of endorphins and subsequently cause the body to stop producing its own endorphins so that without the drug, there is no protection from pain. Methadone is made from opium but does not produce the feelings of euphoria produced by morphine and heroin. Methadone can be used to attempt to control heroin dependency. In addition to methadone treatment, heroin addiction is treated with behavioral therapies such as contingency management therapies and cognitive approaches such as cognitive-behavior interventions.

Hallucinogens are psychogenic drugs that create false sensory perceptions, also known as hallucinations. **Lysergic acid diethylamide (LSD)** is synthesized from a grain fungus and is one of the most potent hallucinogens. Phenyl cyclohexyl piperdine or **PCP** is a synthesized drug that can act as a hallucinogen, stimulant, depressant, or analgesic depending on the dosage. PCP has also been shown to lead to acts of violence against others or suicide. **MDMA** or Ecstasy is an amphetamine that also produces hallucinations. Because of their stimulant and hallucinogenic properties, PCP and MDMA are now classified as stimulatory hallucinogenics. Naturally occurring hallucinogenics include **mescaline**, **psilocybin**, and **marijuana**. The effects of marijuana are more mild than other hallucinogens, yet marijuana use can lead to a powerful psychological dependency.

Sleep deprivation is a serious and pervasive problem in the United States and has been linked to a large percentage of fatal road accidents in addition to higher levels of stress, anxiety, and depression. Causes of sleep deprivation include sleep apnea, narcolepsy, sleepwalking, night terrors, and personal choice.

STUDY HINTS

1. Use the space below to create a visual summary of the brain wave and physiological changes that occur as your body moves from an awake state through the stages of sleep typical for one night of sleep. Use arrows to indicate the progression through the stages throughout the course of a night.

Stage	Brain wave activity	Other descriptions
Awake		
non-REM Stage 1		
non-REM Stage 2		
non-REM Stage 3		
non-REM Stage 4		
REM		

2. The textbook introduces six different sleep disorders. Pretend that you have each of the sleep disorders and write a brief description of a particular episode you experienced due to the disorder.

sleepwalking

I don't remember anything that happened but in the morning my mother told me that about 50 minutes after I had fallen asleep (right when I would be in the deepest stage of sleep, Stage 4) I walked past her in the kitchen and I was carrying a bath towel. I put the towel in the refrigerator, looked right at her, and then went back to bed in my bedroom. Supposedly I do this type of thing quite often.

night terrors

_____

_____

_____

REM behavior
disorder

_____

_____

_____

insomnia

_____

_____

_____

apnea

_____

_____

_____

narcolepsy

_____

_____

_____

Stage	Brain wave activity	Other descriptions
Awake	beta	
non-REM Stage 1	alpha	hypnic jerk occurs here
non-REM Stage 2	theta	sleep spindles are seen in this stage
non-REM Stage 3	delta waves	initial appearance of delta waves, they make up minority of brain wave activity
non-REM Stage 4	more than 50 percent delta waves	deepest stage of sleep, hardest to wake the person up, sleepwalking and night terrors occur in this stage
REM	beta	skeletal muscles are paralyzed (except for people with REM behavior disorder), eyes dart back and forth rapidly below the eyelids

LEARNING OBJECTIVES

4.1   What does it mean to be conscious, and are there different levels of consciousness?

4.2   Why do people need to sleep, and how does sleep work?

4.3   What are the different stages of sleep, including the stage of dreaming and its importance?

4.4   How do sleep disorders interfere with normal sleep?

4.5   Why do people dream, and what do they dream about?

4.6   How does hypnosis affect consciousness?

4.7   What is the difference between a physical dependence and a psychological dependence on a drug?

4.8   How do stimulants and depressants affect consciousness, and what are the dangers associated with taking them, particularly alcohol?

4.9   What are some of the effects and dangers of using narcotics and hallucinogens, including marijuana?

4.10 How serious is the problem of sleep deprivation?

PRACTICE EXAM

For the following multiple choice questions, select the answer you feel best answers the question.

1.   What term do psychologists use to designate our personal awareness of feelings, sensations, and thoughts?
     a)   thinking
     b)   cognition
     c)   conscience
     d)   consciousness

2.   A biological cycle, or rhythm, that is approximately 24 hours long is a(n) _____ cycle.
     a)   infradian
     b)   circadian
     c)   diurnal
     d)   ultradian

3. The hormone melatonin reaches peak levels in the body during the _____.
   a) morning
   b) early evening
   c) afternoon
   d) night

4. Sid is taking part in research on the effects of sleep deprivation; he has been without sleep for 75 hours. Right now researchers have asked him to sit in front of a computer screen and hit a button each time he sees the letter "S" on the screen. A few days ago, Sid was a whiz at this task; however, he is doing very poorly today. How are sleep researchers likely to explain Sid's poor performance?
   a) Due to the sleep deprivation, Sid does not understand the task.
   b) Microsleeps are occurring due to the sleep deprivation, and he is asleep for brief periods of time.
   c) He is determined to ruin the research because of the suffering he is enduring at the hands of the researchers.
   d) He is probably dreaming that he is somewhere else and has no interest in responding to the "here and now."

5. According to this theory, sleep is a product of evolution.
   a) restorative theory
   b) adaptive theory
   c) psychoanalytic theory
   d) dream theory

6. If the EEG record reveals evidence of very small and very fast waves, you are likely to conclude that the sleeping person is
   a) really not sleeping and is awake.
   b) in Stage 2.
   c) in Stage 3.
   d) in Stage 4.

7. Each of the following is true of sleepwalking EXCEPT _____.
   a) more boys than girls sleepwalk
   b) sleepwalking is more common among children than adults
   c) waking a sleepwalker is difficult
   d) waking a sleepwalker is dangerous

8. For several months, Ted has been taking increasingly larger doses of barbiturate sleeping pills to treat insomnia. He just decided to quit taking any barbiturate sleeping pills. What is likely to happen to Ted when he stops taking the barbiturate sleeping pills?
   a) He will become depressed.
   b) He will experience the REM rebound.
   c) He will increase his intake of caffeine.
   d) He will suffer the symptoms of narcolepsy.

9. REM paralysis
   a) is a myth.
   b) only occurs in the elderly.
   c) prevents the acting out of dreams.
   d) may become permanent.

10. REM behavior disorder results from
    a) too much sleep.
    b) not enough sleep.
    c) failure of the pons to block brain signals to the muscles.
    d) deterioration of the medial hypothalamus.

11. What is the rationale for the use of "sleepwalking" as a defense for committing a crime?
    a) It was too dangerous to awaken the sleepwalking criminal.
    b) The suspect actually suffers from REM behavior disorder and was unknowingly acting out a dream.
    c) High levels of anxiety and stress were created by the sleep deprivation caused by the sleepwalking episodes.
    d) The suspect was highly susceptible to suggestion at the time of the crime.

12. Mary is having insomnia. Which piece of advice would you give to help her deal with it?
    a) Take sleeping pills.
    b) Go to bed every night at the same time.
    c) Study in bed and then go immediately to sleep.
    d) Don't do anything but sleep in your bed.

13. Sleep apnea is a disorder characterized by _____.
    a) difficulty falling or remaining asleep
    b) nodding off without warning in the middle of the day
    c) difficulty breathing while asleep
    d) experiencing temporary paralysis immediately after waking up from sleep

14. What two categories of dream content did Sigmund Freud describe?
    a) poetic and realistic
    b) literal and symbolic
    c) latent and manifest
    d) delusional and hallucinatory

15. The activation-information-mode model suggests
    a) events which occur during waking hours may influence dreams.
    b) nothing influences dreams.
    c) activation-synthesis is all wrong.
    d) dreams have more latent content than once thought.

16. According to the text, girls and women tend to dream about
    a) animals.
    b) cars.
    c) people they know.
    d) strangers.

17. A social interaction in which one person responds to suggestions offered by another person for experiences involving alterations in perception, memory, and voluntary action defines
    a) hypnosis
    b) meditation
    c) truth induction
    d) extrasensory perception

18. Tests of "hypnotic susceptibility" have been found to _____.
     a)   be similar for almost everyone
     b)   make use of a series of suggestions
     c)   be almost completely inherited
     d)   use deception

19. Hypnosis can
     a)   give people superhuman strength.
     b)   reliably enhance accuracy of memory.
     c)   regress people back to childhood.
     d)   induce amnesia.

20. The idea of "hidden observer" was suggested by
     a)   Freud.
     b)   Watson.
     c)   Hilgard.
     d)   Kirsch.

21. Psychoactive drugs are
     a)   drugs that speed up activity in the central nervous system.
     b)   drugs capable of influencing perception, mood, cognition, or behavior.
     c)   drugs that slow down activity in the central nervous system.
     d)   drugs derived from the opium poppy which relieve pain and produce euphoria.

22. Psychological dependence is best described as
     a)   a desire to take a drug.
     b)   drug tolerance and signs of withdrawal when deprived of the drug.
     c)   needing a drug to maintain a feeling of emotional or psychological well-being.
     d)   feelings of euphoria following the ingestion of a drug.

23. Drugs that speed up the functioning of the nervous system are called
     a)   stimulants.
     b)   depressants.
     c)   narcotics.
     d)   psychogenics.

24. The most addictive and dangerous (as defined by the number of deaths caused by the drug) stimulant in use today is _____.
     a)   alcohol
     b)   amphetamine
     c)   nicotine
     d)   cocaine

25. Cathy has just taken a drug that has caused her heart rate and breathing to slow down considerably. Most likely, Cathy has taken a(n)
     a)   amphetamine.
     b)   barbiturate.
     c)   narcotic.
     d)   hallucinogen.

26. Your doctor has decided to give you a prescription for a drug to reduce your anxiety levels. Most likely your doctor will prescribe a
    a) narcotic.
    b) hallucinogen.
    c) depressant.
    d) stimulant.

27. Which of the following is classified as a depressant?
    a) cocaine
    b) alcohol
    c) heroin
    d) marijuana

28. Jane has a loss of equilibrium, decreased sensory and motor capabilities, and double vision. According to the table in the text, how many drinks has Jane had?
    a) 1-2
    b) 3-5
    c) 6-7
    d) 8-10

29. Morphine, heroin, and methadone
    a) are stimulants.
    b) are derived from opium.
    c) are often used with ADHD.
    d) increase the action of the central nervous system.

30. LSD is similar to which of the following drugs?
    a) cocaine
    b) methadone
    c) PCP
    d) CHT

31. Bill is taken to the emergency room of the hospital after he reports hearing dogs screaming and seeing fire shooting across his shirt and pants. Assuming his condition is due to a drug overdose, which type of drug did Bill most likely consume?
    a) a depressant
    b) a stimulant
    c) a narcotic
    d) a hallucinogen

32. One of the greatest risks of using marijuana is
    a) physical dependency.
    b) psychological dependency.
    c) weight gain.
    d) heart attack.

33. A significant loss of sleep, resulting in problems in concentration and irritability, is known as
    a) sleep apnea.
    b) narcolepsy.
    c) sleep deprivation.
    d) night terrors.

PRACTICE EXAM ANSWERS

1. d Consciousness is defined as personal awareness of feelings, sensation, and thoughts. Your <u>conscience</u> is your sense of morality or right and wrong.

2. b If you break down the word, "circa" means about or around (such as circa 1960) and "dia" means day. So circa-dia means about one day long.

3. d High melatonin levels is one of the signals for our body that it is time to sleep. The release of melatonin is controlled by signals coming from the suprachiasmatic nucleus, which is light sensitive. In this way, the release of melatonin follows the light-dark patterns of the day.

4. b Microsleeps are brief episodes of sleep that we enter and exit rapidly. Sleep deprivation often leads to decreased performance in simple tasks.

5. b Adaptive theory states that a species sleeps during the time when its predators are most likely to be out hunting, thus increasing the likelihood of survival for that species.

6. a The faster the brain wave activity, the more alert and awake the person is. Another option would have been that the person was in REM sleep where fast small brain wave activity is also seen.

7. d Waking the sleepwalker is not dangerous, it just might be hard to do since they are in Stage 4 deep sleep.

8. b Barbiturate sleeping pills interfere with REM sleep, so since Ted has been deprived of REM he is likely to spend a longer than usual amount of time in REM for the next few nights. This phenomenon is known as REM rebound.

9. c During REM sleep the pons sends messages to the spinal cord that inhibits the movements of skeletal muscles.

10. c REM behavior disorder occurs when REM paralysis does not work and a person acts out their dreams. The paralysis is mediated by the pons in the brainstem.

11. b The sleepwalking defense is actually referring to a suspect thought to have REM behavior disorder.

12. d The idea is that the only association you should have with your bed is sleeping and this will make it easier for you to fall asleep when you get in bed.

13. c Sleep apnea is a sleeping disorder in which a person actually stops breathing for brief periods throughout the night.

14. c Freud thought dreams had two levels – the actual content that he called the manifest content and then the real meaning which he called the latent content.

15. a The activation-synthesis model proposes that dreams are caused by the activation of the cortex by lower areas of the brain.

16. c Women tend to dream about both men and women as well as people they know, while men tend to dream about men.

17. a This is simply another way of describing a state of consciousness in which the person is especially susceptible to suggestion.

18. b The tests used to determine how likely it is for a person to be hypnotized generally include a list of suggestions.

19. d Hypnosis has only been found to induce temporary amnesia, reduce pain, and alter sensory perceptions.

20. c Ernst Hilgard suggested that hypnosis was possible because the subject dissociates himself into a part that is aware of what is going on (the hidden observer) and a part that is unaware.

21. b The rest of the choices describe a specific category of psychoactive drug.

22. c Choice c is the definition for psychological dependence.

23. a Stimulants speed up heart rate, blood pressure, breathing, among other activities.

24. c Nicotine has been linked to nearly 430,000 deaths per year in the U.S. alone.

25. b Barbiturate is the only drug listed that is a depressant.

26.   c   The depressants known as the mild tranquilizers, or benzodiazepines, are often prescribed to lower anxiety levels.
27.   b   Alcohol slows down the activity of the central nervous system.
28.   d   See the table in the textbook.
29.   b   All narcotics are derived from the opium poppy. All three of the drugs listed are classified as narcotics.
57.   c   Methadone shares some of the properties of heroin but does not produce the feelings of euphoria.
30.   c   LSD and PCP are both hallucinogens.
31.   d   Hallucinogens produce false sensory perceptions.
32.   b   The effect of psychological dependence can be very powerful.
33.   c   Sleep deprivation affects a large number of people in the U.S. today

CHAPTER GLOSSARY

activation-information mode model (AIM)	revised version of the activation-synthesis explanation of dreams in which information that is accessed during waking hours can have an influence on the synthesis of dreams.
activation-synthesis hypothesis	explanation of dreaming that states that dreams are created by the higher centers of the cortex to explain the activation by the brainstem of cortical cells during REM sleep periods.
adaptive theory	theory of sleep proposing that animals and humans evolved sleep patterns to avoid predators, sleeping when predators are most active.
alcohol	depressant drug resulting from fermentation or distillation of various kinds of vegetable matter.
alpha waves	brain waves that indicate a state of relaxation or light sleep.
altered states of consciousness	state in which there is a shift in the quality or pattern of mental activity as compared to waking consciousness.
amphetamines	stimulants that are synthesized (made) in laboratories rather than being found in nature.
barbiturates	depressant drugs that have a sedative effect.
benzodiazepines	depressant drugs that lower anxiety and reduce stress.
beta waves	brain waves that indicate a state of being awake and alert.
caffeine	a mild stimulant found in coffee, tea, and several other plant-based substances.
circadian rhythm	a cycle of bodily rhythm that occurs over a 24-hour period.
cocaine	a natural stimulant derived from the leaves of the coca plant.
consciousness	a person's awareness of everything that is going on around him or her at any given moment.
delta waves	long, slow waves that indicate the deepest stage of sleep.
depressants	drugs that decrease the functioning of the nervous system.
hallucinogens	drugs that cause false sensory messages, altering the perception of reality.
heroin	narcotic drug derived from opium that is extremely addictive.
hypnic jerk	an involuntary muscle twitch which often occurs during the transition from wakefulness to sleep.
hypnosis	state of consciousness in which the person is especially susceptible to suggestion.
insomnia	the inability to get to sleep, stay asleep, or get a good quality of sleep.
latent content	term coined by Sigmund Freud to identify the real or "hidden" meaning of a dream.

lysergic acid diethylamide (LSD)	powerful synthetic hallucinogen.
manifest content	term coined by Sigmund Freud to identify the actual or "apparent" content of a dream.
marijuana	mild hallucinogen derived from the leaves and flowers of a particular type of hemp plant.
MDMA	designer drug that can have both stimulant and hallucinatory effects.
melatonin	hormone released from the pineal gland that is associated with the sleep-wake cycle.
mescaline	natural hallucinogen derived from the peyote cactus buttons.
methadone	narcotic drug derived from opium used to treat heroin addiction.
microsleeps	brief episodes of sleep lasting only a few seconds.
morphine	narcotic drug derived from opium, used to treat severe pain.
narcolepsy	sleep disorder in which a person falls immediately into REM sleep during the day, without warning.
narcotics	a class of opium-related drugs that suppress the sensation of pain by binding to and stimulating the nervous system's natural receptor sites for endorphins.
nicotine	a natural stimulant and the active ingredient in tobacco.
night terrors	relatively rare disorder in which the person experiences extreme fear and screams or runs around during deep sleep, without waking fully.
nightmares	bad dreams occurring during REM sleep.
non-REM sleep	any of the stages of sleep that do not include REM.
opium	substance derived from the opium poppy from which all narcotic drugs are derived.
phenyl cyclohexyl piperdine (PCP)	synthesized drug now used as an animal tranquilizer and which can cause stimulant, depressant, narcotic, or hallucinogenic effects.
physical dependence	a physical state in which rapid discontinuation of consumption of a particular drug leads to a condition of withdrawal.
psilocybin	natural hallucinogen found in certain mushrooms.
psychoactive drug	drugs that alter thinking, perception, and memory.
psychological dependence	the feeling that a drug is needed to continue a feeling of emotional or psychological well-being.
rapid eye movement (REM) sleep	stage of sleep in which the eyes move rapidly under the eyelids and the person is typically experiencing a dream.
REM behavior disorder	a rare disorder in which the mechanism that blocks the movement of the voluntary muscles fails to function, allowing the person to thrash around and even get up and act out nightmares.
REM paralysis	the inability to move the voluntary muscles during REM sleep.
REM rebound	increased amounts of REM sleep after being deprived of REM sleep on earlier nights.
restorative theory	theory of sleep proposing that sleep is necessary to the physical health of the body and serves to replenish chemicals and repair cellular damage.
sleep apnea	disorder in which the person stops breathing for nearly half a minute or more during sleep.
sleep deprivation	any significant loss of sleep, resulting in problems in concentration and irritability.
sleep spindles	bursts of brain wave activity seen on the EEG during Stage 2 sleep.
sleepwalking (somnambulism)	occurring during the deep sleep of Stage 4 non-REM sleep, an episode of moving around or walking around in one's sleep.

social-cognitive explanation	theory that assumes that people who are hypnotized are not in an altered state but are merely playing the role expected of them in the situation.
stimulants	drugs that increase the functioning of the nervous system.
suprachiasmatic nucleus (SCN)	area in the hypothalamus that is sensitive to daylight and controls the body's sleep-wake cycle.
theta waves	brain waves indicating the early stages of sleep.
waking consciousness	state in which thoughts, feelings, and sensations are clear, organized, and the person feels alert.
withdrawal	physical symptoms that can include nausea, pain, tremors, crankiness, and high blood pressure, resulting from a lack of an addictive drug in the body systems.

4.2   p. 141

hypothalamus contains the suprachiasmatic nucleus (SCN)
- SCN is sensitive to light—influences pineal gland's secretion of melatonin (↑ melatonin = ↑ sleepiness)
- light through eyes relayed to SCN; SCN signals pineal gland to stop producing melatonin (↓ melatonin = ↑ alertness / ↓ sleepiness)
- SCN also influences body temperature (↓ temperature = ↑ sleepiness)

Altered States—Sleep: The Necessity of Sleep

(sleep is one of the body's daily (circadian) biological rhythms; sleep–wake cycle controlled by the brain including the hypothalamus and the neurotransmitter serotonin)

people can live without sleep for a while, can't live without it altogether
- **sleep deprivation**
- **amount of sleep needed**
- **adaptive theory of sleep**
- **restorative theory of sleep**

Presleep
Awake, alert
Beta waves
Awake, relaxed
Alpha waves

4.3–4   p. 149

consist of both REM (rapid eye movement) and non-REM stages
- **non-REM Stage 1**
- **non-REM Stage 2**
- **non-REM Stages 3 & 4**
- **REM sleep**

Non-REM
Sleep stage 1
Theta waves
Sleep stage 2   Sleep Spindle
Spindle (burst of activity)
Sleep stage 3
Sleep stage 4
Delta waves

REM
REM stage

Altered States—Sleep: Stages and Disorders

Table 4.1 Common Sleep Disorders

NAME OF DISORDER	PRIMARY SYMPTOMS
Somnambulism	Sitting, walking, or performing complex behavior while asleep
Night terrors	Extreme fear, agitation, screaming while asleep
Restless leg syndrome	Uncomfortable sensations in legs causing movement and loss of sleep
Nocturnal leg cramps	Painful cramps in calf or foot muscles
Hypersomnia	Excessive daytime sleepiness
Circadian rhythm disorders	Disturbances of the sleep–wake cycle such as lag and shift work
Enuresis	Urinating while asleep in bed

people can live without sleep for a while, can't live without it altogether
- **insomnia**
- **sleep apnea**
- **narcolepsy**

"On your application it says you have narcolepsy. What is that?"

CAST OF DREAM
THE MONSTER . . . . . . YOUR FATHER
KIND WOMAN . . . . . . YOUR MOTHER
POLICEMAN . . . . YOUR ANALYST
FIRST STRANGER . . . YOUR BROTHER
SECOND STRANGER . . YOUR SISTER
LITTLE BOY . . . . . YOU

4.5   p. 152

Dreams

Why do we dream?
- **Freud's interpretation:** wish fulfillment—conflicts, events, and desires represented in symbolic form in dreams
- **activation–synthesis hypothesis**

What do people dream about? typically about events that occur in everyday life; most in color; content influenced by gender and culture

4.6   p. 156

Altered States: Hypnosis
(state of consciousness during which person is more susceptible to suggestion)

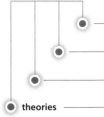

- can be assessed by scale of hypnotic susceptibility

- induction typically involves relaxed focus and "permission to let go"; person being hypnotized is in control and cannot be hypnotized against his or her will

- can be used in therapy—help people deal with pain, anxiety, or cravings (e.g., food, drug)

- **theories**
  - **dissociation:** one part of mind is aware of actions/activities taking place, while the "hypnotized" part is not
  - **social-cognitive theory** suggests that people assume roles based on expectations for a given situation

Table 4.3 Facts About Hypnosis

HYPNOSIS CAN:	HYPNOSIS CANNOT:
Create amnesia for whatever happens during the hypnotic session, at least for a brief time (Bowers & Woody, 1996).	Give people superhuman strength. (People may use their full strength under hypnosis, but it is no more than they had before hypnosis.
Relieve pain by allowing a person to remove conscious attention from the pain (Holroyd, 1996).	Reliably enhance memory. (There's an increased risk of false memory retrieval because of the suggestible state hypnosis creates.)
Alter sensory perceptions. (Smell, hearing, vision, time sense, and the ability to see visual illusions can all be affected by hypnosis.)	Regress people back to childhood. (Although people may act like children, they do and say things children would not.)
Help people relax in situations that normally would cause them stress, such as flying on an airplane (Muhlberger et al., 2001).	Regress people to some "past life." There is no scientific evidence for past life regression (Lilienfeld et al., 2004)

Table 4.5 Blood Alcohol Level and Behavior Associated with Amounts of Alcohol

A drink is a drink. Each contains half an ounce of alcohol.
So a drink is . . .

- 1 can of beer (12 oz. 4–5% alcohol)
- 1 glass of wine (4 oz. 12% alcohol)
- 1 shot of most liquors (1 oz. 40–50% alcohol)

At times "a drink" is really the equivalent of more than just one drink, like when you order a drink with more than one shot of alcohol in it, or you do a shot followed by a beer.

AVERAGE NUMBER OF DRINKS	BLOOD ALCOHOL LEVEL	BEHAVIOR
1–2 drinks	.05%	Feeling of well-being
		Release of inhibitions
		Judgment impaired
		Coordination and level of alertness lowered
		Increased risk of collision while driving
3–5 drinks	.10%	Reaction time significantly slowed
		Muscle control and speech impaired
		Limited night and side vision
		Loss of self-control
		Crash risk greatly increased
6–7 drinks	.15%	Consistent and major increases in reaction time
8–10 drinks	.20%	Loss of equilibrium and technical skills
		Sensory and motor capabilities depressed
		Double vision and legal blindness (20/20)
		Unfit to drive for up to 10 hours
10–14 drinks	.20% and .25%	Staggering and severe motor disturbances
10–14 drinks	.30%	Not aware of surroundings
10–14 drinks	.35%	Surgical anesthesia
		Lethal dosage for a small percentage of people
14–20 drinks	.40%	Lethal dosage for about 50% of people
		Severe circulatory/respiratory depression
		Alcohol poisoning/overdose

Source: Adapted from the *Moderate Drinking Skills Study Guide.* (2004). Eau-Claire, WI: University of Wisconsin.

4.7–9   p. 168

Why do some people continue to use or become addicted to psychoactive drugs?

"Nowadays, Hal is ninety-nine per cent caffeine-free."

- **physical dependence:** user's body needs a drug to function; drug tolerance and withdrawal are warning signs/symptoms

- **psychological dependence:** user believes drug is needed to function

Altered States: Psychoactive Drugs
(drugs that alter thinking, perception, or memory)

- **types**

stimulants
increase functioning of nervous system
- **amphetamines**
- **cocaine**
- **nicotine**
- **caffeine**

depressants
have sedative effect
- **barbiturates**
  major tranquilizers
- **benzodiazepines**
  minor tranquilizers—
  Valium, Xanax, Halcion,
  Activan, Librium, Rohypnol
- **alcohol**

narcotics
euphoria-producing and
pain relieving drugs derived
from opium
- **morphine**
- **heroin**
- **methadone**
  does not produce euphoria;
  used to treat heroin addiction

hallucinogens
alter brain's interpretation of sensations
- **manufactured**
  - **LSD**
  - **PCP**
  - **MDMA (Ectasy)**
- **nonmanufactured**
  - **mescaline**
  - **psilocybin**
  - **marijuana**

_____
_____
_____
_____
_____
_____
_____
_____
_____
_____

State of consciousness	Brief description
waking	*state in which you are aware of your thoughts and feelings and you feel alert*

List as many different states of consciousness as you can and provide a brief description of each. The first example has already been completed. Be sure that your chart includes the states of consciousness such as sleep, hypnosis, daydreaming, meditation, and drugged. See the textbook for descriptions of each state

_____
_____
_____
_____
_____
_____
_____
_____
_____
_____
_____
_____

4.2　Sleep

_____

_____

_____

_____

_____

_____

_____

_____

_____

Figure 4.1 **Sleep Patterns of Infants and Adults**

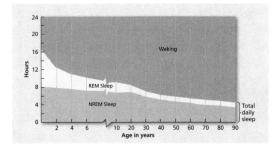

4.3　Sleep Stages

_____

_____

_____

_____

_____

_____

_____

_____

_____

_____

_____

Figure 4.2 **8-Hour Sleep Cycle**

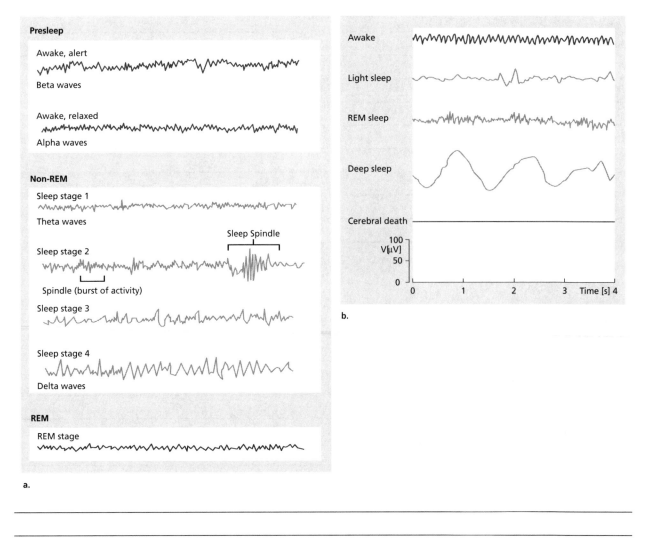

Presleep

Awake, alert

Beta waves

Awake, relaxed

Alpha waves

Non-REM

Sleep stage 1

Theta waves

Sleep stage 2

Sleep Spindle

Spindle (burst of activity)

Sleep stage 3

Sleep stage 4

Delta waves

REM

REM stage

a.

Awake

Light sleep

REM sleep

Deep sleep

Cerebral death

100
V[μV]
50

0

0   1   2   3   Time [s] 4

b.

Figure 4.3 **A Typical Night's Sleep**

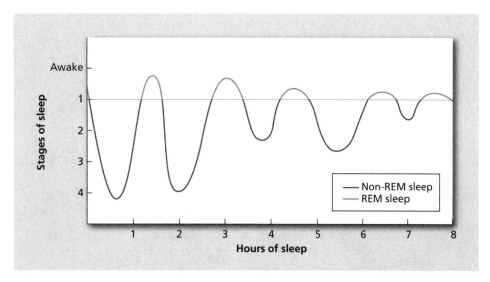

_____
_____
_____
_____
_____
_____
_____
_____
_____
_____
_____
_____
_____

4.4 **Sleep Disorders**

_____
_____
_____
_____
_____
_____
_____
_____
_____
_____
_____
_____
_____

Table 4.1 **Common Sleep Disorders**

Table 4.1 **Common Sleep Disorders**

NAME OF DISORDER	PRIMARY SYMPTOMS
Somnambulism	Sitting, walking, or performing complex behavior while asleep
Night terrors	Extreme fear, agitation, screaming while asleep
Restless leg syndrome	Uncomfortable sensations in legs causing movement and loss of sleep
Nocturnal leg cramps	Painful cramps in calf or foot muscles
Hypersomnia	Excessive daytime sleepiness
Circadian rhythm disorders	Disturbances of the sleep–wake cycle such as jet lag and shift work
Enuresis	Urinating while asleep in bed

_____
_____
_____
_____
_____
_____
_____
_____
_____
_____

4.5  Dreams

_____
_____
_____
_____
_____
_____
_____
_____
_____
_____
_____

_____

_____

_____

_____

_____

_____

_____

_____

_____

_____

Table 4.2 **Sample Items from the Stanford Hypnotic Susceptibility Scale: Form A (SHSS:A)**

Table 4.2	Sample Items from the Stanford Hypnotic Susceptibility Scale: Form A (SHSS:A)	
1. Postural sway	5. Finger lock	9. Hallucination (fly)
2. Eye closure	6. Arm rigidity (left arm)	10. Eye catalepsy
3. Hand lowering (left)	7. Hands moving together	11. Posthypnotic (changes chairs)
4. Immobilization (right arm)	8. Verbal inhibition (name)	12. Amnesia

Source: Hilgard, E. (1965). _Hypnotic Susceptibility_. New York: Harcourt, Brace & World.

_____

_____

_____

_____

_____

_____

_____

_____

_____

_____

Table 4.3 **Facts about Hypnosis**

Table 4.3 Facts about Hypnosis	
HYPNOSIS CAN:	**HYPNOSIS CANNOT:**
Create amnesia for whatever happens during the hypnotic session, at least for a brief time (Bowers & Woody, 1996).	Give people superhuman strength. (People may use their full strength under hypnosis, but it is no more than they had before hypnosis.)
Relieve pain by allowing a person to remove conscious attention from the pain (Holroyd, 1996).	Reliably enhance memory. (There's an increased risk of false memory retrieval because of the suggestible state hypnosis creates.)
Alter sensory perceptions. (Smell, hearing, vision, time sense, and the ability to see visual illusions can all be affected by hypnosis.)	Regress people back to childhood. (Although people may *act* like children, they do and say things children would not.)
Help people relax in situations that normally would cause them stress, such as flying on an airplane (Muhlberger et al., 2001).	Regress people to some "past life." There is no scientific evidence for past life regression (Lilienfeld et al., 2004).

_____
_____
_____
_____
_____
_____
_____
_____
_____

4.7 Drug Dependence

_____
_____
_____
_____
_____
_____
_____
_____
_____
_____
_____

Table 4.4 **Average Caffeine Content of Some Beverages**

Table 4.4   Average Caffeine Content of Some Beverages

PRODUCT (8 OZ. EXCEPT AS NOTED)	CAFFEINE (MILLIGRAMS)
Brewed coffee	60–120
Decaffeinated coffee	2–4
Espresso/cappuccino (1 oz.)	30–50
Tea brewed 1 minute	9–33
Tea brewed 3 minutes	20–46
Tea brewed 5 minutes	20–50
Iced tea (8 oz./12 oz.)	15–24/22–36
Hot cocoa	3–32
Milk chocolate (1 oz.)	1–15
Dark chocolate (1 oz.)	5–35
Jolt soda (8 oz./12 oz.)	47/71
Mountain Dew (8 oz./12 oz.)	36/54
Coca-Cola (8 oz./12 oz.)	31/46
Pepsi (8 oz./12 oz.)	24/36

Source: Barone and Roberts (1996).

Table 4.5 **Blood Alcohol Level and Behavior Associated with Amounts of Alcohol**

Table 4.5   Blood Alcohol Level and Behavior Associated with Amounts of Alcohol

A drink is a drink. Each contains half an ounce of alcohol.
So a drink is . . .

- 1 can of beer (12 oz. 4–5% alcohol)
- 1 glass of wine (4 oz. 12% alcohol)
- 1 shot of most liquors (1 oz. 40–50% alcohol)

At times "a drink" is really the equivalent of more than just one drink, like when you order a drink with more than one shot of alcohol in it, or you do a shot followed by a beer.

AVERAGE NUMBER OF DRINKS	BLOOD ALCOHOL LEVEL	BEHAVIOR
1–2 drinks	.05%	Feeling of well-being
		Release of inhibitions
		Judgment impaired
		Coordination and level of alertness lowered
		Increased risk of collision while driving
3–5 drinks	.10%	Reaction time significantly slowed
		Muscle control and speech impaired
		Limited night and side vision
		Loss of self-control
		Crash risk greatly increased
6–7 drinks	.15%	Consistent and major increases in reaction time
8–10 drinks	.20%	Loss of equilibrium and technical skills
		Sensory and motor capabilities depressed
		Double vision and legal blindness (20/200)
		Unfit to drive for up to 10 hours
10–14 drinks	.20% and .25%	Staggering and severe motor disturbances
10–14 drinks	.30%	Not aware of surroundings
10–14 drinks	.35%	Surgical anesthesia
		Lethal dosage for a small percentage of people
14–20 drinks	.40%	Lethal dosage for about 50% of people
		Severe circulatory/respiratory depression
		Alcohol poisoning/overdose

Source: Adapted from the *Moderate Drinking Skills Study Guide.* (2004). Eau-Claire, WI: University of Wisconsin.

Drug category	Examples	Action on nervous system
Stimulants	*caffeine, cocaine, nicotine, amphetamines (such as Benzedrine, Methedrine, Dexedrine)*	*increases activity, speeds up heart rate, speeds up breathing, raises blood pressure and suppresses appetite. Can produce feelings of power, happiness, energy, increased alertness*
Depressants		
Narcotics		
Hallucinogens		

_____
_____
_____
_____
_____
_____
_____
_____
_____
_____
_____
_____
_____
_____
_____
_____
_____
_____
_____
_____
_____
_____
_____
_____
_____
_____
_____
_____

Table 4.6 How Drugs Affect Consciousness

Table 4.6 How Drugs Affect Consciousness			
DRUG CLASSIFICATION	**COMMON NAME**	**MAIN EFFECT**	**ADVERSE EFFECTS**
Depressants			
Alcohol	Beer, wine, spirits	Relaxation	Alcoholism, health problems, depression, increased risk of accidents, death
Barbiturates (tranquilizers)	Nembutal, Seconal		Addiction, brain damage, death
Stimulants			
Amphetamines	Methamphetamine, speed, Ritalin, Dexedrine	Stimulation, excitement	Risk of addiction, stroke, fatal heart problems, psychosis
Cocaine	Cocaine, crack		Risk of addiction, stroke, fatal heart problems, psychosis
Nicotine	Tobacco		Addiction, cancer
Caffeine	Coffee, tea		Caffeinism, high blood pressure
Narcotics			
Opiates	Morphine, heroin	Euphoria	Addiction, death
Psychedelics and Hallucinogens			
	Marijuana, hashish, LSD, Ecstasy	Distorted consciousness, altered perception	Possible permanent memory problems, bad "trips," suicide, overdose, and death

NOTES

NOTES

YOU KNOW YOU ARE READY FOR THE TEST IF YOU ARE ABLE TO...
- Define learning.
- Explain what classical conditioning is, how it works, and how it was discovered.
- Describe the mechanisms of operant conditioning, its application in the real world, and the researchers who contributed to our understanding of the process.
- Introduce cognitive learning theory.
- Define observational learning and describe Bandura's classic experiments in the area of observational learning.

RAPID REVIEW

Learning is the process that allows us to adapt to the changing conditions of the environment around us and is defined as any relatively permanent change in behavior brought about by experience or practice (as opposed to changes brought about by maturation). Ivan Pavlov, a Russian physiologist, discovered one of the simplest forms of learning called **classical conditioning**. In classical conditioning, an organism learn to make a reflex response to a stimulus other than the original stimulus that produced the response in the first place. The original stimulus is called the **unconditioned (or "unlearned") stimulus (UCS)** and the reflex response is the **unconditioned response (UCR)**. If a **neutral stimulus (NS)** is repeatedly paired with the UCS, it will eventually produce the same kind of reflexive response. At this point, the NS is called a **conditioned stimulus (CS)** and the response is called a **conditioned, or learned, response (CR)**. The repeated pairing of the NS and UCS is known as acquisition. In order for classical conditioning to occur, the CS must occur before the UCS, the CS and UCS must occur close together in time, the CS and UCS must be paired together repeatedly, and the CS should be distinctive. Two other principles of classical conditioning are **stimulus generalization**, the ability of a stimulus that resembles the CS to produce a CR and **stimulus discrimination**, learning to respond to different stimuli in different ways. In classical conditioning, **extinction** occurs after the CS is repeatedly presented without the UCS and no longer produces a CR. **Spontaneous recovery** occurs when the CS is presented after being absent for a period of time and produces a mild CR. When a powerful conditioned stimulus is paired with a neutral stimulus, the conditioned stimulus itself can function as a UCS and turn the neutral stimulus into a second conditioned stimulus. This process is called **higher-order conditioning**.

John Watson demonstrated a particular type of classical conditioning called **conditional emotional response** with Little Albert and his learned phobia of white rats. **Vicarious conditioning** occurs when a person becomes classically conditioned simply by watching someone else respond to a stimulus. **Conditioned taste aversions** are a unique form of classical conditioning that can occur with only one neutral stimulus – unconditioned stimulus pairing. Conditioning is believed to occur so rapidly due to the **biological preparedness** of most mammals. Pavlov suggested that classical conditioning works through the process of **stimulus substitution**, in that the close pairing in time of the CS with the UCS eventually leads to the CS serving as a substitute stimulus for the UCS and activating the same brain area as the UCS. Psychologists who agree with the **cognitive perspective**, such as Robert Rescorla, suggested that the CS must provide some information about the upcoming UCS and that it is this expectancy that causes the association to occur.

Operant conditioning is a type of learning more strongly associated with voluntary behavior and is based on Edward Thorndike's work with cats and the puzzle box. Based on his research, Thorndike formulated the **Law of Effect** which states that if a response is followed by a pleasurable consequence it will tend to be repeated and if a response is followed by an unpleasant consequence it will tend not to be repeated. B.F. Skinner expanded on Thorndike's Law of Effect and coined the term operant conditioning for this type of learning, since the term **operant** refers to any voluntary behavior. While classical conditioning focuses on what happens *before* the response, the key to operant conditioning is what happens *after* the response, or in other words, the consequence. **Reinforcement** is a consequence that is pleasurable and strengthens the response that came before it. There are two types of reinforcers, **primary**

reinforcers satisfy basic needs and don't need to be learned. **Secondary reinforcers** get their reinforcing power through prior associations with a primary reinforcer and thus are learned. Reinforcement works by adding a pleasurable consequence after a response occurs (**positive reinforcement**) or removing something unpleasant after a response occurs (**negative reinforcement**). Both positive and negative reinforcement increase the likelihood that the response will occur again.

Punishment, on the other hand, always decreases the likelihood of a response. Punishment is any consequence of a response that causes that response to be less likely to happen again. While reinforcement strengthens a response that already exists, the goal of punishment is often to eliminate the response, which is usually a much harder task. Typically punishment only temporarily suppresses the response. **Punishment by application** describes the situation in which a response is followed by the addition of something unpleasant. Punishment by application is not the most effective way to modify behavior and has a number of serious drawbacks. **Punishment by removal** occurs when a response is followed by the removal of something pleasant. Punishment can be made more effective if it is administered immediately after the undesired behavior, is administered consistently, and is paired with reinforcement for the right behavior.

Shaping involves the use of operant conditioning to reward **successive approximations** until the desired response is obtained. Operant conditioning has several parallels with classical conditioning such as, **extinction** involves the removal of the reinforcement and **spontaneous recovery** occurs when an organism attempts a previously learned response in order to receive a reward. In addition, a **discriminative stimulus** is defined as any stimulus that provides an organism with a signal or cue for making a certain response in order to get reinforcement. In the lab, researchers found that even though animals could be operantly conditioned to perform certain tasks, they often had a tendency to go back to their genetic, or natural, way of doing things. This tendency to revert to genetically controlled patterns is called **instinctive drift**.

An important principle that Skinner discovered is that the timing of reinforcement can make a significant difference on how fast a response is learned. **Continuous reinforcement** occurs when a reinforcer is presented after every response. **Partial reinforcement** occurs when a reinforcer is given after some, but not all, of the correct responses. Partial reinforcement takes longer to go through extinction, or in other words, is more resistant to extinction. This is known as the **partial reinforcement effect**. The timing of partial reinforcement is referred to as the **schedule of reinforcement**. There are four different schedules of reinforcement: **fixed ratio**, **variable ratio**, **fixed interval**, and **variable interval**. A ratio schedule occurs when a reinforcer depends on the number of responses that are made. In an interval schedule, reinforcers are presented after a certain period of time has passed. If the reinforcers are always given after a set period of time or number of responses, the schedule is said to be fixed. If the reinforcer is given after varying periods of time or numbers of responses the schedule is labeled as variable.

The term **behavior modification** is used to describe the process of using operant conditioning to change behavior. A **token economy** involves the use of tokens to modify behavior. **Time-outs** are an example of punishment by removal where the child is removed from a situation where they could get attention from others. **Applied behavior analysis or ABA** uses shaping techniques to obtain a desired behavior and is particularly successful with children with disorders such as autism. The technique called **biofeedback** uses operant conditioning to modify involuntary behaviors such as blood pressure and heart rate. When this technique is used to try to change brain wave activity it is referred to as **neurofeedback**.

Cognitive learning theorists focus on the mental processes (or cognitions) that occur during learning. Edward Tolman studied the phenomenon of **latent learning** in rats placed in a maze but not reinforced for finding their way out. He found that when the rats were subsequently reinforced, learning occurred much faster than for rats who had never been in the maze. Martin Seligman studied a phenomenon he called **learned helplessness** in dogs. He found that dogs classically conditioned to a tone followed by a painful shock would not later try to escape the shock when provided the opportunity. Seligman extended the concept of learned helplessness to humans in an attempt to explain depression. A third cognitive psychologist, Wolfgang Köhler, studied the phenomenon of **insight learning** in animals. Köhler believed insight learning involved a sudden perception of relationships that could not be gained through trial and error learning. All three theories of learning are related in that they focus on what's going on inside the learner's mind during the learning process as opposed to the external stimuli and rewards of classical and operant conditioning.

A third category of learning is that of **observational learning**, or the learning of a new behavior by observing someone else who is performing that behavior. The term **learning/performance distinction** describes the fact that learning can take place without actual performance. Albert Bandura has been a major contributor to the study of observational learning and conducted a series of classic studies observing children's learned behaviors with a blow-up "Bobo" doll. Bandura concluded that four elements were needed for observational learning to occur, the four elements are attention, memory, imitation, and motivation.

STUDY HINTS

1. Many students get confused with the terms of classical conditioning. There are four major components to this type of learning, unconditioned stimulus (UCS), conditioned stimulus (CS), unconditioned response (UCR) and conditioned response (CR). The best way to keep these terms straight is to ask yourself two questions.

   1. **Is the event I am interested in a stimulus or a response?**

   2. **Is the stimulus/response something that was learned or something that occurs naturally, by instinct.**

   The first question is the easiest way to break down the information. If an event is a stimulus, it will cause something else to happen. List some examples of stimuli here.

   _____

   You might have mentioned any number of stimuli including events such as a bright light, a puff of air, a loud siren, a soft whisper, a touch on your arm, the smell of cookies, a written word. The list is quite large. A stimulus is any event that causes a response.

   Now that you have a good feeling for what stimuli are, try listing some examples of some possible responses.

   _____

   You might have mentioned events such as blinking your eyes, laughing, crying, jumping up, heart rate increasing, feeling scared, raising your hand, driving faster. A response is any behavior (inside or outside of your body) that can be observed.

   Once you determine if your event is a stimulus or response, the second question is fairly easy. Is the stimulus something the subject had to learn how to respond to? If so, then it would be a learned or conditioned stimulus. If the stimulus is something that causes the response automatically, then it is an unlearned or unconditioned stimulus. The same rule applies for the responses. If this is a response that does not occur by instinct, but instead has been learned through experience, then this is a learned or conditioned response. If the response happens the first time you encounter the stimulus, as an instinct, then it is an unlearned or unconditioned response. Now try some examples and see how you do.

A puff of air is aimed at your eye and you blink.
    The event we are interested in is: the blink

        Question 1: Is this a stimulus or a response?

        _____

                        If you wrote response, then you are correct.
                        Blinking is a behavior that we can observe.

        Question 2: Is this response learned or unlearned?

        _____

                        If you wrote unlearned, then you are correct.
                        Blinking to a puff of air is an instinct.

Now you can fill in the blanks.
    The first answer tells you this is a response, so it is either a CR or a UCR.
    The second answer tells you this is unlearned or unconditioned, so it must be a UCR.

Now circle the right term:

	Stimulus	Response
Learned	CS	CR
Unlearned	UCS	UCR

Try some more on your own.

~~~~~~

A picture of a piece of chocolate cake causes your mouth to water.
    The event we are interested in is: the picture of the cake

        Question 1: Is this a stimulus or a response?

        _____

        Question 2: Is this response learned or unlearned?

        _____

Now circle the right term:

	Stimulus	Response
Learned	CS	CR
Unlearned	UCS	UCR

~~~~~~

Your heart speeds up as you see a police car pull up behind you.
   The event we are interested in is: <u>your heart speeding up</u>

   Question 1: Is this a stimulus or a response?

   _____

   Question 2: Is this response learned or unlearned?

   _____

Now select the right term:

	Stimulus	Response
Learned	CS	CR
Unlearned	UCS	UCR

~~~~~~

A loud noise causes someone to jump.
   The event we are interested in is: <u>the loud noise</u>

   Question 1: Is this a stimulus or a response?

   _____

   Question 2: Is this response learned or unlearned?

   _____

Now select the right term:

	Stimulus	Response
Learned	CS	CR
Unlearned	UCS	UCR

~~~~~~

You should have selected the following
   blinking your eyes is a UCR
   the piece of cake is a CS
   your heart speeding up is a CR
   the loud noise is a UCS

2.   Negative reinforcement and punishment are often confused. In negative reinforcement, something bad is taken away. In punishment by removal, something good or desirable is taken away. Most people would enjoy being negatively reinforced but would be upset about being punished. Work through the following scenarios to determine whether the person is being negatively reinforced or punished. The first one has been completed for you.

Behavior	Consequence	Is something good or bad taken away?	Is this negative reinforcement or punishment?	Will the behavior increase or decrease?
Taking an aspirin for a headache.	Headache goes away.	*bad*	*negative reinforcement*	*increase*
Running a red light.	Driver's license is taken away.			
Cleaning your room so that you are no longer grounded.	You are no longer grounded.			
Drinking coffee in the morning when you are very tired.	You no longer feel tired.			
Staying out past your curfew.	Your parents ground you.			
Getting in a fight with a friend.	Your friend will not talk to you anymore.			
Fastening your seatbelt when the buzzer is making a noise.	The buzzer stops.			
Driving your car until it runs out of gas.	You can't drive your car anymore.			
Your boyfriend nags you until you take him out to dinner.	The nagging stops.			

Suggested answers

Behavior	Consequence	Is something good or bad taken away?	Is this negative reinforcement or punishment?	Will the behavior increase or decrease?
Taking an aspirin for a headache.	Headache goes away	*bad*	*negative reinforcement*	*increase*
Running a red light.	Driver's license is taken away.	*good*	*punishment*	*decrease*
Cleaning your room so that you are no longer grounded.	You are no longer grounded.	*bad*	*negative reinforcement*	*increase*
Drinking coffee in the morning when you are very tired.	You no longer feel tired.	*bad*	*negative reinforcement*	*increase*
Staying out past your curfew.	Your parents ground you.	*good*	*punishment*	*decrease*
Getting in a fight with a friend.	Your friend will not talk to you anymore.	*good*	*punishment*	*decrease*
Fastening your seatbelt when the buzzer is making a noise.	The buzzer stops.	*bad*	*negative reinforcement*	*increase*
Driving your car until it runs out of gas.	You can't drive your car anymore.	*good*	*punishment*	*decrease*
Your boyfriend nags you until you take him out to dinner.	The nagging stops.	*bad*	*negative reinforcement*	*increase*

LEARNING OBJECTIVES

5.1   What does the term learning really mean?

5.2   How was classical conditioning first studied, and what are the important elements and characteristics of classical conditioning?

5.3   What is a conditioned emotional response, and how do cognitive psychologists explain classical conditioning?

5.4   How does operant conditioning occur, and what were the contributions of Thorndike and Skinner?

5.5   What are the important concepts in operant conditioning?

5.6   What are some of the problems with using punishment?

5.7   What are the schedules of reinforcement?

5.8   How do operant stimuli control behavior, and what kind of behavior is resistant to operant conditioning?

5.9   What is behavior modification, and how can behavioral techniques be used to modify involuntary biological responses?

5.10 How do latent learning, learned helplessness, and insight relate to cognitive learning theory?

5.11 What occurs in observational learning, including findings from Bandura's classic Bobo doll study and the four elements of observational learning?

5.12 What is a real-world example of the use of conditioning?

PRACTICE EXAM

For the following multiple choice questions, select the answer you feel best answers the questions.

1.   _____ is any relatively permanent change in behavior brought about by experience or practice.
    a)   Learning
    b)   Adaptation
    c)   Memory enhancement
    d)   Muscle memory

2.   The researcher responsible for discovering classical conditioning was
    a)   Skinner.
    b)   Tolman.
    c)   Kohler.
    d)   Pavlov.

3.   Which of the following correctly describes the process of classical conditioning?
    a)   pairing a stimulus that naturally causes a certain response with a second stimulus that naturally causes the same response
    b)   pairing a stimulus that naturally causes a certain response with a second stimulus that does not naturally cause that response
    c)   presenting a pleasurable stimulus after the occurrence of a specific response
    d)   presenting an unpleasant stimulus after the occurrence of a specific response

4.   When Pavlov placed meat powder or other food in the mouths of canine subjects, they began to salivate. The salivation was a/an
    a)   unconditioned response.
    b)   unconditioned stimulus.
    c)   conditioned response.
    d)   conditioned stimulus.

5. Judy would sometimes discipline her puppy by swatting its nose with a rolled-up newspaper. One day she brought the newspaper into the house still rolled up, and her puppy ran from her in fear. By pairing the rolled paper with the swat, Judy's puppy had developed a(n) _____ response to the rolled-up paper.
    a) generalized
    b) conditioned
    c) unconditioned
    d) discriminative

6. You decide you want to try to classically condition your pet dog. What is the correct order that you should use to present the stimuli to your dog.
    a) unconditioned stimulus – neutral stimulus
    b) neutral stimulus – neutral stimulus
    c) neutral stimulus – unconditioned stimulus
    d) present the unconditioned stimulus only

7. After you successfully classically conditioned your pet dog, you repeatedly presented the conditioned stimulus without ever pairing it with the unconditioned stimulus. Over time, your dog stops performing the conditioned response. What has happened?
    a) extinction
    b) spontaneous recovery
    c) generalization
    d) stimulus discrimination

8. John Watson and his colleague, Rosalie Rayner, offered a live, white rat to Little Albert and then made a loud noise behind his head by striking a steel bar with a hammer. The white rat served as the _____ in their study.
    a) discriminative stimulus
    b) counterconditioning stimulus
    c) conditioned stimulus
    d) unconditioned stimulus

9. Pavlov discovered classical conditioning through his study of
    a) cats escaping from a puzzle box.
    b) primate research into problem solving.
    c) digestive secretions in dogs.
    d) lever pressing responses of rats.

10. Television advertisers have taken advantage of the fact that most people experience positive emotions when they see an attractive, smiling person. This association is an example of
    a) operant conditioning.
    b) a conditioned emotional response.
    c) negative reinforcement.
    d) punishment.

11. The current view of why classical conditioning works the way it does, by cognitive theorists such as Rescorla, adds the concept of _____ to the conditioning process.
    a) generalization
    b) habituation
    c) memory loss
    d) expectancy

12. "If a response is followed by a pleasurable consequence, it will tend to be repeated. If a response is followed by an unpleasant consequence, it will tend not to be repeated." This is a statement of
_____.
   a) the law of positive reinforcement
   b) Rescorla's cognitive perspective
   c) Thorndike's Law of Effect
   d) Garcia's conditional emotional response

13. Kenra has a new pet cat and decides to modify her cat's behavior by administering pleasant and unpleasant consequences after her cat's behaviors. Kenra is using the principles of
   a) observational learning.
   b) operant conditioning.
   c) classical conditioning.
   d) insight learning.

14. A box used in operant conditioning of animals, which limits the available responses and thus increases the likelihood that the desired response will occur, is called a _____.
   a) trial box
   b) response box
   c) Watson box
   d) Skinner box

15. A negative reinforcer is a stimulus that is_____ and thus_____ the probability of a response.
   a) removed; increases
   b) removed; decreases
   c) presented; increases
   d) presented; decreases

16. The partial reinforcement effect refers to the fact that a response that is reinforced after some, but not all, correct responses will be.
   a) more resistant to extinction than a response that receives continuous reinforcement (a reinforcer for each and every correct response).
   b) less resistant to extinction than a response that receives continuous reinforcement (a reinforcer for each and every correct response).
   c) more variable in its resistance to extinction than a response that receives continuous reinforcement (a reinforcer for each and every correct response).
   d) totally resistant to extinction unlike a response that receives continuous reinforcement (a reinforcer for each and every correct response).

17. Which example best describes the fixed interval schedule of reinforcement?
   a) receiving a paycheck after two weeks of work
   b) receiving a bonus after selling 20 cell phones
   c) giving your dog a treat every time he comes when you call him
   d) giving your dog a treat every third time he comes when you call him

18. Which schedule of reinforcement should you select if you would like to produce the highest number of responses with the least number of pauses between the responses?
    a) fixed ratio
    b) variable ratio
    c) fixed interval
    d) variable interval

19. When a stimulus is removed from a person or animal and it decreases the probability of response that is known as _____.
    a) positive punishment
    b) punishment by removal
    c) negative reinforcement
    d) negative punishment

20. Your child has begun drawing on the walls of your house and you would like this activity to stop. Which of the following actions would, at least temporarily, decrease the occurrence of the behavior in your child?
    a) use insight learning to get your child to stop drawing on the wall
    b) use classical conditioning to create a positive association with drawing on the wall
    c) negatively reinforce your child after she draws on the wall
    d) punish your child after she draws on the wall

21. An example of a discriminative stimulus might be a
    a) a stop sign.
    b) the stimulus that acts as a UCS in classical conditioning.
    c) the white rat in Watson's Little Albert study of producing phobias.
    d) none of these.

22. In their 1961 paper on instinctive drift, the Brelands determined that three assumptions most Skinnerian behaviorists believed in were not actually true. Which is one of the assumptions that were NOT true?
    a) The animal comes to the laboratory a tabula rasa, or "blank slate," and can therefore be taught anything with the right conditioning.
    b) Differences between species of animals are insignificant.
    c) All responses are equally able to be conditioned to any stimulus.
    d) All of these were not true.

23. Applied behavior analysis or ABA has been used with autistic children. The basic principle of this form of behavior modification is _____.
    a) partial reinforcement
    b) classical conditioning
    c) negative punishment
    d) shaping

24. Biofeedback is an application of _____.
    a) classical conditioning
    b) operant conditioning
    c) social learning
    d) preparedness

25. Cognition refers to
    a)   behavior that is observable and external.
    b)   behavior that is directly measurable.
    c)   the mental events that take place while a person is behaving.
    d)   memories.

26. The idea that learning occurs, and is stored up, even when behaviors are not reinforced is called _____.
    a)   insight
    b)   latent learning
    c)   placebo learning
    d)   innate learning

27. A researcher places dogs in a cage with metal bars on the floor. The dogs are randomly given electric shocks and can do nothing to prevent them or stop them. Later, the same dogs are placed in a cage where they can escape the shocks by jumping over a low hurdle. When the shocks are given, the dogs do not even try to escape. They just sit and cower. This is an example of _____.
    a)   learned helplessness
    b)   stimulus discrimination
    c)   aversive conditioning
    d)   vicarious learning

28. The "aha!" experience is known as
    a)   latent learning.
    b)   insight learning.
    c)   thoughtful learning.
    d)   serial enumeration.

29. If you learn how to fix your car by watching someone on TV demonstrate the technique, you are acquiring that knowledge through
    a)   latent learning.
    b)   operant conditioning.
    c)   classical conditioning.
    d)   observational learning.

30. In Bandura's study with the Bobo doll, the children in the group that saw the model punished did not imitate the model at first. They would only imitate the model if given a reward for doing so. The fact that these children had obviously learned the behavior without actually performing it is an example of
    a)   latent learning.
    b)   operant conditioning.
    c)   classical conditioning.
    d)   insight learning.

31. In Bandura's study of observational learning, the abbreviation AMIM stands for
    a)   attention, memory, imitation, motivation.
    b)   alertness, motivation, intent, monetary reward.
    c)   achievement, momentum, initiative, memory.
    d)   achievement, motivation, intellectual capacity, memory.

32. Which of the following real-world situations is using the principles of classical conditioning?
    a) giving a child a star for completing her homework assignment
    b) sending a child to time-out for stealing his friend's toy truck
    c) grounding a child until she gets her room cleaned
    d) a hungry child smiling at the sight of the spoon her dad always uses to feed her lunch

PRACTICE EXAM ANSWERS

1. a   This is the definition of learning given in the textbook and restated in the summary.
2. d   Skinner developed the theory of operant conditioning and both Kohler and Tolman focused on cognitive learning.
3. b   Classical conditioning occurs when you pair a neutral stimulus (NS) with an unconditioned stimulus (UCS). After repeated pairings, the NS now causes a response similar to the naturally occurring response. The stimulus is now called a conditioned stimulus and the response is the conditioned response.
4. a   An unconditioned response is a response that occurs naturally and does not have to be learned. When food is placed in a dog's mouth, the dog will naturally begin to salivate.
5. b   A conditioned response is a response that has been learned through association. Originally, the rolled-up newspaper did not cause a response of fear in the puppy, but after repeated pairings with a swat, it now causes the fear response.
6. c   For classical conditioning to occur, the neutral stimulus must be repeatedly paired with an unconditioned stimulus. In addition, the neutral stimulus must be presented *before* the unconditioned stimulus.
7. a   Extinction occurs when the CS is continuously presented without the UCS.
8. c   First, decide if the rat is a stimulus or a response. Obviously, the rat is a stimulus. Then figure out if the rat naturally, or instinctively, will cause the response of fear or if the response needs to be learned. If it needs to be learned, then the stimulus is a conditioned stimulus.
9. c   Pavlov was a Russian physiologist who won a Nobel prize for his study of the digestive system in dogs. It was during this research that he observed the phenomenon of classical conditioning and devoted the rest of his years in research to the study of classical conditioning.
10. b   The association between attractive people and feelings of happiness is learned through classical conditioning and is specifically referred to as a conditioned emotional response since it deals with a response of emotion. Notice that all the other choices were related to operant conditioning.
11. d   Expectancy is the idea that the conditioned stimulus has to provide some information about the upcoming unconditioned stimulus, so that we are *expecting* the UCS to occur.
12. c   Thorndike developed this principle through his study of animals escaping from puzzle boxes.
13. b   This is a modified form of the definition of operant conditioning.
14. d   The Skinner box was designed by B.F. Skinner and typically included an apparatus for the animal to move (such as a lever to press) and a mechanism for delivering a reward to the animal.
15. a   Always start with the fact that reinforcement always increases the response. This immediately eliminates options b and d. Negative reinforcement occurs when an unpleasant stimulus is removed, making a the correct choice.
16. a   If a response is resistant to extinction, that means that the person will continue making that response even when it is not followed by a reinforcer.

17. a   Fixed means that the reinforcement will always be presented after the same period of time or number of responses. Interval means that you are dealing with the passage of time.

18. b   The ratio schedule produces the most rapid responses since the reward depends on making a certain number of responses. The variable schedule reduces the pauses after receiving the reinforcer because the next reward could be given at any time.

19. b   Remember that punishment decreases behavior and reinforcement increases behavior. Since the question is asking about a behavior decrease, it must be talking about punishment. Removing a stimulus is described as punishment by removal.

20. d   Once again, you would like the behavior to decrease so you should select punishment.

21. a   A discriminative stimulus is defined as a stimulus that provides a cue that a response might lead to reinforcement. It is a term used with operant conditioning.

22. d   The Brelands questioned all three of these assumptions.

23. d   ABA rewards closer and closer approximations to the desired behavior, which is the definition of shaping.

24. b   The change in physiological state is the response and the light or tone serves as the reinforcement.

25. c   Cognitive psychologists focus on our thought process and mental activities.

26. b   The word latent means something that's present but not visible.

27. a   Learned helplessness was studied by Seligman as a potential animal model of depression.

28. b   With this type of learning, you have a sudden realization or "insight."

29. d   Observational learning occurs when you learn a new behavior or new knowledge through the observation of a model.

30. a   Latent learning occurs when a new behavior has been acquired but the behavior is not performed, as the children in Bandura's experiment did not imitate the model until they were encouraged and rewarded to do so.

31. a   Since all the selections match the abbreviation, try to think about what skills would be needed to learn by observation. First of all, you need to watch the person you are trying to learn from. Choices c and d can be eliminated because they don't list any skill that would assist with the observation. Choice b can then be eliminated if you realize that observational learning can occur without any rewards being offered.

32. d   Choices a-c are all examples of operant conditioning.

CHAPTER GLOSSARY

acquisition	in classical conditioning, the repeated pairing of a neutral stimulus with an unconditioned stimulus in order to produce a conditioned response.
Albert Bandura	1925-present. conducted a series of classic studies on how children model aggressive behavior towards an inflatable Bobo doll and developed the concept of observational learning.
applied behavior analysis (ABA)	modern term for a form of behavior modification that uses shaping techniques to mold a desired behavior or response.
B.F. Skinner	1904–1990. proponent of behaviorist perspective and pioneer in the field of operant conditioning.
behavior modification	the use of operant conditioning techniques to bring about desired changes in behavior.
biofeedback	the use of feedback about biological conditions to bring involuntary responses, such as blood pressure and relaxation, under voluntary control.

biological preparedness	referring to the tendency of animals to learn certain associations, such as taste and nausea, with only one or few pairings due to the survival value of the learning.
classical conditioning	learning to make a reflex response to a stimulus other than the original, natural stimulus that normally produces the reflex.
cognitive learning	learning model that focuses on the mental processes required for the acquisition of new behaviors
cognitive perspective	modern theory in psychology that focuses on mental processes and the study of conscious experiences
conditional emotional response	emotional response that has become classically conditioned to occur to learned stimuli, such as a fear of dogs or the emotional reaction that occurs when seeing an attractive person.
conditioned response (CR)	learned reflex response to a conditioned stimulus.
conditioned stimulus (CS)	stimulus that becomes able to produce a learned reflex response by being paired with the original unconditioned stimulus.
conditioned taste aversions	development of a nausea or aversive response to a particular taste because that taste was followed by a nausea reaction, occurring after only one association.
continuous reinforcement	the reinforcement of each and every correct response.
discriminative stimulus	any stimulus, such as a stop sign or a doorknob, that provides the organism with a cue for making a certain response in order to obtain reinforcement.
Edward Thorndike	1874–1949. discovered the law of effect and laid the groundwork for operant conditioning through his work with puzzle boxes.
Edward Tolman	1886–1959. developed several theories of cognitive learning including the concept of latent learning.
extinction	in classical conditioning, the disappearance or weakening of a learned response following the removal or absence of the unconditioned stimulus.
extinction	in operant conditioning, the disappearance or weakening of a learned response following the removal of a reinforcer.
fixed interval	schedule of reinforcement in which the interval of time that must pass before reinforcement becomes possible is always the same.
fixed ratio	schedule of reinforcement in which the number of responses required for reinforcement is always the same.
higher-order conditioning	occurs when a strong conditioned stimulus is paired with a neutral stimulus, causing the neutral stimulus to become a second conditioned stimulus.
insight learning	the sudden perception of relationships among various parts of a problem, such as an "aha!" experience, allowing the solution to the problem to come quickly.
instinctive drift	tendency for an animal's behavior to revert to genetically controlled patterns.
Ivan Pavlov	1849–1936. a Russian physiologist who first described the phenomenon now known as classical conditioning.
latent learning	learning that remains hidden until its application becomes useful.
Law of Effect	law stating that if a response is followed by a pleasurable consequence, it will tend to be repeated, and if followed by an unpleasant consequence, it will tend to not be repeated.

learned helplessness	the tendency to fail to act to escape from a situation because of a history of repeated failures in the past.
learning	relatively permanent change in behavior due to experience or practice.
learning/performance distinction	referring to the observation that learning can take place without actual performance of the learned behavior.
Martin Seligman	1942-presesnt. cognitive learning theorist who conducted a series of studies on learned helplessness in dogs.
negative reinforcement	the reinforcement of a response by the removal, escape from, or avoidance of an unpleasant stimulus.
neurofeedback	a form of biofeedback using brain-scanning devices to provide feedback about brain activity in an effort to modify behavior.
neutral stimulus (NS)	stimulus that has no effect on the desired response.
observational learning	learning new behavior by watching a model perform that behavior.
operant	any behavior that is voluntary.
operant conditioning	the learning of voluntary behavior through the effects of pleasant and unpleasant consequences to responses.
partial reinforcement	the reinforcement of some, but not all, of the correct responses.
partial reinforcement effect	the tendency for a response that is reinforced after some, but not all, correct responses to be very resistant to extinction.
positive reinforcement	the reinforcement of a response by the addition or experiencing of a pleasure stimulus.
primary reinforcers	any reinforcer that is naturally reinforcing by meeting a basic biological need, such as hunger, thirst, or touch.
punishment	any event or object that, when following a response, makes that response less likely to happen again.
punishment by application	the punishment of a response by the addition or experiencing of an unpleasant stimulus.
punishment by removal	the punishment of a response by the removal of a pleasurable stimulus.
reinforcement	the strengthening of a response that occurs when that response is followed by a pleasurable consequence.
reinforcer	any event or object that, when following a response, increases the likelihood of that response occurring again.
schedule of reinforcement	timing of reinforcement for correct responses.
secondary reinforcers	any reinforcer that becomes reinforcing after being paired with a primary reinforcer, such as praise, tokens, or gold stars.
shaping	the reinforcement of simple steps in behavior that lead to a desired, more complex behavior.
spontaneous recovery	the reappearance of a learned response after extinction has occurred.
stimulus discrimination	the tendency to stop making a generalized response to a stimulus that is similar to the original conditioned stimulus because the similar stimulus is never paired with the unconditioned stimulus.
stimulus generalization	the tendency to respond to a stimulus that is similar to the original conditioned stimulus with the conditioned response.
stimulus substitution	original theory in which Pavlov stated that classical conditioning occurred because the conditioned stimulus became a substitute for the unconditioned stimulus by being paired closely together.
successive approximations	small steps in behavior, one after the other, that lead to a particular goal behavior.
time-out	behavior modification technique where subject is removed from all sources of attention. An example of punishment by removal.

token economy	type of behavior modification in which desired behavior is rewarded with tokens that can then be used to acquire items of value.
unconditioned response (UCR).	an involuntary response to a naturally occurring or unconditioned stimulus.
unconditioned stimulus (UCS)	a naturally occurring stimulus that leads to an involuntary response.
variable interval	schedule of reinforcement in which the interval of time that must pass before reinforcement becomes possible is different for each trial or event.
variable ratio	schedule of reinforcement in which the number of responses required for reinforcement is different for each trial or event.
vicarious conditioning	classical conditioning of a reflex response or emotion by watching the reaction of another person.
Wolfgang Köhler	1887–1967. co-founder of Gestalt psychology, studied problem-solving in animals and promoted the concept of insight learning.

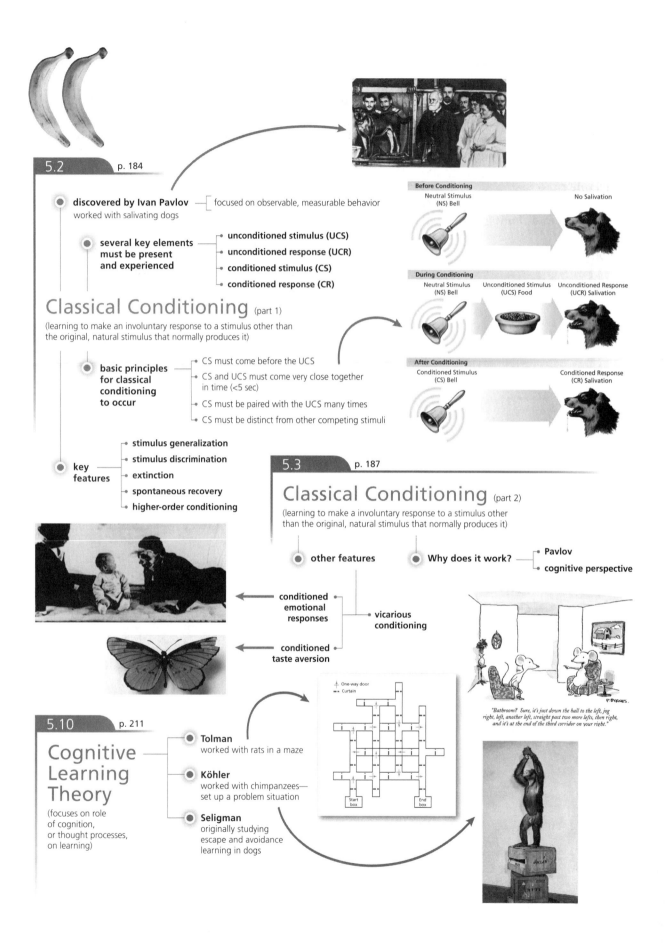

discovered by Ivan Pavlov — focused on observable, measurable behavior
worked with salivating dogs

several key elements must be present and experienced
- unconditioned stimulus (UCS)
- unconditioned response (UCR)
- conditioned stimulus (CS)
- conditioned response (CR)

Classical Conditioning (part 1)

(learning to make an involuntary response to a stimulus other than the original, natural stimulus that normally produces it)

basic principles for classical conditioning to occur
- CS must come before the UCS
- CS and UCS must come very close together in time (<5 sec)
- CS must be paired with the UCS many times
- CS must be distinct from other competing stimuli

key features
- stimulus generalization
- stimulus discrimination
- extinction
- spontaneous recovery
- higher-order conditioning

Before Conditioning
Neutral Stimulus (NS) Bell   No Salivation

During Conditioning
Neutral Stimulus (NS) Bell   Unconditioned Stimulus (UCS) Food   Unconditioned Response (UCR) Salivation

After Conditioning
Conditioned Stimulus (CS) Bell   Conditioned Response (CR) Salivation

Classical Conditioning (part 2)

(learning to make a involuntary response to a stimulus other than the original, natural stimulus that normally produces it)

other features

Why does it work?
- Pavlov
- cognitive perspective

- conditioned emotional responses
- conditioned taste aversion

vicarious conditioning

"Bathroom? Sure, it's just down the hall to the left, jog right, left, another left, straight past two more lefts, then right, and it's at the end of the third corridor on your right."

Cognitive Learning Theory

(focuses on role of cognition, or thought processes, on learning)

Tolman
worked with rats in a maze

Köhler
worked with chimpanzees— set up a problem situation

Seligman
originally studying escape and avoidance learning in dogs

One-way door
Curtain
Start box
End box

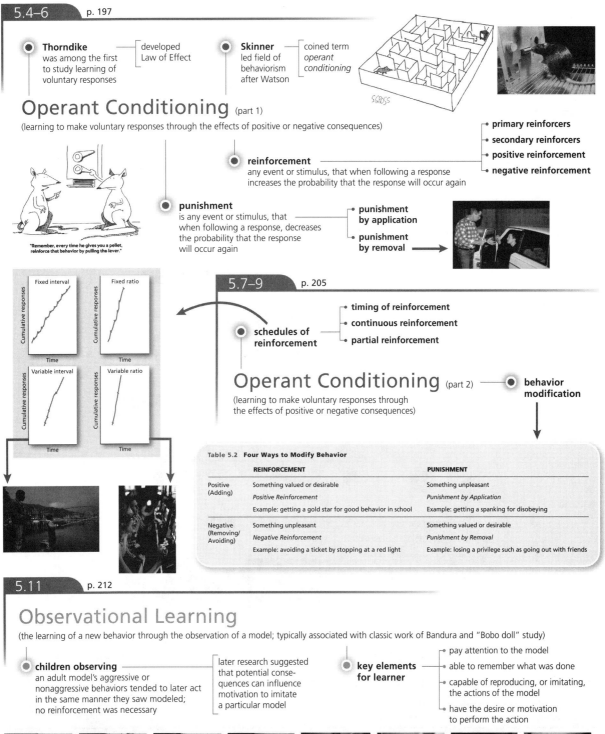

Thorndike
was among the first
to study learning of
voluntary responses

— developed
Law of Effect

Skinner
led field of
behaviorism
after Watson

— coined term
*operant
conditioning*

SGROSS

Operant Conditioning (part 1)
(learning to make voluntary responses through the effects of positive or negative consequences)

reinforcement
any event or stimulus, that when following a response
increases the probability that the response will occur again

- **primary reinforcers**
- **secondary reinforcers**
- **positive reinforcement**
- **negative reinforcement**

"Remember, every time he gives you a pellet, reinforce that behavior by pulling the lever."

punishment
is any event or stimulus, that
when following a response, decreases
the probability that the response
will occur again

- **punishment by application**
- **punishment by removal**

Fixed interval

Fixed ratio

Variable interval

Variable ratio

Cumulative responses / Time

schedules of reinforcement

- **timing of reinforcement**
- **continuous reinforcement**
- **partial reinforcement**

Operant Conditioning (part 2)
(learning to make voluntary responses through
the effects of positive or negative consequences)

behavior modification

Table 5.2 **Four Ways to Modify Behavior**

	REINFORCEMENT	PUNISHMENT
Positive (Adding)	Something valued or desirable	Something unpleasant
	Positive Reinforcement	*Punishment by Application*
	Example: getting a gold star for good behavior in school	Example: getting a spanking for disobeying
Negative (Removing/ Avoiding)	Something unpleasant	Something valued or desirable
	Negative Reinforcement	*Punishment by Removal*
	Example: avoiding a ticket by stopping at a red light	Example: losing a privilege such as going out with friends

Observational Learning
(the learning of a new behavior through the observation of a model; typically associated with classic work of Bandura and "Bobo doll" study)

children observing
an adult model's aggressive or
nonaggressive behaviors tended to later act
in the same manner they saw modeled;
no reinforcement was necessary

— later research suggested
that potential conse-
quences can influence
motivation to imitate
a particular model

**key elements
for learner**

- pay attention to the model
- able to remember what was done
- capable of reproducing, or imitating, the actions of the model
- have the desire or motivation to perform the action

_____
_____
_____
_____
_____
_____
_____
_____
_____
_____
_____

Figure 5.1 **Classical Conditioning**

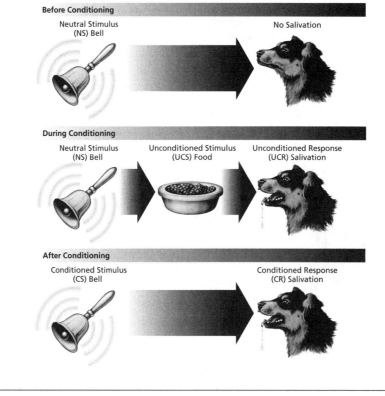

Before Conditioning
Neutral Stimulus (NS) Bell → No Salivation

During Conditioning
Neutral Stimulus (NS) Bell → Unconditioned Stimulus (UCS) Food → Unconditioned Response (UCR) Salivation

After Conditioning
Conditioned Stimulus (CS) Bell → Conditioned Response (CR) Salivation

_____
_____
_____
_____
_____
_____
_____

Figure 5.3 **Extinction and Spontaneous Recovery**

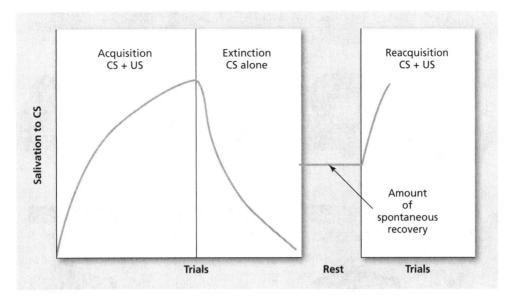

Figure 5.4 **Higher-Order Conditioning**

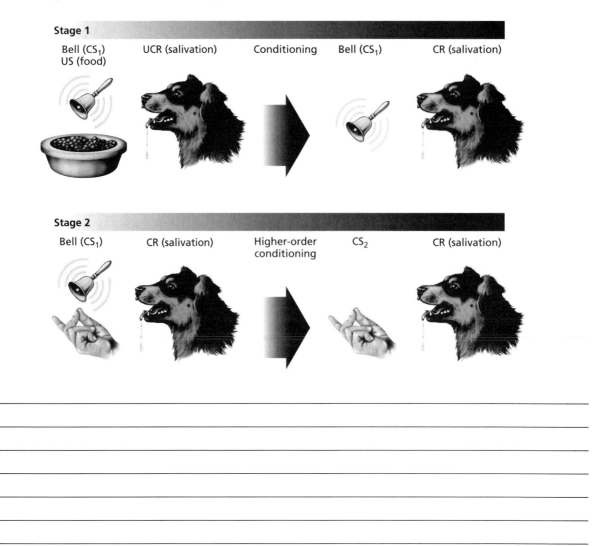

5.4–5.6 Operant Conditioning

Figure 5.7 **A Typical Skinner Box**

_____
_____
_____
_____
_____
_____
_____
_____
_____
_____

Table 5.1 **Comparing Two Kinds of Conditioning**

Table 5.1 Comparing Two Kinds of Conditioning

OPERANT CONDITIONING	CLASSICAL CONDITIONING
End result is an increase in the rate of an already occurring response.	End result is the creation of a new response to a stimulus that did not normally produce that response.
Responses are voluntary.	Responses are involuntary and reflexive.
Consequences are important in forming an association.	Antecedent stimuli are important in forming an association.
Reinforcement should be immediate.	CS must occur immediately before the UCS.
An expectancy develops for reinforcement to follow a correct response.	An expectancy develops for UCS to follow CS.

_____
_____
_____
_____
_____
_____
_____
_____
_____
_____
_____
_____
_____
_____

Table 5.2 **Four Ways to Modify Behavior**

Table 5.2

	REINFORCEMENT	PUNISHMENT
Positive (Adding)	Something valued or desirable	Something unpleasant
	Positive Reinforcement	*Punishment by Application*
	Example: getting a gold star for good behavior in school	Example: getting a spanking for disobeying
Negative (Removing/Avoiding)	Something unpleasant	Something valued or desirable
	Negative Reinforcement	*Punishment by Removal*
	Example: avoiding a ticket by stopping at a red light	Example: losing a privilege such as going out with friends

_____
_____
_____
_____
_____
_____

Table 5.3 **Negative Reinforcement Versus Punishment by Removal**

Table 5.3   Negative Reinforcement Versus Punishment by Removal

EXAMPLE OF NEGATIVE REINFORCEMENT	EXAMPLE OF PUNISHMENT BY REMOVAL
Stopping at a red light to avoid getting in an accident.	Losing the privilege of driving because you got into too many accidents.
Mailing an income tax return by April 15 to avoid paying a penalty.	Having to lose some of your money to pay the penalty for late tax filing.
Obeying a parent before the parent reaches the count of "three" to avoid getting a scolding.	Being "grounded" (losing your freedom) because of disobedience.

_____
_____
_____
_____
_____
_____

_____
_____
_____
_____
_____
_____
_____
_____
_____
_____
_____

Figure 5.8 **Schedules of Reinforcement**

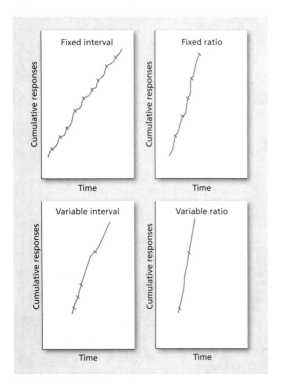

_____
_____
_____
_____
_____
_____
_____
_____
_____
_____
_____
_____
_____
_____
_____
_____
_____
_____
_____

Figure 5.10 **Learning Curves for Three Groups of Rats**

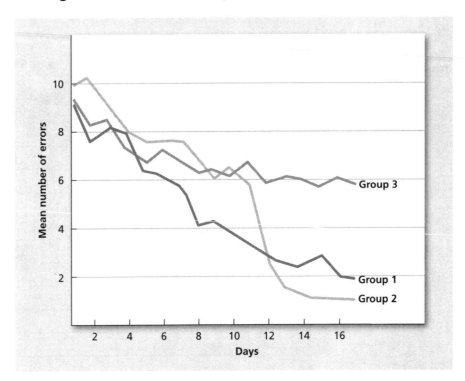

YOU KNOW YOU ARE READ FOR THE TEST IF YOU ARE ABLE TO...

- Introduce the study of memory including the basic processes of encoding, storage, and retrieval as well as current theories of how memory works.
- Discuss the information-processing theory of memory in detail including the concepts of sensory, short-term, and long-term memory.
- Identify the basic mechanisms and limitations in the retrieval of information including false memories.
- Describe Ebbinghaus's work on forgetting and proposed explanations for forgetting.
- Explain the biological processes thought to underlie memory and the deterioration of memory.

RAPID REVIEW

Memory can be thought of as an active system that receives information from the senses, organizes and alters it as it stores it, and then retrieves information from storage. All the current models of memory involve the three processes of **encoding**, **storage**, and **retrieval**.

Three models or theories about memory are discussed in the text. One is the **levels-of-processing model**, which proposes that how long a memory will be remembered depends on the depth to which it was processed. A second model is the **parallel distributed processing model**, which proposes that memories are created and stored across a network of neural circuits simultaneously, or in other words, in a parallel fashion. The third and currently most accepted model of memory is the **information-processing model**, which proposes that memory is divided into three components – **sensory**, **short term**, and **long term**. Sensory memory is the first stage of memory and involves information from our sensory systems. Visual sensory memory is called **iconic memory** and was studied extensively by George Sperling through the use of the partial report method. The capacity of iconic memory is everything that can be seen at one time and the duration is around half a second. **Eidetic imagery**, also known as photographic memory, is the ability to access visual sensory memory over a long period of time. Iconic memory is useful for allowing the visual system to view the surroundings as continuous and stable. **Echoic memory** is the memory of auditory information and has the capacity of what can be heard at any one moment and has a duration of about two seconds.

The information-processing model proposes that information moves from sensory memory to short-term memory through the process of **selective attention**. This process explains the phenomenon of the cocktail party effect, when you are at a party and hear your name in a conversation across the room. Another name for short-term memory is **working memory**, and some researchers propose that short-term memory consists of a central control process along with a visual "sketch pad" and auditory "recorder." George Miller studied the capacity of short-term memory using the digit-span memory test and discovered that people can store an average of seven chunks of information (plus or minus two) in their short-term memory. **Chunking** is the process of reorganizing the information into meaningful units. The duration of short-term memory is between 10-30 seconds without rehearsal. **Maintenance rehearsal** describes the process of continuing to pay attention to a piece of information, such as reciting a name over and over again in your head.

Long-term memory is the third stage of memory proposed by the information-processing theory and has an essentially unlimited capacity and duration. Information may by encoded into long-term memory through **elaborative rehearsal**, a way of transferring information by making it meaningful. Long-term memories can be divided into two types, procedural and declarative. **Procedural, or nondeclarative, memories** are memories for skill and habits, in other words, memories for things people can *do*. **Declarative memories** are memories of facts, or things people can *know*. There are two types of declarative memories, semantic and episodic. **Semantic memory** is memory for the meanings of words and concepts while **episodic memory** is the memory of events or "episodes." Procedural memories appear to be stored in the cerebellum and amygdala, while declarative memories most likely involve the frontal and temporal lobes. Procedural memory is sometimes referred to as **implicit memory**, and declarative memory can be thought of as **explicit memory**. Explicit memories are easily verbalized, while implicit memories are nearly impossible to state in words. It is not entirely clear how the brain organizes information in long-term memory. The **semantic network model** suggests that information is stored in the brain in a connected fashion with related concepts physically close to each other.

Retrieval describes the process of pulling memories out of long-term memory. A **retrieval cue** is a stimulus that aids in the process of remembering. When the environment in which you learned an item serves as a retrieval cue, it is referred to as **encoding specificity**. If an emotional state serves as a retrieval cue, it is called **state-dependent learning**. Information can be retrieved through the process of **recall**, such as filling in the blanks, or **recognition**, such as multiple choice questions in which the correct answer only needs to be "recognized." Not all information can be recalled equally well. The **serial position effect** describes the finding that information at the beginning and end of a list is more likely to be remembered than the information in the middle. The **primacy effect** proposes that the information at the beginning of the list is remembered due to rehearsal, while the **recency effect** proposes that the information at the end of the list is remembered due to the fact that it is still in short-term memory. Recognition is usually a much easier task than recall since the retrieval cue is the actual piece of information you are trying to remember, yet retrieval errors are still made when using recognition. A **false positive** occurs when someone recognizes a piece of information as a memory even though it did not happen. For example, a witness says they saw broken glass at the scene of an accident, when there was no glass broken in the accident. Elizabeth Loftus has spent over 30 years investigating the reliability of eyewitness memories and has found that what people see and hear about an event after the fact can affect the accuracy of their memories for that event. **Automatic encoding** is a term used to describe the memory process when we aren't actively paying attention to the information. A **flashbulb memory** is a specific type of automatic encoding that occurs when an unexpected and often emotional event occurs. Flashbulb memories typically contain a great deal of information including many details but might not be as accurate as they appear.

The retrieval of memories is a much more **constructive process** than most people assume. Several factors affect the accuracy of information retrieval. One factor is the **misinformation effect** in which false information presented after an event influences the memory of that event. When suggestions from others create inaccurate or false memories, this is referred to as the **false memory syndrome**. The false memory syndrome has frequently been observed while people are under hypnosis. Research by Loftus has suggested that in order for an individual to interpret a false event as a true memory, the event must seem plausible and the individual should be given information that supports the belief that the event could have happened to them personally. **Hindsight bias** is the tendency of people to falsely believe that they would have been able to accurately predict a result.

Herman Ebbinghaus was one of the first scientists to systematically study the process of forgetting. Using lists of **nonsense syllables**, he discovered that most forgetting occurs in the initial hour after the material is learned. He presented his findings in a visual graph called the **curve of forgetting**. There are at least four different causes for forgetting. **Encoding failure** occurs when the information does not make it past the initial encoding process and never really becomes a memory. Another possible cause of forgetting is the **decay** (or **disuse**) of the **memory trace** in short-term memory or the disuse of the information in long-term memory. The final two causes of forgetting discussed in the textbook have to do with interference. **Proactive interference** occurs when information from the past disrupts newly learned information. **Retroactive interference** occurs when the newly learned information interferes with the memories of the information from the past. Ebbinghaus found he could greatly improve memory if he spaced out his study sessions, a technique called **distributed practice**, as opposed to "cramming" or trying to learn all the information the night before the exam.

It is still unclear exactly how memories are physically stored in the brain. The concept of the physical change that takes place in the brain when memories are formed is called the engram, and scientists continue their search for the engram. In general, there is strong evidence to suggest that long-term procedural memories are stored in the cerebellum, while long-term declarative memories are stored in the frontal and temporal lobes. Storage of short-term memories has been associated with the prefrontal cortex and the temporal lobe. The process of physically storing a memory in your brain is called **consolidation** and could consist of a number of changes including an increase in receptor sties, increased sensitivity at the synapse, changes on the dendrites, or changes in proteins in the neuron. The hippocampus has been found to play an important role in the formation of new memories. This fact was mainly discovered by observing patients with damage to the hippocampus and noting their inability to form any new memories. A man named H.M. is the most famous of these patients. H.M.'s hippocampi were removed during a surgical procedure to reduce the severity of his epileptic seizures. After the surgery, H.M. could not form any new declarative memories. H.M. could, however, still form new procedural memories. **Amnesia** is a disorder which is characterized by severe memory loss, such as that of H.M.'s and can take one of two forms. **Retrograde amnesia** is an inability to retrieve memories from the past, while **anterograde amnesia** is an inability to form any new memories. An inability to remember events from the first few years of life has been described as **infantile amnesia** and may be due to the implicit, or nonverbal, nature of those memories.

     Alzheimer's disease is one type of dementia that is associated with severe memory loss. Currently there is no cure for Alzheimer's disease but researchers are working hard to find one. Several possibilities include drugs that block the breakdown of acetylcholine, chemicals within the gingko biloba herb, drugs that stimulate nerve growth, and statins or drugs that lower cholesterol.

STUDY HINTS

1.   Two of the most important concepts presented in this chapter consist of a three-part model. One concept is the basic processes involved in memory – encoding, storage, and retrieval. The other concept is the information-processing model of memory which consists of sensory, short-term, and long-term memory. Students often get these ideas confused. To help you clarify the concepts, correctly identify the components of the information-processing model in the diagram below. Remember that encoding, storage, and retrieval can happen at each of these stages. List an example of encoding, storage, and retrieval for each stage.

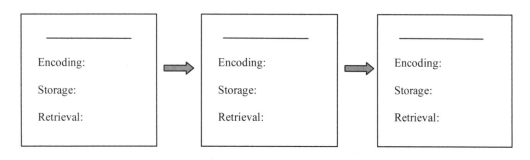

2.   Long-term memory can be divided into two basic types of memory – procedural and declarative. Declarative memories can be further broken down into episodic and semantic. To help you understand the difference between these types of memories, come up with a specific memory from your own life and write it in the appropriate box.

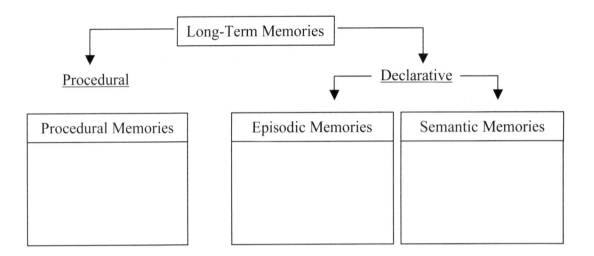

Suggested answers for Study Hint 1

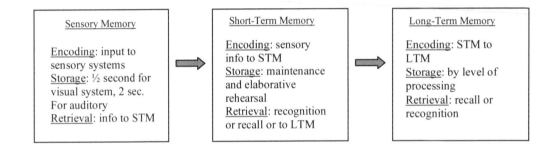

Suggested answers for Study Hint 2

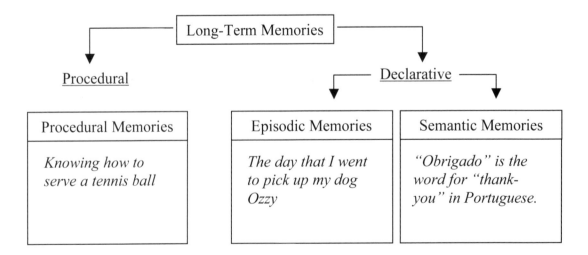

LEARNING OBJECTIVES

6.1 What are the three processes of memory and the different models of how memory works?

6.2 How does sensory memory work?

6.3 What is short-term memory, and how does it differ from working memory?

6.4 How is long-term memory different from other types of memory?

6.5 What are the various types of long-term memory, and how is information stored in long-term memory organized?

6.6 What kinds of cues help people remember?

6.7 How do the retrieval processes of recall and recognition differ, and how reliable are our memories of events?

6.8 How are long-term memories formed, and what kinds of problems do people experience as a result?

6.9 What is false memory syndrome?

6.10 Why do we forget?

6.11 How and where are memories formed in the brain?

6.12 How does amnesia occur, and what is Alzheimer's disease?

PRACTICE EXAM

For the following multiple choice questions, select the answer you feel best answers the question.

1. _____ is defined as an active system that receives information from the senses, organizes and alters it as it stores it away, and then retrieves the information from storage.
   a) Classical conditioning
   b) Operant conditioning
   c) Learning
   d) Memory

2. _____ is retention of memory for some period of time.
   a) Encoding
   b) Storage
   c) Retrieval
   d) Evaluation

3. Janie is taking an exam in her history class. On the exam there is a question that asks her to state and discuss the five major causes of the Trans-Caspian War (whatever that was!). Janie remembers four of them. She knows there is a fifth but time is up. As Janie is walking down the stairs, all of a sudden, she remembers that fifth point but it is too late. Janie had a problem with
   a) encoding.
   b) storage.
   c) retrieval.
   d) evaluation.

4. The processes of encoding, storage, and retrieval are seen as part of the _____ model of memory.
   a) Information-processing
   b) levels-of-processing
   c) parallel distributed processing
   d) All of the above are correct.

5. The "levels-of-processing" concept of Craik and Lockhart would suggests that which of the following questions would lead to better memory of the word "frog"?
   a) "Does it rhyme with blog?"
   b) "Is it in capital letters?"
   c) "Is it written in cursive?"
   d) "Would it be found in a pond?"

6. In the parallel distributed processing model of memory,

    a) information is simultaneously stored across a network that stretches across the brain.
    b) information is stored simultaneously in unconnected regions of the brain.
    c) information is associated in sets of classically conditioned neurons across the neocortex.
    d) None of these are correct.

7. The three parts of the information-processing model of memory are
    a) sensory memory, short-term memory, and long-term memory.
    b) CS, UCS, UR, CR.
    c) encoding, storage, retrieval.
    d) shallow, medium, deep processing.

8. Which memory system provides us with a very brief representation of all the stimuli present at a particular moment?
    a) primary memory
    b) sensory memory
    c) long-term memory
    d) short-term memory

9. Your friend asks you a question, and just as you say "What?" you realize what the person said. Which part of your memory was maintaining your friend's words?
    a) iconic sensory memory
    b) echoic sensory memory
    c) short-term memory
    d) long-term memory

10. Someone a short distance away, to whom you have been paying no attention, quietly speaks your name, and suddenly you are attending to that conversation. This is an example of _____ .
    a) Broadbent's process of selective memory
    b) the Phi phenomenon
    c) the cocktail party phenomenon
    d) cue-controlled inhibition

11. _____ is synonymous with short-term memory.
    a) Shadow memory
    b) Working memory
    c) Secondary memory
    d) Sensory registers

12. Your professor asks you to get up in front of the class and repeat a long list of numbers that she reads to you. If you are not given a chance to repeat the numbers to yourself as she reads them, what is the longest list of numbers you will most likely to be able to remember?
    a) 2
    b) 7
    c) 12
    d) 25

13. You try to remember a phone number by repeating it over and over to yourself. What type of rehearsal are you using?
    a) condensed
    b) permanent
    c) elaborative
    d) maintenance

14. Of the following, which is the most similar to the concept of long-term memory?
    a) a revolving door
    b) a filing cabinet
    c) a desk top
    d) a computer keyboard

15. Long-term memories are encoded in terms of
    a) sounds.
    b) visual images.
    c) meanings of words and concepts.
    d) all of the above.

16. Procedural memories are to _____ memories as declarative memories are to _____ memories.
    a) implicit; explicit
    b) explicit; implicit
    c) general knowledge; personal facts
    d) personal facts; general knowledge

17. Which of the following types of LTM are forms of explicit memory?
    a) procedural
    b) semantic
    c) episodic
    d) both (b) and (c)

18. As a young child, you spent hours on your skateboard. After several years of not skating, you jump on your board as if you never missed a day. The long-term memory of how to skate is an example of what type of memory?
    a) explicit
    b) episodic
    c) semantic
    d) procedural

19. As you are skating down the street on your skateboard, you think back to the day you accidentally skated into a parked car and had to go the hospital to get stitches. The memory of this event would be described as a(n) _____ memory.
    a) procedural
    b) implicit
    c) episodic
    d) semantic

20. According to the semantic network model, it would take more time to answer "true" to which sentence?
    a) "A salmon is an animal."
    b) "A salmon is a fish."
    c) "A canary is a bird."
    d) All of these would take the same time.

21. If memory was like the sea, we could say that _____ is long-term memory, _____ are the memories, and _____ are retrieval cues.
    a) the sea, fish, hooks
    b) a boat, worms, fish
    c) a boat, hooks, worms
    d) an island, worms, fishing poles

22. Which of the following concepts describes why it is best to take a test in the same room in which you learned the material?
    a) state-dependent learning
    b) encoding specificity
    c) tip of the tongue phenomenon
    d) cocktail party effect

23. While you were studying for your history final, you were very angry at your roommate for playing her music too loud. If you wanted to maximize your ability to remember the information on the final, what mood should you be in while you are taking the final?
    a) happy
    b) sad
    c) angry
    d) surprised

24. Under most circumstances, when you are intentionally trying to remember an item of information, _____ is an easier task than _____.
    a) recognition; recall
    b) recall; recognition
    c) priming; the savings method
    d) the savings method; priming

25. When the sound of the word is the aspect that cannot be retrieved, leaving only the feeling of knowing the word without the ability to pronounce it, this is known as _____.
    a) encoding failure
    b) extinction of acoustic storage
    c) auditory decay
    d) the tip of the tongue effect

26. The test you are taking right now requires which type of memory retrieval process?
    a) recall
    b) recognition
    c) encoding
    d) echoic

27. False positives occur when a person incorrectly "matches" a stimulus that is merely similar to a real memory. One major problem with eyewitness testimony is that
    a) extinction of auditory memories causes the witness to forget what was said.
    b) witnesses are prone to habituate to the courtroom and forget what happened.
    c) false positives can cause eyewitness testimony to be quite inaccurate.
    d) None of these are true.

28. Is eyewitness testimony usually accurate?
    a) Yes, because seeing is believing.
    b) No, because eyewitnesses are not usually honest.
    c) Yes, because eyewitnesses are very confident about their testimony.
    d) No, because there is a great possibility of a "false positive" identification.

29. For more than 30 years, the most influential researcher into eyewitness memory has been _____.
    a) Broadbent
    b) Sperling
    c) Loftus
    d) Treisman

30. Flashbulb memories _____.
    a) are not subject to periodic revision
    b) usually concern events that are emotionally charged
    c) are almost always highly accurate
    d) usually concern events from early childhood

31. In this view, memories are literally "built" from the pieces stored away at encoding. This view is called _____.
    a) constructive processing
    b) hindsight bias
    c) adaptation of memory traces
    d) flashbulb integration

32. Which of the following phenomena provides support for the concept that memories are reconstructed as they are retrieved or remembered?
    a) tip of the tongue
    b) hindsight bias
    c) cocktail party effect
    d) retrograde amnesia

33. Which of the following is an example of the misinformation effect?
    a) forgetting where you left your keys
    b) falsely remembering that a friend was wearing a jacket after being asked what color your friend's jacket was
    c) remembering a traumatic event from childhood
    d) telling someone a lie

34. Which of the following statements about hypnosis is <u>NOT</u> true?
    a) Subjects cannot always distinguish between memories which they have always had and new "memories" recently recovered under hypnosis.
    b) Hypnotic age regression appears to increase the accuracy of childhood recall.
    c) The impact of hypnosis on the reliability of later memory depends on the type of question asked. Open-ended questions cause less memory "contamination" than closed-ended, leading questions.
    d) Some pseudomemories (false memories) suggested by hypnosis do not persist after the hypnosis.

35. Which of the following techniques are used by therapists to implant a false memory?
    a) hypnosis, drugs, and suggestion
    b) partial reinforcement, rewards, and punishments
    c) presentations of images of the person's problems, presented in a subliminal fashion
    d) All of these are used.

36. Which of these is viewed as the major problem in the repressed-memory controversy?
    a) guaranteeing the right to sue alleged abusers
    b) therapists' unwillingness to help recover memories
    c) deliberate deception on the part of those who claim abuse
    d) distinguishing true repressed memories from false memories

37. Ebbinghaus found that information is forgotten
    a) more rapidly as time goes by.
    b) gradually at first, then increasing in speed of forgetting.
    c) quickly at first, then tapering off gradually.
    d) most quickly one day after learning.

38. Retroactive interference as used in the study of memory refers to when
    a) older information already in memory interferes with the retrieval of newer information.
    b) newer information interferes with the retrieval of older information.
    c) the information is not attended to and fails to be encoded.
    d) information that is not accessed decays from the storage system over time.

39. Shalissa has two exams today. One is in French and the other is in history. Last night she studied French before history. When she gets to her history test, all she can remember is French! Shalissa's memory is suffering from _____.
    a) cue-dependent forgetting
    b) proactive interference
    c) decay
    d) retroactive interference

40. In the famous case of H. M., after having part of his brain removed, he could no longer _____.
    a) pay attention to specific stimuli
    b) retrieve memories
    c) form new memories
    d) make sense of memories

41. The physical processes that occur when a memory is formed are called
   a) consolidation.
   b) actuation.
   c) potentiation.
   d) depolarization.

42. When a person's _____ is damaged or removed, anterograde amnesia results.
   a) hippocampus
   b) prefrontal lobe
   c) amygdala
   d) cerebellum

43. Which of these is an example of what has been called infantile amnesia?
   a) At age 25 Betty can recall only good memories of what happened when she was 4 to 5 years old.
   b) When he is 10 years old John has no memory of a family vacation that occurred when he was 2 years old.
   c) When faced with a horrible stressor, some people return to an earlier stage of development such as infancy for the comfort that it provides.
   d) Despite the fact that Alice began to learn how to play the violin when she was 3, she has very little skill now that she is in her 30s.

44. There currently is a cure for Alzheimer's disease.
   a) True.
   b) False.

PRACTICE EXAM ANSWERS

1. d Memory involves the three processes of encoding, storage, and retrieval. All three other choices deal with the process of learning.

2. b When you store something, you keep it (or retain it) for a certain period of time. In the study of memory, the term "storage" involves keeping or retaining information for a certain period of time.

3. c Retrieval is the process of pulling information back out of memory.

4. d Encoding, storage, and retrieval are the basic processes for memory and are a component of ALL the theories on exactly how memory works.

5. d The levels-of-processing model proposes that the "deeper" the level of processing, the more likely it is to be remembered. This means that the more meaning or significance you can give to a piece of information, the better you remember it. Associating a frog with the place it lives is the most meaningful association of all the four choices.

6. a The name of the model describes the theory. The parallel distributed model proposes a series of networks that work in parallel in the brain.

7. a As mentioned in Question 4, all models of memory include the concepts of encoding, storage, and retrieval. The aspects of the information-processing model that make it unique are the concepts of sensory, short-term, and long-term memory.

8. b Sensory memory is the briefest of all the memory stages proposed by the information-processing model. Visual sensory memory lasts only about one-half a second.

9. b Echoic memory is the memory of sounds. It should be easy to remember if you just think of an "echo" for echoic.

10.   c   The cocktail party effect is a demonstration of our selective attention abilities. Obviously, you are processing all of the information but you are only "attending to" a small portion of it. One place this phenomenon is likely to occur is at a party, thus the name "cocktail party effect."

11.   b   Short-term memory is thought to be the place where memories either enter long-term memory or disappear. The idea is that if we work with the information, using memory techniques or rehearsal strategies, then the information will be retained in long-term memory.

12.   b   The amount of information we can retain in short-term memory was studied by George Miller and presented in a paper called "The magic number 7 plus or minus two."

13.   d   Maintenance rehearsal is one of the most basic methods to remember something and involves simply repeating the information over and over. Elaborative rehearsal is more complex and involves forming an association with the information.

14.   b   Long-term memory is where information is stored for an indefinite amount of time. If you look at the choices for this question, the only item that accommodates the storage of anything for a long period of time is a filing cabinet.

15.   d   Memories are encoded in terms of all these components. One theory suggests that each component of a memory is actually stored in a different place in the brain.

16.   a   Procedural memories (such as how to ride a bike) are hard to verbalize just as implicit memories are hard to verbalize. If something is explicit, that means it is very clear and obvious, just as declarative memories (like the memory of your first kiss) are very easy to identify.

17.   d   Semantic memories are memories of facts such as the capital of the United States. Episodic memories are memories of episodes, such as your last birthday celebration.

18.   d   Procedural memories are memories for procedures (or habits and skills).

19.   c   This is a memory of a specific episode.

20.   a   In selection a you are having to move across two categories – salmon to fish to animal. Whereas in selections b and c, you are only moving across one category – salmon to fish and canary to bird.

21.   a   Try to consider the most important aspects of long-term memory, memories, and retrieval cues. Long-term memory can hold a large amount of information like the sea, a boat, or an island. The memories are what are found in long-term memory. We find fish in the sea but we don't typically store a large number of worms or hooks in a boat or worms in an island. Just to make sure you are correct, retrieval cues are used to pull out the memories, hooks can pull out worms. None of the other options make sense (fish don't pull out worms, worms don't pull out hooks, and fishing poles don't pull out worms). So the correct choice is a.

22.   b   Encoding specificity refers to your physical surroundings and how they can act as retrieval cues for information.

23.   c   State-dependent learning refers to your emotional state and how being in the same mood during retrieval as you were during the encoding process can help you remember more information.

24.   a   Recognition simply requires "recognizing" the right answer. This means you are given all the options and you simply select the correct choice.

25.   d   Tip of the tongue phenomena gives us one clue as to how retrieval works.

26.   b   You are given the right answer and you simply have to select it from choices a-d.

27.   c   The work of Elizabeth Loftus has demonstrated that false positives among eyewitnesses are more frequent than we used to believe.

28.   d   Although eyewitness testimony can be accurate, there is always the possibility of false positives.

29.   c   Elizabeth Loftus is one of the most influential researchers into false memories.

30. b Flashbulb memories can be altered over time.
31. a Constructive processing assumes that all the pieces of a memory are stored in different locations and "re-assembled" every time the memory is retrieved.
32. b In hindsight bias, our memory of a past event is influenced by new information.
33. b The misinformation effect occurs when a leading question or statement actually alters your memory of an event.
34. b Studies on memories retrieved under hypnosis have failed to find an increase in accuracy for recalling childhood events.
35. a Therapists have mainly used hypnosis, drugs, or suggestion to implant false memories.
36. d Often an individual cannot distinguish between their own true memories and false memories.
37. c Most forgetting occurs within the first hour after the material is learned.
38. b Retroactive interference occurs when the new information gets in the way or "interferes" with the already learned material.
39. b Proactive interference occurs with the already learned material interferes with the new information.
40. c After H.M's hippocampus was removed, he lost the ability to move memories from short-term to long-term memory.
41. a The term consolidation refers to the physical basis of memories. Researchers are still working to determine the precise details of consolidation.
42. a Anterograde amnesia is described as the inability to form any new memories. Just like the case of H.M., when a person's hippocampus is removed or damaged, anterograde amnesia is often the result.
43. b Infantile amnesia refers to the inability to remember events that occurred during the first one to two years of your life.
44. b Although researchers have made a tremendous amount of progress toward our understanding of Alzheimer's disease, there still is no cure for the disease.

CHAPTER GLOSSARY

Alzheimer's disease	the most common form of dementia in elderly people, leads to severe cognitive loss due to the deterioration of brain tissue.
amnesia	disorder characterized by severe memory loss.
anterograde amnesia	loss of memory from the point of injury or trauma forward, or the inability to form new long-term memories.
automatic encoding	tendency of certain kinds of information to enter long-term memory with little or no effortful encoding.
chunking	the process of regrouping material in memory in order to combine smaller pieces into one larger unit.
cocktail party effect	the ability to focus our listening attention on a single conversation among a large amount of background noise.
consolidation	the changes that take place in the structure and functioning of neurons when an engram is formed.
constructive processing	referring to the retrieval of memories in which those memories are altered, revised, or influenced by newer information.
curve of forgetting	a graph showing a distinct pattern in which forgetting is very fast within the first hour after learning a list and then tapers off gradually.
decay	loss of memory due to the passage of time, during which the memory trace is not used.
declarative memory	type of long-term memory containing information that is conscious and known.

distributed practice	spacing the study of material to be remembered by including breaks between study periods.
disuse	another term to describe memory decay which suggests that memories that are not used will eventually decay and disappear.
echoic memory	the brief memory of something a person has just heard.
eidetic imagery	the ability to access a visual memory for 30 seconds or more.
elaborative rehearsal	a method of transferring information from STM into LTM by making that information meaningful in some way.
Elizabeth Loftus	psychologist working on memory and how it can be influenced, she is known for her work with false memories.
encoding	the set of mental operations that people perform on sensory information to convert that information into a form that is usable in the brain's storage systems.
encoding failure	failure to process information into memory.
encoding specificity	the tendency for memory of information to be improved if related information (such as surroundings or physiological state) available when the memory is first formed is also available when the memory is being retrieved.
episodic memory	type of declarative memory containing personal information not readily available to others, such as daily activities and events.
explicit memory	memory that is consciously known, such as declarative memory.
false memory syndrome	a condition in which a person has a memory that is objectively false but strongly believed to be true.
false positive	error of recognition in which people think that they recognize some stimulus that is not actually in memory.
flashbulb memory	type of automatic encoding that occurs because an unexpected event has strong emotional associations for the person remembering it.
George Miller	1920-present. published a paper in 1956 called "The magical number seven plus or minus two" which described the capacity of short-term memory without rehearsal.
George Sperling	psychologist who first studied iconic memory and discovered the duration of iconic memory is around half a second.
H.M.	famous patient who lost the ability to form new memories after surgical removal of his hippocampi.
Herman Ebbinghaus	German psychologist who was a pioneer in the study of human memory. Made extensive use of nonsense syllables in his studies.
hindsight bias	the tendency to falsely believe, through revision of older memories to include newer information, that one could have correctly predicted the outcome of an event.
iconic memory	visual sensory memory, lasting only a fraction of a second.
implicit memory	memory that is not easily brought into conscious awareness, such as procedural memory.
infantile amnesia	the inability to retrieve memories from much before the age of 3.
information-processing model	model of memory that assumes the processing of information for memory storage is similar to the way a computer processes memory, in a series of 3 stages.
levels-of-processing model	model of memory that assumes information that is more "deeply processed," or processed according to its meaning rather than just the sound or physical characteristics of the word or words, will be remembered more efficiently and for a longer period of time.

long-term memory	the system of memory into which all the information is placed to be kept more or less permanently.
maintenance rehearsal	practice of saying some information to be remembered over and over in one's head in order to maintain it in short-term memory.
memory	an active system that receives information from the senses, organizes and alters it as it stores it away, and then retrieves the information from storage.
memory trace or engram	physical change in the brain that occurs when a memory is formed.
misinformation effect	the tendency of misleading information presented after an event to alter the memories of the event itself.
nonsense syllables	consonant-vowel-consonant combinations that can be pronounced but have no semantic meaning.
parallel distributed processing model	a model of memory in which memory processes are proposed to take place at the same time, over a large network of neural connections.
primacy effect	tendency to remember information at the beginning of a body of information better than the information that follows.
proactive interference	memory retrieval problem that occurs when older information prevents or interferes with the retrieval of newer information.
procedural (nondeclarative) memory	type of long-term memory including memory for skills, procedures, habits, and conditioned responses. These memories are not conscious but are implied to exist because they affect conscious behavior.
recall	type of memory retrieval in which the information to be retrieved must be "pulled" from memory with very few external cues.
recency effect	tendency to remember information at the end of a body of information better than the information ahead of it.
recognition	the ability to match a piece of information or a stimulus to a stored image or fact.
retrieval	getting information that is in storage into a form that can be used.
retrieval cue	a stimulus for remembering.
retroactive interference	memory retrieval problem that occurs when newer information prevents or interferes with the retrieval of older information.
retrograde amnesia	loss of memory from the point of some injury or trauma backwards, or loss of memory for the past.
selective attention	the ability to focus on only one stimulus from among all sensory input.
semantic memory	type of declarative memory containing general knowledge, such as knowledge of language and information learned in formal education.
semantic network model	model of memory organization which assumes that information is stored in the brain in an connected fashion, with concepts that are related to each other stored physically closer to each other than concepts that are not highly related.
sensory memory	the very first stage of memory, the point at which information enters the nervous system through the sensory systems.
serial position effect	tendency of information at the beginning and end of a body of information to be remembered more accurately than information in the middle of the body of information.
short-term (working) memory	the memory system in which information is held for brief periods of time while being used.
state-dependent learning	the ability to retrieve information more readily when a person is in the same emotional state they were in when the information was learned.
storage	holding onto information for some period of time.

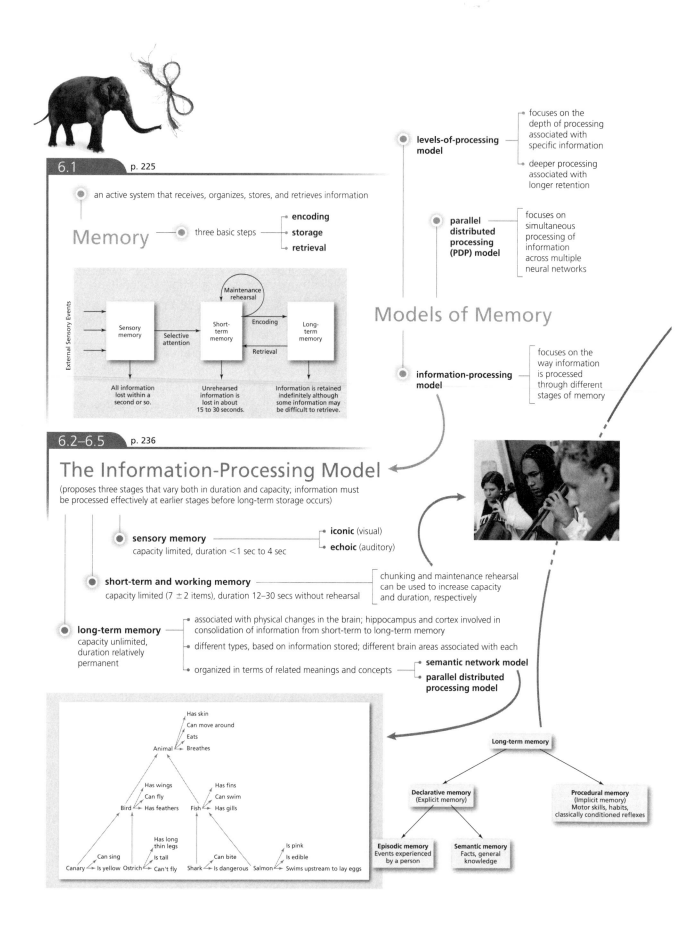

levels-of-processing model
- focuses on the depth of processing associated with specific information
- deeper processing associated with longer retention

parallel distributed processing (PDP) model
- focuses on simultaneous processing of information across multiple neural networks

Models of Memory

information-processing model
- focuses on the way information is processed through different stages of memory

an active system that receives, organizes, stores, and retrieves information

Memory — three basic steps
- encoding
- storage
- retrieval

External Sensory Events

Maintenance rehearsal

Sensory memory → Selective attention → Short-term memory → Encoding → Long-term memory

Retrieval

All information lost within a second or so.

Unrehearsed information is lost in about 15 to 30 seconds.

Information is retained indefinitely although some information may be difficult to retrieve.

The Information-Processing Model

(proposes three stages that vary both in duration and capacity; information must be processed effectively at earlier stages before long-term storage occurs)

sensory memory
capacity limited, duration <1 sec to 4 sec
- iconic (visual)
- echoic (auditory)

short-term and working memory
capacity limited (7 ±2 items), duration 12–30 secs without rehearsal
- chunking and maintenance rehearsal can be used to increase capacity and duration, respectively

long-term memory
capacity unlimited, duration relatively permanent
- associated with physical changes in the brain; hippocampus and cortex involved in consolidation of information from short-term to long-term memory
- different types, based on information stored; different brain areas associated with each
- organized in terms of related meanings and concepts
  - **semantic network model**
  - **parallel distributed processing model**

Has skin
Can move around
Eats
Animal — Breathes

Has wings
Can fly
Bird — Has feathers

Has fins
Can swim
Fish — Has gills

Has long thin legs
Can sing
Canary — Is yellow
Is tall
Ostrich — Can't fly

Can bite
Shark — Is dangerous

Is pink
Is edible
Salmon — Swims upstream to lay eggs

Long-term memory

Declarative memory (Explicit memory)

Procedural memory (Implicit memory) Motor skills, habits, classically conditioned reflexes

Episodic memory Events experienced by a person

Semantic memory Facts, general knowledge

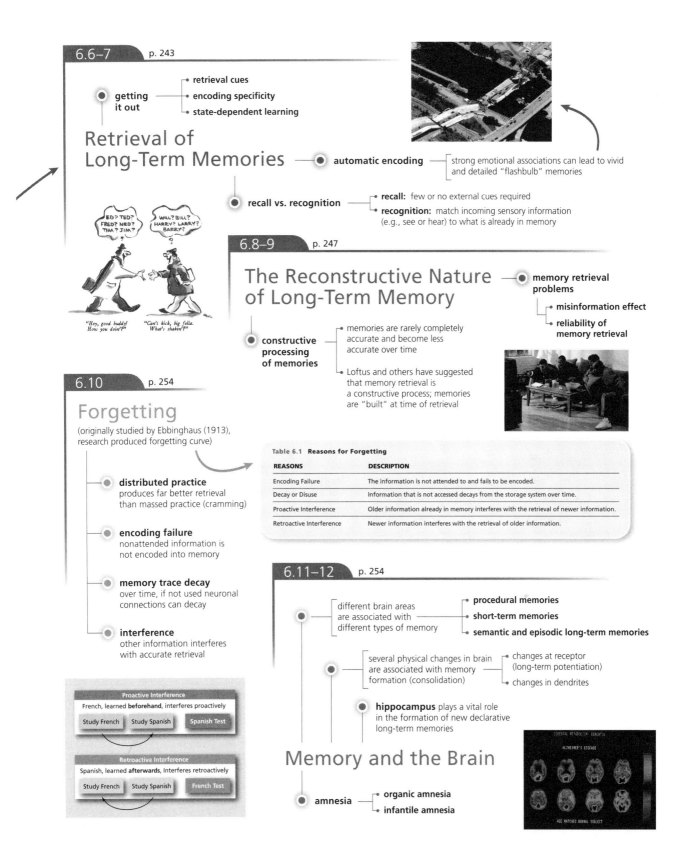

6.6–7   p. 243

- **getting it out**
  - retrieval cues
  - encoding specificity
  - state-dependent learning

Retrieval of Long-Term Memories

- **automatic encoding** — strong emotional associations can lead to vivid and detailed "flashbulb" memories

- **recall vs. recognition**
  - **recall:** few or no external cues required
  - **recognition:** match incoming sensory information (e.g., see or hear) to what is already in memory

"Hey, good buddy! How you doin'?"

"Can't kick, big fella. What's shakin'?"

6.8–9   p. 247

The Reconstructive Nature of Long-Term Memory

- **memory retrieval problems**
  - misinformation effect
  - reliability of memory retrieval

- **constructive processing of memories**
  - memories are rarely completely accurate and become less accurate over time
  - Loftus and others have suggested that memory retrieval is a constructive process; memories are "built" at time of retrieval

6.10   p. 254

Forgetting

(originally studied by Ebbinghaus (1913), research produced forgetting curve)

- **distributed practice**
  produces far better retrieval than massed practice (cramming)

- **encoding failure**
  nonattended information is not encoded into memory

- **memory trace decay**
  over time, if not used neuronal connections can decay

- **interference**
  other information interferes with accurate retrieval

Table 6.1 Reasons for Forgetting

REASONS	DESCRIPTION
Encoding Failure	The information is not attended to and fails to be encoded.
Decay or Disuse	Information that is not accessed decays from the storage system over time.
Proactive Interference	Older information already in memory interferes with the retrieval of newer information.
Retroactive Interference	Newer information interferes with the retrieval of older information.

6.11–12   p. 254

- different brain areas are associated with different types of memory
  - procedural memories
  - short-term memories
  - semantic and episodic long-term memories

- several physical changes in brain are associated with memory formation (consolidation)
  - changes at receptor (long-term potentiation)
  - changes in dendrites

- **hippocampus** plays a vital role in the formation of new declarative long-term memories

Memory and the Brain

Proactive Interference
French, learned **beforehand**, interferes proactively

| Study French | Study Spanish | Spanish Test |

Retroactive Interference
Spanish, learned **afterwards**, Interferes retroactively

| Study French | Study Spanish | French Test |

- **amnesia**
  - organic amnesia
  - infantile amnesia

Figure 6.1 **Three-Stage Process of Memory**

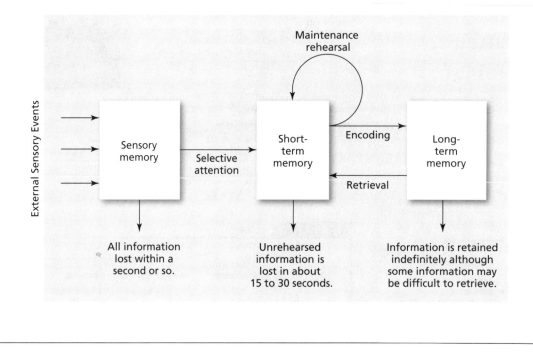

Figure 6.2 **Iconic Memory Test**

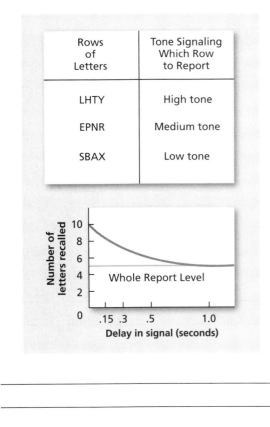

Rows of Letters	Tone Signaling Which Row to Report
LHTY	High tone
EPNR	Medium tone
SBAX	Low tone

Figure 6.3 **Digit-Span Test**

6 8 2 5

5 7 2 1 4

3 5 9 7 2 1

9 2 5 4 6 3 8

2 8 3 7 1 5 6 9

7 3 2 4 9 6 8 5 1

6 5 4 7 8 9 3 2 1 7

_____

_____

_____

_____

_____

_____

_____

_____

_____

_____

6.4–6.5 Long–Term Memory

_____

_____

_____

_____

_____

_____

_____

_____

_____

_____

_____

Figure 6.5 **Types of Long-Term Memories**

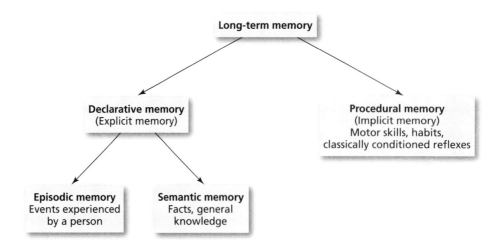

Figure 6.6 **An Example of a Semantic Network**

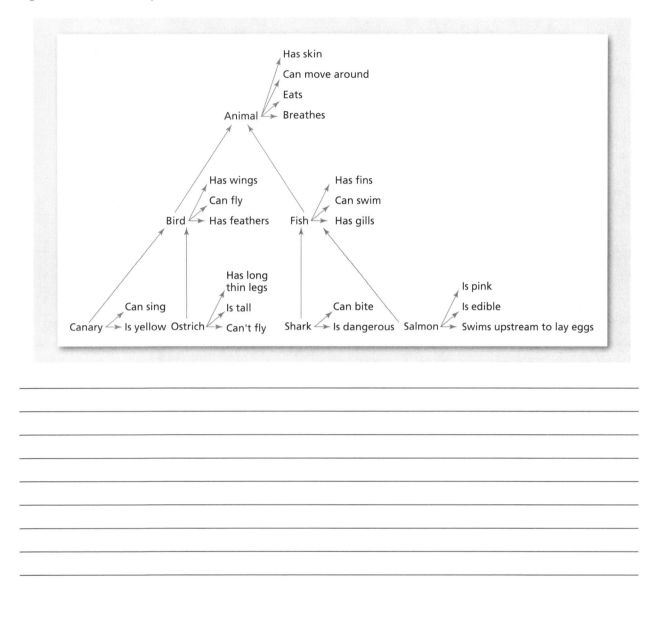

_____
_____
_____
_____
_____
_____
_____
_____
_____
_____

6.6–6.7 **Retrieval**

_____
_____
_____
_____
_____
_____
_____
_____
_____
_____

Figure 6.7 **Recall of Target Words in Two Contexts**

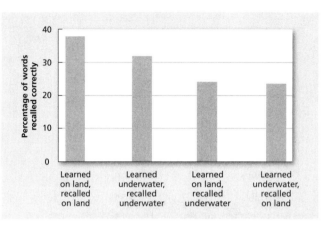

_____
_____
_____
_____
_____
_____

Figure 6.8 **Serial Position Effect**

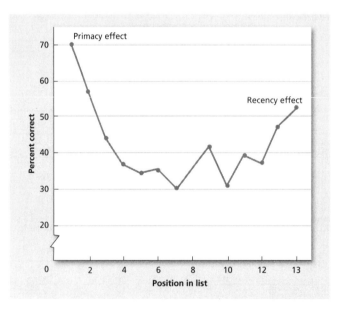

_____
_____
_____
_____
_____
_____

6.8–6.9 Reconstructive Nature of Memory

6.10 Forgetting

Figure 6.9 **Curve of Forgetting**

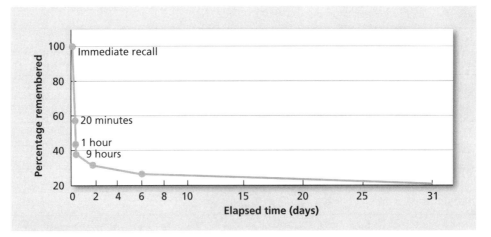

Figure 6.11 **Proactive and Retroactive Interference**

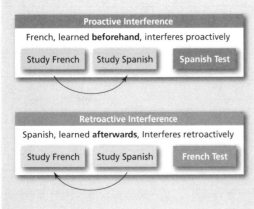

Table 6.1 **Reasons for Forgetting**

Table 6.1   **Reasons for Forgetting**

REASON	DESCRIPTION
Encoding Failure	The information is not attended to and fails to be encoded.
Decay or Disuse	Information that is not accessed decays from the storage system over time.
Proactive Interference	Older information already in memory interferes with the retrieval of newer information.
Retroactive Interference	Newer information interferes with the retrieval of older information.

6.11–6.12 Biology of Memory

NOTES

YOU KNOW YOU ARE READY FOR THE TEST IF YOU ARE ABLE TO...

- Introduce the concept of cognition, as it relates to mental images, concepts and problem solving.
- Describe artificial intelligence and creative thinking.
- Discuss the measurement of intelligence including the Stanford-Binet and Wechsler intelligence tests, test construction issues, and the determination of developmental delay.
- Describe several prominent theories of intelligence including the concepts of giftedness, mental retardation, heredity, and environment.
- Explain the basis of language and the relationship between language and thought processes.

RAPID REVIEW

Thinking, or **cognition**, can be defined as mental activity that goes on in the brain when a person is processing information. Cognition includes both verbal and nonverbal processes. Two examples of cognition are **mental images**, which are picture-like representations that stand in for objects or events, and **concepts**, or ideas that represent a class of objects. Concepts can be ranked from general to specific by applying the terms **superordinate**, **basic level** type, and **subordinate**. **Formal concepts** are defined by specific rules, while **natural concepts** are formed as a result of experience. A **prototype** is a specific example of a concept that closely resembles the defining features of a concept. Concepts are formed through experience and culture and have an impact on our thinking.

Problem solving involves using our thoughts or cognitions to reach a goal and consists of at least four different techniques. **Trial-and-error** problem solving makes use of mechanical solutions. When someone uses **algorithms** to problem-solve they are following step-by-step procedures to solve the problem. **Heuristics** are general "rules of thumb" that can be applied to many situations. **Means-end analysis** is an example of one type of heuristic where the difference between where you are and where you want to be is determined and then steps are taken to reduce that difference. **Insight** consists of solving the problem by having a sudden moment of inspiration or "aha!" moment. **Artificial intelligence** is the creation of a machine that can think like a human, and is represented today through computer program such as Deep Blue.

Some factors that interfere with problem solving include **functional fixedness**, which is when a person thinks about objects only in terms of their typical uses; **mental sets** which are tendencies to use the same problem-solving strategies that worked in the past; and **confirmation bias**, which consists of the search for evidence that fits your beliefs while ignoring any contradictory information. **Creativity** occurs when a person solves a problem by combining ideas and behaviors in a new way. Many methods of problem solving utilize **convergent thinking,** which assumes that one single answer exists for the problem. **Divergent thinking** is the opposite process of convergent thinking. When an individual uses divergent thinking, he or she starts from one point and comes up with many possibilities or ideas based on that point.

Intelligence can be defined as the ability to learn from one's experiences, acquire knowledge, and use resources effectively in adapting to new situations or solving problems. Currently, there is still much disagreement on exactly what is meant by the term "intelligence." In 1904, Charles Spearman proposed that intelligence was split between two abilities. The first ability was a general intelligence, labeled the **g factor**, and the other was a specific intelligence referred to as the **s factor**. Spearman believed that both the g and s factors could be measured using standardized intelligence tests. Howard Gardner, on the other hand, proposed that at least nine different kinds of intelligence exist. Robert Sternberg proposed the **triarchic theory of intelligence**, which states that intelligence can be divided into three types; **analytical**, **creative**, and **practical intelligence**.

In France in 1916, Alfred Binet and Theodore Simon developed the first formal test for intelligence in order to determine a child's mental age. The Stanford-Binet test used a ratio of mental age to chronological age to determine an individual's **intelligence quotient** or **IQ**. In the U.S., the Wechsler intelligence tests are now used more frequently that the Stanford-Binet and IQ scores are now based on individual **deviation IQ scores** rather than a ratio. The Wechsler tests are designed for specific age groups and can be administered individually. To determine the quality of a psychological test, you need to look at the test's **validity**, **reliability**, and procedure used to obtain the **norms**. Validity refers to how well the test measures what it claims to measure, while reliability indicates the test's ability to produce the same result when given to the same person under similar conditions. Norms are determined by the standardization group selected by the researchers and should be a representative sample of the population who will be taking the test. All psychological tests should also be examined for the cultural biases. Adrian Dove created an intelligence test call the Dove Counterbalance General Intelligence Test (also known as the Chitling Test) to demonstrate the cultural biases present in many of the intelligence tests currently in use.

Mental retardation, now more commonly referred to as **developmental delay**, occurs in about 3 percent of the U.S. population and is defined by an IQ score of 70 (two standard deviations below the mean) or lower along with adaptive behaviors significantly below the expected level for the person's age group. Diagnosis of developmental delay is determined by the person's intellectual and adaptive behavior skills, psychological and emotional levels, physical health considerations, and environmental factors. Developmental delay is classified from mild to moderate, severe, and profound. The three most common biological causes of developmental delay are Down syndrome, fetal alcohol syndrome, and fragile X syndrome.

Individuals who receive scores of 130 or above on intelligence tests are referred to as **gifted**. Lewis Terman conducted a longitudinal study of the traits and behaviors of over 1,500 gifted children. The children were known as Terman's Termites and his findings showed that many of the common myths about the "nutty genius" were unfounded.

More recently, the concept of **emotional intelligence** has been suggested as an important factor for success in life. Further research in this area is still needed. The role of a person's environment or nurture, and heredity, also referred to as nature, on the development of intelligence continues to be debated. Studies of identical and fraternal twins raised together and apart have provided one method for investigating the role of nature and nurture.

Language is defined as a system for combining symbols (such as words) so that an unlimited number of meaningful statements can be made for the purpose of communicating with others and can be analyzed at many levels. **Semantics** is the rules for determining the meaning of words and sentences. **Phonemes** are the most basic units of sounds used in a specific language, **morphemes** combine the units of sound into the smallest units that have meaning, **grammar** includes all the rules for combining morphemes into words, and **syntax** is the rules for combining words into sentences. **Pragmatics** deals with the practical aspects of communicating with others. The relationship between language and thought has been studied extensively. The Sapir-Whorf hypothesis, also known as the **linguistic relativity hypothesis**, proposes that the words people use determine how they think about themselves and the world. An opposing theory, known as **cognitive universalism**, proposes that certain ways of thinking are shared among all groups of people and influence the development of language in similar ways. Animals other than humans demonstrate a diverse ability to communicate but it is unclear whether or not they have the capability for language as demonstrated by the ability to use abstract symbols to communicate. Kanzi, a bonobo chimpanzee, has demonstrated an ability to understand about 150 spoken English words. However, none of the animals studied to date appear to have been able to use and comprehend syntax.

Researchers have found that "exercising" the brain with activities such as reading, taking classes, and working on crossword puzzles can help increase the ability of the brain to build and maintain new neurons and connections. This potential for brain growth and repair is called **cognitive reserve**.

STUDY HINTS

1. In this chapter, you were presented with four different approaches to problem solving. In order to better understand how these approaches differ from each other, take the following problem and come up with an example of how you could solve the problem using each of the four different approaches.

    Problem: You are packing up to move to college and you have one more box to fit in the trunk of your car but it looks like there is simply no room left. You don't want to leave the box behind. How will you solve this problem?

Approach	Solution
trial and error	
algorithm	
heuristics	
insight	

2. The two most commonly used methods to assess any psychological test are to determine the validity and reliability of the test. Examine the following test descriptions and determine whether the test has a potential problem with its reliability or validity.

Example	Validity or Reliability Issue?
A personality test gives a very different score for the same person when they retake it six months later.	
An individual takes an online IQ test that measures how long she can hold her breath.	
A 5-year-old child is diagnosed as developmentally delayed based on his IQ scores, but when he is brought back and given the same test, his scores fall in the above average range.	

Suggested answers to Question 1

Approach	Solution
trial and error	*Keep placing the box in various places and positions in your car until you find one that works.*
algorithm	*Go online and find a website that deal with physics. Enter in the dimensions of your car and the exact dimensions of every box and item that you are trying to fit in your car. Get a printout of the optimal placement for each box and follow it step by step to fit everything in.*
heuristics	*Think back to how your mom always told you to pack the big things first and then squeeze the little ones in. Take your boxes out and pack them again using this general rule of thumb to guide you.*
insight	*Sit back with your friends for a few minutes and relax. As you are talking with your friends, all of a sudden you remember that your family has a "Big Mac" container that will attach to the top of the car. Strap the container on, place your box in the container, and take off for school.*

Suggested answers to Question 2

Example	Validity or Reliability Issue?
A personality test gives a very different score for the same person when they retake it six months later.	*reliability – the scores are not consistent over time for the same person*
An individual takes an online IQ test that measures how long she can hold her breath.	*validity – does holding your breath give a very accurate assessment of your IQ?*
A 5-year-old child is diagnosed as developmentally delayed based on his IQ scores, but when he is brought back and given the same test, his scores fall in the above average range.	*This question illustrates that without reliability a test will also lack validity. The test scores are inconsistent over time, which indicates that the test is not really measuring what it claims to measure since we assume that intelligence is a fairly constant factor.*

LEARNING OBJECTIVES

7.1 *How are mental images and concepts involved in the process of thinking?*

7.2 *What are the methods people use to solve problems and make decisions, and can a machine be made to think like a person?*

7.3 *Why does problem solving sometimes fail, and what is meant by creative thinking?*

7.4 *How do psychologists define intelligence, and how do various theories of intelligence differ?*

7.5 *How is intelligence measured, and how are intelligence tests constructed?*

7.6 *What is mental retardation, and what are its causes?*

7.7 *What defines giftedness, and does being intellectually gifted guarantee success in life?*

7.8 *What is the influence of heredity and environment on the development of intelligence?*

7.9 *How is language defined, and what are its different elements and structure?*

7.10 *Does language influence the way people think, and are animals capable of learning language?*

7.11 *What are some ways to improve thinking?*

For the following multiple choice questions, select the answer you feel best answers the question.

1. Mental images _____.
    a) represent abstract ideas
    b) have a picture-like quality
    c) consist entirely of unconscious information
    d) are always prototypes

2. If three people used mental images to tell you how many windows they each had in their individual houses, which person would take the longest to answer?
    a) the person with two windows in his or her house
    b) the person with eight windows in his or her house
    c) the person with twelve windows in his or her house
    d) They would all take the same amount of time to answer.

3. Concepts are ideas that represent _____.
    a) a class or category of objects, events, or activities
    b) thoughts, images, muscle patterns of behavior
    c) higher-order conditioning and secondary reinforcers
    d) none of these

4. A very general form of a concept, such as "vegetable" represents which concept level?
    a) subordinate
    b) superordinate
    c) basic level
    d) hyperordinate

5. The trial-and-error method of solving problems is also known as
    a) the use of a heuristic device.
    b) the use of algorithms.
    c) the mechanical solution.
    d) the A.I. Solution.

6. Zach could not remember the four-digit combination needed to open the lock on his bicycle. After struggling to figure out what to do, he turned to start the long walk home and all of a sudden he remembered the combination to the lock. The problem-solving strategy Zach used would be best described as
    a) trial-and-error.
    b) algorithm.
    c) a heuristic.
    d) insight.

7. Which of the following examples would qualify as artificial intelligence according to the definition given in the textbook?
    a) a "smart" toaster that pops up when the toast starts to burn
    b) a global positioning system installed in a car that can tell the driver exactly where she is located and how to get to her desired destination
    c) a door that automatically opens when someone steps in front of it
    d) a computerized black jack program that uses heuristics to attempt to beat its opponents

8. The tendency for people to persist in using problem-solving patterns that have worked for them in the past is known as
   a) mental set.
   b) confirmation bias.
   c) creativity.
   d) divergent thinking.

9. Luann needs to hammer a nail into the wall but the only tool she can find in the house is a screwdriver. Luann's inability to see how the handle of the screwdriver could be used as a hammer, best represents the concept of
   a) functional fixedness.
   b) confirmation bias.
   c) creativity.
   d) artificial bias.

10. The ability to produce solutions to problems that are unusual, inventive, novel, and appropriate is called _____.
    a) creativity
    b) insight
    c) heuristics
    d) latent learning

11. Which of the following activities would NOT increase your creativity?
    a) keeping a journal
    b) brainstorming
    c) subject mapping
    d) convergent thinking

12. The ability to understand the world, think rationally or logically, and use resources effectively when faced with challenges or problems, or the characteristics needed to succeed in one's culture is the psychologist's working definition of _____.
    a) divergent problem solving
    b) creative thinking
    c) heuristic usage
    d) intelligence

13. Measuring intelligence by testing is a rather new concept in the history of the world. It is roughly_____ years old.
    a) 50
    b) 100
    c) 200
    d) 500

14. An 8-year-old child who scored like an average 10-year-old on an intelligence test would have a mental age of _____ and an IQ of _____.
    a) eight; 80
    b) eight; 125
    c) ten; 100
    d) ten; 125

15. Because of the need to measure the IQ of people of varying ages, newer IQ tests base their evaluation of IQ on_____.
    a) mental age alone
    b) deviation scores from the mean of the normal distribution
    c) giving extra points for older folks to compensate for their slower processing times
    d) none of these

16. If a test consistently produces the same score when administered to the same person under identical conditions, that test can be said to be high in
    a) reliability.
    b) validity.
    c) accuracy.
    d) norms.

17. Denny has a flat upper lip, wide-set eyes, and problems with his heart in addition to being mildly retarded. Denny most likely suffers from
    a) Down syndrome.
    b) fetal alcohol syndrome.
    c) fragile X syndrome.
    d) cretinism.

18. Which two of the following aspects are included in the definition of developmental delay?
    a) IQ scores and adaptive behavior
    b) age and socioeconomic status
    c) race and country of origin
    d) Only IQ scores are considered.

19. Which of the following statements about the gifted is true?
    a) They are more likely to suffer from mental illnesses.
    b) They are physically weaker than nongifted persons.
    c) They are often skilled leaders.
    d) They are socially unskilled.

20. Which was NOT a finding of the Terman and Oden (1974) study of gifted kids?
    a) They were socially well adjusted.
    b) They were more resistant to mental illness.
    c) They were clearly much more likely to be females.
    d) They were average in weight, height, and physical attractiveness.

21. Sternberg has found that _____ intelligence is a good predictor of success in life, but has a low relationship to _____ intelligence.
    a) practical; analytical
    b) practical; creative
    c) analytical; practical
    d) academic; creative

22. What three types of intelligence constitute Sternberg's triarchic theory of intelligence?
    a) global, intuitive, and special
    b) general, global, and specific
    c) analytical, creative, and practical
    d) mathematical, reasoning, and verbal

23. The "g" in Spearman's g factor of intelligence stands for
    a) gifted intelligence.
    b) general intelligence.
    c) graded intelligence.
    d) The g does not stand for anything.

24. If intelligence is determined primarily by heredity, which pair should show the highest correlation between IQ scores?
    a) fraternal twins
    b) identical twins
    c) brothers and sisters
    d) parents and children

25. If a researcher believed that <u>nature</u> was the most important factor in determining an individual's intelligence level, she would most closely agree with which of the following statements?
    a) Intelligence is largely inherited from your parents.
    b) Intelligence has no relationship to your biological family.
    c) The environment is the most important factor in determining a child's intelligence level.
    d) A child's intelligence can be greatly increased by providing stimulating toys throughout infancy.

26. Language, by definition,
    a) is symbolic.
    b) can be written, spoken, or signed.
    c) is capable of an infinite set of meaningful utterances.
    d) all of these

27. The basic units of sound are called
    a) morphemes.
    b) phonemes.
    c) semantics.
    d) syntax.

28. Syntax is
    a) a system of rules for combining words and phrases to form sentences.
    b) the smallest units of meaning within a language.
    c) the basic units of sound.
    d) the rules to determine the meaning of words.

29. The linguistic relativity hypothesis suggests that _____.
    a) one's language determines the pattern of one's thinking and view of the world
    b) one's thinking and view of the world determines the structure of one's language
    c) we decide which objects belong to a concept according to what is most probable or sensible, given the facts at hand
    d) perception of surface structure precedes deep structure in understanding a sentence

30. Which theory would support the idea that certain concepts are shared by all people regardless of the language spoken?
    a) Sapir-Whorf hypothesis
    b) linguistic relativity hypothesis
    c) cognitive universalism
    d) heuristic theory

31. Dolphins, according to TV and movies, are very intelligent and have strong language abilities. They might even be able to talk! However, which statement is true from the research?
    a) Dolphins have been shown to master syntax.
    b) Dolphins have the language abilities of a 3-year-old.
    c) Dolphin communication with parrots has been firmly established.
    d) None of these are true.

32. You are worried about your aging parents. Perhaps they might develop senile dementia. Thus you suggest
    a) they stop reading as it will tire their brains out faster.
    b) they start a program of extreme physical exercise to push more blood through their brains.
    c) they need to start reading, doing puzzles, getting involved in a hobby, etc., to exercise their brains.
    d) Nothing will help – don't bother to suggest anything.

PRACTICE EXAM ANSWERS

1. b Mental images are mental representations of objects that have a picture-like quality.
2. c Research has found that if the individuals used mental images to answer the question, they would actualize visualize the house and have to count the windows, so the person with the most windows would take the longest time to answer.
3. a The definition for concepts is that they are ideas that represent a class or category of objects or events.
4. b Superordinate is the highest or most general level of a concept. Basic level is the level most commonly used (such as potato or lettuce), subordinate is the most specific such as a russet potato or romaine lettuce.
5. c Again, this is asking for the straight definition of trial-and-error problem solving.
6. d Insight problem solving occurs when you get a sudden inspiration that leads you to the solution to your problem.
7. d Artificial intelligence is defined as a machine that thinks like a human; in particular, you can pay attention to the problem-solving skills of the machine. The first three examples are all simple procedures the machines are programmed to perform, but the last example represents an active problem-solving ability.
8. a A mental set exists when someone continues to use the same approaches that worked in the past. Confirmation bias occurs when someone pays attention to information that confirms his ideas and ignores any contradictory input.
9. a Functional fixedness occurs when an individual is *fixed* on only one *function* of a particular object.
10. a This is the definition of creativity.

11. d Convergent thinking occurs when you assume there is only one single answer or solution to a problem. Typically, convergent thinking decreases creative ability.
12. d As can be seen, intelligence is a broad idea that can be difficult to define.
13. b Alfred Binet started testing children in France in 1916.
14. d The IQ is based on a mental age of 10 divided by a chronological age of 8 and multiplied by 100. This gives an IQ = 125.
15. b Deviation IQ scores are based on the norms of a representative sample of the population (also known as the standardization group).
16. a Reliability indicates a test consistency, while validity indicates accuracy, or how well the test measures what it says it measures.
17. b Denny most likely suffers from fetal alcohol syndrome.
18. a The diagnosis of developmental delay is based on IQ scores as well as how well the individual is able to function in day-to-day life.
19. c C is the only true statement, the other three statements are myths that have not been supported by research.
20. c There were actually slightly more males than females in the sample of subjects selected for the Terman study.
21. a Sternberg has found that practical intelligence is a good predictor of success in life, but has a low relationship to analytical intelligence.
22. c Sternberg proposed that intelligence should actually be broken down into three components that can be thought of as book smarts, street smarts, and creativity.
23. b Spearman proposed a two-factor theory of intelligence. The g factor was for general intelligence and the s factor was for specific intelligence.
24. b Identical twins should show the strongest correlation since they share 100 percent of the same genes.
25. a Nature refers to the influence of heredity on behaviors and traits. A is the only selection that focuses on inheritance of genes.
26. d The definition of language includes all three of these attributes.
27. b Phonemes are the basic units of sound.
28. a Syntax refers to the rules we use to form meaningful sentences.
29. a *Linguistic relativity* hypothesis (also referred to as the Sapir-Whorf hypothesis) states that our thought processes are *relative* to the *language* (or linguistic setting) in which we grew up.
30. c Cognitive universalism proposes that our basic thought processes, or cognitions, are universally shared by all people.
31. d Chimpanzees have demonstrated a vocabulary equal to a 2-year-old child, but no animal to date has demonstrated the ability to use and comprehend syntax.
32. c In some ways the brain can be thought of as a muscle, in which increased activity can actually strengthen the brain.

CHAPTER GLOSSARY

Alfred Binet	1857–1911. French psychologist who developed the first formal test for intelligence.
algorithms	very specific, step-by-step procedures for solving certain types of problems.
analytical intelligence	the ability to break problems down into component parts, or analysis, for problem solving.

basic level type	an example of a type of concept around which other, similar concepts are organized, such as "dog," "cat," or "pear."
Charles Spearman	1863–1945. English psychologist who proposed the two-factor theory of intelligence consisting of the g factor and the s factor.
cognition (thinking)	mental activity that goes on in the brain when a person is organizing and attempting to understand information, and communicating information to others.
cognitive reserve	the ability of the brain to build and maintain new neurons and the connections between them.
cognitive universalism	theory that concepts are universal and influence the development of language.
concepts	ideas that represent a class or category of objects, events, or activities.
confirmation bias	the tendency to search for evidence that fits one's beliefs while ignoring any evidence that does not fit those beliefs.
convergent thinking	type of thinking in which a problem is seen as having only one answer, and all lines of thinking will eventually lead to that single answer, using previous knowledge and logic
creative intelligence	the ability to deal with new and different concepts and to come up with new ways of solving problems.
creativity	the process of solving problems by combining ideas or behavior in new ways.
developmental delay	condition in which a person's behavioral and cognitive skills exist at an earlier developmental stage than the skills of others who are the same chronological age. A more acceptable term for mental retardation.
deviation IQ score	a type of intelligence measure which assumes that IQ is normally distributed around a mean of 100 with a standard deviation of about 15.
divergent thinking	type of thinking in which a person starts from one point and comes up with many different ideas or possibilities based on that point.
emotional intelligence	the awareness of and ability to manage one's own emotions as well as the ability to be self-motivated, able to feel what others feel, and socially skilled.
formal concepts	concepts that are defined by specific rules or features.
functional fixedness	a block to problem solving that comes from thinking about objects in terms of only their typical functions.
g factor	the ability to reason and solve problems, or general intelligence.
gifted	the two percent of the population falling on the upper end of the normal curve and typically possessing an IQ of 130 or above.
grammar	the system of rules by which the symbols of language are arranged.
heuristics	a general strategy that may help narrow down the possible solutions for a problem. Also known as a "rule of thumb."
Howard Gardner	1943-present. cognitive psychologist who has acted as a major proponent on the concept of multiple intelligences. Current theory suggests that nine types of intelligence exist.
insight	when the solution to a problem comes suddenly, also referred to as a "aha!" moment.
intelligence	the ability to learn from one's experiences, acquire knowledge, and use resources effectively in adapting to new situations or solving problems.

intelligence quotient (IQ)	a number representing a measure of intelligence, resulting from the division of one's mental age by one's chronological age and then multiplying that quotient by 100.
language	a system for combining symbols (such as words) so that an unlimited number of meaningful statements can be made for the purpose of communicating with others.
Lewis Terman	1877–1956. Cognitive psychologist well known for his longitudinal study of gifted children, affectionately referred to as Terman's Termites.
linguistic relativity hypothesis (Sapir-Whorf hypothesis)	the theory that thought processes and concepts are controlled by language.
means-end analysis	heuristic in which the difference between the starting situation and the goal is determined and then steps are taken to reduce that difference.
mental images	mental representations that stand in for objects or events and have a picture-like quality.
mental set	the tendency for people to persist in using problem-solving patterns that have worked for them in the past.
morphemes	the smallest units of meaning within a language.
natural concepts	concepts people form as a result of their experiences in the real world.
nature	the role a person's heredity plays in his or her development.
norms	the standards used to assess the score of any individual who completes a standardized test.
nurture	the role a person's environment plays in his or her development.
phonemes	the basic units of sound in language.
practical intelligence	the ability to use information to get along in life and become successful.
pragmatics	aspects of language involving the practical aspects of communicating with others, or the social "niceties" of language.
problem solving	process of cognition that occurs when a goal must be reached by thinking and behaving in certain ways.
prototype	an example of a concept that closely matches the defining characteristics of a concept.
reliability	the tendency of a test to produce the same scores again and again each time it is given to the same people.
Robert Sternberg	1949–present. proposed the triarchic theory of intelligence which states that intelligence is composed of three different abilities.
s factor	the ability to excel in certain areas, or specific intelligence.
semantics	the rules for determining the meaning of words and sentences.
standardization group	a randomly selected group chosen to represent the population for whom a psychological test is intended. Norms are calculated based off on the scores of the standardization group.
subordinate	the most specific category of a concept, such as one's pet dog or a pear in one's hand.
superordinate	the most general form of a type of concept, such as "animal" or "fruit."
syntax	the system of rules for combining words and phrases to form grammatically correct sentences.

trial and error	problem-solving method in which one possible solution after another is tried until a successful one is found.
triarchic theory of intelligence	Sternberg's theory that there are three kinds of intelligences: analytical, creative, and practical.
validity	the degree to which a test actually measures what it's supposed to measure.

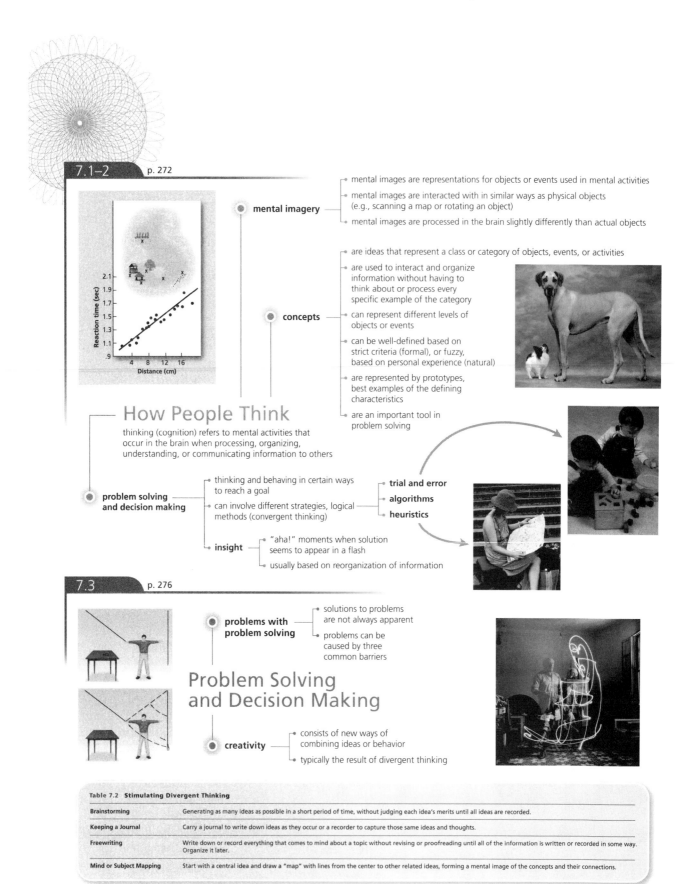

7.1–2   p. 272

mental imagery
- mental images are representations for objects or events used in mental activities
- mental images are interacted with in similar ways as physical objects (e.g., scanning a map or rotating an object)
- mental images are processed in the brain slightly differently than actual objects

concepts
- are ideas that represent a class or category of objects, events, or activities
- are used to interact and organize information without having to think about or process every specific example of the category
- can represent different levels of objects or events
- can be well-defined based on strict criteria (formal), or fuzzy, based on personal experience (natural)
- are represented by prototypes, best examples of the defining characteristics
- are an important tool in problem solving

How People Think

thinking (cognition) refers to mental activities that occur in the brain when processing, organizing, understanding, or communicating information to others

problem solving and decision making
- thinking and behaving in certain ways to reach a goal
- can involve different strategies, logical methods (convergent thinking)
  - trial and error
  - algorithms
  - heuristics

insight
- "aha!" moments when solution seems to appear in a flash
- usually based on reorganization of information

7.3   p. 276

problems with problem solving
- solutions to problems are not always apparent
- problems can be caused by three common barriers

Problem Solving and Decision Making

creativity
- consists of new ways of combining ideas or behavior
- typically the result of divergent thinking

Table 7.2 Stimulating Divergent Thinking	
Brainstorming	Generating as many ideas as possible in a short period of time, without judging each idea's merits until all ideas are recorded.
Keeping a Journal	Carry a journal to write down ideas as they occur or a recorder to capture those same ideas and thoughts.
Freewriting	Write down or record everything that comes to mind about a topic without revising or proofreading until all of the information is written or recorded in some way. Organize it later.
Mind or Subject Mapping	Start with a central idea and draw a "map" with lines from the center to other related ideas, forming a mental image of the concepts and their connections.

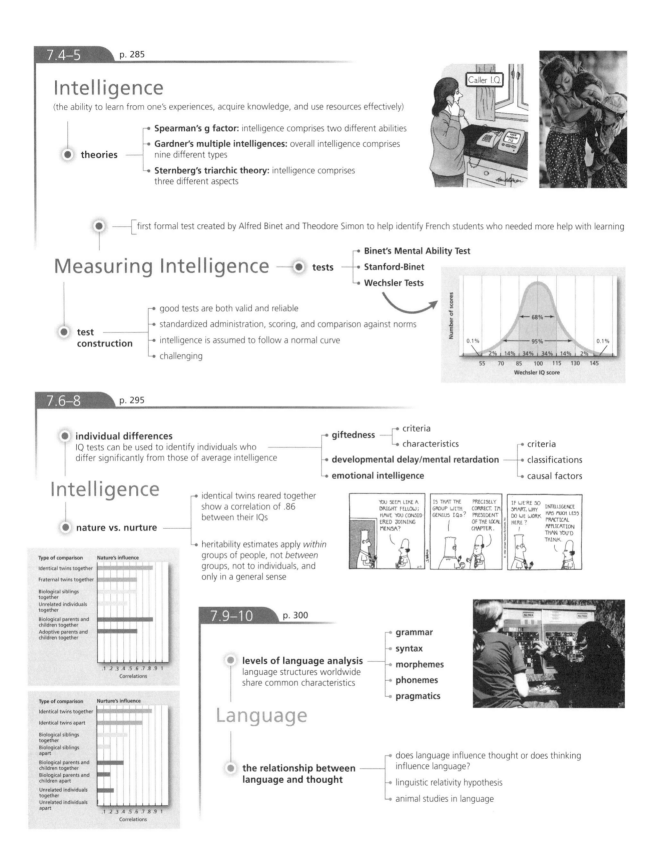

Intelligence
(the ability to learn from one's experiences, acquire knowledge, and use resources effectively)

theories
- **Spearman's g factor:** intelligence comprises two different abilities
- **Gardner's multiple intelligences:** overall intelligence comprises nine different types
- **Sternberg's triarchic theory:** intelligence comprises three different aspects

first formal test created by Alfred Binet and Theodore Simon to help identify French students who needed more help with learning

Measuring Intelligence

tests
- **Binet's Mental Ability Test**
- **Stanford-Binet**
- **Wechsler Tests**

test construction
- good tests are both valid and reliable
- standardized administration, scoring, and comparison against norms
- intelligence is assumed to follow a normal curve
- challenging

individual differences
IQ tests can be used to identify individuals who differ significantly from those of average intelligence

- **giftedness**
  - criteria
  - characteristics
- **developmental delay/mental retardation**
  - criteria
  - classifications
  - causal factors
- **emotional intelligence**

Intelligence

nature vs. nurture
- identical twins reared together show a correlation of .86 between their IQs
- heritability estimates apply *within* groups of people, not *between* groups, not to individuals, and only in a general sense

levels of language analysis
language structures worldwide share common characteristics
- grammar
- syntax
- morphemes
- phonemes
- pragmatics

Language

the relationship between language and thought
- does language influence thought or does thinking influence language?
- linguistic relativity hypothesis
- animal studies in language

Figure 7.1 **Kosslyn's Fictional Island**

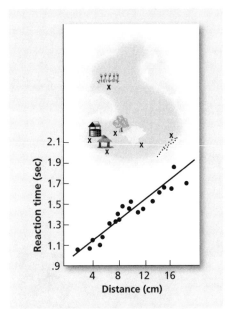

Table 7.1 **From Prototypes to Atypical Examples (Most Typical to Least Typical)**

Table 7.1   From Prototypes to Atypical Examples (Most Typical to Least Typical)

VEHICLES	FRUITS
Car	Orange
Bus	Apple
Train	Peach
Bicycle	Grape
Airplane	Strawberry
Boat	Grapefruit
Wheelchair	Watermelon
Sled	Date
Skates	Tomato
Elevator	Olive

Source: Adapted from Rosch & Mervis (1975), p. 576.

_____
_____
_____
_____
_____
_____
_____
_____
_____
_____

7.3   Problems in Problem Solving

_____
_____
_____
_____
_____
_____
_____
_____
_____
_____
_____

Table 7.2 **Stimulating Divergent Thinking**

Table 7.2 Stimulating Divergent Thinking	
Brainstorming	Generate as many ideas as possible in a short period of time, without judging each idea's merits until all ideas are recorded.
Keeping a Journal	Carry a journal to write down ideas as they occur or a recorder to capture those same ideas and thoughts.
Freewriting	Write down or record everything that comes to mind about a topic without revising or proofreading until all of the information is written or recorded in some way. Organize it later.
Mind or Subject Mapping	Start with a central idea and draw a "map" with lines from the center to other related ideas, forming a mental image of the concepts and their connections.

_____
_____
_____
_____
_____
_____
_____
_____
_____
_____
_____
_____
_____

 **Intelligence**

_____
_____
_____
_____
_____
_____
_____
_____
_____
_____
_____

Table 7.3 Gardner's Nine Intelligences

Table 7.3   Gardner's Nine Intelligences

TYPE OF INTELLIGENCE	DESCRIPTION	SAMPLE OCCUPATION
Verbal/linguistic	Ability to use language	Writers, speakers
Musical	Ability to compose and/or perform music	Musicians, even those who do not read musical notes but can perform and compose
Logical/mathematical	Ability to think logically and to solve mathematical problems	Scientists, engineers
Visual/spatial	Ability to understand how objects are oriented in space	Pilots, astronauts, artists, navigators
Movement	Ability to control one's body motions	Dancers, athletes
Interpersonal	Sensitivity to others and understanding motivation of others	Psychologists, managers
Intrapersonal	Understanding of one's emotions and how they guide actions	Various people-oriented careers
Naturalist	Ability to recognize the patterns found in nature	Farmers, landscapers, biologists, botanists
Existentialist	Ability to see the "big picture" of the human world by asking questions about life, death, and the ultimate reality of human existence	Various careers, philosophical thinkers

Table 7.4 **Paraphrased Items from the Stanford-Binet Intelligence Test**

Table 7.4   Paraphrased Items from the Stanford-Binet Intelligence Test

	TYPE OF ITEM	DESCRIPTION OF ITEM
2	Board with three differently shaped holes	Child can place correct shape into matching hole on board.
4	Building block bridge	Child can build a simple bridge out of blocks after being shown a model.
7	Similarities	Child can answer such questions as "In what way are a ship and a car alike?"
9	Digit reversal	Child can repeat four digits backwards.
Average adult	Vocabulary	Child can define 20 words from a list.

*Age at which item typically is successfully completed.
Source: Roid, G. H. (2003).

Table 7.5 **Paraphrased Sample Items from the Wechsler Adult Intelligence Scale (WAIS–IV)**

Table 7.5   Paraphrased Sample Items from the Wechsler Adult Intelligence Scale (WAIS–IV)

VERBAL SCALE	
Information	What is steam made of? What is pepper? Who wrote *Tom Sawyer*?
Comprehension	Why is copper often used in electrical wire? What is the advantage of keeping money in a bank?
Arithmetic	Three women divided eighteen golf balls equally among themselves. How many golf balls did each person receive?
	If two buttons cost $.15, what will be the cost of a dozen buttons?
Similarities	In what way are a circle and a triangle alike? In what way are a saw and a hammer alike?
Vocabulary	What is a hippopotamus? What does "resemble" mean?
PERFORMANCE SCALE	
Picture Arrangement	A story is told in three or more cartoon panels placed in the incorrect order; put them together to tell the story.
Picture Completion	Point out what's missing from each picture.
Block Design	After looking at a pattern or design, try to arrange small cubes in the same pattern.
Object Assembly	Given pieces with part of a picture on each, put them together to form objects such as a hand or a profile.
Digit Symbol	Learn a different symbol for each number and then fill in the blank under the number with the correct symbol. (This test is timed.)

Simulated items similar to those in the *Wechsler Adult Intelligence Scale*, Third Edition (1997).

Table 7.6 **Sample of the Dove Counterbalance General Intelligence Test**

Table 7.6   Sample of the Dove Counterbalance General Intelligence Test

1. A "handkerchief head" is:
    a. a cool cat,   d. a hoddi,
    b. a porter,   e. a preacher.
    c. an Uncle Tom,

2. Cheap chitlings (not the kind you purchase at a frozen food counter) will taste rubbery unless they are cooked long enough. How soon can you quit cooking them to eat and enjoy them?
    a. 45 minutes,
    b. 2 hours,
    c. 24 hours,
    d. 1 week (on a low flame),
    e. 1 hour.

3. What are the "Dixie Hummingbirds"?
    a. part of the KKK,
    b. a swamp disease,
    c. a modern gospel group,
    d. a Mississippi Negro paramilitary group,
    e. deacons.

4. "Money don't get everything it's true"
    a. but I don't have none and I'm so blue,
    b. but what it don't get I can't use,
    c. so make do with what you've got,
    d. but I don't know that and neither do you.

The answers are as follows:

1. c.   2. c.   3. c.   4. b.

Source: Dove, A. (1971).

Figure 7.4 **The Normal Curve**

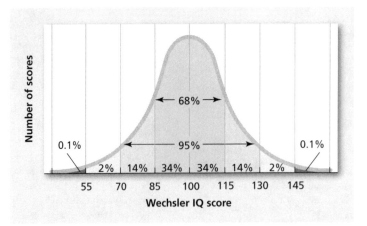

_____
_____
_____
_____
_____
_____
_____
_____
_____
_____
_____
_____
_____
_____

7.6–7.7 **Mental Retardation and Giftedness**

_____
_____
_____
_____
_____
_____
_____
_____
_____
_____

Table 7.7 **Classifications of Developmental Delay**

Table 7.7   **Classifications of Developmental Delay**

CLASSIFICATION	RANGE OF IQ SCORES	ADAPTIVE LIMITATIONS	PERCENTAGE OF DEVELOPMENTALLY DELAYED POPULATION
Mild	55–70	Can reach sixth-grade skill level. Capable with training of living independently and being self-supporting. (This category makes up the vast majority of those with developmental delays.)	90%
Moderate	40–55	Can reach second-grade skill level. Can work and live in sheltered environments with supervision.	6%
Severe	25–40	Can learn to talk and perform basic self-care but needs constant supervision.	3%
Profound	Below 25	Very limited ability to learn, may only be able to learn very simple tasks, poor language skills and limited self-care.	1%

Source: Table based on classifications in DSM-IV-TR (American Psychiatric Association, 2000).

7.8 Nature/Nurture

Figure 7.5 **Correlations Between IQ Scores of Persons with Various Relationships**

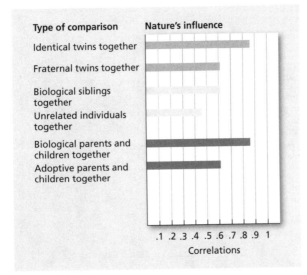

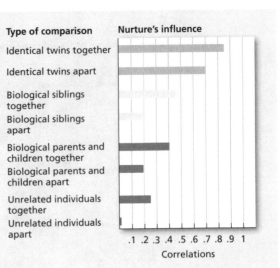

7.9–7.10 **Language**

Use the chart below to write a brief explanation of each component and come up with a specific example.

Component	Explanation	Example
phonemes		
morphemes		
grammar		
syntax		
pragmatics		

_____
_____
_____
_____
_____
_____
_____
_____
_____
_____
_____

7.11 Cognitive Health

_____
_____
_____
_____
_____
_____
_____
_____
_____
_____
_____

NOTES

YOU KNOW YOU ARE READY FOR THE TEST IF YOU ARE ABLE TO...

- Introduce the research methods and major issues in developmental psychology, including the nature versus nurture controversy.
- Describe the stages of prenatal development and potential hazards.
- Discuss the theories of Piaget and Vygotsky with regards to cognitive development.
- Describe the physical and cognitive development in infancy and childhood including language development.
- Explain the concept of personality including the idea of temperament, attachment theory, and Erikson's psychosocial model.
- Identify the major stages of development in adolescence and adulthood.
- Discuss three theories of aging and Kübler-Ross's stages of dying.
- Understand how ADHD affects adults.

RAPID REVIEW

Human development is the scientific study of the changes that occur in people as they age from conception to death. Since age cannot be directly manipulated by a researcher, developmental psychologists have had to develop alternative methods to investigate the effects of aging on psychological processes. Three common methods used are **longitudinal**, **cross-sectional**, and **cross-sequential** studies. Longitudinal studies have the advantage of following the same subject across time but are limited due to the amount of time and money required to complete the study and the problem of attrition. Cross-sectional studies are cheaper, faster, and easier to conduct since they gather information from different age groups at one particular period of time; however, results from these studies may be confounded due to individual and history differences. Cross-sequential studies are a combination of longitudinal and cross-sectional techniques and often represent an ideal compromise. One of the biggest debates among developmental psychologists is the question of **nature** versus **nurture**. Nature refers to the influence of everything you inherited genetically from your biological parents and nurture refers to the influence your environment has had on your development. More recently, the question of interest has switched from nature *versus* nurture to the interaction of nature *and* nurture. Behavioral genetics is the field of science that studies the interactions of nature, or genes, and nurture, or the environment.

Genetics is the science of heredity and involves the study of DNA, genes, and chromosomes. **DNA (deoxyribonucleic acid)** is the smallest unit of the three and are strands of molecules linked together like a twisted ladder. The links are made up of amines and their names are abbreviated with the letters A, T, G, and C. The next largest unit are the **genes**, which are sections of the ladder containing instructions on how to make a specific protein. One way to think of genes is as individual recipes for proteins. The biggest unit is the **chromosomes**, which are long strands of DNA twisted together and wound up in coils. The chromosomes are found in the nucleus of all the cells of your body except red blood cells. Humans have a total of 46 chromosomes, 23 from the mother's egg and 23 from the father's sperm. Each chromosome from the mother matches a chromosome from the father to form 23 pairs. Both chromosomes in the pair have the same genes (for example, each chromosome contains a gene for hair color). Even though they contain the same gene, the instructions on that gene might be slightly different; for example, one of the genes has the instructions for blonde hair while the other gene contains the instructions for brown hair. The first 22 pairs of chromosomes are called autosomes, and the last pair (the 23rd) contains the instructions for determining sex and are called the sex chromosomes. **Dominant genes** are the genes that are more likely to influence the trait. **Recessive genes** are not as strong and will only get their instructions carried out if the other chromosome in the pair also contains a recessive gene. In reality, almost all traits are determined by multiple gene pairs. This is called polygenic inheritance. Some diseases result from problems with recessive genes and are only expressed when both parents have the recessive gene, while some disorders result from the fact that there are the wrong number of chromosomes in the fertilizing egg or sperm.

Many people believe that **conception** represents the beginning of life. **Fertilization** occurs when the sperm penetrates the egg (or **ovum**). The result is a single cell with 46 chromosomes (23 from the sperm and 23 from the egg). This cell is called a **zygote**. **Monozygotic (or identical) twins** result from the zygote splitting into two separate masses early in the division process. **Dizygotic (or fraternal) twins** result from two eggs being fertilized by two separate sperm. Siamese twins are more properly referred to as **conjoined twins** and result from an incomplete separation of the zygotic mass. Britty and Abby Hensel are an example of conjoined twins. The **germinal period** of pregnancy is the first two weeks after fertilization during which the zygote migrates down to the uterus and attaches to the uterine wall. The placenta and umbilical cord both begin to develop during this period. The **embryonic period** lasts from about Week 2 to Week 8 after which the **embryo** is about one inch long with primitive eyes, nose, lips, teeth, arms and legs. **Critical periods** are times in development during which an environmental influence can impact the development of the fetus. Different organs and structures have different critical periods. The environmental influences that can impact the development of the fetus are called **teratogens**. The **fetal period** lasts from the eighth week after conception to the end of the pregnancy. Tremendous growth of the **fetus** occurs during this time. A baby born before the 38th week of pregnancy is considered preterm and is at risk for survival, especially if he or she weighs less than five and a half pounds. Most miscarriages, also called spontaneous abortions, occur in the first three months of a pregnancy.

Infants have a large number of capabilities even immediately after birth. Most infants are able to perform five innate reflexes. Touch is the most well developed sense followed by smell and taste. Vision is the least functional of the senses. The rods are developed at birth but cones must develop over a six-month time period. At birth, an infant's vision is most clear seven to ten inches from their face. Also, infants appear to show a preference for the human voice and human faces. Due to a recent trend of many parents choosing not to give immunization shots to their children, there is a growing concern over the possibility of widespread epidemics. Most immunizations are made from the dead virus and cannot cause an infection in the recipient. No link has been found between autism and immunization.

The brain triples in weight during the first two years of life with the increase being caused by the expansion of existing cells not the growth of new ones. Jean Piaget believed that the primary factor in the development of a child's cognitive abilities was the child's interactions with objects in the environment. Piaget believed that children form mental concepts or **schemes** as they experience new situations and events. He proposed four stages of **cognitive development** from infancy to adolescence. The **sensorimotor stage**, lasting from infancy to age 2, involves the use of the senses and muscles to learn about the environment and includes the development of **object permanence** and symbolic thought. The **preoperational stage** lasts from age 2 to 7 and involve language and concept development through the process of asking questions. Children in this stage display the ability of symbolic thought through make-believe play and also display characteristics of **egocentrism**, **centration**, and **irreversibility**. The **concrete operational** stage lasts from age 7 to 12 and includes the development of concepts such as **conservation** and reversible thinking. However, children in this stage are still unable to deal with abstract concepts such as freedom or love. The **formal operational stage** is the final stage of cognitive development, according to Piaget, and lasts from the age of 12 on. During this stage abstract, hypothetical thinking develops. Research suggests that about one-half of the adults in the U.S. reach this stage of cognitive development. Piaget's concepts have been successfully applied in schools but have also been criticized for their emphasis on distinct stages of development, overemphasis on egocentrism, and failure to mention the role of the family or social environment in the child's development.

Lev Vygotsky was a Russian psychologist who felt the primary factor in development was the social environment. He proposed a concept called **scaffolding** in which a more highly skilled person give the learner help and then stops as the learner develops on his own. Vygotsky believed that each child has a **zone of proximal development** or ZPD, which is the difference between what a child can do alone and what he or she can do with the help of a teacher. Vygotsky's principles have been applied in the classroom through the use of cooperative learning and reciprocal teaching.

Psychologists interested in information-processing theory have investigated the memory capabilities of the developing infant and have found that infants demonstrate memory from birth, 4- to 5-year-olds appear to be able to store about three items in their short-term memory and have both episodic and procedural memories in long-term memory. Language development appears to be an important step in cognitive development and facilitates the development of symbolic thinking. The stages of language development experienced by all speakers includes <u>cooing</u> around 2 months of age, <u>babbling</u> at 6 months of age, one-word speech or <u>holophrases</u> around 1 year of age, <u>telegraphic speech</u> at around a year and a half, and then whole sentences.

Temperament refers to the behavioral and emotional characteristics observed in infancy. Several researchers have suggested the existence of three types of temperaments, easy, difficult, and slow to warm up. **Attachment** is the emotional bond between an infant and caregiver. Mary Ainsworth and others studied attachment using the Strange Situation and observed four attachment styles, secure, avoidant, ambivalent, and disorganized/disoriented. Harry Harlow studied the nature of attachment behaviors by observing Rhesus monkeys interact with two different "surrogate" mothers. He found that **contact comfort** was an important factor in attachment.

<u>Erik Erikson</u>, who originally trained as a Freudian psychoanalyst, proposed an eight-stage theory of development that occurred over the entire life span. Each stage involved an emotional crises in the individual's social interactions. The first four stages occurred during infancy and childhood and consisted of the crises of **trust versus mistrust**, **autonomy versus shame and doubt**, **initiation versus guilt**, and **industry versus inferiority**. Most children begin to understand **gender** differences around the age of 2 and begin to develop their own **gender identity**.

Adolescence is the period of time from around age 14 to the early 20s and is most clearly identified by the physical changes that occur in **puberty**. Mentally, many adolescents are moving into Piaget's formal operational stage of development, which includes the ability to think in the abstract and to consider hypothetical situations. At the same time, adolescents still demonstrate a considerable amount of egocentric thinking as can be seen in the thought processes of the **personal fable**, in which the adolescent feels they are different from all others, and the **imaginary audience**, where the adolescent is convinced that everyone is looking at him or her.

<u>Lawrence Kohlberg</u> proposed a theory about the development of moral thinking and divided the development into three levels, **pre-conventional**, during which the individual conforms to social norms; **conventional**, during which time the consequences determine morality; and **post-conventional**, during which a person's individual moral principles determine right and wrong. The social crisis proposed by Erikson for the period of adolescence is that of **identity versus role confusion**.

Adulthood can be roughly identified as the time period from the early 20s until death. Middle age is often associated with an increase in health problems and includes the events of **menopause** for women and **andropause** for men. Cognitive abilities do not decline overall but the speed of processing does appear to slow down and people tend to have a harder time retrieving specific information from their memory. Erikson proposed three psycho-social developmental stages for adulthood. The stages are **intimacy versus isolation**, **generativity versus stagnation**, and **ego integrity versus despair**. Parenting is a significant part of many people's adulthood. Diana Baumrind proposed three basic parenting styles, **authoritarian**, **permissive**, and **authoritative**. Permissive parents can either be **permissive neglectful** or **permissive indulgent**.

There are a number of theories as to why our bodies physically age. The cellular clock theory suggests that cells are limited in the number of times they can reproduce. The wear-and-tear theory proposes that aging is a result of outside stressors such as physical exertion and bodily damage. The free radical theory states that as people get older, more and more free radicals accumulate in their bodies. Socially, the **activity theory** suggests that elderly people adjust more positively to aging when they remain active in some way.

Elizabeth Kübler-Ross proposed a well-known theory of the dying process. Based on her work with dying patients, Kübler-Ross felt that people experienced a series of five different emotions including denial, anger, bargaining, depression, and acceptance. Others see dying as more of a process rather than a series of stages.

In the last few decades, researchers have begun to realize that **attention deficit hyperactivity disorder (ADHD)** often persists into adulthood. Many treatments are currently available for adult ADHD.

1. Perhaps the most influential theory on cognitive development is Jean Piaget's theory. He proposed four stages of cognitive development. To enhance your learning of these stages, fill in the chart below. Try to fill it in as much as possible without going back to your notes and/or the textbook. The first stage has been filled in as an example.

Stage	Age	Characteristics	How would you test to see if someone is in this stage?
Sensorimotor	*0-2 years*	• Children explore using their sensory and motor systems. • Develop object permanence.	*Hide a toy under a blanket and see if the child looks under the blanket for the toy.*

2. Another major theory of development is the theory proposed by Erik Erikson. Erikson's theory focuses more on the development of personality, with each stage marked by a crisis that needs to be resolved. The crisis typically involves the social interactions of the individual and is represented by the two extremes of the possible outcomes (for example, industry versus inferiority). One way to keep track of these stages is to realize that the labels follow a pattern of "desirable outcome versus undesirable outcome." Also, they reflect the social activities that are typically going on at that age. Fill in the chart below to help you understand Erikson's theory of development.

Age	Social Activities	Desirable Outcome	Undesirable Outcome

0-1 years	being fed, taken care of by someone else	sense of _trust_	sense of _mistrust_

Suggested answers for Study Hint 1

Stage	Age	Characteristics	How would you test to see if someone is in this stage?
Sensorimotor	0-2 years	• Children explore using their sensory and motor systems. • Develop object permanence.	Hide a toy under a blanket and see if the child looks under the blanket for the toy.
Preoperational	2-7 years	• A lot of egocentric thinking. • Children can represent objects mentally. • Engage in make-believe play. • Do not understand concepts of conservation. • Tend to focus on one aspect of an object	Ask the child if she would rather have two quarters or five pennies (she will probably want the five pennies). See if the child can play a make-believe game.
Concrete Operational	7-12 years	• Show an understanding for the principles of conservation. • Demonstrate logical thinking and can solve analogies • Focus mostly on concrete objects and ideas.	Divide a string of clay into five pieces and see if the child thinks there is as much clay in the five pieces as there was in the one string.
Formal Operational	12 years and on	• Can use abstract reasoning to solve problems. • Able to consider hypothetical situations.	Ask the child an abstract question and see how she responds. An example of a question could be "What if snow were black?"

Suggested answers for Study Hint 2

Age	Social Activities	Desirable Outcome	Undesirable Outcome
0-1 years	being fed, taken care of by someone else	sense of trust	sense of mistrust
1-3 years	Learning to walk, talk, dress yourself, etc.	sense of autonomy (feeling that you are in control of your own body)	sense of shame and doubt
3-5 years	going to preschool, being responsible to obey family rules, learning your role as a member of a family	sense of initiative	sense of guilt or irresponsibility
5-12 years	going to school, completing school assignments, participating in social activities with peers	sense of industry (feeling capable of completing your work)	sense of inferiority or incompetence
12-18 years	deciding "what you want to be when you grow up" choosing a career path, selecting your own group of friends	sense of identity	feeling of role confusion, unsure of who you are

18-40 years	finding a partner to form a life-long commitment, succeeding in a career	sense of intimacy, feel comfortable forming close relationships	sense of isolation, not able to form close ties with others
40-60 years	focus on career and family. Perhaps grandchildren begin to enter the picture. Begin thinking of the legacy that you will leave for your children and/or the future generation	sense of generativity, or succeeding in creating something that will benefit others in the future	sense of stagnation, or feeling that you have done nothing for the next generation
60 years and on	dealing with retirement from your career, family might be more involved in their own lives, facing the fact of death among those in your social group	sense of ego integrity, or a sense of acceptance of your life and acceptance of death.	sense of despair about your life and a fear of your inevitable death.

LEARNING OBJECTIVES

8.1   What are some of the special research methods used to study development?

8.2   What is the relationship between heredity and environmental factors in determining development?

8.3   How do chromosomes, genes, and DNA determine a person's characteristics or disorders, and what causes multiple births?

8.4   What happens during the germinal, embryonic, and fetal periods of pregnancy, and what are some hazards in prenatal development?

8.5   What kind of physical changes take place in infancy and childhood?

8.6   What are three ways of looking at cognitive development, and how does language develop?

8.7   How do infants and children develop personalities and form relationships with others, and what are Erikson's stages of psychosocial development for children?

8.8   What are the physical, cognitive, and personality changes that occur in adolescence, including concepts of morality and Erikson's search for identity?

8.9   What are the physical, cognitive, and personality changes that occur during adulthood and aging, including Erikson's last three psychosocial stages and patterns of parenting?

8.10 How do psychologists explain why aging occurs, and what are the stages of death and dying?

8.11 How does attention deficit hyperactivity disorder affect adults?

PRACTICE EXAM

For the following multiple choice questions, select the answer you feel best answers the question.

1.   A researcher who selects a sample of people of varying ages and studies them at one point in time is, by definition, using the _____ method.
   a)   cohort design
   b)   longitudinal design
   c)   behavior genetics design
   d)   cross-sectional design

2.   Which of the following is an example of a longitudinal study?
   a)   observing three groups of children (ages 2, 6, and 12) for a two-hour period
   b)   observing three groups of children (ages 2, 6, and 12) for a two-week period
   c)   observing a group of 30 children at age 2 and again at age 6 and once more when the children turn 12 years of age.
   d)   surveying a group of middle-aged adults, half male and half female.

3. What relatively new field investigates the influence of genes and heredity on behavior?
   a) psychobiology
   b) neuropsychology
   c) behavioral genetics
   d) psychoanalysis

4. When a researcher discusses the contributions of "nature" on development, she is referring to the effects of your
   a) environment.
   b) heredity.
   c) social interactions.
   d) teratogens.

5. Which of the following is a special molecule that contains the genetic material of the organism?
   a) DNA
   b) gene
   c) chromosomes
   d) amines

6. Which of the following is essentially a "recipe" or set of instructions for making a protein?
   a) DNA
   b) a chromosome
   c) a gene
   d) an enzyme

7. Why are males more likely than females to exhibit sex-linked traits?
   a) Males' X chromosome may not have a necessary dominant gene.
   b) Females are actually the stronger sex.
   c) Females have a protective enzyme in their sex hormones.
   d) Males' Y chromosome may not have a necessary dominant gene.

8. Dizygotic twins are formed from one egg and two sperm.
   a) True
   b) False

9. Monozygotic twins _____.
   a) are genetically identical
   b) are genetically different
   c) will be of a different sex
   d) are more likely to occur when a woman is taking fertility drugs

10. Brittany and Abby Hensel are a type of twin referred to as_____.
    a) nonidentical
    b) dizygotic
    c) fraternal
    d) conjoined

11. The specialized organ that provides nourishment and filters away waste products from the developing baby is called the _____.
    a) placenta
    b) uterus
    c) umbilical cord
    d) embryo

12. What are some of the common consequences to a child if the mother smoked while pregnant?
    a) increased birth weight and lethargy
    b) lower birth weight and short stature
    c) severe hearing loss and heart defects
    d) severely deformed limbs and muscle spasms

13. The longest prenatal period during which tremendous growth occurs and the organs continue to develop and become functional is called_____.
    a) germinal
    b) embryonic
    c) fetal
    d) gestational

14. In the _____ reflex, the baby moves its head toward any light touch to its face.
    a) sucking
    b) startle
    c) rooting
    d) grasping

15. Which sense is the most well developed at birth?
    a) taste
    b) touch
    c) sight
    d) hearing

16. Which of the following statements about immunizations is true?
    a) Children who are given an immunization are fairly likely to get the disease itself.
    b) Immunizations almost always cause bad reactions.
    c) Immunizations are needed even if the disease has been eliminated.
    d) Some immunizations cause autism in children.

17. Your little sister picks up objects, feels every part of them, and then puts them in her mouth. What stage of Jean Piaget's model of cognitive development does this behavior suggest?
    a) concrete operations
    b) sensorimotor
    c) preoperational
    d) formal operations

18. A theory that looks at the way people deal with the information that comes in through the senses is called_____.
    a) information-processing theory
    b) sensorimotor intelligence
    c) habituation
    d) metamemory

19. Which of the following would a child in Piaget's preoperational stage of cognitive development NOT be able to do?
    a) mentally represent an object
    b) play make-believe
    c) see the world from someone else's perspective
    d) use symbolic thought

20. Vygotsky's idea that children develop cognitively when someone else helps them by asking leading questions and providing examples is called
    a) scaffolding.
    b) centration.
    c) conservation.
    d) metamemory.

21. The first noticeable signs of language development in infants is
    a) babbling.
    b) cooing.
    c) telegraphic speech.
    d) holophrases.

22. By about 12 months, most infants _____.
    a) begin to use intonation in their language
    b) build a vocabulary of one-word phrases, or holophrases
    c) begin to distinguish, in their language, between themselves and others
    d) begin to form two- and three-word sentences

23. Infants in different cultures and of different languages experience a different series of stages in language development.
    a) True
    b) False

24. If an infant in Mary Ainsworth's Strange Situation was unwilling to explore, became very upset by the stranger, and demanded to be picked up by his mother but then kicked to get away, he would most likely be classified as
    a) secure
    b) avoidant
    c) ambivalent
    d) disorganized-disoriented

25. Chester is irritable, loud, and negative most of the time. He really doesn't like when new people pick him up and hold him and has irregular sleeping, eating, and waking schedules. What temperament does he exhibit?
    a) active
    b) slow-to-warm-up
    c) difficult
    d) easy

26. Erikson's theory of social development viewed the ages of 3 to 6, his third stage, as being characterized by the major challenge of _____.
    a) identity versus role diffusion
    b) industry versus inferiority
    c) initiative versus guilt
    d) autonomy versus shame and doubt

27. According to Erikson, when children between the ages of 5 and 12 succeed at learning new skills, they develop a sense of _____; and if they fail to develop new abilities, they feel _____.
    a) shame; doubt
    b) trust; guilty
    c) industry; inferior
    d) identity; despair

28. _____theorists believe that gender identity is learned through direct reinforcement and observational learning.
    a) Social learning
    b) Cognitive
    c) Psychoanalytic
    d) Humanistic

29. The growth spurt for boys typically begins at age_____.
    a) 9
    b) 12
    c) 10
    d) 15

30. Fifteen-year-old Todd is writing an impassioned novel about growing up in America. In his novel he describes his experiences in a way that portrays himself as unique and special, such that no one has ever thought such deep thoughts or experienced such ecstasy before. Todd's writings most clearly reflect _____.
    a) his sense of autonomy
    b) the personal fable
    c) the period of rebellion common to all adolescents
    d) his developing sense of conscience

31. Which of the following questions would an adolescent who has NOT reached Piaget's stage of formal operations have trouble thinking about?
    a) What date did Columbus arrive in America?
    b) How many 2-inch pieces can a 10-inch rope be cut into?
    c) What if you had been born to different parents?
    d) What is the definition of democracy?

32. Jeremy is 17 years old. According to Erikson, his chief task will be acquiring a sense of _____.
    a) identity
    b) intimacy
    c) generativity
    d) autonomy

33. The cessation of menstruation and ovulation is called _____.
    a) climacteric
    b) perimenopause
    c) menopause
    d) andropause

34. All of the following are reasons why middle adults experience changes in memory EXCEPT _____.
    a) stress
    b) more information to remember
    c) more information stored in memory
    d) hardening of the arteries

35. A young adult who is having difficulty trusting others is most likely still trying to resolve Erikson's stage of
    a) autonomy vs. shame and doubt
    b) ego integrity vs. despair
    c) industry vs. inferiority
    d) intimacy vs. isolation

36. Which of the following is an example of generativity?
    a) completing a crossword puzzle
    b) becoming a mentor
    c) getting married
    d) finding your own identity

37. The _____ theory of aging suggests that unstable oxygen molecules cause damage to the structure of cells, increasing with age.
    a) wear-and-tear
    b) cellular clock
    c) disengagement
    d) free radical

38. Which theory correctly explains why the aging process occurs?
    a) cellular clock theory
    b) free radical theory
    c) wear-and-tear theory
    d) No theory to date has thoroughly explained the aging process.

39. Several weeks of diagnostic tests have revealed the cancer has spread throughout Barry's body. His physician suggested that he "take care of important matters." Barry realizes his family's home needs repairs, so he arranges to have that done right away. To relieve his family of the agony of planning his funeral, he has made all the arrangements. Barry told his minister he has a good life and just wants to make sure he provides for his family after his death. This description fits the stage Kübler-Ross called _____.
    a) denial
    b) acceptance
    c) bargaining
    d) depression

40. Attention deficit hyperactivity disorder has not been observed to occur in adults.
    a) True
    b) False

PRACTICE EXAM ANSWERS

1. d   D is correct. Cross-sectional design studies several different age groups at the same time.

2. b   B is correct because a longitudinal study involves the study of a group of individuals at two or more time points in their lives. It may be helpful to remember that a <u>long</u>itudinal study takes a <u>long</u> time to complete

3. c   Genetics is a field that investigates the effects of genes and environmental influences on behavior, whereas psychobiology is the study of the biological bases of behavior.

4. b   Nature refers to everything you inherit biologically. Nurture refers to the effects of your surroundings, or environment.

5. a   DNA, genes, and chromosomes all contain the genetic material of an organism, but DNA is the only molecule listed.

6. c   A gene is a section of DNA that contains instructions for making proteins. Chromosomes are large strands of DNA that contain many genes.

7. d   In the 23rd pair of chromosomes, females have an XX pair and males have an XY pair. The Y chromosome is smaller than the X chromosome and so some genes on the X chromosome don't have a "match" on the Y chromosome. Because there is no competition, a recessive gene on the X chromosome is more likely to be expressed in males than in females.

8. b   "Di" means two, and zygotic is referring to the zygote which is formed when the egg and sperm unite. Dizygotic (or fraternal) twins are formed from two eggs and two sperm.

9. a   Monozygotic twins are formed from one egg and one sperm ("mono" means one). After the egg and sperm unite they split to form two zygotes. Because all the DNA comes from the same egg and sperm, monozygotic twins are genetically identical.

10. d   Conjoined twins (commonly referred to as Siamese twins) are physically joined due to the fact that the zygotes do not completely separate from each other.

11. a   The placenta provides protection and nourishment to the fetus.

12. b   Multiple studies have found that babies of mothers who smoked are smaller in weight and height than babies from mothers who didn't smoke.

13. c   The fetal period is the longest and last stage of prenatal development and is when the most growth occurs in the fetus.

14. c   The rooting reflex is thought to help the baby with breast-feeding.

15. b   Touch and taste are fairly well developed at birth, with touch being the most highly developed. The sense of sight takes the longest to fully develop after birth.

16. c   Even if the disease has been eliminated in a specific area or country, there are possibilities of infection from other countries.

17. b   The sensorimotor stage involves exploring the world through the use of the sensory and motor systems. During the sensorimotor stage infants interact deliberately with objects by chewing, grasping, and tasting them It is the first of Piaget's four stages of cognitive development.

18. a   Information-processing theory looks at the way in which people deal with the information that comes in through the senses. Metamemory is one's knowledge about the workings of memory and memory strategies.

19. c   In the preoperational stage of development, children are still very egocentric and have a very hard time seeing the world from someone else's viewpoint.

20. a   Scaffolding is the process of helping a child develop by providing the framework for learning.

21. b   Cooing is the first visible sign of language development in infants, followed by babbling, holophrases, and then telegraphic speech.

22. b By about one year of age, children are communicating one-word "phrases." Telegraphic speech, which consists of two- or three-word sentences, usually develops around one and a half to two years of age.
23. b It appears that all infants experience the same stages of language development.
24. c The ambivalent child exhibits ambivalent behaviors towards his or her mother. An example is begging to be picked up by the mother and then struggling to get away from the mother once he or she is picked up.
25. c Difficult babies tend to be irritable, are not comfortable with change, and have irregular schedules.
26. c Initiative vs. guilt is Erikson's third stage of development. Autonomy vs. shame and doubt is the second stage, and industry vs. inferiority is the fourth stage.
27. c Industry vs inferiority is Erikson's fourth stage of development and corresponds closely with the primary school years.
28. a Social learning theorists focus on how personality is learned.
29. b Boys show a growth spurt around age 12, whereas girls typically show a growth spurt earlier, around age 10.
30. b The personal fable describes a phenomenon commonly seen in adolescents in which they feel that no one else has experienced the emotions or thoughts that they are currently experiencing.
31. c The key to Piaget's fourth and final stage of cognitive development is the ability to consider hypothetical and abstract situations. The question in choice c is the only question requiring abstract thought.
32. a Erikson believed most of the adolescent years involved the crisis of identity vs. role confusion.
33. c Menopause is the correct answer. Perimenopause is the term used to describe the period of five to ten years during which a woman's reproductive system begins to decline.
34. d Memory changes during middle age have not been found to be associated with physical decline.
35. d Erikson proposed the stage of intimacy vs. isolation for young adults as they try to form intimate relations with others and learn to trust in someone other than themselves.
36. b Generativity involves helping a younger generation and engaging in activities that will leave a legacy.
37. d Radicals are oxygen molecules in the cells that are thought to cause damage.
38. d None of the theories to date have thoroughly explained the aging process.
39. b Kübler-Ross described the stage of acceptance as an emotional state of acknowledging one's impending death and being at peace with the idea.
40. b ADHD has been observed in adults with increasing frequency in recent years.

CHAPTER GLOSSARY

activity theory	theory of adjustment to aging that suggests older people are happier if they remain active in some way.
adolescence	the period of life from about age 13 to the early twenties, during which a young person is no longer physically a child but is not yet an independent, self-supporting adult.
andropause	gradual changes in the sexual hormones and reproductive system of males.
attachment	the emotional bond between an infant and the primary caregiver.

attention deficit hyperactivity disorder (ADHD)	disorder characterized by lack of impulse control, inability to concentrate and hyperactivity.
authoritative	parenting style that involves combining firm limits on behavior combined with love, warmth, affection, respect, and a willingness to listen.
authoritiarian	parenting style that is rigid, demanding, controlling, uncompromising, and overly concerned with rules.
autonomy versus shame and doubt	second stage of personality development in which the toddler strives for physical independence.
babbling	consonant and vowel sounds representing the second stage of language development, usually occurring around 6 months of age
centration	in Piaget's theory, the tendency of a young child to focus on only one feature of an object while ignoring other, relevant features.
chromosome	tightly wound strand of genetic material (or DNA).
cognitive development	the development of thinking, problem solving, and memory.
conception	the moment at which a female becomes pregnant.
concrete operational stage	third stage of cognitive development in which the school-age child becomes capable of logical thought processes, but is not yet capable of abstract thinking.
conjoined twins	often called Siamese twins, occurring from an incomplete separation of the zygotic cells.
conservation	in Piaget's theory, the ability to understand that simply changing the appearance of an object does not change the object's nature.
contact comfort	variable of tactile sensation that was proposed by Harry Harlow to be an important component in the formation of attachment.
conventional morality	second level of Kohlberg's stages of moral development in which the child's behavior is governed by conforming to the society's norms of behavior.
cooing	vowel-like sounds made by babies around 2 months of age representing the first stage of language development.
critical periods	times during which some environmental influence can have an impact on the development of the infant.
cross-sectional design	research design in which several different age groups of participants are studied at one particular point in time.
cross-sequential design	research design in which participants are first studied by means of a cross-sectional design, but also followed and assessed for a period of no more than six years.
dizygotic twins	often called fraternal twins, occurring when two eggs each get fertilized by two different sperm, resulting in two zygotes in the uterus at the same time.
DNA (deoxyribonucleic acid)	special molecule that contains the genetic material of the organism.
dominant gene	referring to a gene that actively controls the expression of a trait.
ego integrity versus despair	eighth and final stage of Erikson's model of development in which the goal is to develop a sense of wholeness that comes from having lived a full life and the ability to let go of regrets, the final completion of the ego.
egocentrism	the inability to see the world through anyone else's eyes.
Elizabeth Kübler-Ross	1926–2004 Swiss psychiatrist known for her work with dying patients and her proposed theory of five stages of dying.
embryo	name for the developing organism from 2 weeks to 8 weeks after fertilization.

embryonic period	the period from 2 to 8 weeks after fertilization, during which the major organs and structures of the organism develop.
Erik Erikson	1902–1994. developmental psychologist trained in the methods of psychoanalysis who proposed a theory of personality development based on a series of emotional crises.
fertilization	the union of the ovum and sperm.
fetal period	the time from about 8 weeks until the birth of the child.
fetus	name for the developing organism from 8 weeks after fertilization to the birth of the baby.
formal operational stage	Piaget's last stage of cognitive development in which the adolescent becomes capable of abstract thinking.
gender	the behavior associated with being male or female.
gender identity	perception of one's gender and the behavior that is associated with that gender.
gene	section of DNA having the same arrangement of chemical elements.
generativity versus stagnation	seventh stage of Erikson's model of personality development in which the crisis involves providing guidance to one's children or the next generation, contributing to the well-being of the next generation through career or volunteer work or developing a sense of stagnation.
genetics	the science of inherited traits.
germinal period	first 2 weeks after fertilization, during which the zygote moves down to the uterus and begins to implant in the lining.
holophrases	single word utterances seen universally in the stages of language development.
human development	the scientific study of the changes that occur in people as they age, from conception until death.
identity versus role confusion	fifth stage of personality development in which the adolescent must find a consistent sense of self.
imaginary audience	type of thought common to adolescents in which young people believe that other people are just as concerned about the adolescent's thoughts and characteristics as they themselves are.
industry versus inferiority	fourth stage of personality development in which the adolescent strives for a sense of competence and self-esteem.
initiative versus guilt	third stage of personality development in which the preschool-aged child strives for emotional and psychological independence, and attempts to satisfy curiosity about the world.
intimacy versus isolation	sixth stage of Erikson's model of personality development in which an emotional and psychological closeness that is based on the ability to trust, share, and care, while still maintaining one's sense of self is developed.
irreversibility	in Piaget's theory, the inability of the young child to mentally reverse an action.
Jean Piaget	1896–1980 Swiss developmental psychologist who proposed a four-stage theory of cognitive development based on the concept of mental operations.
Lawrence Kohlberg	1927–1987 developmental psychologist known for his theory on the development of moral reasoning.
Lev Vygotsky	1896–1934 Russian developmental psychologist who emphasized the role of the social environment on cognitive development and proposed the idea of zones of proximal development.

longitudinal design	research design in which one participant or group of participants is studied over a long period of time.
menopause	the cessation of ovulation and menstrual cycles and the end of a woman's reproductive capability.
monozygotic twins	identical twins formed when one zygote splits into two separate masss of cells, each of which develops into a separate embryo.
nature	the influence of our inherited characteristics on our personality, physical growth, intellectual growth, and social interactions.
nurture	the influence of the environment on personality, physical growth, intellectual growth, and social interactions.
object permanence	the knowledge that an object exists even when it is not in sight.
ovum	the female sex cell, or egg.
permissive	parenting style in which the parent puts very few demands on the child for behavior.
permissive indulgent	permissive parenting style in which the parents seem to be too involved with their children, allowing them to act any way they wish.
permissive neglectful	permissive parenting style in which the parents are not involved with their children.
personal fable	type of thought common to adolescents in which young people believe themselves to be unique and protected from harm.
polygenic inheritance	a trait or characteristic that is determined by more than one gene pair.
post-conventional morality	third level of Kohlberg's stages of moral development in which the person's behavior is governed by moral principles that have been decided upon by the individual and which may be in disagreement with accepted social norms.
pre-conventional morality	first level of Kohlberg's stages of moral development in which the child's behavior is governed by the consequences of the behavior.
preoperational stage	Piaget's second stage of cognitive development in which the preschool child learns to use language as a means of exploring the world.
puberty	the physical changes that occur in the body as sexual development reaches its peak.
recessive gene	referring to a gene that only influences the expression of a trait when paired with an identical gene.
scaffolding	process in which a more skilled learner gives help to a less skilled learner, reducing the amount of help as the less skilled learner becomes more capable.
scheme	a mental concept formed through experiences with objects and events.
sensorimotor stage	Piaget's first stage of cognitive development in which the infant uses its senses and motor abilities to interact with objects in the environment.
telegraphic speech	type of speech in words are left out of a sentence but the meaning of the sentence remains, such as "want cookie" to mean "I would like a cookie."
temperament	the behavioral characteristics that are fairly well established at birth, such as easy, difficult, and slow-to-warm-up.
teratogen	any factor that can cause a birth defect.
trust versus mistrust	first stage of personality development in which the infant's basic sense of trust or mistrust develops as a result of consistent or inconsistent care.
zone of proximal development (ZPD)	Vygotsky's concept of the difference between what a child can do alone and what that child can do with the help of a more skilled teacher.
zygote	cell resulting from the uniting of the ovum and sperm.

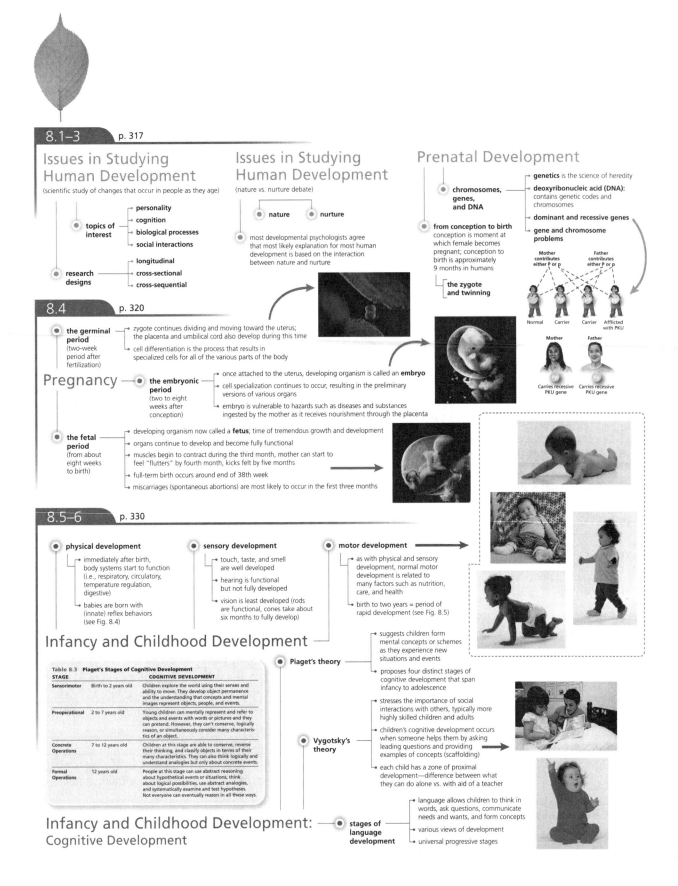

p. 317

Issues in Studying Human Development
(scientific study of changes that occur in people as they age)

- topics of interest
  - personality
  - cognition
  - biological processes
  - social interactions

- research designs
  - longitudinal
  - cross-sectional
  - cross-sequential

Issues in Studying Human Development
(nature vs. nurture debate)

- nature
- nurture

- most developmental psychologists agree that most likely explanation for most human development is based on the interaction between nature and nurture

Prenatal Development

- chromosomes, genes, and DNA
  - genetics is the science of heredity
  - deoxyribonucleic acid (DNA): contains genetic codes and chromosomes
  - dominant and recessive genes
  - gene and chromosome problems

- from conception to birth
  conception is moment at which female becomes pregnant; conception to birth is approximately 9 months in humans
  - the zygote and twinning

Mother contributes either P or p

Father contributes either P or p

Normal | Carrier | Carrier | Afflicted with PKU

Mother | Father

Carries recessive PKU gene | Carries recessive PKU gene

p. 320

8.4

- the germinal period (two-week period after fertilization)
  - zygote continues dividing and moving toward the uterus; the placenta and umbilical cord also develop during this time
  - cell differentiation is the process that results in specialized cells for all of the various parts of the body

Pregnancy

- the embryonic period (two to eight weeks after conception)
  - once attached to the uterus, developing organism is called an **embryo**
  - cell specialization continues to occur, resulting in the preliminary versions of various organs
  - embryo is vulnerable to hazards such as diseases and substances ingested by the mother as it receives nourishment through the placenta

- the fetal period (from about eight weeks to birth)
  - developing organism now called a **fetus**; time of tremendous growth and development
  - organs continue to develop and become fully functional
  - muscles begin to contract during the third month, mother can start to feel "flutters" by fourth month, kicks felt by five months
  - full-term birth occurs around end of 38th week
  - miscarriages (spontaneous abortions) are most likely to occur in the first three months

p. 330

8.5-6

- physical development
  - immediately after birth, body systems start to function (i.e., respiratory, circulatory, temperature regulation, digestive)
  - babies are born with (innate) reflex behaviors (see Fig. 8.4)

- sensory development
  - touch, taste, and smell are well developed
  - hearing is functional but not fully developed
  - vision is least developed (rods are functional, cones take about six months to fully develop)

- motor development
  - as with physical and sensory development, normal motor development is related to many factors such as nutrition, care, and health
  - birth to two years = period of rapid development (see Fig. 8.5)

Infancy and Childhood Development

- Piaget's theory
  - suggests children form mental concepts or schemes as they experience new situations and events
  - proposes four distinct stages of cognitive development that span infancy to adolescence

- Vygotsky's theory
  - stresses the importance of social interactions with others, typically more highly skilled children and adults
  - children's cognitive development occurs when someone helps them by asking leading questions and providing examples of concepts (scaffolding)
  - each child has a zone of proximal development—difference between what they can do alone vs. with aid of a teacher

- stages of language development
  - language allows children to think in words, ask questions, communicate needs and wants, and form concepts
  - various views of development
  - universal progressive stages

Infancy and Childhood Development:
Cognitive Development

Table 8.3 Piaget's Stages of Cognitive Development

STAGE		COGNITIVE DEVELOPMENT
Sensorimotor	Birth to 2 years old	Children explore the world using their senses and ability to move. They develop object permanence and the understanding that concepts and mental images represent objects, people, and events.
Preoperational	2 to 7 years old	Young children can mentally represent and refer to objects and events with words or pictures and they can pretend. However, they can't conserve, logically reason, or simultaneously consider many characteristics of an object.
Concrete Operations	7 to 12 years old	Children at this stage are able to conserve, reverse their thinking, and classify objects in terms of their many characteristics. They can also think logically and understand analogies but only about concrete events.
Formal Operations	12 years old	People at this stage can use abstract reasoning about hypothetical events or situations, think about logical possibilities, use abstract analogies, and systematically examine and test hypotheses. Not everyone can eventually reason in all these ways.

- involves development of personality, relationships, and a sense of being male or female; process begins in infancy and continues into adulthood
  - **important early concepts**
    - infants demonstrate personality through their temperament (e.g., easy, difficult, slow to warm up), which can also affect and is affected by parenting and the environment
    - attachment (emotional bond between infant and a primary caregiver) is very important; different attachment styles have been identified by Ainsworth and others (e.g., secure, avoidant, ambivalent, disorganized-disoriented) that appear to be similar, but not identical, across different cultures
  - **Erikson's theory**
    - suggests development occurs in a series of eight stages (see Table 8.4)
    - at each stage an emotional crisis must be successfully met for normal development to occur
  - **gender role development**
    - most children begin to realize difference between sexes at about age two
    - knowing expectations for gender and development of gender identity takes much longer and is influenced by both biology and cultural expectations

Infancy and Childhood Development:
Psychosocial Development

Table 8.4   Erikson's Psychosocial Stages of Development

STAGE	DEVELOPMENTAL CRISIS	SUCCESSFUL DEALING WITH CRISIS	UNSUCCESSFUL DEALING WITH CRISIS
1. Infant Birth to 1 year old	**Trust Versus Mistrust** Babies learn to trust or mistrust others based on whether or not their needs—such as food and comfort—are met.	If babies' needs are met, they learn to trust people and expect life to be pleasant.	If babies' needs are not met, they learn not to trust.
2. Toddler 1 to 3 years old	**Autonomy Versus Shame and Doubt** Toddlers realize that they can direct their own behavior.	If toddlers are successful in directing their own behavior, they learn to be independent.	If toddlers' attempts at being independent are blocked, they learn self-doubt and shame for being unsuccessful.
3. Preschool Age 3 to 5 years old	**Initiative Versus Guilt** Preschoolers are challenged to control their own behavior, such as controlling their exuberance when they are in a restaurant.	If preschoolers succeed in taking responsibility, they feel capable and develop initiative.	If preschoolers fail in taking responsibility, they feel irresponsible, anxious, and guilty.
4. Elementary School Age 5 to 12 years old	**Industry Versus Inferiority** When children succeed in learning new skills and obtaining new knowledge, they develop a sense of industry, a feeling of competence arising from their work and effort.	When children succeed at learning new skills, they develop a sense of industry, a feeling of competence and self-esteem arising from their work and effort.	If children fail to develop new abilities, they feel incompetent, inadequate, and inferior.
5. Adolescence 13 to early twenties	**Identity Versus Role Confusion** Adolescents are faced with deciding who or what they want to be in terms of occupation, beliefs, attitudes, and behavior patterns.	Adolescents who succeed in defining who they are and finding a role for themselves develop a strong sense of identity.	Adolescents who fail to define their identity become confused and withdraw or want to inconspicuously blend in with the crowd.
6. Early Adulthood Twenties and thirties	**Intimacy Versus Isolation** The task facing those in early adulthood is to be able to share who they are with another person in a close, committed relationship.	People who succeed in this task will have satisfying intimate relationships.	Adults who fail at this task will be isolated from other people and may suffer from loneliness.
7. Middle Adulthood Forties and fifties	**Generativity Versus Stagnation** The challenge is to be creative, productive, and nurturant of the next generation.	Adults who succeed in this challenge will be creative, productive, and nurturant, thereby benefiting themselves, their family, community, country, and future generations.	Adults who fail will be passive, self-centered, feel that they have done nothing for the next generation, and feel that the world is no better off for their being alive.
8. Late Adulthood Sixties and beyond	**Ego Integrity Versus Despair** The issue is whether a person will reach wisdom, spiritual tranquility, a sense of wholeness, and acceptance of his or her life.	Elderly people who succeed in addressing this issue will enjoy life and not fear death.	Elderly people who fail will feel that their life is empty and will fear death.

- **physical development**
  - increase in height and changes in both primary and secondary sex characteristics
  - occurs as the result of glandular and hormonal activities
  - tends to occur about two years after beginning of growth spurt
- **cognitive development**
  - final maturation of the frontal lobes allows cognitive advances (e.g., abstract thought/Piaget's formal operations)
  - despite advances, still have egocentric thought that emerges in a variety of ways

Adolescence
(period of life from about age 13 to early 20s)

- **moral development**
  - understanding of what is "right" and "wrong"
  - early theory was proposed by Kohlberg; suggested three levels of moral development
  - other researchers (e.g., Gilligan) suggest that Kohlberg's ideas applied more to males; others suggest that assessment was based on hypothetical, rather than real-life, dilemmas
- **psychosocial development**
  - adolescence is largely marked by the search for a consistent sense of self or personal identity
  - Erikson: the psychosocial crisis that must be resolved is identity vs. role confusion
  - parent/teen conflict to be expected

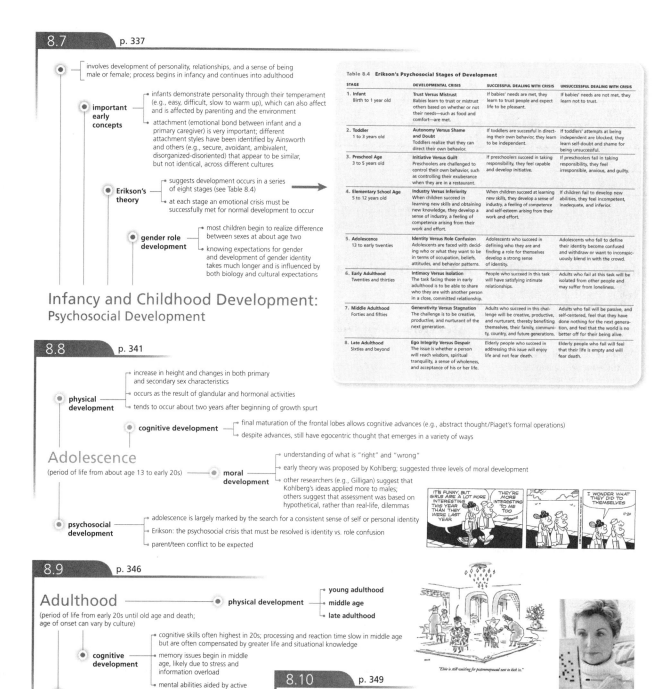

Comic panels: "IT'S FUNNY, BUT GIRLS ARE A LOT MORE INTERESTING THIS YEAR THAN THEY WERE LAST YEAR" / "THEY'RE MORE INTERESTING TO ME TOO" / "I WONDER WHAT THEY DID TO THEMSELVES" 11-20

Adulthood
(period of life from early 20s until old age and death; age of onset can vary by culture)

- **physical development**
  - young adulthood
  - middle age
  - late adulthood
- **cognitive development**
  - cognitive skills often highest in 20s; processing and reaction time slow in middle age but are often compensated by greater life and situational knowledge
  - memory issues begin in middle age, likely due to stress and information overload
  - mental abilities aided by active cognitive engagement (challenging crossword puzzles, reading, etc.) and physical activity
- **psychosocial development**
  - typical life concerns involve career, relationships, family, and approaching old age
  - Erikson's stage

"Elsie is still waiting for postmenopausal zest to kick in."

Adulthood: Aging

- **theories on aging**
  vary focus from biological changes to influence on external stressors
  - cellular clock theory
  - wear-and-tear theory
- **activity theory**
  - positive psychological adjustment associated with continued activity and involvement
- **stages of death and dying**
  (based on work of Kübler-Ross)
  - denial
  - anger
  - bargaining
  - depression
  - acceptance

_____

_____

_____

_____

_____

_____

_____

_____

_____

_____

Table 8.1 **A Comparison of Three Developmental Research Designs**

Table 8.1 A Comparison of Three Developmental Research Designs		
CROSS-SECTIONAL DESIGN **Different** participants of various ages are compared at one point in time to determine age-related *differences*.	**Group One:** 20-year-old participants **Group Two:** 40-year-old participants **Group Three:** 60-year-old participants	Research done in 2005
LONGITUDINAL DESIGN The **same** participants are studied at various ages to determine age-related *changes*.	**Study One:** 20-year-old participants	Research done in 1965
	Study Two: Same participants are now 40 years old	Research done in 1985
	Study Three: Same participants are now 60 years old	Research done in 2005
CROSS-SEQUENTIAL DESIGN **Different** participants of various ages are compared at several points in time, for a period of no more than six years to determine both age-related *differences* and age-related *changes*.	**Study One:** Group One: 20-year-old participants Group Two: 40-year-old participants	Research done in 1965
	Study Two: Group One: participants are now 25 Group Two: participants are now 45	Research done in 1970

_____

_____

_____

_____

_____

_____

_____

_____

_____

_____

_____
_____
_____
_____
_____
_____
_____
_____
_____
_____
_____

Figure 8.1 **DNA Molecule**

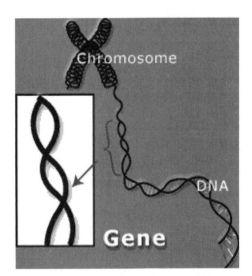

_____
_____
_____
_____
_____
_____
_____
_____
_____
_____
_____
_____
_____
_____
_____
_____
_____
_____
_____
_____
_____
_____

Figure 8.2 **Dominant and Recessive Ganaes and PKU**

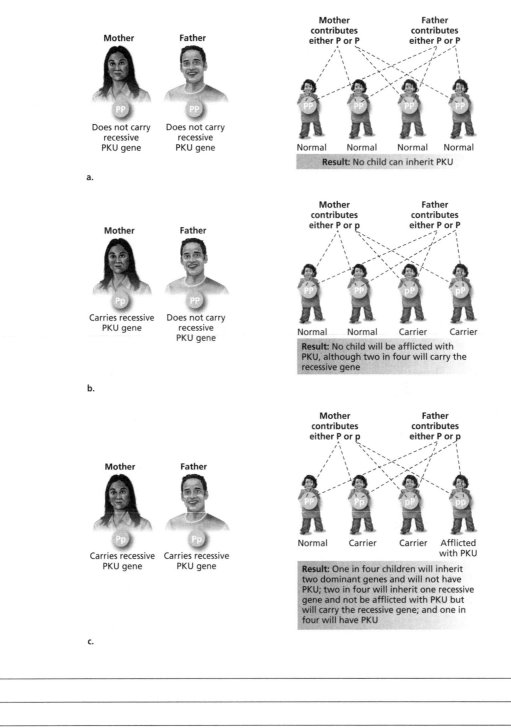

a.

Mother — Does not carry recessive PKU gene (PP)
Father — Does not carry recessive PKU gene (PP)

Mother contributes either P or P
Father contributes either P or P

Normal (PP) — Normal (PP) — Normal (PP) — Normal (PP)

Result: No child can inherit PKU

b.

Mother — Carries recessive PKU gene (Pp)
Father — Does not carry recessive PKU gene (PP)

Mother contributes either P or p
Father contributes either P or P

Normal (PP) — Normal (PP) — Carrier (pP) — Carrier (pP)

Result: No child will be afflicted with PKU, although two in four will carry the recessive gene

c.

Mother — Carries recessive PKU gene (Pp)
Father — Carries recessive PKU gene (Pp)

Mother contributes either P or p
Father contributes either P or p

Normal (PP) — Carrier (Pp) — Carrier (pP) — Afflicted with PKU (pp)

Result: One in four children will inherit two dominant genes and will not have PKU; two in four will inherit one recessive gene and not be afflicted with PKU but will carry the recessive gene; and one in four will have PKU

_____
_____
_____
_____
_____
_____
_____
_____
_____

Figure 8.3 **Monozygotic and Dizygotic Twins**

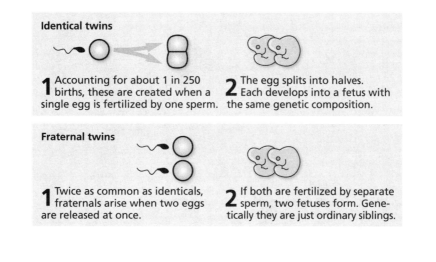

Identical twins

1 Accounting for about 1 in 250 births, these are created when a single egg is fertilized by one sperm.

2 The egg splits into halves. Each develops into a fetus with the same genetic composition.

Fraternal twins

1 Twice as common as identicals, fraternals arise when two eggs are released at once.

2 If both are fertilized by separate sperm, two fetuses form. Genetically they are just ordinary siblings.

_____
_____
_____
_____
_____
_____
_____
_____
_____
_____
_____
_____

Table 8.2 **Common Teratogens**

Table 8.2 **Common Teratogens**	
TERATOGENIC AGENT	**EFFECT ON DEVELOPMENT**
Rubella	Blindness, deafness, heart defects, brain damage
Marijuana	Irritability, nervousness, tremors; infant is easily disturbed, startled
Cocaine	Decreased height, low birth weight, respiratory problems, seizures, learning difficulties; infant is difficult to soothe
Alcohol	Fetal alcohol syndrome (mental retardation, delayed growth, facial malformation), learning difficulties, smaller than normal heads
Nicotine	Miscarriage, low birth weight, stillbirth, short stature, mental retardation, learning disabilities
Mercury	Mental retardation, blindness
Syphilis	Mental retardation, deafness, meningitis
Caffeine	Miscarriage, low birth weight
Radiation	Higher incidence of cancers, physical deformities
High Water Temperatures	Increased chance of neural tube defects

_____
_____
_____
_____
_____
_____
_____
_____
_____
_____
_____

8.5　Infancy and Childhood Physical Development

_____
_____
_____
_____
_____
_____
_____
_____
_____
_____
_____

Figure 8.4 **Five Infant Reflexes**

a.   b.   c.

d.   e.

_____
_____
_____
_____
_____
_____
_____
_____
_____
_____
_____
_____
_____
_____
_____
_____
_____
_____
_____
_____
_____

Figure 8.5 **Six Motor Milestones**

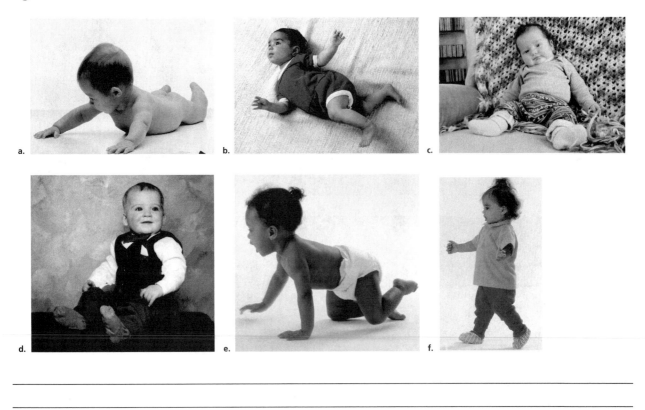

a.   b.   c.

d.   e.   f.

_____
_____
_____
_____
_____
_____
_____
_____
_____
_____

8.6 **Infancy and Childhood Cognitive Development**

_____
_____
_____
_____
_____
_____
_____
_____
_____
_____

Table 8.3 **Piaget's Stages of Cognitive Development**

Table 8.3 Piaget's Stages of Cognitive Development

STAGE		COGNITIVE DEVELOPMENT
Sensorimotor	Birth to 2 years old	Children explore the world using their senses and ability to move. They develop object permanence and the understanding that concepts and mental images represent objects, people, and events.
Preoperational	2 to 7 years old	Young children can mentally represent and refer to objects and events with words or pictures and they can pretend. However, they can't conserve, logically reason, or simultaneously consider many characteristics of an object.
Concrete Operations	7 to 12 years old	Children at this stage are able to conserve, reverse their thinking, and classify objects in terms of their many characteristics. They can also think logically and understand analogies but only about concrete events.
Formal Operations	12 years old to adulthood	People at this stage can use abstract reasoning about hypothetical events or situations, think about logical possibilities, use abstract analogies, and systematically examine and test hypotheses. Not everyone can eventually reason in all these ways.

Figure 8.6 **Conservation Experiment**

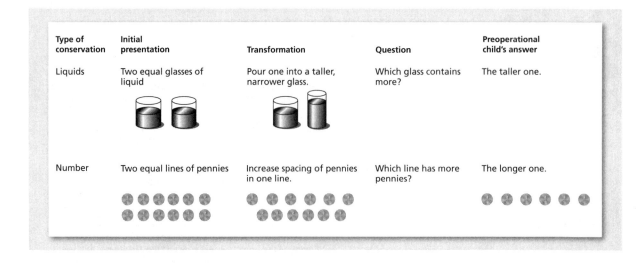

Type of conservation	Initial presentation	Transformation	Question	Preoperational child's answer
Liquids	Two equal glasses of liquid	Pour one into a taller, narrower glass.	Which glass contains more?	The taller one.
Number	Two equal lines of pennies	Increase spacing of pennies in one line.	Which line has more pennies?	The longer one.

8.7 Infancy and Childhood Psychosocial Development

Table 8.4 Erikson's Psychosocial Stages of Development

Table 8.4 Erikson's Psychosocial Stages of Development

STAGE	DEVELOPMENTAL CRISIS	SUCCESSFUL DEALING WITH CRISIS	UNSUCCESSFUL DEALING WITH CRISIS
1. **Infant** Birth to 1 year old	**Trust Versus Mistrust** Babies learn to trust or mistrust others based on whether or not their needs—such as food and comfort—are met.	If babies' needs are met, they learn to trust people and expect life to be pleasant.	If babies' needs are not met, they learn not to trust.
2. **Toddler** 1 to 3 years old	**Autonomy Versus Shame and Doubt** Toddlers realize that they can direct their own behavior.	If toddlers are successful in directing their own behavior, they learn to be independent.	If toddlers' attempts at being independent are blocked, they learn self-doubt and shame for being unsuccessful.
3. **Preschool Age** 3 to 5 years old	**Initiative Versus Guilt** Preschoolers are challenged to control their own behavior, such as controlling their exuberance when they are in a restaurant.	If preschoolers succeed in taking responsibility, they feel capable and develop initiative.	If preschoolers fail in taking responsibility, they feel irresponsible, anxious, and guilty.
4. **Elementary School Age** 5 to 12 years old	**Industry Versus Inferiority** When children succeed in learning new skills and obtaining new knowledge, they develop a sense of industry, a feeling of competence arising from their work and effort.	When children succeed at learning new skills, they develop a sense of industry, a feeling of competence and self-esteem arising from their work and effort.	If children fail to develop new abilities, they feel incompetent, inadequate, and inferior.
5. **Adolescence** 13 to early twenties	**Identity Versus Role Confusion** Adolescents are faced with deciding who or what they want to be in terms of occupation, beliefs, attitudes, and behavior patterns.	Adolescents who succeed in defining who they are and finding a role for themselves develop a strong sense of identity.	Adolescents who fail to define their identity become confused and withdraw or want to inconspicuously blend in with the crowd.
6. **Early Adulthood** Twenties and thirties	**Intimacy Versus Isolation** The task facing those in early adulthood is to be able to share who they are with another person in a close, committed relationship.	People who succeed in this task will have satisfying intimate relationships.	Adults who fail at this task will be isolated from other people and may suffer from loneliness.
7. **Middle Adulthood** Forties and fifties	**Generativity Versus Stagnation** The challenge is to be creative, productive, and nurturant of the next generation.	Adults who succeed in this challenge will be creative, productive, and nurturant, thereby benefiting themselves, their family, community, country, and future generations.	Adults who fail will be passive, and self-centered, feel that they have done nothing for the next generation, and feel that the world is no better off for their being alive.
8. **Late Adulthood** Sixties and beyond	**Ego Integrity Versus Despair** The issue is whether a person will reach wisdom, spiritual tranquility, a sense of wholeness, and acceptance of his or her life.	Elderly people who succeed in addressing this issue will enjoy life and not fear death.	Elderly people who fail will feel that their life is empty and will fear death.

_____
_____
_____
_____
_____
_____

_____

_____

_____

_____

_____

_____

_____

_____

_____

_____

_____

Table 8.5 **Kohlberg's Three Levels of Morality**

Table 8.5   **Kohlberg's Three Levels of Morality**

LEVEL OF MORALITY	HOW RULES ARE UNDERSTOOD	EXAMPLE
Preconventional morality (typically very young children)	The consequences determine morality; behavior that is rewarded is right; that which is punished is wrong.	A child who steals a toy from another child and does not get caught does not see that action as wrong.
Conventional* morality (older children, adolescents, and most adults)	Conformity to social norms is right; nonconformity is wrong.	A child criticizes his or her parent for speeding because speeding is against the stated laws.
Postconventional morality (about 20 percent of the adult population)	Moral principles determined by the person are used to determine right and wrong and may disagree with societal norms.	A reporter who wrote a controversial story goes to jail rather than reveal the source's identity.

*The term *conventional* refers to general standards or norms of behavior for a particular society, which will differ from one social group or culture to another.

_____

_____

_____

_____

_____

_____

_____

_____

_____

_____

_____

_____

_____

_____
_____
_____
_____
_____
_____
_____
_____
_____
_____
_____

Table 8.6 **Erikson's Psychosocial Adolescent and Adult Stages**

Table 8.6   Erikson's Psychosocial Adolescent and Adult Stages

STAGE	DEVELOPMENTAL CRISIS	SUCCESSFUL DEALING WITH CRISIS	UNSUCCESSFUL DEALING WITH CRISIS
5. Adolescence 13 to early twenties	**Identity Versus Role Confusion** Adolescents are faced with deciding who or what they want to be in terms of occupation, beliefs, attitudes, and behavior patterns.	Adolescents who succeed in defining who they are and find a role for themselves develop a strong sense of identity.	Adolescents who fail to define their identity become confused and withdraw or want to inconspicuously blend in with the crowd.
6. Early Adulthood Twenties and thirties	**Intimacy Versus Isolation** The task facing those in early adulthood is to be able to share who they are with another person in a close, committed relationship.	People who succeed in this task will have satisfying intimate relationships.	Adults who fail at this task will be isolated from other people and may suffer from loneliness.
7. Middle Adulthood Forties and fifties	**Generativity Versus Stagnation** The challenge is to be creative, productive, and nurturant of the next generation.	Adults who succeed in this challenge will be creative, productive, and nurturant, thereby benefiting themselves, their family, community, country, and future generations.	Adults who fail will be passive, and self-centered, feel that they have done nothing for the next generation, and feel that the world is no better off for their being alive.
8. Late Adulthood Sixties and beyond	**Ego Integrity Versus Despair** The issue is whether a person will reach wisdom, spiritual tranquility, a sense of wholeness, and acceptance of his or her life.	Elderly people who succeed in addressing this issue will enjoy life and not fear death.	Elderly people who fail will feel that their life is empty and will fear death.

Source: Erikson, 1950/1963, 1968.

_____
_____
_____
_____
_____
_____
_____

8.10 Aging

8.11 ADHD

NOTES

YOU KNOW YOU ARE READY FOR THE TEST IF YOU ARE ABLE TO...

- Introduce the concept of motivation and discuss the major theories proposed to explain motivated behavior.
- Discuss the specific motivation of hunger and examine the physiological and social components in addition to common eating disorders.
- Describe the three elements of emotion and present six theories on how emotions are processed.
- Explain what the positive psychology movement is.

RAPID REVIEW

Motivation is the process by which activities are started, directed, and continued so that physical or psychological needs or wants are met. When motivation comes from outside the self it is called **extrinsic motivation**, on the other hand, if a person does something because it is satisfying in some internal manner, the motivation is called **intrinsic motivation**. Several theories have been proposed to explain the process of motivation including the theories of instinct, drive-reduction, needs, arousal, incentive, humanistic, and self-determination. **Instinct approach** suggests that people are motivated by biologically determined internal forces. Unfortunately, instinct theory only describes behavior and is unable to explain why people did what they did. The **drive-reduction approach** proposes that a **need**, or requirement, produces a **drive** and that people act in order to reduce these drives. The drives can be **primary drives** such as hunger and thirst or **acquired (secondary) drives** such as the need for money. The rationale for drive-reduction includes the idea that the body has a tendency to try to maintain a steady state referred to as **homeostasis**. When the body is out of balance, a need develops and the tension provides the drive to reduce the need and return the body to a state of balance. Drive-reduction theory, however, cannot explain why people would increase their internal tension by doing things like parachuting out of an airplane. **Need theory** attempts to explain motivation by understanding three specific needs, the **need for achievement (nAch), need for affiliation (nAff)**, and **need for power (nPow)**. **Arousal theory** suggests that people are motivated to maintain an optimal level of arousal or tension. The level of arousal is achieved by increasing or decreasing stimulation and is driven by a proposed **stimulus motive**. The **Yerkes-Dodson law** demonstrates that for an easy task, performance is best when arousal is a little higher than average, whereas for a difficult task, performance is best when arousal is a little below average. Individuals who consistently seek out high levels of arousal have been labeled as **sensation seekers**. According to **incentive approaches** of motivation, peoples actions are determined by the rewards or **incentives** for their behaviors. **Expectancy-value theories** are a subset of incentive theories that assume a person's expectancies, or beliefs about what will happen in the future, need to be taken into account in order to understand his or her motivation.

Abraham Maslow was a major proponent of the humanistic approach to motivation and proposed a hierarchy of needs that individuals must fulfill before they can reach the highest need of **self-actualization** where a person reaches his or her fullest potential. According to Maslow, basic needs such as hunger and thirst must be satisfied before the higher level needs can be achieved. Also, Maslow referred to the times in which self-actualization is attained as **peak experiences**. Another theory of motivation similar to Maslow's is the **self-determination theory** that proposes that there are three inborn and universal needs that humans work to satisfy. These needs are the need for autonomy, competence, and relatedness.

One specific area of motivation that has been studied extensively is the motivation to eat, also known as hunger. The hunger drive can be divided into physiological and social components. Physiologically, **insulin** and **glucagons** are hormones that regulate the level of glucose in the bloodstream. Insulin increases blood sugar levels which leads to feelings of hunger. Several areas in the hypothalamus also play an important role in regulating eating behavior, perhaps by influencing the specific weight that our bodies try to maintain, or our **weight set point**. Another factor that influences the weight set point is the **basal metabolic rate**, which decreases as we age, causing a corresponding increase in the weight set point. The social factors that influence hunger include the times of day when a person typically eats, using food to reduce stress or provide comfort, and the appeal of a tempting dessert item. Some problems associated with eating behaviors are **obesity**, in which a person weighs 20 percent over his or her ideal weight; **anorexia nervosa**, in which a person weighs 15 percent less than his or her ideal weight; and **bulimia**, in which a person develops a cycle of overeating, followed by deliberate vomiting. A hormone called **leptin** may play a role in controlling how hungry an individual feels.

Emotions can be defined as the "feeling" aspect of consciousness, characterized by a certain physical arousal, a certain behavior, and an inner awareness of feelings. As can be seen in the definition, emotions can be divided into three components: physiology, behaviors, and subjective experience. Different emotions have been found to be associated with different physiological reactions. The amygdala has been found to play a role in the regulation of emotions in humans as well as other animals. The behaviors of emotions include facial expressions, body movements, and other actions. Research has supported the idea that at least seven basic facial expressions are recognized and mimicked in cultures around the world. However, the **display rules**, or exactly when, where, and how these emotions can be expressed, appears to differ across cultures. The subjective experience of emotions involves the cognitive process of assigning a label, such as happy, to your feelings. Several theories have been developed in an attempt to explain the process humans use to label our emotions. **Common sense theory** suggests that a stimulus causes a particular emotion to occur which then leads to the behavioral and physiological response. The **James-Lange theory** of emotion proposes that a stimulus leads to a particular physiological response which then leads to the subjective experience of an emotion. The **Cannon-Bard theory** suggests that the physical and subjective experience of emotions occur at the same time. A stimulus leads to activation of the thalamus which then simultaneously activates the sympathetic nervous system and higher cortical areas which interpret the signal as a particular emotion. Schachter and Singer proposed the **cognitive arousal theory** which proposes that after a stimulus occurs our body has a physical reaction and we make a cognitive appraisal of the situation. Based on feedback from both these sources, we then come up with a subjective label for the emotion we are experiencing. The **facial feedback hypothesis** assumes that facial expressions provide feedback to the brain regarding the emotion being expressed and can then intensify or even cause the emotion. Lazarus's **cognitive-mediational theory** of emotion suggests that following a stimulus, we engage in a cognitive appraisal of the situation which then triggers a subjective experience of an emotion followed by a physiological response.

The **positive psychology movement** is a new perspective in psychology that recommends shifting the focus of psychology away from the negative and more towards the positive. In his book *The Pursuit of Happiness*, David G.Myers, a major proponent of positive psychology, suggests a number of ways to try to increase your emotional response of happiness. Some of the suggestions include acting happy, getting enough sleep, and exercising.

STUDY HINTS

1. By far, the most confusing concept of this chapter is keeping track of the theories of emotion. The following hints are designed to help you work through this process. To start with, try filling in the following table correctly. Remember when we are discussing emotions there are several components we are interested in. The theories vary according to which component comes first. The components are
    *   physiological experience of emotion (increased heart rate, sweating, etc.)
    *   subjective experience of emotion (the "feeling" of happiness, sadness, or anger)
    *   cognitive appraisal (using your thought process to assess the situation)
    *   subcortical brain activity (not considered cognitive types of action)

    Using these key components, fill in the following table. The first row has already been filled in for you.

Theory	Event	1st response	2nd response	3rd response
Common Sense	*stimulus (dog barking)*	*subjective experience (fear)*	*physiological experience (increased heart rate)*	
James-Lange Theory				
Cannon-Bard Theory				
Schachter-Singer Theory				
Facial Feedback Hypothesis				
Cognitive-mediational Theory				

2. Now look over the chart you just completed. Which of the theories are similar and which are different? Can you come up with a way to group the theories together based on similarity?

As you learned in the chapter on memory, processing the information in this manner will help you better retain the material and make retrieval for the exam an easier process. Try grouping the theories into the following three categories:

Category 1: Physiological experience occurs after you "feel" the emotion

_____

_____

Category 2: "Feeling" the emotion occurs after the physiological changes

_____

_____

_____

Category 3: "Feeling" the emotion and the physiological changes occur at the same time

_____

Suggested answers for Question 1

Theory	Event	1st response	2nd response	3rd response
Common Sense	*stimulus (dog barking)*	*subjective experience (fear)*	*physiological experience (increased heart rate)*	
James-Lange Theory	*stimulus (dog barking)*	*physiological (increased heart rate)*	*subjective (fear)*	
Cannon-Bard Theory	*stimulus (dog barking)*	*subcortical brain activity*	*physiological and subjective at the same time*	
Schachter-Singer Theory	*stimulus (dog barking)*	*physiological response (increased heart rate)*	*cognitive appraisal (there is a scary-looking dog barking at me)*	*subjective experience (fear)*
Facial Feedback Hypothesis	*stimulus (dog barking)*	*facial expression of fear*	*subcortical brain activity*	*subjective experience (fear)*
Cognitive-mediational Theory	*stimulus (dog barking)*	*cognitive appraisal (there is a scary-looking dog barking at me)*	*subjective experience (fear)*	*physiological experience (increased heart rate)*

Suggested answers for Question 2
Category 1: Physiological experience occurs after you "feel" the emotion

_____*common sense theory*_____

_____*cognitive-mediational theory*_____

Category 2: "Feeling" the emotion occurs after the physiological changes

_____ _James-Lange theory_____

_____ _Schachter-Singer theory of cognitive arousal_____

_____ _facial feedback hypothesis_____

Category 3: "Feeling" the emotion and the physiological changes occur at the same time

_____ _Cannon-Bard theory_____

LEARNING OBJECTIVES

9.1 How do psychologists define motivation, and what are the key elements of the early instinct and drive-reduction approaches to motivation?

9.2 What are the characteristics of the three types of needs?

9.3 What are the key elements of the arousal and incentive approaches to motivation?

9.4 How do Maslow's humanistic approach and self-determination theory explain motivation?

9.5 *What happens in the body to cause hunger, and how do social factors influence a person's experience of hunger?*

9.6 What are some problems in eating behavior, and how are they affected by biology and culture?

9.7 What are the three elements of emotion?

9.8 How do the James-Lange and Cannon-Bard theories of emotion differ?

9.9 What are the key elements in cognitive arousal theory, the facial-feedback hypothesis, and the cognitive-mediational theory of emotion?

9.10 What is the positive psychology movement?

PRACTICE EXAM

For the following multiple choice questions, select the answer you feel best answers the question.

1. The process by which activities are started, directed, and continued so that physical or psychological needs or wants are met is called
    a) motivation.
    b) emotion.
    c) achievement.
    d) synergy.

2. Which statement about motivation is **true**?
    a) A motive energizes and directs behavior.
    b) We are always aware of motivational processes.
    c) Different motives always lead to different behaviors.
    d) Two people motivated by the same factor will satisfy that motive through similar means.

3. In the early 20th century, psychologists were inclined to explain motivated behavior by attributing it to _____.
    a) emotions
    b) incentives
    c) learned responses
    d) instincts

4. William McDougal proposed ____ instincts for humans early in the 20th century.
    a) 5
    b) 9
    c) 18
    d) 24

5. Each of the following is a valid criticism of instinct theories of motivation EXCEPT _____.
    a) human behavior is rarely rigid, inflexible, and found throughout the species
    b) instinct theories name behaviors without pinpointing their origins
    c) they were the dominant explanation for human behavior early in the 20th century
    d) description is more important than explanation.

6. Salmon swimming upstream to spawn are an example of _____.
    a) incentives
    b) motives
    c) instinct
    d) needs

7. Drives serve to activate responses that are aimed at reducing the drive, thereby returning the body to a more normal state called
    a) stability.
    b) equilibrium.
    c) homeostasis.
    d) physiological balance.

8. Some psychologists believe that behavior is motivated by the body's attempts to achieve a state of balance in which the body functions effectively, or in _____.
    a) reciprocity
    b) acquiescence
    c) propinquity
    d) homeostasis

9. Primary drives are _____.
    a) exceptions to the drive-reduction principle
    b) learned
    c) influenced by stimuli within the body
    d) influenced by stimuli outside the body

10. Monica put all her time and energy into getting into the acting club because her main goal in life "was to be a famous star!" Monica's drive to be famous was a(n) _____ drive.
    a) primary
    b) reflexive
    c) tertiary
    d) secondary

11. Homeostasis is like a
    a) scale.
    b) thermostat.
    c) carburetor.
    d) bicycle.

12. Your text discusses all of the following needs EXCEPT
    a) achievement.
    b) affiliation.
    c) power.
    d) sex.

13. Which of the following is correct for people high in need achievement?
    a) They look for careers which make a lot of money.
    b) They look for careers and hobbies that allow others to evaluate them.
    c) They look for careers which require little education.
    d) They look for careers which will make them famous.

14. According to Carol Dweek, need achievement is closely related to
    a) genetics.
    b) geography.
    c) luck.
    d) personal factors.

15. In arousal theory, people are said to have a(n) _____ level of tension.
    a) ultimate
    b) lower
    c) optimal
    d) high

16. Indiana Jones goes off to foreign lands in search of artifacts hidden in dangerous places and guarded by fierce protectors. Dr. Jones would be described as _____ in arousal theory.
    a) a sensation seeker
    b) nAff
    c) fool-hardy
    d) high nPow

17. As a class assignment you are required to collect advertising slogans and describe how they may be relevant to concepts in psychology. You select the Jell-O slogan, "There's always room for Jell-O," and describe in class that it is relevant to one of the theories of motivation. Which theory?
    a) instinctive
    b) incentive
    c) drive-reduction
    d) optimum-level

18. One interesting thing about incentive approaches is that incentives
    a) exist inside a narrow collection of internal stimuli.
    b) exist independently of any need or level of arousal.
    c) exist inside a narrow collection of internal stimuli.
    d) only work for adults.

19. Jill is motivated by money and the things money will bring her. Jack is motivated by doing good things, and his incentives are based on that idea and belief. What theory incorporates both these types of motivational causes?
    a) sensation seeking theory
    b) entity theory
    c) increment theory
    d) expectancy-value theory

20. According to Abraham Maslow, developing one's full potential to its fullest extent results in
    a) safety.
    b) self-esteem.
    c) belongingness.
    d) self-actualization.

21. Which of the following does NOT show the motivating power of self-actualization?
    a) Joan wants to live in a house with all the modern conveniences so that she may have more time to seek fulfillment from her career and family.
    b) Frank feels that he is a good salesman because he likes what he does and knows how to do it well.
    c) Barbara knows that, as a teacher, she is a good person because she realizes the importance of imparting knowledge to society.
    d) Mark works hard as an attorney only so that he can attract more clients, more money, and be secure in the knowledge that his family can survive.

22. Self-determination theory (SDT) best fits which type of motivation?
    a) the need for affiliation
    b) intrinsic motivation
    c) extrinsic motivation
    d) a mastery goal

23. Intrinsic motivation is defined as
    a) the pursuit of an activity for external rewards.
    b) the pursuit of an activity for its own sake.
    c) the pursuit of an activity to relieve the state of tension caused by deprivation.
    d) the pursuit of an activity in order to be judged favorably by others.

24. One factor in hunger seems to be the increase in _____ that occurs after we begin to eat.
    a) cholesterol
    b) lipoproteins
    c) insulin
    d) glucose

25. The ventromedial hypothalamus (VMH) may be involved in
    a) increasing hunger.
    b) decreasing hunger.
    c) processing low fats.
    d) food allergies.

26. The lateral hypothalamus (LH) may be involved in
    a) stoppage of eating.
    b) the onset of eating.
    c) processing low fats.
    d) food allergies.

27. Anna Nicole weighed about 125 lbs most of her adult life. However, it seemed like whenever Anna Nicole gained weight it was easy to lose and get back to 125. But when she wanted to go below 125 it took forever and even the slightest deviation from her diet got her back to 125. What explanation would you give Anna Nicole?
    a) Use better diet products.
    b) Start a reality TV show.

c) Her weight, 125, is her set point. Leave it alone.
d) Her BMR is causing all the problems.

28. The concept of "comfort food" suggests that food
    a) may be influenced by social factors.
    b) has genetic ways to comfort.
    c) may release hormones and neurotransmitters that are comforting.
    d) is reflexive.

29. Which component of hunger is most likely contributing to the fact that sometimes a person who has just had a late breakfast will still feel hungry at noon?
    a) social
    b) behavioral
    c) physiological
    d) intrinsic

30. Obesity is defined as someone who is at least ___ percent or more over the ideal body weight.
    a) 10
    b) 20
    c) 30
    d) 40

31. Which individual has the highest risk for developing anorexia nervosa?
    a) lower-class 26-year-old European man
    b) an upper-class 16-year-old American boy
    c) a lower-class 26-year-old European woman
    d) an upper-class 16-year-old American girl

32. An eating disorder characterized by binges of eating followed by self-induced vomiting is called _____.
    a) anorexia nervosa
    b) bulimia
    c) Karposi's anemia
    d) Huntington's chorea

33. All of the following statements are correct about bulimia EXCEPT
    a) individuals with bulimia have a distorted view of how much food is too much food.
    b) bulimia is not as damaging as anorexia nervosa.
    c) binge eating and vomiting are common symptoms.
    d) individuals with bulimia have a distorted body image.

34. You are a hormone. You are secreted into the bloodstream by fatty tissue and your job is to signal the hypothalamus that the body has enough food, reducing appetite and increasing the feeling of being full. Who are you?
    a) adrenalin
    b) peptic acid
    c) leptin
    d) lippotor

35. What Latin word connects both motive and emotion?
    a) emote
    b) move

c)   mote
d)   mate

36. Paul Ekman and his colleagues gathered abundant evidence supporting the universality of _____ basic facial expressions of emotion.
     a)   three
     b)   five
     c)   seven
     d)   nine

37. According to Ekman, which of the following is NOT one of the universal facial expressions?
     a)   disgust
     b)   fear
     c)   contempt
     d)   shame

38. To explain the human universality and variability of emotions, Ekman and his associates
     a)   developed a concept of "display rules," which are rules for emotional expression.
     b)   developed an inter-observer system to make sure that observers defined expressions reliably.
     c)   interviewed all participants in order to assess unexpressed feelings and motivations.
     d)   monitored the brain waves of participants to determine which hemisphere had higher activation.

39. Which one of the following is NOT one of the three elements of emotion discussed in the text?
     a)   physiology
     b)   labeling
     c)   behavior
     d)   environment

40. Which theory states that a stimulus triggers physiological changes that produce emotion?
     a)   Cannon-Bard theory
     b)   James-Lange theory
     c)   Schachter-Singer theory
     d)   commonsense view of emotions

41. Which statement is most consistent with the James-Lange theory of emotion?
     a)   "I run because I'm afraid."
     b)   "I'm laughing because I am happy."
     c)   "I'm crying because I'm sad."
     d)   "I'm anxious because I perspire."

42. What is the correct sequence of events in emotional response according to the Cannon-Bard theory?
     a)   stimulus --> emotion --> physiological changes
     b)   stimulus --> physiological changes --> emotion
     c)   physiological changes --> stimulus --> emotion
     d)   stimulus --> emotion AND physiological changes (simultaneous)

43. "I think I'm afraid, therefore I am afraid" is a statement that is most consistent with which of the following theories?
     a)   the James-Lange theory
     b)   activation theory

c)	cognitive arousal theory
d)	the Cannon-Bard theory

44.	You just finished a cup of very strong coffee which causes your body to have a general feeling of arousal. That afternoon you attend the funeral of a friend. According to Schachter and Singer, which of the following would most likely occur?
a)	Your emotion would be happy in spite of the funeral because of the arousal.
b)	You would work very hard to control your emotion.
c)	Your emotion would be sad since the context would affect your labeling.
d)	Your emotional state would be impossible to predict.

45.	According to the theory of emotion proposed by Schachter and Singer, what is the most important determinant of your subjective experience of emotion?
a)	physiological reactions
b)	cognitive appraisal of the situation
c)	facial expressions
d)	intensity of the stimulus

46.	In the classic study of emotion conducted by Schachter and Singer, after receiving the epinephrine, the subjects placed in the room with the angry man reported feeling
a)	angry.
b)	happy.
c)	both angry and happy.
d)	No emotions were reported.

47.	Which recent study below casts doubt on the facial feedback hypothesis?
a)	a woman with a paralyzed face still responded emotionally to slides meant to stimulate emotions
b)	a blind woman still responded emotionally to slides meant to stimulate emotions
c)	a woman paralyzed from the waist down still responded emotionally to slides meant to stimulate emotions
d)	a woman with Down syndrome still responded emotionally to slides meant to stimulate emotions

48.	According to the facial feedback hypothesis, if you would like to make yourself feel more happy you should
a)	spend time with friends.
b)	talk to a counselor.
c)	think about all the positive aspects of your life.
d)	smile.

49.	"I see a dog but it is behind a fence and I don't have anything to worry about so I feel calm" is a statement that is most consistent with which of the following theories?
a)	James-Lange theory
b)	Cannon-Bard theory
c)	Schachter-Singer theory
d)	cognitive-mediational theory

50.	According to the cognitive-mediational theory, which factor would be most important in determining whether you feel nervous when asked to speak in front of the class?
a)	your physiological reaction to the request
b)	activation of subcortical brain activity

c)   your cognitive appraisal of the situation
d)   your change in blood pressure

51. Positive psychology is best defined as
     a)   psychology which only focuses on positive test results (that is, those tests that actually show a difference between two groups).
     b)   a movement in psychology which emphasizes the positive aspects of the human experience as opposed to the negative.
     c)   a movement in psychology that attempts to incorporate simple mathematical functions as a means of understanding human behavior.
     d)   an area in psychology that promotes a theory for treating depressed patients in which the patient is encouraged to think positively.

52. Which of the following is NOT a suggestion given by David Myers in his book *The Pursuit of Happiness*?
     a)   Spend time alone.
     b)   Take control of your time.
     c)   Nurture your spiritual self.
     d)   Keep a gratitude journal.

PRACTICE EXAM ANSWERS

1.	a	This is the definition in the text. If you answered b, then you are confusing emotion with motivation.
2.	a	This is simply the definition of motive.
3.	d	Instinct theory was one of the first proposed theories of motivation in psychology. Be careful not to confuse incentive with instincts!
4.	c	McDougal proposed a total of 18 basic instincts.
5.	c	This is not a criticism but simply a statement. For d, the criticism was that description is LESS important than explanation.
6.	c	Instincts are innate biologically determined behaviors.
7.	c	Homeostasis is the term psychologists and physiologists use to refer to the body's state of balance. Equilibrium means the same thing but is not the term used by psychologists.
8.	c	Homeostasis is a sense of balance.
9.	c	These internal stimuli would include things such as hunger or thirst.
10.	c	Secondary drives are drives that we acquire through learning. The drive to be famous is learned.
11.	b	A is not correct because a scale only has one direction.
12.	d	The three needs discussed with regard to motivation were the needs for achievement, affiliation, and power.
13.	b	High achievers need feedback from others.
14.	d	There was no mention of genetics in her theory, but there was considerable discussion about an individual's sense of self and views on intelligence.
15.	c	Arousal theory argues that arousal should be neither too high nor too low.
16.	a	His actions indicate that he needs a higher level of arousal than most people.
17.	b	Incentive theory suggests that we often eat food items because of their reward value and not simply because we are hungry.
18.	b	Incentives motivate behavior whether or not we have a specific need and regardless of our arousal level.
19.	d	Expectancy value theory states that the values of a person determine his or her motivation levels.

20. d   Self-actualization is at the top of Maslow's hierarchy of needs.

21. d   This is the only situation in which the person is focusing on basic needs for himself and his family. In all the other examples, the individuals were focused on growth needs.

22. b   Self-determination theory is characterized by intrinsic motivations.

23. b   All the other motivations are based on external factors. Intrinsic motivation deals with forces within the individual.

24. c   Insulin is associated with feelings of hunger and is related to blood sugar levels.

25. b   When the ventromedial hypothalamus was removed in experimental animals, the animals no longer controlled their eating and became extremely obese.

26. b   When the lateral hypothalamus was removed in experimental animals, the animals stopped eating and had to be force-fed food.

27. c   The set point is the level of weight the body tends to maintain.

28. a   Social factors in hunger include the social cues associated with food.

29. a   Social factors can have a strong impact on feelings of hunger.

30. b   This percentage was discussed in your textbook and arrived at by health professionals.

31. d   According to government statistics, white upper-class females in the U.S. show the highest prevalence rates for anorexia.

32. b   This is the definition given in the textbook. Note that the vomiting distinguishes bulimia from anorexia.

33. b   Although the damage from bulimia is different than that from anorexia, it is still a very dangerous disorder.

34. c   Leptin appears to be the hormone that causes you to feel full.

35. b   This is the definition given in your textbook.

36. c   The research found seven facial expressions that appear to be universal.

37. d   Shame was not found in all cultures. The seven facial expressions he did find were anger, fear, disgust, happiness, surprise, sadness, and contempt.

38. a   Ekman found that display rules tend to vary across cultures, whereas the recognition of basic emotions tends to be universal.

39. d   Emotion was broken down into its physical, behavioral, and subjective (or labeling) components.

40. b   The James-Lange theory states that the changes in our body come first, followed by our subjective experience of an emotion.

41. d   The physiological change comes before the experience of the emotion.

42. c   Cannon-Bard believed the subjective and physiological experience occurred simultaneously.

43. c   The cognitive aspect (or thinking component) is the factor that determines your emotions according to the cognitive arousal theory.

44. c   According to Schachter and Singer, the coffee causes an arousal and then you seek environmental cues to come up with a label for your arousal.

45. b   See the answer to number 44.

46. a   In accordance with Schachter and Singer's theory, the participants use the environmental cues of an angry co-subject to determine that their own arousal was due to anger as well.

47. a   If her face is paralyzed, she would not be able to send feedback to her brain regarding her facial expression and thus her emotions would be significantly reduced according to the facial feedback hypothesis.

48. d   The facial feedback hypothesis proposes that our brain receives feedback on our facial expressions which then serves to enhance whatever emotion we are expressing.

49. d   The cognitive-mediational theory believes that we first assess the situation before we have a subjective experience of emotion or a physiological reaction.

50. c   See the answer to number 49.

51. b This is the definition given in your textbook.
52. a Myers suggests spending time with others and those you care about.

CHAPTER GLOSSARY

Abraham Maslow	1908-1970. American psychologist who was a major proponent of the humanistic movement in psychology.
acquired (secondary) drives	those drives that are learned through experience or conditioning, such as the need for money or social approval.
amygdala	brain structure located near the hippocampus, responsible for fear responses and memory of fear.
anorexia nervosa	a condition in which a person reduces eating to the point that a weight loss of 15 percent below the ideal body weight or more occurs.
arousal theory of motivation	theory of motivation in which people are said to have an optimal (best or ideal) level of tension that they seek to maintain by increasing or decreasing stimulation.
basal metabolic rate	the rate at which the body burns energy when the organism is resting.
bulimia	a condition in which a person develops a cycle of "binging" or overeating enormous amounts of food at one sitting, and "purging" or deliberately vomiting after eating.
Cannon-Bard theory of emotion	theory in which the physiological reaction and the emotion are assumed to occur at the same time.
cognitive arousal theory	theory of emotion in which both the physical arousal and the labeling of that arousal based on cues from the environment must occur before the emotion is experienced.
cognitive-mediational theory	theory of emotion in which a stimulus must be interpreted (appraised) by a person in order to result in a physical response and an emotional reaction.
common sense theory	idea held by most people that a stimulus leads to the subjective experience of an emotion which then triggers a physiological response.
display rules	learned ways of controlling displays of emotion in social settings.
drive	a psychological tension and physical arousal arising when there is a need that motivates the organism to act in order to fulfill the need and reduce the tension.
drive-reduction theory	approach to motivation that assumes behavior arises from physiological needs which cause internal drives to push the organism to satisfy the need and reduce tension and arousal.
emotion	the "feeling" aspect of consciousness, characterized by a certain physical arousal, a certain behavior that reveals the emotion to the outside world, and an inner awareness of feelings.
expectancy-value theories	a type of incentive theory that assumes the actions of humans cannot be predicted without understanding the beliefs, values, and the importance that a person attaches to those beliefs and values at any given moment.
extrinsic motivation	type of motivation in which a person performs an action because it leads to an outcome that is separate from or external to the person.
facial feedback hypothesis	theory of emotion which assumes that facial expressions provide feedback to the brain concerning the emotion being expressed, which in turn causes and intensifies the emotion.
glucagons	hormones that are secreted by the pancreas to control the levels of fats, proteins, and carbohydrates in the body by increasing the level of glucose in the bloodstream.
hierarchy of needs	a theory of motivation proposed by Maslow which suggests that as people meet their basic needs they seek to satisfy successively higher needs as laid out in the hierarchy.
homeostasis	the tendency of the body to maintain a steady state.

humanistic theory of motivation	theories of motivation which focus on human potential and the drive to be the best a person can be.
hypothalamus	small structure in the brain located below the thalamus and directly above the pituitary gland, responsible for motivational behavior such as sleep, hunger, thirst, and sex.
incentive theory of motivation	theories of motivation in which behavior is explained as a response to the external stimulus and its rewarding properties.
incentives	things that attract or lure people into action.
instinct approach of motivation	approach to motivation that assumes people are governed by instincts similar to those of other animals.
instincts	the biologically determined and innate patterns of behavior that exist in both people and animals.
insulin	a hormone secreted by the pancreas to control the levels of fats, proteins, and carbohydrates in the body by reducing the level of glucose in the bloodstream.
intrinsic motivation	type of motivation in which a person performs an action because the act itself is rewarding or satisfying in some internal manner.
James-Lange theory of emotion	theory in which a physiological reaction leads to the labeling of an emotion.
leptin	a hormone that, when released into the bloodstream, signals the hypothalamus that the body has had enough food and reduces the appetite while increasing the feeling of being full.
motivation	the process by which activities are started, directed, and continued so that physical or psychological needs or wants are met.
need	a lack of some material (such as food or water) that is required for survival of the organism.
need for achievement (nAch)	a need which involves a strong desire to succeed in attaining goals, not only realistic ones but also challenging ones.
need for affiliation (nAff)	the need for friendly social interactions and relationships with others.
need for power (nPow)	the need to have control or influence over others.
needs theory of motivation	theory of motivation that examines the three specific needs for achievement, affiliation, and power.
obesity	condition in which a person weighs 20 percent or more over their ideal weight.
peak experiences	according to Maslow, times in a person's life during which self-actualization is temporarily achieved.
positive psychology	a viewpoint that recommends shifting the focus of psychology away from the negative aspects to a more positive focus on strengths, well-being, and the pursuit of happiness.
primary drives	those drives that involve needs of the body such as hunger and thirst.
Schachter and Singer	two psychologists responsible for proposing the cognitive arousal theory of emotions.
self-actualization	according to Maslow, the seldom-reached point at which people have sufficiently satisfied the lower needs and achieved their full human potential.
self-determination theory (SDT)	theory of human motivation in which the social context of an action has an effect on the type of motivation existing for the action.
sensation seeker	someone who needs more arousal than the average person.
stimulus motive	a motive that appears to be unlearned but causes an increase in stimulation. An example of this motive is curiosity.
weight set point	the particular level of weight that the body tries to maintain.
Yerkes-Dodson law	predicts that a certain level of arousal will be motivating, but too much arousal or too little arousal will decrease motivation. The optimal level of arousal appears to depend on the individual and the difficulty of the task.

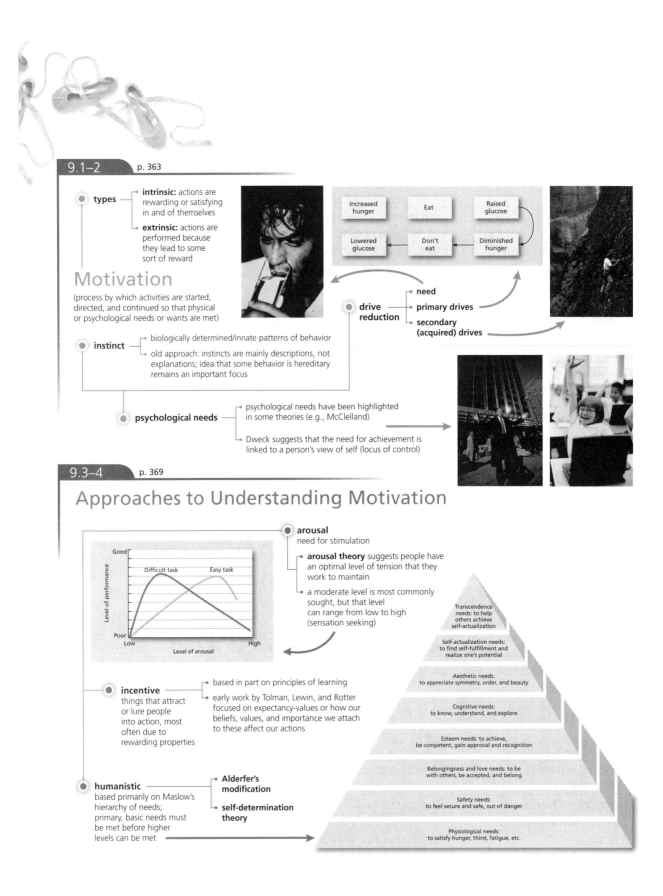

types
- **intrinsic:** actions are rewarding or satisfying in and of themselves
- **extrinsic:** actions are performed because they lead to some sort of reward

Motivation

(process by which activities are started, directed, and continued so that physical or psychological needs or wants are met)

instinct
- biologically determined/innate patterns of behavior
- old approach: instincts are mainly descriptions, not explanations; idea that some behavior is hereditary remains an important focus

| Increased hunger | Eat | Raised glucose |
| Lowered glucose | Don't eat | Diminished hunger |

drive reduction
- need
- primary drives
- secondary (acquired) drives

psychological needs
- psychological needs have been highlighted in some theories (e.g., McClelland)
- Dweck suggests that the need for achievement is linked to a person's view of self (locus of control)

Approaches to Understanding Motivation

arousal
need for stimulation

- **arousal theory** suggests people have an optimal level of tension that they work to maintain
- a moderate level is most commonly sought, but that level can range from low to high (sensation seeking)

[Graph: Level of performance (Poor to Good) vs. Level of arousal (Low to High), showing curves for "Difficult task" and "Easy task"]

incentive
things that attract or lure people into action, most often due to rewarding properties
- based in part on principles of learning
- early work by Tolman, Lewin, and Rotter focused on expectancy-values or how our beliefs, values, and importance we attach to these affect our actions

humanistic
based primarily on Maslow's hierarchy of needs; primary, basic needs must be met before higher levels can be met
- **Alderfer's modification**
- **self-determination theory**

Transcendence needs: to help others achieve self-actualization

Self-actualization needs: to find self-fulfillment and realize one's potential

Aesthetic needs: to appreciate symmetry, order, and beauty

Cognitive needs: to know, understand, and explore

Esteem needs: to achieve, be competent, gain approval and recognition

Belongingness and love needs: to be with others, be accepted, and belong

Safety needs: to feel secure and safe, out of danger

Physiological needs: to satisfy hunger, thirst, fatigue, etc.

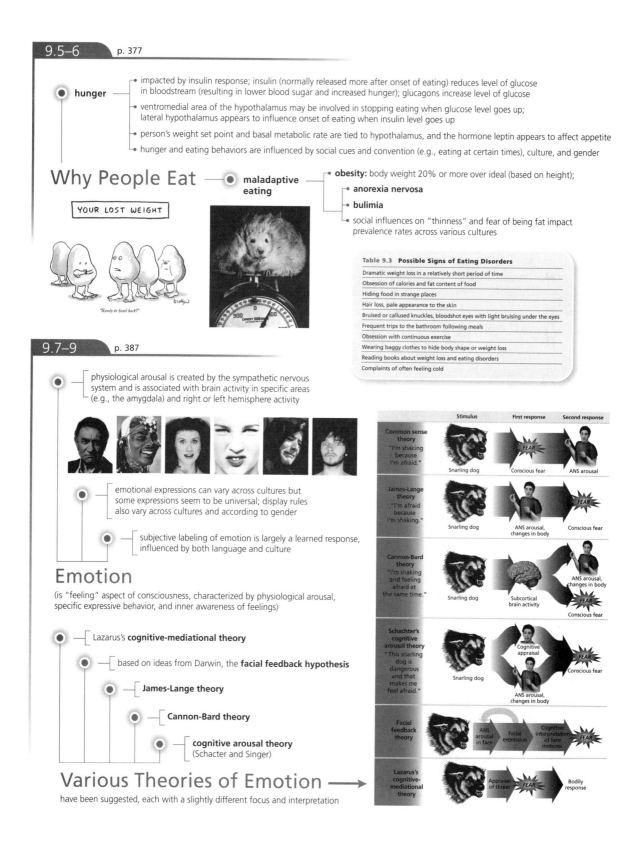

- **hunger**
  - impacted by insulin response; insulin (normally released more after onset of eating) reduces level of glucose in bloodstream (resulting in lower blood sugar and increased hunger); glucagons increase level of glucose
  - ventromedial area of the hypothalamus may be involved in stopping eating when glucose level goes up; lateral hypothalamus appears to influence onset of eating when insulin level goes up
  - person's weight set point and basal metabolic rate are tied to hypothalamus, and the hormone leptin appears to affect appetite
  - hunger and eating behaviors are influenced by social cues and convention (e.g., eating at certain times), culture, and gender

Why People Eat

- **maladaptive eating**
  - **obesity:** body weight 20% or more over ideal (based on height);
  - **anorexia nervosa**
  - **bulimia**
  - social influences on "thinness" and fear of being fat impact prevalence rates across various cultures

YOUR LOST WEIGHT

"Ready to head back?"

Table 9.3 Possible Signs of Eating Disorders

Dramatic weight loss in a relatively short period of time

Obsession of calories and fat content of food

Hiding food in strange places

Hair loss, pale appearance to the skin

Bruised or callused knuckles, bloodshot eyes with light bruising under the eyes

Frequent trips to the bathroom following meals

Obsession with continuous exercise

Wearing baggy clothes to hide body shape or weight loss

Reading books about weight loss and eating disorders

Complaints of often feeling cold

- physiological arousal is created by the sympathetic nervous system and is associated with brain activity in specific areas (e.g., the amygdala) and right or left hemisphere activity

- emotional expressions can vary across cultures but some expressions seem to be universal; display rules also vary across cultures and according to gender

- subjective labeling of emotion is largely a learned response, influenced by both language and culture

Emotion

(is "feeling" aspect of consciousness, characterized by physiological arousal, specific expressive behavior, and inner awareness of feelings)

- Lazarus's **cognitive-mediational theory**
- based on ideas from Darwin, the **facial feedback hypothesis**
- **James-Lange theory**
- **Cannon-Bard theory**
- **cognitive arousal theory** (Schacter and Singer)

Various Theories of Emotion →

have been suggested, each with a slightly different focus and interpretation

	Stimulus	First response	Second response
Common sense theory "I'm shaking because I'm afraid."	Snarling dog	FEAR Conscious fear	ANS arousal
James-Lange theory "I'm afraid because I'm shaking."	Snarling dog	ANS arousal, changes in body	FEAR Conscious fear
Cannon-Bard theory "I'm shaking and feeling afraid at the same time."	Snarling dog	Subcortical brain activity	ANS arousal, changes in body / FEAR Conscious fear
Schachter's cognitive arousal theory "This snarling dog is dangerous and that makes me feel afraid."	Snarling dog	Cognitive appraisal / ANS arousal, changes in body	FEAR Conscious fear
Facial feedback theory		ANS arousal in face → Facial expression → Cognitive interpretation of face motions	FEAR
Lazarus's cognitive-mediational theory		Appraisal of threat → FEAR	Bodily response

Figure 9.1 **Homeostasis**

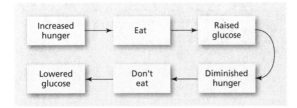

Figure 9.2 **Arousal and Performance**

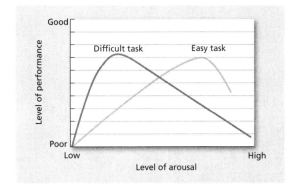

Table 9.1 **Sample Items from the Zuckerman-Kuhlman Personality Questionnaire**

Table 9.1 Sample Items from the Zuckerman-Kuhlman Personality Questionnaire	
SCALE ITEM	**SENSATION SEEKING**
I sometimes do "crazy" things just for fun.	High
I prefer friends who are excitingly unpredictable.	High
I am an impulsive person.	High
Before I begin a complicated job, I make careful plans.	Low
I usually think about what I am going to do before doing it.	Low

Source: Adapted from Zuckerman, M. (2002).

Figure 9.3 **Maslow's Hierarchy of Needs**

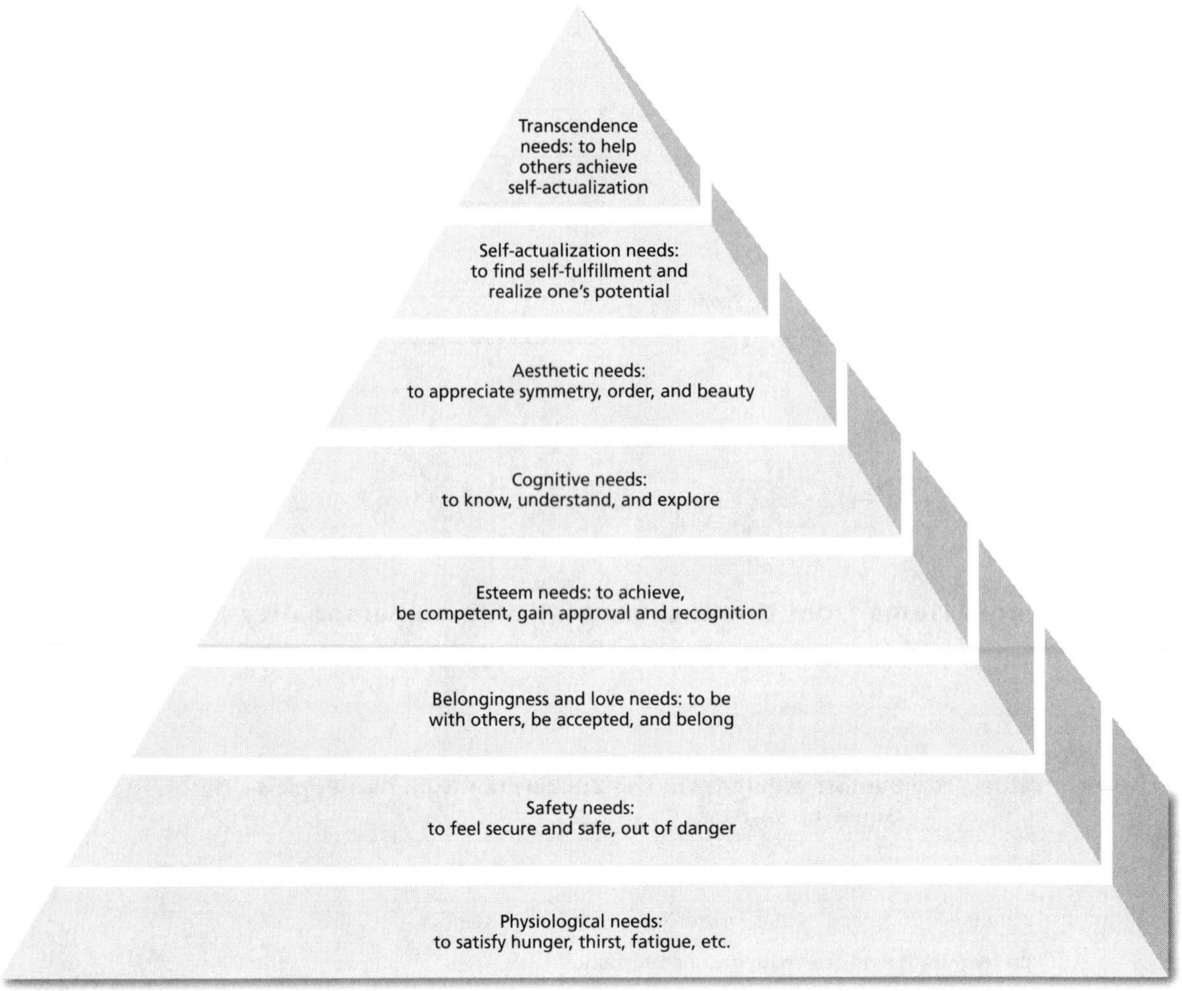

Transcendence needs: to help others achieve self-actualization

Self-actualization needs: to find self-fulfillment and realize one's potential

Aesthetic needs: to appreciate symmetry, order, and beauty

Cognitive needs: to know, understand, and explore

Esteem needs: to achieve, be competent, gain approval and recognition

Belongingness and love needs: to be with others, be accepted, and belong

Safety needs: to feel secure and safe, out of danger

Physiological needs: to satisfy hunger, thirst, fatigue, etc.

_____
_____
_____
_____
_____
_____
_____
_____
_____
_____
_____
_____
_____
_____
_____
_____

_____
_____
_____
_____
_____
_____
_____
_____
_____

Table 9.2 **Average Basal Metabolic Rates for a Female and Male**

Table 9.2 Average Basal Metabolic Rates for a Female and Male				
AGE RANGE	AGES 10–18	AGES 19–30	AGES 31–60	AGES 61–80
Female (5½ ft.)	1,770*	1,720	1,623	1,506
Male (6 ft.)	2,140	2,071	1,934	1,770

*Numbers in the table represent the number of calories a person needs to consume each day to maintain body weight (without exercise).

_____
_____
_____
_____
_____
_____
_____
_____
_____
_____
_____

Table 9.3 **Possible Signs of Eating Disorders**

Table 9.3   **Possible Signs of Eating Disorders**
Dramatic weight loss in a relatively short period of time
Obsession with calories and fat content of food
Hiding food in strange places
Hair loss, pale appearance to the skin
Bruised or callused knuckles, bloodshot eyes with light bruising under the eyes
Frequent trips to the bathroom following meals
Obsession with continuous exercise
Wearing baggy clothes to hide body shape or weight loss
Reading books about weight loss and eating disorders
Complaints of often feeling cold

_____
_____
_____
_____
_____
_____
_____
_____
_____
_____
_____

 **Emotion**

_____
_____
_____
_____
_____
_____
_____
_____
_____
_____
_____

Figure 9.5 **Facial Expressions of Emotion**

a.   b.   c.

d.   e.   f.

_____

_____

_____

_____

_____

_____

_____

_____

_____

_____

_____

_____

_____

_____

_____

_____

_____

_____

_____

_____

_____

_____

_____

Figure 9.12 **Comparison of Theories of Emotion**

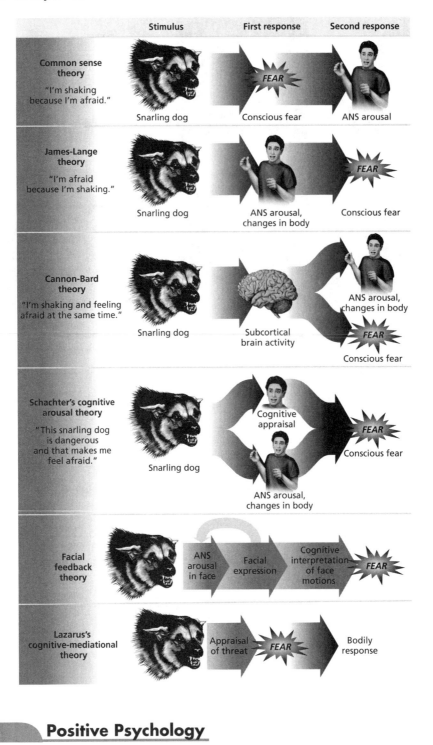

	Stimulus	First response	Second response

Common sense theory
"I'm shaking because I'm afraid."
Snarling dog — Conscious fear (FEAR) — ANS arousal

James-Lange theory
"I'm afraid because I'm shaking."
Snarling dog — ANS arousal, changes in body — Conscious fear (FEAR)

Cannon-Bard theory
"I'm shaking and feeling afraid at the same time."
Snarling dog — Subcortical brain activity — ANS arousal, changes in body / FEAR Conscious fear

Schachter's cognitive arousal theory
"This snarling dog is dangerous and that makes me feel afraid."
Snarling dog — Cognitive appraisal / ANS arousal, changes in body — FEAR Conscious fear

Facial feedback theory
ANS arousal in face — Facial expression — Cognitive interpretation of face motions — FEAR

Lazarus's cognitive-mediational theory
Appraisal of threat — FEAR — Bodily response

9.10 Positive Psychology

_____

_____

_____

_____

_____

_____

YOU KNOW YOU ARE READY FOR THE TEST IF YOU ARE ABLE TO...

- Discuss physical sex differences between males and females.
- Describe the psychological gender differences between males and females including gender development and gender stereotypes.
- Introduce three of the most influential studies on sexual behavior in the United States.
- Explain the concept of sexual orientation.
- Describe the physical and psychological problems that can lead to sexual dysfunction.
- Discuss the most common sexually transmitted diseases in the United States.

RAPID REVIEW

Sex is defined as the physical differences between males and females. **Primary sex characteristics** are those physical characteristics that are present at birth and are directly involved in human reproduction. In the female, the primary sex characteristics include the **vagina**, **uterus**, and **ovaries**. In the male the primary sex characteristics include the **penis**, the **testes** (also called the testicles), the **scrotum**, and the **prostate gland**. In the female embryo, the development of the gonads into ovaries causes the release of **estrogen** which leads to the development of the remaining sex organs, while in the male, the development of the gonads into testes leads to the release of **androgens** and further development of the male sex organs. **Secondary sex characteristics** develop during **puberty** and are indirectly involved in human reproduction. Female secondary sex characteristics include a growth spurt after the first **menstrual cycle**, enlarged breasts, maturation of **mammary glands**, wider hips, pubic hair, and fat deposits on the buttocks and thighs. Male secondary sex characteristics include a deepening voice, facial chest and pubic hair, development of coarser skin texture, and a growth spurt.

Approximately 1 out of 1,500 children in the U.S. are born with ambiguous sexual organs, a condition previously referred to as **hermaphroditism**, but now more commonly called **intersexed**. Many physicians view the condition as an abnormality that should be repaired by sexual reassignment surgery. However, many intersexed individuals feel that the decision regarding surgery should be made by the individual themselves when they are old enough to make their own choice.

Gender is defined as the psychological aspects of being feminine or masculine. **Gender roles** are a culture's expectation for behavior of a person who is perceived as male or female, and **gender typing** is the process by which individuals learn their expected gender role. A person's sense of being female or male is called their **gender identity** and is influenced by both biology and environment. For example, some researchers believe that exposure to certain hormones during fetal development influences gender identity in addition to the strong environmental pressures of family and friends to behave in the "expected" manner. **Social learning theory** proposes that individuals learn their gender identities by observing the behaviors of the people around them and being rewarded for imitating the appropriate gender behavior. **Gender schema theory** suggests that children acquire their gender role by organizing their own behavior around their internalized schema of "boy" or "girl." A **gender stereotype** is a generalization about males or females that ignores individual differences. Female gender stereotypes often include characteristics such as illogical, emotional, sensitive, nurturing, while male gender stereotypes can include characteristics such as aggressive, logical, decisive, and unemotional. **Sexism** refers to prejudice about males and females. **Benevolent sexism** refers to the acceptance of positive stereotypes about males and females. Psychologist Sandra Bem coined the term **androgyny** to describe people who display both male and female characteristics. With regard to cognitive differences between gender, men tend to perform better than women on certain spatial tasks, while women tend to perform better than men on tests of perceptual speed. Researchers are still investigating the relative contributions of the environment and heredity on these gender differences. With regard to communication, women tend to use a "relate" style of communication while men often use a "report" style.

Three landmark studies have provided much of the information available today in the U.S. about human sexuality. In 1957, <u>William Masters and Virginia Johnson</u> conducted the first direct observational study on the physical aspects of the human sexual response by recording the physiological reactions of 700 female and male volunteers while they were engaged in sexual intercourse or masturbation. Their research led them to propose four stages of the sexual response cycle: **excitement**, **plateau**, **orgasm**, and **resolution**, respectively. Men show a **refractory period** after the fourth phase during which time they cannot achieve erection. The valuable research of Masters and Johnson has helped a tremendous number of individuals but was extremely controversial when it was originally published. In 1948, <u>Alfred Kinsey</u> published his findings from a large survey of adult sexual behavior in the United States. His findings were based on face-to-face interviews with participants and included details about the frequency of behaviors such as masturbation, anal sex, premarital sex, and sexual orientation. Some have criticized the Kinsey study on the basis of methodological issues. The next large-scale study of human sexual behavior was published in 1993 by <u>Samuel Janus and Cynthia Janus</u>. The *Janus Report* described sexual behaviors in the U.S. based on the survey responses of 3,000 individuals from across the U.S. In addition to topics examined previously, The *Janus Report* also looked at **sexual deviance** among other new topics.

Sexual orientation refers to a person's sexual attraction for members of a particular sex. The term **heterosexual** refers to people who are sexually attracted to members of the opposite physical sex, and the term **homosexual** refers to individuals who are attracted to members of their own physical sex. A person who is **bisexual** may be either male or female and is attracted to both sexes. A great deal of time and energy has been invested into answering the question of whether sexual orientation is learned or inherited from your parents. A well-known study by Simon LeVay found differences in posthumous hypothalamus size between heterosexual and homosexual men. Although this study was corroborated by a similar study in sheep, both studies are correlational in nature and do not tell us the actual cause of sexual orientation.

A **sexual dysfunction** is a problem with sexual functioning or the actual physical workings of the sex act and can be caused by a number of factors. **Organic or stress-induced dysfunctions** are the sexual problems that are caused by physical disorders or by psychological distress. The sexual problems can be in three areas of sexual activity: sexual interest, arousal, and response. **Paraphilia** is a sexual dysfunction in which the person achieves sexual arousal and fulfillment through sexual behavior that is unusual or socially unacceptable. **Pedophilia** is a sexual deviancy that involves recurring sexual thoughts about or behaviors toward children who have not yet entered puberty. Pedophilia is illegal and considered immoral in almost every culture. A **pedophile** is a person with pedophilia. **Transvestism** is a dysfunction in which the individual receives sexual pleasure from dressing in the clothing of the opposite sex.

Sexually transmitted diseases or STDs are any disease that is spread through sexual contact. Some common STDs in the United States include **chlamydia**, **syphilis**, **gonorrhea**, **genital herpes**, **genital warts**, and AIDS (or **acquired immune deficiency syndrome**). AIDS is cause by the **human immunodeficiency virus** (HIV) which wears down the body's immune system, making the individual highly susceptible to infections. The virus can be transmitted from person to person through exposure to blood, vaginal fluid, semen, and breast milk. There are no documented cases of the spread of AIDS through tears or saliva. In the United States, approximately 900,000 have the virus and about 300,000 of those individuals have developed AIDS. The medications used to treat the virus are called antiretrovirals and work by slowing down the action of the virus. Researchers are working on a vaccine that would prevent HIV infection.

Individuals can protect themselves from STDs by using condoms, having a sexual relationship with one uninfected partner, not sharing needles or other drug equipment, having regular exams for STDs, learning the common symptoms of STDs, talking openly with your partner about diseases and condom use, and realizing that abstinence is the only 100 percent effective prevention.

STUDY HINTS

1. This chapter introduced three of the most important studies on human sexuality conducted to date. Use the following table to help you summarize the details of these studies

Researcher(s)	Date of Study	Method Used	Major Findings

2. Try matching each of the STDs listed on the left with the correct set of symptoms on the right.

chlamydia

initial symptoms of a painless open sore that usually appears on the penis or around or in the vagina. If untreated, may go on to more advanced stages, including a transient rash and, eventually, serious involvement of the heart and central nervous system

syphilis

infection caused by the herpes simplex virus, which causes a painful rash of fluid-filled blisters on the genitals

gonorrhea

affects the genitals of both sexes, causes burning or difficulty with urination, itching, and a yellow or green discharge. It is easily treated with antibiotics.

genital herpes

lesions produced by the human papillomavirus (HPV) and transmitted through sexual contact. The lesions may be raised and bumpy, or flat and almost impossible to see.

genital warts

causes damage to the female and male reproductive systems resulting in infertility, may remain undetected for long periods of time

acquired immune deficiency syndrome (AIDS)

viral disorder that causes deterioration of the immune system and eventually results in death due to complicating infections that the body can no longer fight

Suggested Answers for Question 1

Researcher(s)	Date of Study	Method Used	Major Findings
Masters and Johnson	late 1950's published in 1957	direct observation in a laboratory	four phases of human sexual response. Men and women both go through the four phases but men have a refractory period that is not typically seen in women.
Alfred Kinsey	1948	one-on-one personal interviews	sexual orientation was seen more along a continuum. Frequency of masturbation, premarital and extramarital sex was much higher than many people previously thought.
Samuel Janus and Cynthia Janus	1993	one-on-one interviews as well as mass questionnaires	findings on typical sexual behavior as well was sexual deviance, single people's sexual behavior, marriage, divorce, and decisions to have children

Answers for Question 2

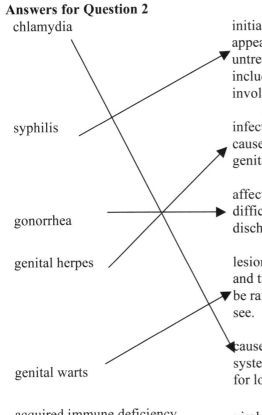

chlamydia

syphilis

gonorrhea

genital herpes

genital warts

acquired immune deficiency
syndrome (AIDS)

initial symptoms of a painless open sore that usually
appears on the penis or around or in the vagina. If
untreated, may go on to more advanced stages,
including a transient rash and, eventually, serious
involvement of the heart and central nervous system

infection caused by the herpes simplex virus, which
causes a painful rash of fluid-filled blisters on the
genitals

affects the genitals of both sexes, causes burning or
difficulty with urination, itching, and a yellow or green
discharge. It is easily treated with antibiotics.

lesions produced by the human papillomavirus (HPV)
and transmitted through sexual contact. The lesions may
be raised and bumpy, or flat and almost impossible to
see.

causes damage to the female and male reproductive
systems resulting in infertility, may remain undetected
for long periods of time

viral disorder that causes deterioration of the immune
system and eventually results in death due to
complicating infections that the body can no longer
fight

LEARNING OBJECTIVES

10.1 What are the physical differences between
females and males?

10.2 What is gender, and how can biology and
learning influence gender role
development?

10.3 How do gender roles develop, and how can
they be influenced by stereotypes or an
emphasis on androgyny?

10.4 How do men and women differ in thinking,
social behavior, and personality?

10.5 What happens in the bodies of women and
men during sexual intercourse?

10.6 What did the early and most recent surveys
of human sexual behavior reveal?

10.7 How do different sexual orientations
develop?

10.8 How do physical and psychological sexual
problems differ?

10.9 What are sexually transmitted diseases, and
what can be done to prevent the spread of
these disorders?

PRACTICE EXAM

For the following multiple choice questions, select the answer you feel best answers the question.

1. The growth spurt in <u>female</u> puberty usually starts at around _____ years of age.
    a) 8-10
    b) 10-12
    c) 12-14
    d) 14-16

2. Which of the following is NOT a secondary sex characteristic in males?
   a) facial and chest hair
   b) deepening voice
   c) development of coarser skin texture
   d) the prostate gland

3. _____ is the process by which people learn their culture's preferences and expectations for proper "masculine" and "feminine" behavior.
   a) Gender role
   b) Gender identity
   c) Gender typing
   d) Gender stereotyping

4. Whereas _____ can be defined as the physical characteristics of being female or male, _____ is defined as the psychological aspects of being feminine or masculine.
   a) sex; gender
   b) gender roles; gender identity
   c) gender typing; gender
   d) gender; sex

5. Traditional views of gender roles are more likely found in
   a) collectivist cultures.
   b) individualistic cultures.
   c) countries like the Netherlands, Germany, Italy, and England.
   d) None of these answers are correct.

6. If an individual's gender identity was completely determined by the DNA he or she inherited, we would say that gender identity is determined by
   a) nature.
   b) nurture.
   c) both nature and nurture.
   d) We would not be able to say.

7. When children observe their same-sex parents behaving in certain ways and imitate that behavior, a psychologist uses which theory to explain the situation?
   a) Freudian psychoanalysis
   b) Piaget's theory of development
   c) gender schema theory
   d) social learning theory

8. A child who develops her identity and organizes her behavior around a mental concept of "girl" is relying on
   a) simple imitation.
   b) positive reinforcement.
   c) social pressures.
   d) a gender schema.

9. Desperate for help with her computer, Dana calls her fiancé, thinking that he will know what to do because he is a man, and men are natural fixers. Dana's thinking in this instance is an example of
   a) androgyny.
   b) schema error.
   c) benevolent sexism.
   d) negative stereotyping.

10. Stereotypes about males and females consist of only negative characteristics
   a) True
   b) False

11. Psychologist Sandra Bem (1975, 1981) developed the concept of _____.
   a) androgyny
   b) benevolent sexism
   c) social learning theory
   d) ambiguity

12. MRI technology has demonstrated that men listen with _____.
   a) the right hemisphere of the brain
   b) the left hemisphere of the brain
   c) both hemispheres of the brain
   d) There is no consistent pattern of listening.

13. One difference that has been reported in the communication styles of men and women is that
   a) no differences have been found in communication styles.
   b) men talk more than women.
   c) men are more likely to switch topics frequently.
   d) women are more likely to interrupt.

14. Approximately how many children in the U.S. are born with both male and female sex organs?
   a) 1 out of 100
   b) 1 out of 1,500
   c) 1 out of 100,000
   d) There are currently no estimates of the number.

15. The final phase of the sexual response is _____.
   a) excitement
   b) plateau
   c) orgasm
   d) resolution

16. The research of Masters and Johnson represents the first major contribution to our understanding of
   a) common sexual behaviors.
   b) prevalence of sexually transmitted diseases.
   c) common sexual disorders.
   d) the physical response during sexual activity.

17. One seemingly amazing aspect of Masters and Johnson's research program concerning human sexual response was _____.
    a) their ability to get senior citizens to volunteer as subjects in the first studies
    b) that the study was funded by churches open to discovering ways to prevent masturbation
    c) that they were able to convince the newspapers to keep the research secret for a long period of time
    d) None of these are correct.

18. The Kinsey Report, which was published in 1948 by Alfred Kinsey and reported on common sexual behaviors of adults in U.S., was based on what type of research method?
    a) direct observation
    b) anonymous surveys
    c) experimental laboratory studies
    d) one-on-one personal interviews

19. According to Kinsey, what percentage of husbands reported anal sex with their wives?
    a) 11 percent
    b) 14 percent
    c) 92 percent
    d) 26 percent

20. The first large-scale study of human behavior to be done after the Kinsey and Masters and Johnson reports was conducted by _____.
    a) Janus and Janus
    b) Hite and Rose
    c) Hilton and Paris
    d) Erickson and Schlomo

21. If homosexuality were definitively found to be due to genetic or hormonal influences, then _____.
    a) discrimination against homosexuals would be equivalent to racism or sexism
    b) it would no longer be seen as a matter of simple choice
    c) society could no longer demand that homosexuals change their behavior
    d) All of these are true.

22. When a person refers to himself or herself as "heterosexual" or "homosexual," the person is referring to his or her
    a) sexual identity.
    b) sex.
    c) gender identity.
    d) sexual orientation.

23. A controversial study by Simon LeVay found that the _____ was significantly larger in heterosexual men than in homosexual men or women.
    a) hypothalamus
    b) hippocampus
    c) cerebral cortex
    d) corpus callosum

24. Jaime enjoys sexual activity with his partner. However, he cannot reach an orgasm during sexual intercourse even though fully aroused. Jaime is suffering from _____.
    a) male erectile disorder
    b) male orgasmic disorder
    c) dyspareunia
    d) premature ejaculation

25. Aaliyah became sexually aroused or gratified through rubbing up against an unwilling person, usually in a crowded public place. He has a condition known as _____.
    a) foyeurism
    b) frotteurism
    c) necrophilia
    d) transvestism

26. _____ is a disorder in which an individual achieves sexual arousal and fulfillment through sexual behavior that is unusual or not socially acceptable.
    a) Schizophrenia
    b) Borderline personality disorder
    c) Gender identity disorder
    d) Paraphilia

27. Which cause of a sexually transmitted disease is hardest to treat?
    a) bacterial
    b) fungal
    c) viral
    d) All are equally difficult to treat.

28. AIDS can be passed from one individual to the next through each of the following ways EXCEPT
    a) vaginal fluid.
    b) semen.
    c) tears.
    d) blood.

29. AIDS is caused by
    a) a bacterial infection.
    b) an air-borne fungus.
    c) a viral infection.
    d) The cause is not yet known.

30. Shallice has had several sexual partners in the past year. What is the BEST advice you could give her about how she can lower the odds of contracting a sexually transmitted disease in the future?
    a) Use condoms.
    b) Learn the symptoms of the common sexually transmitted diseases.
    c) Practice abstinence.
    d) All of these are good advice.

PRACTICE EXAM ANSWERS
1. b   The female growth spurt starts at around age 10-12, while the male growth spurt starts at around age 12-14.
2. d   The prostate gland is a primary sex characteristic in males.

3.   c   Gender typing is the process of learning proper masculine and feminine behaviors. Gender roles are the actual expectations each culture has for males and females, and gender identity is the individuals' sense of being male or female.

4.   a   Sex refers to physical differences and gender refers to psychological and social differences.

5.   a   Several research studies have supported the idea that collectivist cultures, such as those found in many Asian and South American countries, display more traditional views on gender roles.

6.   a   Nature refers to inherited, biological differences, while nurture refers to the effects of the environment.

7.   d   Social learning theory emphasizes observational learning which is reinforced through attention and positive remarks.

8.   d   A gender schema is a mental concept of what it means to be a "boy" or a "girl."

9.   c   Benevolent sexism is the result of thinking that all men or all women have some particular desirable trait, simply because of their sex.

10.   b   Stereotypes can be both negative and positive.

11.   a   Androgyny describes people who exhibit both male and female typical behaviors.

12.   b   Several studies have shown that males listen primarily with the left hemisphere of the brain, while females tend to show activity in both hemispheres while they are engaged in listening activities.

13.   c   Men are more likely to use a "report" style of communication which involves switching topics frequently, while women are more likely to use a "relate" style of communication.

14.   b   The best estimate to date is that about 1 in every 1,500 children in the U.S. is born with ambiguous sexual genitalia.

15.   d   Masters and Johnson labeled the fourth and final phase of the human sexual response as the "resolution" phase.

16.   d   Masters and Johnson used direct observations in the laboratory to investigate the physical human sexual response.

17.   c   Masters and Johnson were able to convince the newspapers to keep the research secret for almost 12 years.

18.   d   Alfred Kinsey traveled across the country with a team of researchers and conducted one-on-one personal interviews to gather data on sexual behavior.

19.   a   According to Kinsey, 11 percent of husbands reported anal sex with their wives.

20.   a   The Januses did the first major study on common sexual behaviors after Kinsey.

21.   d   If homosexuality were definitively found to be due to genetic or hormonal influences, then it would no longer be seen as a matter of simple choice, society could no longer demand that homosexuals change their behavior, and discrimination against homosexuals would be equivalent to racism.

22.   d   Sexual orientation refers to a person's attraction for members of a particular sex.

23.   a   LeVay's study reported differences in the size of the hypothalamus. The hypothalamus controls the pituitary gland which regulates many important hormonal levels in the body.

24.   b   Jaime does get fully aroused, which means he does have erections and is therefore not suffering from an erectile disorder. Instead he has a condition known as male orgasmic disorder.

25.   b   Frotteurism is the practice of obtaining sexual arousal or gratification by rubbing against an unwilling person.

26.   d   Paraphilias are a group of disorders in which sexual arousal is achieved through unusual or socially unacceptable methods.

27.   c   Bacterial infections can normally be treated with antibiotics but viral diseases are very hard to treat.

28. c   Currently, there are no documented cases of a person becoming infected with AIDS through exposure to tears.
29. c   AIDS is caused by the human immunodeficiency virus, more commonly referred to as HIV.
30. c   Although all of the options are good advice, the best way to prevent STDs is through abstinence.

CHAPTER GLOSSARY

acquired immune deficiency syndrome (AIDS)	sexually transmitted viral disorder that causes deterioration of the immune system and eventually results in death due to complicating infections that the body can no longer fight.
Alfred Kinsey	1894-1956. Regarded by some as the father of the scientific study of human sexuality. Published a series of reports called the Kinsey Reports which described common sexual behaviors in the U.S.
androgens	male sex hormones.
androgyny	characteristic of possessing the most positive personality characteristics of males and females regardless of actual sex.
benevolent sexism	acceptance of positive stereotypes of males and females that leads to unequal treatment.
bisexual	person sexually attracted to both men and women.
chlamydia	sexually transmitted disease which can cause damage to the female and male reproductive systems resulting in infertility. Chlamydia may remain undetected for long periods of time.
estrogen	female sex hormones.
excitement	first phase of sexual arousal during which the pulse rate increases, blood pressure rises, breathing quickens, and the skin may show a rosy flush.
gender	the psychological aspects of being male or female.
gender identity	the individual's sense of being male or female.
gender roles	the culture's expectations for masculine or feminine behavior, including attitudes, actions, and personality traits associated with being male or female in that culture.
gender schema theory	theory of gender identity acquisition in which a child develops a mental pattern, or schema, for being male or female and then organizes observed and learned behavior around that scheme.
gender stereotype	a concept held about a person or group of people that is based on being male or female.
gender typing	the process of acquiring gender role characteristics.
genital herpes	sexually transmitted infection caused by the herpes simplex virus, which causes a painful rash of fluid-filled blisters on the genitals.
genital warts	lesions produced by the human papillomavirus (HPV) and transmitted through sexual contact. The lesions may be raised and bumpy, or flat and almost impossible to see.
gonorrhea	sexually-transmitted disease that affects the genitals of both sexes, gonorrhea causes burning or difficulty with urination, itching, and a yellow or green discharge. It is easily treated with antibiotics.
hermaphroditism	the condition of possessing both male and female sexual organs.
heterosexual	person sexually attracted to the opposite sex.
homosexual	person sexually attracted to the same sex.

human immunodeficiency virus (HIV)	a virus that steadily weakens the body's defense (immune) system until it can no longer fight off infections such as pneumonia, diarrhea, tumors, and other illnesses.
intersexed	a person who possesses ambiguous sexual organs, making it difficult to determine actual sex from a visual inspection at birth.
mammary glands	glands within the breast tissue that produce milk when a woman gives birth to an infant.
menstrual cycle	monthly shedding of the blood and tissue that line the uterus in preparation for pregnancy when conception does not occur.
organic or stress-induced dysfunctions	sexual problem caused by physical disorder or psychological stress.
orgasm	a series of rhythmic contractions of the muscles of the vaginal walls or the penis, also the third and shortest phase of sexual response.
ovaries	the female sexual glands.
paraphilia	a sexual disorder in which the person's preferred method of sexual arousal and fulfillment is through sexual behavior that is unusual or socially unacceptable.
pedophile	a person who has recurring sexual thoughts, fantasies, or engages in sexual actions toward prepubescent (nonsexually mature) children.
pedophilia	deriving sexual arousal and pleasure from touching or having sexual relations with prepubescent (nonsexually mature) children, or fantasizing about such contact.
penis	male external sex organ.
plateau	second phase of sexual arousal during which the physical changes that began in the first phase are continued.
primary sex characteristics	sexual organs present at birth and directly involved in human reproduction.
prostate gland	gland that secretes most of the fluid holding the male sex cells or sperm.
puberty	period during which the secondary sex characteristics begin to develop and the capability of sexual reproduction is attained.
refractory period	time period in males just after orgasm in which the male cannot become aroused or achieve erection.
resolution	the final phase of the sexual response in which the body is returned to a normal state.
Samuel and Cynthia Janus	in 1993, published the most recent nationwide survey of common sexual behaviors. The publication is called *The Janus Report*.
scrotum	external sack that holds the testes.
secondary sex characteristics	sexual organs and traits that develop at puberty and are indirectly involved in human reproduction.
sex	physical properties that distinguish males from females.
sexism	prejudice about males and/or females
sexual deviance	behavior that is unacceptable according to societal norms and expectations.
sexual dysfunction	a problem in sexual functioning.
sexual orientation	a person's sexual attraction preference for members of a particular sex.
sexually transmitted diseases (STDs)	any disease that is spread through sexual contact.
social learning theory	theory of gender identity acquisition which emphasizes learning through observation and imitation of models.

syphilis	sexually transmitted disease with the initial symptom of a painless open sore that usually appears on the penis or around or in the vagina. If untreated, syphilis may go on to more advanced stages, including a transient rash and, eventually, serious involvement of the heart and central nervous system.
testes	the male sex glands.
transvestism	deriving sexual arousal and pleasure from dressing in the clothing of the opposite sex.
uterus	the womb in which the baby grows during pregnancy.
vagina	the tube that leads from the outside of a female's body to the opening of the womb.
Virginia Johnson	b. 1925. Psychologist famous for her pioneering research into the nature of human sexual response and the diagnosis and treatment of sexual disorders and dysfunctions from 1957 until the 1990s.
William Masters	1915-2001. Gynecologist famous for his pioneering research into the nature of human sexual response and the diagnosis and treatment of sexual disorders and dysfunctions from 1957 until the 1990s.

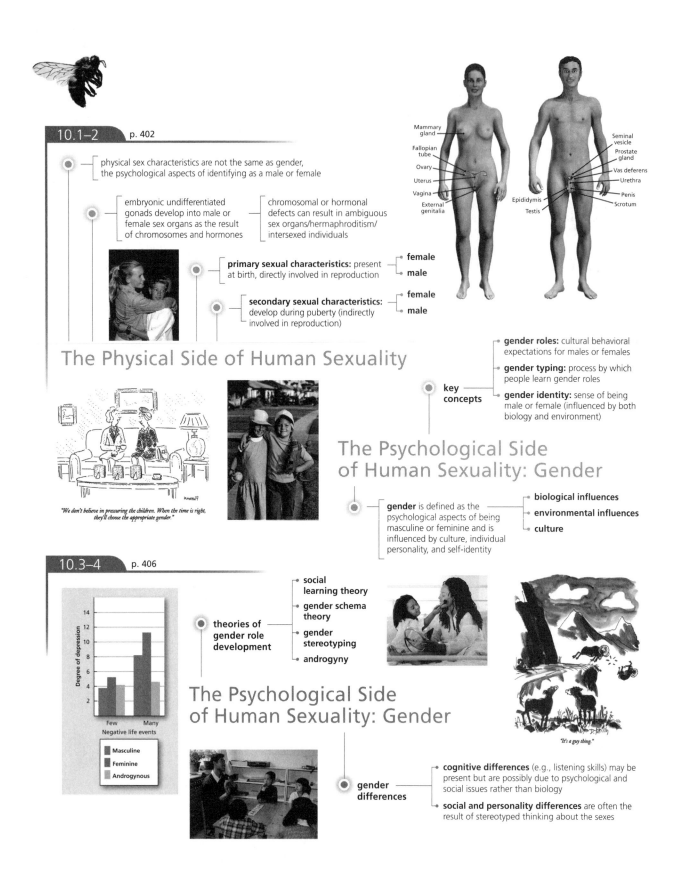

10.1–2   p. 402

physical sex characteristics are not the same as gender, the psychological aspects of identifying as a male or female

embryonic undifferentiated gonads develop into male or female sex organs as the result of chromosomes and hormones

chromosomal or hormonal defects can result in ambiguous sex organs/hermaphroditism/intersexed individuals

primary sexual characteristics: present at birth, directly involved in reproduction
- female
- male

secondary sexual characteristics: develop during puberty (indirectly involved in reproduction)
- female
- male

Mammary gland
Fallopian tube
Ovary
Uterus
Vagina
External genitalia

Seminal vesicle
Prostate gland
Vas deferens
Urethra
Penis
Scrotum
Epididymis
Testis

The Physical Side of Human Sexuality

"We don't believe in pressuring the children. When the time is right, they'll choose the appropriate gender."

key concepts
- **gender roles:** cultural behavioral expectations for males or females
- **gender typing:** process by which people learn gender roles
- **gender identity:** sense of being male or female (influenced by both biology and environment)

The Psychological Side of Human Sexuality: Gender

gender is defined as the psychological aspects of being masculine or feminine and is influenced by culture, individual personality, and self-identity
- **biological influences**
- **environmental influences**
- **culture**

10.3–4   p. 406

Degree of depression

14
12
10
8
6
4
2

Few   Many
Negative life events

- Masculine
- Feminine
- Androgynous

theories of gender role development
- **social learning theory**
- **gender schema theory**
- **gender stereotyping**
- **androgyny**

The Psychological Side of Human Sexuality: Gender

"It's a guy thing."

gender differences
- **cognitive differences** (e.g., listening skills) may be present but are possibly due to psychological and social issues rather than biology
- **social and personality differences** are often the result of stereotyped thinking about the sexes

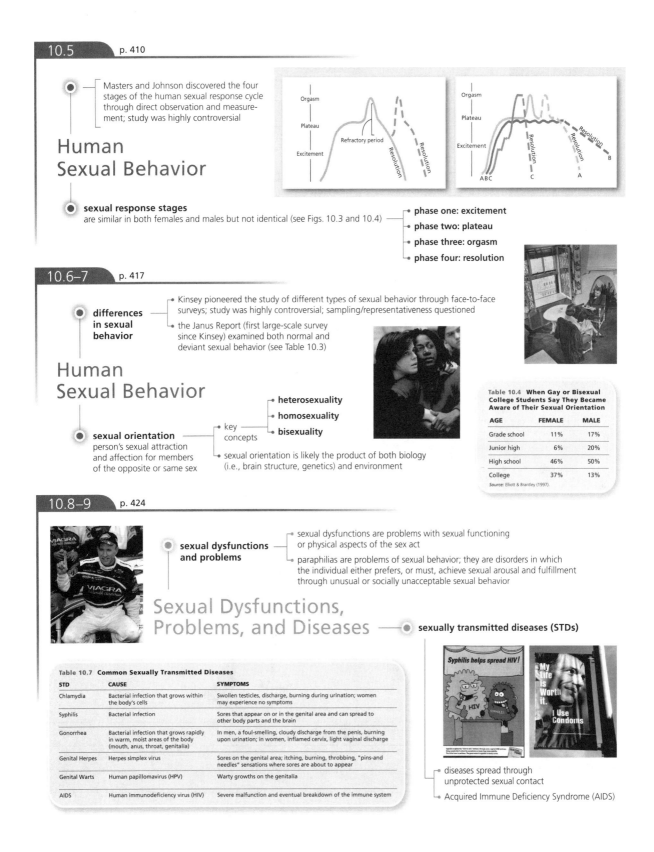

Masters and Johnson discovered the four stages of the human sexual response cycle through direct observation and measurement; study was highly controversial

Human Sexual Behavior

sexual response stages
are similar in both females and males but not identical (see Figs. 10.3 and 10.4)

- **phase one: excitement**
- **phase two: plateau**
- **phase three: orgasm**
- **phase four: resolution**

differences in sexual behavior
- Kinsey pioneered the study of different types of sexual behavior through face-to-face surveys; study was highly controversial; sampling/representativeness questioned
- the Janus Report (first large-scale survey since Kinsey) examined both normal and deviant sexual behavior (see Table 10.3)

Human Sexual Behavior

sexual orientation
person's sexual attraction and affection for members of the opposite or same sex

- key concepts
  - **heterosexuality**
  - **homosexuality**
  - **bisexuality**
- sexual orientation is likely the product of both biology (i.e., brain structure, genetics) and environment

Table 10.4 When Gay or Bisexual College Students Say They Became Aware of Their Sexual Orientation

AGE	FEMALE	MALE
Grade school	11%	17%
Junior high	6%	20%
High school	46%	50%
College	37%	13%

Source: Elliott & Brantley (1997).

sexual dysfunctions and problems
- sexual dysfunctions are problems with sexual functioning or physical aspects of the sex act
- paraphilias are problems of sexual behavior; they are disorders in which the individual either prefers, or must, achieve sexual arousal and fulfillment through unusual or socially unacceptable sexual behavior

Sexual Dysfunctions, Problems, and Diseases

sexually transmitted diseases (STDs)

- diseases spread through unprotected sexual contact
- Acquired Immune Deficiency Syndrome (AIDS)

Table 10.7 Common Sexually Transmitted Diseases

STD	CAUSE	SYMPTOMS
Chlamydia	Bacterial infection that grows within the body's cells	Swollen testicles, discharge, burning during urination; women may experience no symptoms
Syphilis	Bacterial infection	Sores that appear on or in the genital area and can spread to other body parts and the brain
Gonorrhea	Bacterial infection that grows rapidly in warm, moist areas of the body (mouth, anus, throat, genitalia)	In men, a foul-smelling, cloudy discharge from the penis, burning upon urination; in women, inflamed cervix, light vaginal discharge
Genital Herpes	Herpes simplex virus	Sores on the genital area; itching, burning, throbbing, "pins-and needles" sensations where sores are about to appear
Genital Warts	Human papillomavirus (HPV)	Warty growths on the genitalia
AIDS	Human immunodeficiency virus (HIV)	Severe malfunction and eventual breakdown of the immune system

Figure 10.1 **Male and Female Sexual Organs**

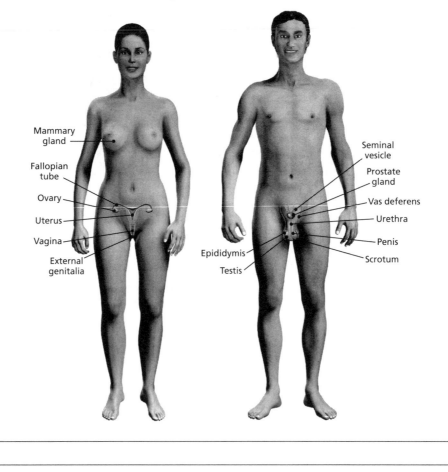

Mammary gland

Fallopian tube

Ovary

Uterus

Vagina

External genitalia

Seminal vesicle

Prostate gland

Vas deferens

Urethra

Penis

Epididymis

Testis

Scrotum

_____
_____
_____
_____
_____
_____
_____
_____
_____

Figure 10.2 **Depression as Influenced by Negative Life Events**

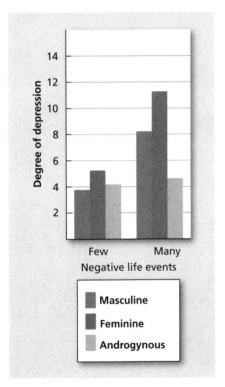

_____
_____
_____
_____
_____
_____
_____
_____
_____
_____
_____

Figure 10.3 **The Male Sexual Response Cycle**

Figure 10.4 **The Female Sexual Response Cycle**

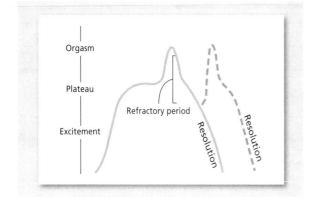

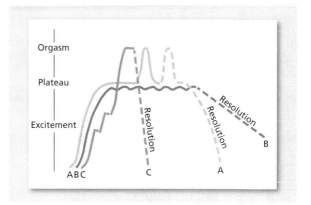

_____
_____
_____
_____
_____
_____
_____
_____
_____
_____
_____
_____
_____
_____
_____
_____

Table 10.1 Kinsey and Colleagues' (1948) Rating Scale for Sexual Orientation

Table 10.1 Kinsey and Colleagues' (1948) Rating Scale for Sexual Orientation

0	1	2	3	4	5	6
Exclusively heterosexual	Predominantly heterosexual; only incidentally homosexual	Predominantly heterosexual; more than incidentally homosexual	Equally hetero-sexual and homosexual	Predominantly homosexual; more than incidentally heterosexual	Predominantly homosexual; only incidentally heterosexual	Exclusively homosexual

Source: Reprinted with permission of the Kinsey Institute for Research in Sex, Gender, and Reproduction, Inc.

Table 10.2 Key Findings from Kinsey's Sexual Behavior Surveys

Table 10.2 Key Findings from Kinsey's Sexual Behavior Surveys

Males reporting anal sex with spouse: 11 percent.

Nearly 46 percent of males had bisexual experiences.

Between 6 and 14 percent of females had bisexual experiences.

Whereas nearly 21 percent of the males had experienced intercourse at age 16, only 6 percent of females had done so.

Males reporting premarital sex: 67 to 98 percent (varied by economic level).

Females reporting premarital sex: 50 percent.

Nearly 50 percent of all married males had some extramarital experiences, whereas 26 percent of married females had extramarital experiences.

About 10 percent of males were predominantly homosexual.

Between 2 and 6 percent of females were predominantly homosexual.

Males who reported masturbating: 92 percent.

Females who reported masturbating: 62 percent.

Gebhard & Johnson (1979/1998).

Table 10.3 **Findings from the Janus Report**

Table 10.3   Findings from the Janus Report

Full sexual relations by age 14: men—19 percent, women—7.5 percent.

Overall, nearly 80 percent of men and 70 percent of women said they had masturbated, with about a quarter to a third saying that it was rarely.

At least one homosexual experience: 22 percent of men, 17 percent of women.

Males reporting premarital sex: 67 percent.

Females reporting premarital sex: 46 percent.

About 40 percent of men and about 26 percent of women reported having had at least one extramarital affair.

About 9 percent of males were predominantly homosexual.

About 5 percent of females were predominantly homosexual.

Janus & Janus (1993).

Table 10.4 **When Gay or Bisexual College Students Say They Became Aware of Their Sexual Orientation**

Table 10.4   When Gay or Bisexual College Students Say They Became Aware of Their Sexual Orientation

AGE	FEMALE	MALE
Grade school	11%	17%
Junior high	6%	20%
High school	46%	50%
College	37%	13%

Source: Elliott & Brantley (1997).

_____

_____

_____

_____

_____

_____

_____

_____

_____

_____

Table 10.5 **Organic or Stress-Induced Dysfunctions**

Table 10.5	**Organic or Stress-Induced Dysfunctions**
Sexual Desire Disorders	Hypoactive Sexual Desire Disorder: Ongoing, abnormally low desire for sexual activity.
	Sexual Aversion Disorder: Fear and disgust of sexual contact.
Sexual Arousal Disorders	Female Sexual Arousal Disorder: Desire for sexual activity is present, but physical discomfort and a lack of pleasure are experienced during sexual activity.
	Male Erectile Disorder: A male cannot maintain an erection long enough to complete the sexual act.
Orgasmic Disorders	Male Orgasmic Disorder: A male cannot achieve orgasm through vaginal stimulation, even though fully aroused.
	Female Orgasmic Disorder: A female cannot achieve an orgasm even though fully aroused.
	Premature Ejaculation: Some men experience orgasm shortly after penetration, which can cause feelings of sexual inadequacy because the partner does not have time to achieve orgasm.
Sexual Pain Disorders	Vaginismus: Persistent contractions of the vaginal muscles, causing sexual intercourse to be painful or impossible.
	Dyspareunia: Pain in the genitals that can occur before, during, or after intercourse can be experienced by either sex.

_____

_____

_____

_____

_____

_____

_____

_____

_____

_____

_____

Table 10.6 **Paraphilias**

Table 10.6	Paraphilias
Festishism	An object or part of the body becomes the focus of sexual interest and arousal, such as shoes, feet, or underwear.
Exhibitionism	The exposure of normally clothed parts of the body to unsuspecting and typically unwilling viewers, such as a "flasher."
Voyeurism	The act of obtaining sexual arousal and gratification through watching other people engage in sexual behavior or undress, such as a "Peeping Tom."
Frotteurism	The act of becoming sexually aroused or gratified through rubbing up against an unwilling person, usually in a crowded public place.
Necrophilia	Fetishism in which the sexual arousal comes from touching or having intercourse with a corpse.
Transvestism	Fetishism in which sexual arousal and pleasure come from wearing the clothing of the opposite sex.

_____

_____

_____

_____

_____

_____

Table 10.7 **Common Sexually Transmitted Diseases**

Table 10.7	Common Sexually Transmitted Diseases	
STD	**CAUSE**	**SYMPTOMS**
Chlamydia	Bacterial infection that grows within the body's cells	Swollen testicles, discharge, burning during urination; women may experience no symptoms
Syphilis	Bacterial infection	Sores that appear on or in the genital area and can spread to other body parts and the brain
Gonorrhea	Bacterial infection that grows rapidly in warm, moist areas of the body (mouth, anus, throat, genitalia)	In men, a foul-smelling, cloudy discharge from the penis, burning upon urination; in women, inflamed cervix, light vaginal discharge
Genital Herpes	Herpes simplex virus	Sores on the genital area; itching, burning, throbbing, "pins-and-needles" sensations where sores are about to appear
Genital Warts	Human papillomavirus (HPV)	Warty growths on the genitalia
AIDS	Human immunodeficiency virus (HIV)	Severe malfunction and eventual breakdown of the immune system

_____

_____

_____

_____

_____

_____

YOU KNOW YOU ARE READY FOR THE TEST IF YOU ARE ABLE TO...

- Define stress and identify the external and psychological factors that influence an individual's experience of stress.
- Discuss the causes of stress.
- Describe the physical reaction to stress and the relation of this reaction to cognitive, personality, and social factors.
- Explain the methods used to cope with stress including those influenced by culture and religion.

RAPID REVIEW

Health psychology is a new area of psychology focusing on how physical activities, psychological traits, and social relationships affect overall health. **Stress** is the physical, emotional, cognitive, and behavioral responses to events that are perceived as threatening or challenging. When a person's stress response is unpleasant or undesirable it is called **distress**, and when it is an optimal amount that helps a person function it is called **eustress**. The events that cause stress are called **stressors** and can be either internal or external events. Stressors can include external events such as catastrophes, major life changes, and hassles, along with internal experiences such as pressure, uncontrollability, and frustration. A **catastrophe** is an unpredictable event that happens on a large scale such as a tornado or flood. Catastrophes are one cause of an anxiety disorder known as **acute stress disorder (ASD)** in which an individual has recurring nightmares, sleep disturbances, and flashbacks of the event. When the symptoms of ASD last for more than one month, the disorder is then called **post-traumatic stress disorder (PTSD).** A number of researchers have suggested that any major life change, such as moving, getting married, getting a new job, would result in stress. Holmes and Rahe developed the **Social Readjustment Rating Scale** (SRRS) to measure the amount of change and thus stress in a person's life. Researchers have found a moderate correlation between scores on the SRRS and physical health. Alternate forms of the SRRS have been designed for specific populations such as the **College Undergraduate Stress Scale** (CUSS) for college students. A majority of the stressors that people have to deal with are the little daily annoyances, or **hassles**. Surveys that measure the number of hassles an individual has to deal with are actually a better predictor of short-term illnesses than the SRRS. The internal experience of **pressure** is also considered a stressor. Pressure is the psychological experience produced by demands and expectations from outside sources. Two additional internal causes of stress are uncontrollability, or a lack of control in a situation, and **frustration**, or being blocked from achieving a desired goal. Typical reactions to frustration include persistence and **aggression**, or actions meant to harm or destroy. **Displaced aggression** occurs when a person takes out his or her frustrations on less threatening, more available targets and is a form of **displacement**. Another possible reaction to frustration is **escape or withdrawal**.

An extreme reaction to stress is **suicide**, or intentionally taking one's own life. Statistics from the Office of the Surgeon General indicate that rates of suicide increase with age, men are more likely to complete a suicide than women, and the most common method of committing suicide is the use of a gun. Symptoms of suicide include feelings of hopelessness, lack of energy, irritability, and sleep disturbances, among others. Some of the ways to help someone who is contemplating suicide is to listen with true concern, stay with them, and call the police for emergency intervention.

Conflict is another source of stress and occurs when a person feels pulled toward two or more goals but can only achieve one of them. In 1935 a researcher by the name of Lewin defined three types of conflict. **Approach-approach conflict** occurs when an individual is attempting to choose between two desirable goals. **Avoidance-avoidance conflict** occurs when someone must choose between two undesirable goals. **Approach-avoidance conflict** describes a single goal that has both desirable and undesirable outcomes. An individual faced with two options in which each option has positive and negative aspects is dealing with a **double approach-avoidance conflict**. If there are more than two options, the conflict is called a **multiple approach-avoidance conflict**.

Psychologist <u>Hans Selye</u> was a pioneer in the study of the physical consequences of exposure to stressors. He proposed that the body goes through a sequence of three stages he called the **general adaptation syndrome**. The initial stage is called <u>alarm</u> and represents the immediate reaction to stress mediated by our <u>sympathetic nervous system</u>. Typical alarm reactions include increased heart rate and blood pressure, and release of sugar into the blood stream. As the stress continues, the body enters the <u>resistance</u> stage during which time the sympathetic nervous system works overtime to give the body more energy. When the body's resources have been exhausted, the <u>parasympathetic nervous system</u> is activated and the body enters the <u>exhaustion</u> stage. Selye believed that it was the prolonged release of stress hormones during the resistance stage that led to the breakdown of the body's **immune system** and the onset of the stress-related physical conditions. Researchers in the field of **psychoneuroimmunology** who study the effects of psychological factors on the immune system have found that stress actually causes an increase in the activity of the immune system. High levels of stress have been linked to increased risk of heart disease. Also, stress has been shown to decrease the amount of **natural killer cells**, which are the cells responsible for fighting cancerous growths.

The **cognitive-mediational theory** of emotions proposed by Richard Lazarus states that the way people think about and appraise a stressor is a major factor in their stress response. The first step in appraising a stressor is called **primary appraisal** and involves estimating the severity of the stressor and classifying it as a threat, challenge, or loss. In **secondary appraisal**, an individual determines what resources he or she has available for dealing with the threat or loss. Personality has also been linked to stress-related health risks. In 1974, Meyer Freidman and Ray Rosenman published a book describing the **Type A** and **Type B** personalities and their link to heart disease. Based on studies of their own patients, Freidman and Rosenman proposed that individuals with Type A personality (a person who is competitive, ambitious, workaholic, with a constant sense of pressure) were more likely to develop heart disease than someone with a Type B personality. Several studies found that the specific trait of hostility in Type A individuals was the best predictor of future heart problems. A third personality type called **Type C** (in which a person holds in their emotions and tends to be pleasant) was later identified and is currently being investigated as to its possible link with cancer rates. Finally, research has suggested a fourth personality type, the **hardy personality**, which is associated with decreased illness due to stress. An individual with a hardy personality shows commitment, displays a sense of control, and sees stresses as challenges to be met and answered. In addition to personality, links have been found between an individual's attitude and his or her physical reactions to stress. Specifically, **pessimists** have been found to have significantly more stress-related health problems than **optimists**. One way to become an optimist is to recognize any negative thoughts you are having and to work to get rid of them.

Social factors also play a key role in the amount of stress an individual experiences. Living in poverty and job stress are two major sources of stress. A serious consequence of job stress is **burnout**, or negative changes in thoughts, emotions, and behaviors as a result of prolonged stress or frustration. **Acculturative stress** describes the stress an individual experiences when having to adapt to a new culture. The method of adaptation can affect the stress level. Some of the methods of adapting to a new culture include integration, assimilation, separation, and marginalization. The effects of negative social factors on health can be minimized by a strong **social support system**, or network of family and friends who can offer help when a person is in need.

Coping strategies are actions that people take to master, tolerate, reduce, or minimize the effects of stressors and include both behavioral and psychological strategies. **Problem-focused coping** occurs when a person tries to eliminate the source of stress or reduce its impact by taking some action, while **emotion-focused coping** involves changing the way you feel or react to a stressor. One example of emotion-focused coping involves the use of **psychological defense mechanisms**, such as denial, repression, rationalization, and projection, among others. Both **concentrative and receptive meditation** have also been found to be effective coping strategies. Culture and religion have also been found to affect an individual's level of stress as well as the strategies used to cope with that stress.

A few ways that individuals can promote wellness in their own lives include exercising, getting involved with others, getting enough sleep, eating healthy foods, reserving time for fun, managing their time, and even breathing deeply.

STUDY HINTS

1. One important component to understanding this chapter is to understand the difference between a stressor and stress. The stressor is the event that causes us to experience stress. The event can be external, such as getting stuck in traffic, or internal, such as worrying about an upcoming exam. Our reaction to the event is called stress and can be physical, emotional, mental, and behavioral. Try coming up with some examples of events that could be considered stressors along with possible stress reactions. The first example has already been completed for you.

Stressor	Stress Reaction
Having to take an exam	*increased heart rate*
_____	_____
_____	_____
_____	_____

2. Many students find the different types of conflicts confusing. Look over the Key Concepts area to refresh yourself on the meaning of each type of conflict and then try to come up with an example from your own life that illustrates each type of conflict. List your examples in the space below.

Approach-Approach Conflict: _____

_____

Approach-Avoidance Conflict: _____

_____

Avoidance-Avoidance Conflict: _____

_____

LEARNING OBJECTIVES

11.1   *How do psychologists define stress?*

11.2   *What kinds of external events can cause stress?*

11.3   *What are some psychological factors in stress?*

11.5   *How do cognitive factors and personality differences affect the experience of stress?*

11.6   *What social factors influence stress reactions?*

11.7   *What are some ways in which people cope with stress reactions?*

11.4 How does stress affect the physical
      functioning of the body and its immune
      system?

11.8 How is coping with stress affected by culture
      and religion?
11.9 What are some ways to promote wellness?

PRACTICE EXAM

For the following multiple choice questions, select the answer you feel best answers the question.

1. The term used to describe the physical, emotional, cognitive, and behavioral responses to events that are viewed as threatening or challenging is _____.
    a) stress
    b) stressors
    c) uncontrollability
    d) pressures

2. The response an individual might have to an unpleasant stressor, such as losing his job, would be called
    a) eustress.
    b) distress.
    c) stress appraisal.
    d) negative stressors.

3. After we have decided that a certain event is a stressor, we must decide how we will deal with it and what resources are available for coping with the stressor. This process is called_____.
    a) primary appraisal
    b) secondary appraisal
    c) stress-related decision
    d) hassle-related decision

4. According to the cognitive-mediational theory of emotions proposed by Richard Lazarus, which of the following would be the best way to reduce the stress of losing a job?
    a) Try to ignore the problem.
    b) Try to understand all the negative implications of the loss.
    c) List all the resources that you do not have available and will need to acquire.
    d) View the loss as a challenge and opportunity to explore a new career.

5. Which of the following is an example of a stressor that would be classified as a hassle according to Richard Lazarus?
    a) getting married
    b) locking your keys in the car
    c) losing your house due to a flood
    d) the death of a family member

6. The Social Readjustment Rating Scale (SRRS) measures stress related to _____.
    a) positive and negative life events
    b) only negative life events
    c) only positive life events
    d) internal stressors

7. Gloria is a tax accountant, who is very busy from January to April 15, which is the tax return filing deadline. She feels that she must work very long hours during this time to meet the April 15 deadline for all of her clients. Gloria is experiencing_____.
   a) anxiety
   b) pressure
   c) overload
   d) cognitive dissonance

8. A woman who had an unpleasant confrontation with her boss and then goes home and yells at the dog would be displaying
   a) uncontrollability.
   b) pressure.
   c) displaced aggression.
   d) catastrophe.

9. Which of the following is a fact about suicide, according to the Office of the Surgeon General of the United States?
   a) Men attempt suicide more than women.
   b) More people die from suicide than from homicide.
   c) The most common method of committing suicide is with pills.
   d) Suicide is a spontaneous act.

10. People who talk about suicide just want attention and won't really follow through with it.
   a) True
   b) False

11. Which of the following is an example of an avoidance-avoidance conflict?
   a) a person who enjoys the ocean has to choose between retiring in the Bahamas or in Tahiti
   b) a student has to decide whether to turn in an unfinished paper and receive a failing grade or hand it in late and lose many points
   c) someone wanting to eat some cake but not wanting the calories
   d) a person who loves chocolate must choose between chocolate cake or chocolate ice cream

12. Trying to decide on taking a trip to the Bahamas which would be very enjoyable but would severely limit the amount of money you would have to spend on other items is an example of a(n)
   a) approach-approach conflict.
   b) approach-avoidance conflict.
   c) avoidance-avoidance conflict.
   d) multiple approach-avoidance conflict.

13. The general adaptation syndrome proposed by Hans Selye describes how we respond to stress with regard to our
   a) psychological reactions.
   b) emotional reactions.
   c) social reactions.
   d) physical reactions.

14. According to Selye, some people may develop illnesses such as high blood pressure or weakened immune system during the _____ stage of the GAS.
    a) alarm
    b) collapse
    c) exhaustion
    d) resistance

15. Stress has been shown to be related to _____.
    a) increased resistance to environmental threats
    b) decreased efficiency of the reticular formation
    c) increased galvanic skin response
    d) decreased efficiency of the body's immune system

16. When stress levels are elevated, the amount of natural killer cells in the body tends to
    a) increase.
    b) decrease.
    c) stay the same.
    d) There is not enough data to say at this point.

17. The Type A behavior pattern is a significant predictor of _____.
    a) mental illness
    b) coronary heart disease
    c) cancer
    d) respiratory illnesses

18. Someone who would be classified as having a Type C personality would be likely to
    a) openly express his or her anger at someone.
    b) try to always look on the bright side of a situation.
    c) display a great deal of hostility when things don't go his or her way.
    d) internalize his or her anger so that no one can see his or her true emotion.

19. _____ is the term used to describe the excessive anger exhibited by drivers in response to ordinary traffic frustration.
    a) Road rage
    b) Conflict
    c) Driving stress
    d) Frustration

20. Pepe moved from Argentina to France. He chose not to learn to speak and write French, continues to maintain his old culture's styles of dress and customs, and lives in a neighborhood where only people from Argentina live. Pepe has used which method of entering the majority culture?
    a) integration
    b) assimilation
    c) separation
    d) marginalization

21. Which method of acculturation would tend to lead to the greatest degree of stress?
    a) integration
    b) assimilation
    c) separation
    d) marginalization

22. Her mother is ill and Vanna is feeling overwhelmed and sad. To cope with this stress of her mother's illness, Vanna has been writing her feelings down in a journal. Vanna is using _____.
    a) problem-focused coping
    b) emotion-focused coping
    c) distraction
    d) reappraisal

23. A student who is failing but does not study because she refuses to believe that the instructor will really assign her an "F" at the end of the term is using the psychological defense mechanism of _____.
    a) repression
    b) denial
    c) projection
    d) rationalization

24. Which of the following examples best illustrates the psychological defense mechanism of projection?
    a) Suzan has a serious gambling addiction but refuses to admit it.
    b) John thinks to himself that he should watch one more hour of TV before starting to study for his big exam so that way he will feel nice and relaxed while he is studying.
    c) Saul plans an elaborate "congratulations party" for the coworker who received the promotion that Saul was desperately hoping to receive.
    d) Alex feels guilty about not doing his part to keep the house clean, but when his wife comes home, he accuses her of being a slob and not helping out enough around the house.

25. Research shows that _____ lowers blood pressure in adolescents and adults.
    a) sensory deprivation
    b) concentrative meditation
    c) sublimation
    d) implosive meditation

26. You are a psychologist working with a new client, an immigrant from China, who is experiencing adjustment problems due to stress. Which of the following are you first going to consider when assessing your client's ability to cope?
    a) use of meditative strategies
    b) use of psychological defense mechanisms
    c) ability to use biofeedback equipment
    d) cultural background.

27. Several studies have found a positive correlation between level of religious commitment and life expectancies.
    a) True
    b) False

28. Eating a healthy breakfast
    a) has been shown to increase the risk of obesity.
    b) has been shown to decrease the ability to concentrate.
    c) has been shown to decrease the risk of obesity.
    d) has been shown to increase the need for a morning nap.

1. a   The response itself is called stress and the event that causes the response is called a stressor.

2. b   The response to negative stressors is called distress and the response to positive stressors or the optimal level of stressors is referred to as eustress.

3. b   Secondary appraisal involves deciding how to deal with a stressor and estimating the resources available for coping with it, while primary appraisal is the first step we take when facing a potential threat; it involves estimating its severity and determining whether it is a challenge or a threat.

4. d   The cognitive-mediational theory of emotions suggests that the way we think about or interpret a stressor is the biggest factor in determining our response.

5. b   Lazarus focused on the minor daily annoyances, such as losing your car keys, as a significant source of stress in our lives.

6. a   The SRRS assumes that any change (either positive or negative) will serve as a stressor in an individual's life.

7. b   Although anxiety may be a result of pressure, Gloria is experiencing pressure as a result of her need to work longer hours to meet a deadline.

8. c   Displaced aggression often occurs when the person or object that a person is really angry at is not an accessible target.

9. b   Although women attempt suicide more frequently than men, men actually complete suicide at a higher rate than women.

10. b   This is a common myth about suicide.

11. b   Avoidance-avoidance conflicts involve having to choose between two undesirable outcomes.

12. b   Approach-avoidance conflicts focus on one decision that has both positive and negative aspects to it.

13. d   The general adaptation syndrome describes our body's physical reactions to stress.

14. d   During the resistance stage, the body uses its resources to fight off the stressor. It is not until the next stage, exhaustion, that bodily resources are so depleted that stress-related diseases can develop.

15. d   Stress is related to decreased efficiency of the immune system.

16. b   Natural killer cells are important cells in the body that server to limit the growth of cancerous cells. During times of stress, the level of natural killer cells tends to decrease, thus increasing the chances of tumor growth.

17. b   The original development of the idea of Type A personality was in order to describe and predict the individuals who were at high risk for heart disease.

18. d   Type C personalities tend to internalize their emotions.

19. a   Driving stress may be what a person with road rage feels, but road rage is the term for excessive anger exhibited by some drivers over ordinary traffic frustration.

20. c   Separation occurs when a person tries to maintain his or her original cultural identity. Assimilation occurs when a person completely gives up his or her old cultural identity and completely adopts the majority culture's ways.

21. d   Marginalization occurs when an individual is not a part of his original culture, nor is he a part of the new culture. This method of acculturation has been found to create the greatest amount of acculturative stress.

22. b   Vanna is coping with her stress by focusing on and thinking about her emotions.

23. b   Denial is the refusal to recognize or acknowledge a threatening situation. Rationalization is the defense mechanism that involves finding excuses for a behavior that is unacceptable.

24. d   Alex is projecting his feelings of guilt onto his wife.

25. b   Concentrative mediation places one in a state of relaxation and lowers blood pressure. There is no such term as implosive mediation.

26.   d   Psychological defense mechanisms are significant but would not be as important in your initial assessment as would cultural background, especially since the client is from a country with a very different culture.
27.   a   Although these studies do not prove a cause and effect relationship, they have shown a correlation between religious affiliation and longevity.
28.   c   Eating a healthy breakfast has been shown to decrease the risk of obesity.

CHAPTER GLOSSARY

acculturative stress	stress resulting from the need to change and adapt one's ways to the majority culture.
acute stress disorder (ASD)	a disorder resulting from exposure to a major stressor, with symptoms of anxiety, recurring nightmares, sleep disturbances, problems in concentration, and moments in which people seem to "relive" the event in dreams and flashbacks for as long as one month following the event.
aggression	actions meant to harm or destroy.
alarm	the first stage of Hans Selye's general adaptation syndrome during which the sympathetic nervous system prepares the body for action.
approach-approach conflict	conflict occurring when a person must choose between two desirable goals.
approach-avoidance conflict	conflict occurring when a person must choose or not choose a goal that has both positive and negative aspects.
avoidance-avoidance conflict	conflict occurring when a person must choose between two undesirable goals.
burnout	negative changes in thoughts, emotions, and behavior as a result of prolonged stress or frustration.
catastrophe	an unpredictable, large-scale event that creates a tremendous need to adapt and adjust as well as overwhelming feelings of threat.
cognitive-mediational theory	theory of emotions proposed by Richard Lazarus that states the way people think about and appraise a stressor is a major factor in their stress response.
College Undergraduate Stress Scale (CUSS)	assessment that measures the amount of stress in a college student's life over a one-year period resulting from major life events.
concentrative meditation	form of meditation in which a person focuses the mind on some repetitive or unchanging stimulus so that the mind can be cleared of disturbing thoughts and the body can experience relaxation.
conflict	psychological experience of being pulled toward or drawn to two or more desires or goals, only one of which may be attained.
coping strategies	actions that people can take to master, tolerate, reduce, or minimize the effects of stressors.
displaced aggression	taking out one's frustrations on some less threatening or more available target, a form of displacement.
displacement	psychological defense mechanism in which emotional reactions and behavioral responses are shifted to targets that are more available or less threatening than the original target.
distress	the effect of unpleasant and undesirable stressors.
double approach-avoidance conflict	conflict in which the person must decide between two goals, with each goal possessing both positive and negative aspects.
emotion-focused coping	coping strategies that change the impact of a stressor by changing the emotional reaction to the stressor.

escape or withdrawal	leaving the presence of a stressor, either literally or by a psychological withdrawal into fantasy, drug abuse, or apathy.
eustress	the effect of positive events, or the optimal amount of stress that people need to promote health and well-being.
exhaustion	the third stage of Hans Selye's general adaptation syndrome during which the parasympathetic nervous system takes over and the body experiences any number of physical illnesses.
frustration	the psychological experience produced by the blocking of a desired goal or fulfillment of a perceived need.
general adaptation syndrome (GAS)	the three stages of the body's physiological reaction to stress, including alarm, resistance, and exhaustion.
Hans Selye	1907–1982. Canadian endocrinologist who studied the physical response to stress and developed the concept of the general adaptation syndrome.
hardy personality	a person who seems to thrive on stress but lacks the anger and hostility of the Type A personality.
hassles	the daily annoyances of everyday life.
health psychology	area of psychology focusing on how physical activities, psychological traits, and social relationships affect overall health and rate of illness.
immune system	the system of cells, organs, and chemicals of the body that respond to attacks from diseases, infections, and injuries.
multiple approach-avoidance conflict	conflict in which the person must decide between more than two goals, with each goal possessing both positive and negative aspects.
natural killer cells	immune system cell responsible for suppressing viruses and destroying tumor cells.
optimists	people who expect positive outcomes.
parasympathetic nervous system	the division of the autonomic nervous system responsible for regulating the routine functions of the body, such as heartbeat, digestion, sleeping.
pessimists	people who expect negative outcomes.
post-traumatic stress disorder (PTSD)	a disorder resulting from exposure to a major stressor, with symptoms of anxiety, nightmares, poor sleep, reliving the event, and concentration problems, lasting for more than one month.
pressure	the psychological experience produced by urgent demands or expectations for a person's behavior that come from an outside source.
primary appraisal	the first step in assessing a stress, or involves estimating the severity of a stressor and classifying it as either a threat or a challenge.
problem-focused coping	coping strategies that try to eliminate the source of a stress or reduce its impact through direct actions.
psychological defense mechanisms	unconscious distortions of a person's perception of reality that reduce stress and anxiety.
psychoneuroimmunology	the study of the effects of psychological factors such as stress, emotions, thoughts, and behavior on the immune system.
receptive meditation	form of meditation in which a person attempts to become aware of everything in immediate conscious experience, or an expansion of consciousness.
resistance	the second stage of Hans Selye's general adaptation syndrome during which the sympathetic nervous system recruits resources to maintain an elevated level of activity and energy.
secondary appraisal	the second step in assessing a threat, involves estimating the resources available to the person for coping with the stressor.
Social Readjustment Rating Scale (SRRS)	assessment that measures the amount of stress in a person's life over a one-year period resulting from major life events.

social support system	the network of family, friends, neighbors, coworkers, and others who can offer support, comfort, or aid to a person in need.
stress	the term used to describe the physical, emotional, cognitive, and behavioral responses to events that are appraised as threatening or challenging.
stressors	events that cause a stress reaction.
suicide	intentionally taking one's own life.
sympathetic nervous system	the division of the autonomic nervous system responsible for mobilizing the body's energy and resources during times of stress and arousal.
Type A personality	person who is ambitious, time-conscious, extremely hard-working, and tends to have high levels of hostility and anger as well as being easily annoyed.
Type B personality	person who is relaxed and laid-back, less driven and competitive than Type A and slow to anger.
Type C personality	pleasant but repressed person, who tends to internalize his or her anger and anxiety and who finds expressing emotions difficult.
uncontrollability	the psychological experience caused by having no ability to change your particular set of circumstances.

stress is the physical, emotional, cognitive, and behavioral response to events that are appraised as threatening or challenging; first studied systematically by Hans Selye

can include physical fatigue, recurring illness, over/under eating, smoking/drinking more than usual, mood swings, irritability, depression, anger, memory and concentration problems

stress-causing events are called stressors; can come from external or internal sources; range from mild to severe

negative events cause distress; positive events cause eustress, the optimal level of stress required to facilitate healthy adaptation and well-being

external stress-causing events may include catastrophes, major life changes, and daily hassles (differ according to developmental stage)

can be assessed systematically (e.g., Social Readjustment Rating Scale, College Undergraduate Stress Scale)

Table 11.1 Sample Items from the Social Readjustment Rating Scale (SRRS)

MAJOR LIFE EVENT	LIFE CHANGE UNITS
Death of spouse	100
Divorce	75
Marital separation	65
Jail term	63
Death of a close family member	63
Personal injury or illness	53
Marriage	50
Dismissal from work	47
Marital reconcilliation	45
Pregnancy	40
Death of close friend	37
Change to different line of work	36
Change in number of arguments with spouse	36
Major mortgage	31
Foreclosure of mortgage or loan	30
Begin or end school	26
Change in living conditions	25
Change in work hours or conditions	20
Change in residence/schools/recreation	19
Change in social activities	18
Small mortgage or loan	17
Vacation	13
Christmas	12
Minor violations of the law	11

Source: Adapted and abridged from Holmes & Rahe (1967).

Stress and Stressors (part 1)

prolonged or acute stress can cause stress-related disorders that have symptoms including anxiety, recurring nightmares, sleep problems, problems concentrating, and "reliving" the experience through flashbacks or dreams

acute stress disorder (ASD): symptoms present for < 1 month

post-traumatic stress disorder (PTSD): symptoms persist > 1 month

pressure urgent demands or expectations and uncontrollability

frustration due to external (losses, rejections, failures, delays) or internal (personal characteristics) factors; can result in several typical responses

persistence

aggression

escape/withdrawal (**suicide** is a drastic form of escape)

Stress and Stressors (part 2)
(psychological stressors are often related to external events)

conflict

approach–approach conflict

avoidance–avoidance conflict

approach–avoidance conflict

multiple approach–avoidance conflicts

the **autonomic nervous system (ANS)** figures prominently in the body's physiological reactions to stress

Hans Selye identified the **general adaption syndrome (GAS)**, the sequence of physiological reactions the body goes through when adapting to a stressor

alarm

resistance

exhaustion

the field of **psychoneuroimmunology** focuses on the effects of stress on the immune system

Physiological Factors

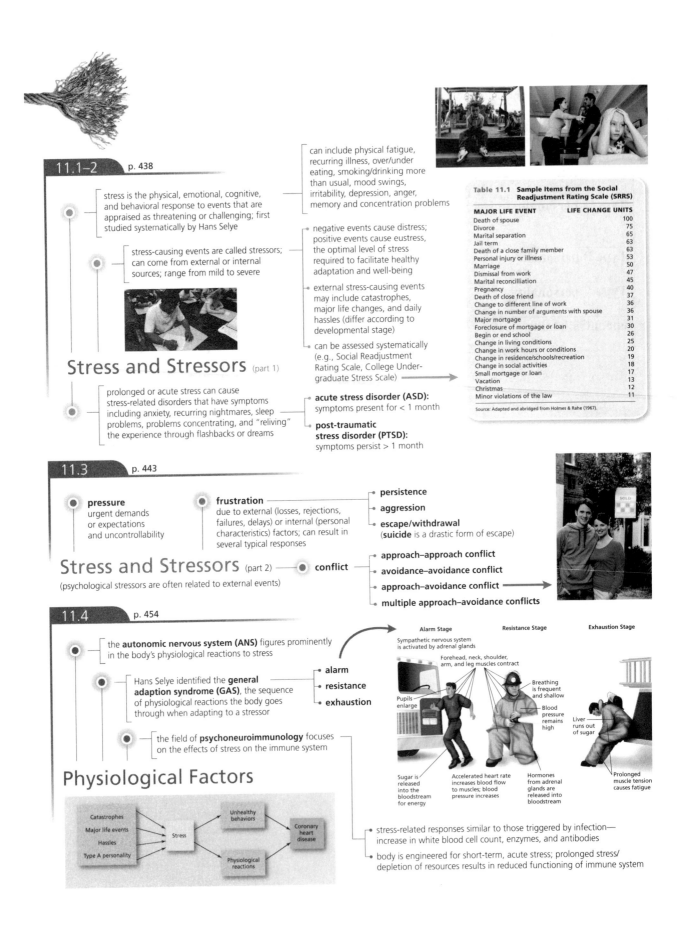

Alarm Stage   Resistance Stage   Exhaustion Stage

Sympathetic nervous system is activated by adrenal glands

Forehead, neck, shoulder, arm, and leg muscles contract

Pupils enlarge

Breathing is frequent and shallow

Blood pressure remains high

Liver runs out of sugar

Sugar is released into the bloodstream for energy

Accelerated heart rate increases blood flow to muscles; blood pressure increases

Hormones from adrenal glands are released into bloodstream

Prolonged muscle tension causes fatigue

Catastrophes / Major life events / Hassles / Type A personality → Stress → Unhealthy behaviors / Physiological reactions → Coronary heart disease

stress-related responses similar to those triggered by infection—increase in white blood cell count, enzymes, and antibodies

body is engineered for short-term, acute stress; prolonged stress/depletion of resources results in reduced functioning of immune system

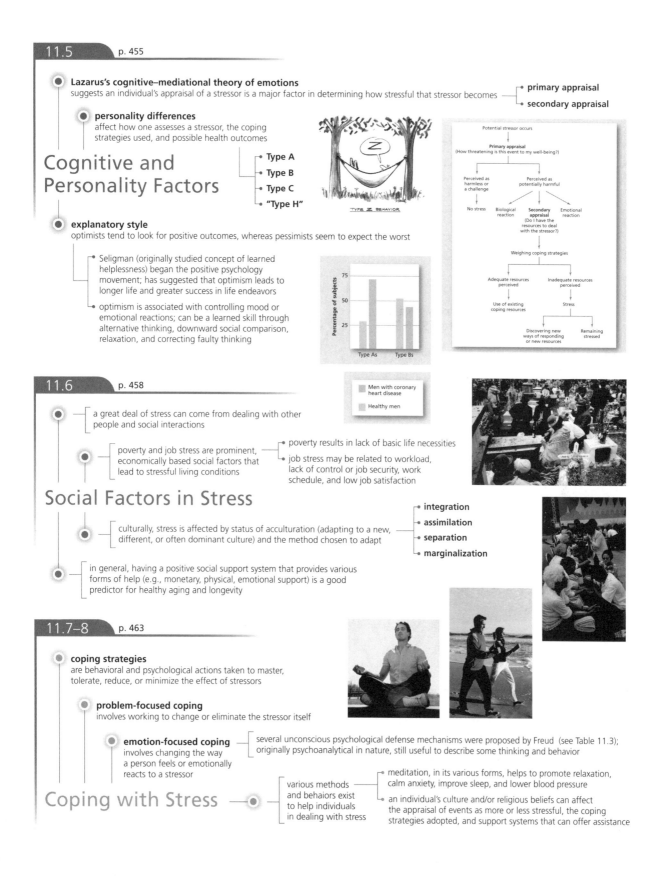

11.5 — p. 455

Lazarus's cognitive–mediational theory of emotions
suggests an individual's appraisal of a stressor is a major factor in determining how stressful that stressor becomes
- primary appraisal
- secondary appraisal

personality differences
affect how one assesses a stressor, the coping strategies used, and possible health outcomes

Cognitive and Personality Factors
- Type A
- Type B
- Type C
- "Type H"

explanatory style
optimists tend to look for positive outcomes, whereas pessimists seem to expect the worst

- Seligman (originally studied concept of learned helplessness) began the positive psychology movement; has suggested that optimism leads to longer life and greater success in life endeavors
- optimism is associated with controlling mood or emotional reactions; can be a learned skill through alternative thinking, downward social comparison, relaxation, and correcting faulty thinking

11.6 — p. 458

- a great deal of stress can come from dealing with other people and social interactions

- poverty and job stress are prominent, economically based social factors that lead to stressful living conditions
  - poverty results in lack of basic life necessities
  - job stress may be related to workload, lack of control or job security, work schedule, and low job satisfaction

Social Factors in Stress

- culturally, stress is affected by status of acculturation (adapting to a new, different, or often dominant culture) and the method chosen to adapt
  - integration
  - assimilation
  - separation
  - marginalization

- in general, having a positive social support system that provides various forms of help (e.g., monetary, physical, emotional support) is a good predictor for healthy aging and longevity

11.7–8 — p. 463

coping strategies
are behavioral and psychological actions taken to master, tolerate, reduce, or minimize the effect of stressors

problem-focused coping
involves working to change or eliminate the stressor itself

emotion-focused coping
involves changing the way a person feels or emotionally reacts to a stressor
- several unconscious psychological defense mechanisms were proposed by Freud (see Table 11.3); originally psychoanalytical in nature, still useful to describe some thinking and behavior

Coping with Stress

various methods and behaviors exist to help individuals in dealing with stress
- meditation, in its various forms, helps to promote relaxation, calm anxiety, improve sleep, and lower blood pressure
- an individual's culture and/or religious beliefs can affect the appraisal of events as more or less stressful, the coping strategies adopted, and support systems that can offer assistance

Table 11.1 **Sample Items from the Social Readjustment Rating Scale (SRRS)**

Table 11.1 **Sample Items from the Social Readjustment Rating Scale (SRRS)**

MAJOR LIFE EVENT	LIFE CHANGE UNITS
Death of spouse	100
Divorce	75
Marital separation	65
Jail term	63
Death of a close family member	63
Personal injury or illness	53
Marriage	50
Dismissal from work	47
Marital reconciliation	45
Pregnancy	40
Death of close friend	37
Change to different line of work	36
Change in number of arguments with spouse	36
Major mortgage	31
Foreclosure of mortgage or loan	30
Begin or end school	26
Change in living conditions	25
Change in work hours or conditions	20
Change in residence/schools/recreation	19
Change in social activities	18
Small mortgage or loan	17
Vacation	13
Christmas	12
Minor violations of the law	11

Source: Adapted and abridged from Holmes & Rahe (1967).

Table 11.2 **College Undergraduate Stress Scale (CUSS)**

Table 11.2 **College Undergraduate Stress Scale (CUSS)**

EVENT	RATING
Being raped	100
Finding out that you are HIV-positive	100
Death of a close friend	97
Contracting a sexually transmitted disease (other than AIDS)	94
Concerns about being pregnant	91
Finals week	90
Oversleeping for an exam	89
Flunking a class	89
Having a boyfriend or girlfriend cheat on you	85
Financial difficulties	84
Writing a major term paper	83
Being caught cheating on a test	83
Two exams in one day	80
Getting married	76
Difficulties with parents	73
Talking in front of a class	72
Difficulties with a roommate	66
Job changes (applying, new job, work hassles)	65
A class you hate	62
Confrontations with professors	60
Maintaining a steady dating relationship	55
Commuting to campus or work, or both	54
Peer pressures	53
Being away from home for the first time	53
Getting straight A's	51
Fraternity or sorority rush	47
Falling asleep in class	40

Source: Adapted from Renner & Mackin (1998).

_____

_____

_____

_____

_____

_____

_____

_____

_____

Figure 11.1 **General Adaptation Syndrome**

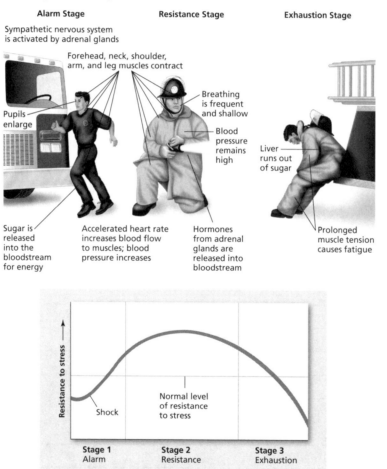

Figure 11.2 **Stress Duration and Illness**

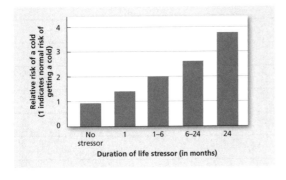

Figure 11.3 **Stress and Coronary Heart Disease**

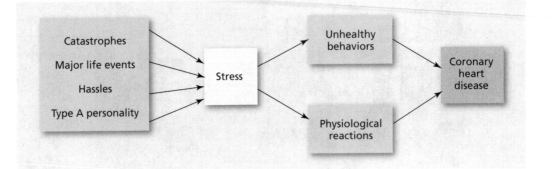

_____
_____
_____
_____
_____
_____
_____
_____

Figure 11.4 **Responses to a Stressor**

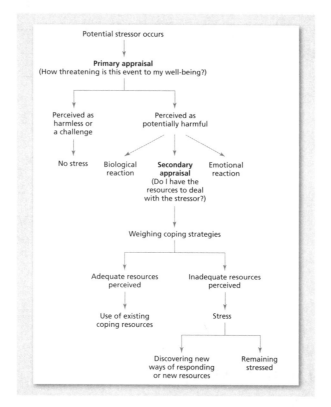

_____
_____
_____
_____
_____
_____
_____
_____

Figure 11.5 **Personality and Coronary Heart Disease**

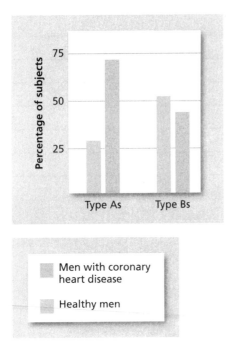

Men with coronary heart disease

Healthy men

11.7–11.9 Coping with Stress

Table 11.3 The Psychological Defense Mechanisms

Table 11.3 The Psychological Defense Mechanisms

DEFENSE MECHANISM AND DEFINITION	EXAMPLE
Denial: refusal to recognize or acknowledge a threatening situation.	Ben is an alcoholic who denies being an alcoholic.
Repression: "pushing" threatening or conflicting events or situations out of conscious memory.	Elise, who was sexually abused as a child, cannot remember the abuse at all.
Rationalization: making up acceptable excuses for unacceptable behavior.	"If I don't have breakfast, I can have that piece of cake later on without hurting my diet."
Projection: placing one's own unacceptable thoughts onto others, as if the thoughts belonged to them and not to oneself.	Keisha is attracted to her sister's husband but denies this and believes the husband is attracted to her.
Reaction formation: forming an emotional reaction or attitude that is the opposite of one's threatening or unacceptable actual thoughts.	Matt is unconsciously attracted to Ben but outwardly voices an extreme hatred of homosexuals.
Displacement: expressing feelings that would be threatening if directed at the real target onto a less threatening substitute target.	Sandra gets reprimanded by her boss and goes home to angrily pick a fight with her husband.
Regression: falling back on childlike patterns as a way of coping with stressful situations.	Four-year-old Jeff starts wetting his bed after his parents bring home a new baby.
Identification: trying to become like someone else to deal with one's anxiety.	Marie really admires Suzy, the most popular girl in school, and tries to copy her behavior and dress.
Compensation (substitution): trying to make up for areas in which a lack is perceived by becoming superior in some other area.	Reggie is not good at athletics, so he puts all of his energies into becoming an academic scholar.
Sublimation: turning socially unacceptable urges into socially acceptable behavior.	Alain, who is very aggressive, becomes a professional hockey player.

NOTES

YOU KNOW YOU ARE READY FOR THE TEST IF YOU ARE ABLE TO...

- Describe the role social influence plays on conformity, compliance, and obedience.
- Discuss the issues of social cognition including the formation and development of attitudes, impressions, and attributions.
- Introduce concepts of social interaction including prejudice, discrimination, interpersonal attraction, aggression, and altruisim.

RAPID REVIEW

Social psychology is the scientific study of how a person's behavior, thoughts, and feelings are influenced by the real, imagined, or implied presence of others. Social psychology can be broadly divided into the areas of social influence, social cognition, and social interaction.

Social influence is the process in which the presence of other people influences the behavior, feelings, and thoughts of an individual. **Conformity** involves changing one's own behavior to more closely match the actions of others. In 1951 Solomon Asch conducted a classic experiment on conformity by having subjects judge the length of a line after hearing a group of confederates all report an obviously incorrect answer. Asch found that the subjects conformed to the group answer around one-third of the time and that conformity increased as the group size increased, up to a group of four confederates. In a later study, Asch found that conformity greatly decreased when at least one confederate gave the right answer. **Groupthink** is a type of conformity in which people feel it is more important to maintain the group's cohesiveness than to consider the facts more realistically. Social influence can also be used to describe the phenomenon of **compliance**, which occurs when people change their behavior as a result of another person or the group asking or directing them to change. **Consumer psychology** is an area of psychology that studies how people get other people to buy things. There are a number of techniques that people use to obtain the compliance of others including the **foot-in-the-door technique**, in which compliance with a small request is followed by a larger request, and the **door-in-the-face technique**, which is the process of making a large request which is almost always refused and then a smaller request that is often agreed to. The door-in-the-face technique relies on the **norm of reciprocity**, which states that if someone does something to you, you should do something in return. Two additional compliance techniques include the **lowball technique** in which the cost of the commitment is increased *after* the commitment is already made and the **that's-not-all technique** in which an offer is made and before the individual can make a decision, something "extra" is added to the offer. In compliance, an individual changes his or her behavior because someone asks him or her; in **obedience**, an individual changes his or her behavior because an authority figure gives him or her an order. Stanley Milgram conducted one of the most famous experiments on obedience in which he measured the number of volts a participant would administer to another participant simply because the experimenter instructed him or her to do so. In reality, no electrical shocks were being administered. Milgram found that about two-thirds of the subjects (65 percent) administered electrical shocks up to a lethal level of 450 volts when instructed to do so. The presence of others can also influence how well an individual performs a specific task in a process. The positive influence of others on performance is called **social facilitation**, while the negative influence is sometimes called **social impairment**. If the task is easy, the presence of others seems to improve performance, but if the task is difficult, the presence of others actually has a negative impact on performance. **Social loafing** describes the tendency for people to put less effort into a simple task when working in a group as opposed to working alone.

Social cognition deals with the ways people think about other people and includes attitudes, impressions, and attributions. An **attitude** can be defined as a tendency to respond positively or negatively toward a certain idea, person, object, or situation. Attitudes are composed of the way people feel, act, and think. The affective component describes the feelings associated with attitudes, the behavior component describes the actions, and the cognitive component describes the thoughts. Attitudes have been found to be only weak predictors of actual behavior. Attitude formation occurs in or as a learning process that occurs through direct contact, direct instruction, interaction with others, and vicarious (or observational) learning. **Persuasion** is the process by which one person tries to change the belief, opinion, position, or course of action of another person through argument, pleading, or explanation. Factors that influence the effectiveness of persuasion include the source, the message, and the target audience. The **elaboration likelihood model** examines how likely it is that an individual will elaborate on a persuasive message and what the outcome of the elaboration will most likely be. When people attend to the content of the message, the model describes it as **central-route processing**, and when people pay attention to information outside of the message content itself, it is referred to as **peripheral-route processing**. **Cognitive dissonance** is a sense of discomfort that occurs when a person's behavior does not match up with that person's attitudes. When a person experiences cognitive dissonance, he or she typically changes the conflicting behavior to match the attitude, changes the attitude to match his or her behavior, or forms new cognitions to justify his or her behavior. **Impression formation** involves the process of forming the first knowledge that a person has concerning another person, in other words, the "first impression." One component of impression formation involves **social categorization**, which is the assignment of a person to a category based on characteristics the person has in common with other people with whom one has had experience in the past. Social categorization can often result in **stereotypes**, or a set of characteristics that people believe are shared by all members of a particular social category. People often form their own categories based on **implicit personality theories**, or sets of assumptions about how different types of people, personality traits, and actions are all related. Most implicit personality theories are formed in childhood. The final aspect of social cognition discussed in the textbook is **attribution**, or the process of explaining one's own behavior and the behavior of others. Fritz Heider originally described **attribution theory** and divided attributions into two categories: **situational causes** were explanations that relied on external causes and **dispositional causes** assume behavior is the result of some internal factor. The **fundamental attribution error** is the most well-known bias of attribution and is the tendency for some people to almost exclusively use dispositional attributes to explain other people's behavior.

Social interaction, or the relationship between people, is the third main area of study in the field of social psychology. When a person holds an unsupported and often negative attitude about the members of a particular group it is called a **prejudice**, and when a person acts differently towards a person based on that attitude it is called **discrimination**. The creation of **in-groups** and **out-groups** can often intensify discrimination. The **realistic conflict** theory states that prejudice and discrimination will be increased between groups that are in conflict. Jane Elliot used her second-grade classroom to demonstrate the power of prejudice and discrimination by dividing her class based on the color of the students' eyes and observing the effects. Conflicts between groups tend to increase as pressures and stresses increase. Often the prejudice exists because of the need for a scapegoat, a person or group who serves as the target for the frustrations and negative emotions of the group with the prejudiced attitude. Several theories have been proposed to explain the formation and persistence of prejudice. **Social identity theory** suggests that the three processes of social categorization, social identification, and **social comparison** are involved in the formation of prejudice attitudes. **Stereotype vulnerability** refers to the effect that a person's knowledge of someone else's stereotyped opinion can have on that person's behavior. The resulting feeling of anxiety is referred to as stereotype threat. The negative impact of stereotype threat on an individual's performance can actually cause a person to act in the way that the stereotype predicts, thus confirming an outside observer's prejudice attitude. **Self-fulfilling prophecy** occurs when a person acts according to his or her existing beliefs and his or her actions make it more likely that his or her beliefs are confirmed. The best defense against prejudice is becoming informed about people who are different from you. **Equal status contact**, in which all individuals involved have the same amount of power in the situation, is crucial for reducing prejudice. Educators have attempted to create situations of equal status in the classroom by setting up **jigsaw classrooms**, in which students have to work together to reach a specific goal. Another area of social interaction discussed in your textbook is **interpersonal attraction**, or liking or having the desire for a relationship with someone else. Several factors are involved in the attraction of one person to another including physical attractiveness, **proximity** (or how close a person is to you physically), similarity, and **reciprocity of liking** (or liking someone who likes you). Robert Sternberg proposed a theory of love that contains three components: intimacy, passion, and commitment. He felt that seven types of love could be described by various combinations of these three components. Two of Sternberg's proposed types of love are **romantic love** and **companionate love**. A very different type of social interaction is that of violence. **Aggression** is defined as any behavior intended to hurt or destroy another person. Social psychologists have examined the role of both biology and the environment on aggression. Twin studies have shown a higher correlation of aggression levels in identical twins than in fraternal twins. Certain areas of the brain have been found to control aggressive responses, and testosterone levels are related to aggression. However, a large portion of human aggression is influenced by learning. Several studies have suggested that taking on a particular **social role** can lead to an increase in aggressive behavior. A number of studies have also supported the link between exposure to violent media and aggression. The final area of social interaction discussed in your textbook is **prosocial behavior**, or socially desirable behavior that benefits others rather than bringing them harm. **Altruism** is a specific type of prosocial behavior in which an individual helps someone else with no expectation of reward. Sometimes the presence of other people can decrease the likelihood of prosocial behavior as can be seen in the **bystander effect** and **diffusion of responsibility**. Bibb Latane and John Darley conducted a series of experiments that found that participants were less likely to respond to an emergency situation where other people were present than when they were alone. Some of the decisions an individual must make when deciding whether to offer help or not include noticing the situation, defining the situation as an emergency, taking responsibility, planning a course of action, and taking action.

Technically, a **cult** refers to any group of people with a particular religious or philosophical set of beliefs and identities; however, most people associate the term cult with a group of people whose beliefs are so different from the mainstream that they are viewed with suspicion.

STUDY HINTS

1. The text introduces four common methods that are used to gain the compliance of another person. In order to better understand the differences among these methods, assume that you are trying to get your friend to come pick you up and then go shopping at the mall with you. In the space below, come up with an example of how you might get your friend to comply with your request using each of the techniques listed.

Technique	Example
Foot-in-the-door	
Door-in-the-face	
Lowball	
That's-not-all	

2. Social psychology contains a large number of well-known researchers along with the famous studies they carried out. It is important to be able to remember which researcher goes with which study. Next to the researchers listed below, briefly describe the experiment they carried out along with the topic they studied. In the final column, come up with a mnemonic to help you remember the information.

Researcher	Experiment	Topic	Mnemonic
Solomon Asch			
Stanley Milgram			
Jane Elliot			
Latané and Darley			
Philip Zimbardo			

LEARNING OBJECTIVES

12.1 What factors influence people to conform to the actions of others?

12.2 How is compliance defined, and what are four common ways to gain the compliance of another?

12.3 What factors make obedience more likely?

12.4 What are the three components of an attitude, how are attitudes formed, and how can attitudes be changed?

12.5 How do people react when attitudes and behavior are not the same?

12.6 What are social categorization and implicit personality theories?

12.7 How do people try to explain the actions of others?

12.8 How are prejudice and discrimination different?

12.9 Why are people prejudiced, and how can prejudice be stopped?

12.10 What factors govern attraction and love, and what are some different kinds of love?

12.11 How is aggressive behavior determined by biology and learning?

12.12 What is altruism, and how is deciding to help someone related to the presence of others?

12.13 Why do people join cults?

PRACTICE EXAM

For the following multiple choice questions, select the answer you feel best answers the question.

1. Vince has always believed children deserve the best prenatal care available. During a class discussion, he hears the first of several speakers express very negative attitudes toward spending tax money on prenatal care for the poor. When it is his turn to speak, he voices an opinion more in keeping with the previous speakers. Vince's behavior is an example of
   a) compliance.
   b) persuasion.
   c) conformity.
   d) obedience.

2. The following researcher conducted a series of studies on conformity that involved having a subject judge the length of three lines after a group of confederates all reported an obviously incorrect answer.
   a) Jane Elliot
   b) Stanley Milgram
   c) Philip Zimbardo
   d) Solomon Asch

3. _____ occurs when people begin to think that it is more important to maintain a group's cohesiveness than to objectively consider the facts.
   a) Groupthink
   b) The lowball technique
   c) Obedience
   d) Social loafing

4. All of the following are causes for groupthink EXCEPT
   a) the belief that the group can do no wrong.
   b) the belief that the group is invulnerable.
   c) the belief that opposition to the group is unsound.
   d) openness to differing opinions.

5. At the supermarket, a demonstrator gives away free samples of a new pizza. He also gives each taster a coupon worth $1 off his or her grocery bill. This manufacturer is depending on the social process of _____ to increase sales.
   a) norm of reciprocity
   b) deindividuation
   c) group polarization
   d) social facilitation

6. Selena is trying to get her boyfriend to wash the dishes for her. To start with, she asks her boyfriend to cook dinner for her. When her boyfriend refuses, she asks, "Well, will you at least wash the dishes then?" To which he readily agrees. Selena has just used the _____.
   a) foot-in-the-door technique
   b) door-in-the-face technique
   c) lowball technique
   d) that's-not-all technique

7. Changing one's behavior due to a direct order of an authority figure is referred to as
   a) compliance.
   b) obedience.
   c) conformity.
   d) persuasion.

8. Imagine 100 individuals are asked to take part in a replication of Milgram's famous study on obedience. How are these 100 people likely to respond?
    a) The majority would administer 450 volts as instructed.
    b) The majority would immediately realize the use of deception and leave.
    c) Most of the women would refuse to obey, whereas almost all of the men would obey.
    d) Most of the participants would work together to force the experimenter to end the experiment.

9. A teacher decides against assigning group projects in which all group members get the same grade. What social psychological phenomenon might the teacher be concerned about?
    a) conformity
    b) social loafing
    c) social influence
    d) social facilitation

10. Ashley has practiced her drum routine over and over. When she gets up to play it at the recital in front of 100 people, she performs it better than she ever has. Her improved performance is an example of
    a) social compliance.
    b) persuasion.
    c) social facilitation.
    d) social impairment.

11. Which of the following is the best example of the behavioral component of an attitude?
    a) Bea feels recycling is a great concept.
    b) Bob is upset when he hears a corporation plans to build a polluting plant near his home.
    c) Bill struggles to understand the arguments both sides present in a debate over a new manufacturing plant.
    d) Betty writes a letter to her senator asking for support of a law making corporations responsible for the pollution they cause.

12. Which of the following is NOT a factor that influences attitude formation?
    a) direct contact with an individual
    b) DNA inherited from your parents
    c) instructions from your parents
    d) observing someone else's actions

13. Kerry's positive attitude toward China, even though she has never been there, seems to be related to the fact that her mother is Chinese and talks about China all the time with Kerry. Which method of attitude formation is involved in this example?
    a) direct contact
    b) direct instruction
    c) interaction with others
    d) classical conditioning

14. Which communicator would likely be most persuasive?
    a) an attractive person who is an expert
    b) a moderately attractive person who is an expert
    c) an attractive person who has moderate expertise
    d) a moderately attractive person who has moderate expertise

15. _____ describes the situation in which people attend to the content of a message.
    a) Central-route processing
    b) Cognitive dissonance
    c) Social facilitation
    d) Peripheral-route processing

16. Which of the following was a finding in the classic study by Festinger and Carlsmith (1959)?
    a) Those who got $1 to perform a boring task said the task was more interesting than did those who got $2.
    b) Those who got $20 to perform a boring task said the task was more interesting than did those who got $1.
    c) Paid groups said the task was less boring than did nonpaid groups.
    d) Women performed the tasks for less money than men.

17. Which of the following represents an example of cognitive dissonance?
    a) a boy learns how to ride a bicycle without the training wheels
    b) a father telling his daughter that he will really only be proud of her if she gets all A's like she did last semester
    c) a student stays up all night to study for an upcoming exam
    d) a woman who is arguing that it is morally wrong to kill animals for food becomes upset when she is asked to explain why she is wearing a leather belt and leather shoes

18. What is the term for the process of developing an opinion about another person?
    a) social interaction
    b) stereotyping
    c) impression formation
    d) interpersonal judgment

19. Toni sees a picture of the new international exchange student and notices that the student looks happy, so Toni automatically assumes that he is also friendly. This automatic assumption about the student's personality is an example of
    a) central-route processing.
    b) implicit personality theory.
    c) cognitive dissonance.
    d) discrimination.

20. The process of explaining one's own behavior and the behavior of other people is called
    _____.
    a) stereotyping
    b) attribution
    c) central-route processing
    d) cognitive dissonance

21. "Look, Officer, I didn't see the stop sign back there because the sun was in my eyes." The police officer responds, "You were not paying attention." How would a social psychologist describe this situation?
    a) Both individuals were making fundamental attribution errors.
    b) Both individuals were making situational attributions.
    c) The driver was making a dispositional attribution; the officer was making a situational attribution.
    d) The driver was making a situational attribution; the officer was making a dispositional attribution.

22. While watching the TV game show "Jeopardy," your roommate says, "The game show host, Alex Trebek, knows all the answers. He must be a genius." You tell your roommate she probably would not have said that if she had attended class the day the instructor discussed the topic of _____.
    a) social facilitation
    b) stereotyping illusions
    c) internal attribution biases
    d) fundamental attribution errors

23. A bank loan officer thinks people who speak with an accent are lazy; consequently, he refuses to grant them loans. The loan officer's belief is an example of _____. His refusal to grant them loans is an example of _____ .
    a) discrimination; prejudice
    b) stereotyping; attribution
    c) attribution; stereotyping
    d) prejudice; discrimination

24. The part of a person's self-concept that is based on his or her identification with a nation, culture, or ethnic group or with gender or other roles in society is called
    a) the fundamental attribution error.
    b) self-serving bias.
    c) ethnocentrism.
    d) social identity.

25. Which of the following does NOT represent an effective method for reducing prejudice?
    a) establishing a jigsaw classroom
    b) bringing diverse groups of people into contact with each other
    c) learning about people who are different from you
    d) establishing equal status contact between different groups of people

26. We tend to ___ attractive people more than we do less attractive people.
    a) like
    b) dislike
    c) ignore
    d) hate

27. When opposites attract it is said that they have _____ characteristics.
    a) proximal
    b) complementary
    c) rewarding
    d) reciprocal

28. Which of the following was NOT a component of Robert Sternberg's theory of love?
    a) intimacy
    b) lust
    c) passion
    d) commitment

29. Behavior that is intended to hurt or destroy another person is referred to as _____ .
    a) empty love
    b) prejudice
    c) aggression
    d) dissonance

30. The fact that a social role can lead to an increase in aggressive behavior points to _____ as a major contributor to aggression.
    a) biology
    b) the environment
    c) DNA
    d) chemical influences

31. What term refers to helping behavior that is performed voluntarily for the benefit of another person, with no anticipation of reward?
    a) altruism
    b) collectivism
    c) interdependence
    d) humanitarianism

32. In a crowded mall parking lot, dozens of people hear a female voice yell, "He's killing me!" Yet, no one calls the police. What is the reason for the lack of action, according to Darley and Latane?
    a) People are too busy to respond.
    b) Most people "do not want to become involved."
    c) The fight-or-flight response is not activated when others are in danger.
    d) There is a diffusion of responsibility.

33. In Latané and Darley's classic 1969 study, they found that _____ of the participants reported the smoke in the room when the two confederates in the room noticed the smoke but then ignored it.
    a) all
    b) three-fourths
    c) one-half
    d) one-tenth

34. All of the following are decision points in helping behavior EXCEPT
    a) noticing.
    b) defining an emergency.
    c) taking responsibility.
    d) diffusion of responsibility.

35. In 1995, there were approximately how many cults in the United States?
    a) 200
    b) 500
    c) 4000
    d) 15,000

PRACTICE EXAM ANSWERS

1. c   Conformity involves going along with the group despite one's real opinion. Compliance would be the case if someone had asked him to voice an opinion in keeping with the previous speakers. In this case, Vince did it on his own as a result of internal pressure to conform.

2. d   D is the correct answer. Asch conducted the well-known studies on conformity. Milgram studied obedience in his famous studies with electrical shock.

3. a   Groupthink describes the thought processes that can dominate a group of individuals.

4. d   Groupthink results in lack of differing opinions. Believing that the group can do no wrong is actually a cause for groupthink.

5. a   The norm of reciprocity involves the tendency of people to feel obligated to give something in return after they have received something. Social facilitation is an increase in performance caused by greater arousal.

6. b   The door-in-the-face technique involves asking for a large request that you know will be refused followed up by a smaller request, which many people then agree to.

7. b   Obedience involves changing your behavior due to an order from "above," while conformity involves changing your behavior to better "fit in" with others around you.

8. a   The Milgram experiment has been repeated at various times, in the United States and in other countries, and the percentage of participants who went all the way consistently remained between 61 and 66 percent. In addition, few differences between males and females have been found.

9. b   The teacher knows that some students will slack off if they are not being evaluated for their individual performance, due to a phenomenon known as social loafing.

10. c   Social facilitation is the term for the positive effect on one's performance caused by the perception that others are watching.

11. d   Writing is an action, or behavior. The fact that Bill struggled to understand indicates that what he is doing is cognitive.

12. b   Attitude formation is believed to occur solely through the learning process and is not considered to be something that is inherited biologically.

13. c   The fact that Kerry's mother talks about China all the time with Kerry and is Chinese indicates that her attitude is the result of interaction with her mother.

14. a   Attractiveness and expertise have been shown to increase persuasiveness.

15. a   In central-route processing, an individual pays attention to the content of the message, whereas in peripheral-route processing, an individual focuses on details other than the main content of the message.

16. a   The group that got paid less used cognitive dissonance to justify their poor pay for telling a lie.

17. d   Cognitive dissonance is an emotional disturbance that occurs when a person's actions don't match his or her statements.

18. c   While stereotyping may be a component of impression formation, it is not the term for the process of developing an opinion about another person.

19. b   Implicit personality theory represents the automatic associations a person makes about personality traits that are assumed to be related.

20. b   An attribute is an explanation for a person's behavior. Stereotypes are preconceived ideas about a group of people.

21. d   The driver attributed his error to something in his situation, the sun; whereas the officer attributed his error to something internal to him, his lack of attention.

22. d   Your roommate attributed something that is situational (Trebek gets the answers ahead of time) to an internal characteristic (genius). Although internal attribution bias sounds correct, it is not a term used in social psychology.

23. d   Prejudice is an unsupported, often negative belief about all people in a particular group, whereas discrimination is an action taken that is based on this belief. In this case, the action is the refusal to grant loans.

24. d   Social identity refers to a person's identity with his or her social group. Ethnocentrism is the process of viewing the world from your own viewpoint and failing to see alternative perspectives.

25. b   Simply bringing groups together normally does not reduce prejudice unless all the members of the group have equal status and power in the group.
26. a   Social psychologists have found that we tend to like attractive people more than unattractive people.
27. b   Things that "complement" each other tend to be opposites. The term proximity refers to nearness.
28. b   Sternberg's theory of love includes the three components of intimacy, passion, and commitment.
29. c   Aggression describes a type of behavior, whereas prejudice refers to a person's attitude.
30. b   The impact of the social role points to learning and the influence of the surrounding environment on an individual's aggressive behavior.
31. a   Altruism is defined as helping others for no personal benefit. Humanitarianism means almost the same thing as altruism but is not the term social psychologists use for the helping behavior that is performed voluntarily for the benefit of another person, with no anticipation of reward.
32. d   According to Latane and Darley most people say they do want to become involved, however often diffusion of responsibility occurs. Diffusion of responsibility is what occurs as each person thinks someone else will call for help, i.e., take responsibility.
33. d   About 1/10th of the participants reported smoke when the confederates in the room noticed the smoke but did nothing about it. This number was much higher when the participants were in the room alone.
34. d   Diffusion of responsibility stops a person from helping and is not considered a decision point.
35. c   The estimate is between 3000-5000 cults in the U.S.

CHAPTER GLOSSARY

aggression	behavior intended to hurt or destroy another person.
altruism	prosocial behavior that is done with no expectation of reward and may involve the risk of harm to oneself.
attitude	a tendency to respond positively or negatively toward a certain person, object, idea, or situation.
attribution	the process of explaining one's own behavior and the behavior of others.
attribution theory	the theory of how people explain behavior.
bystander effect	referring to the effect that the presence of other people has on the decision to help or not help, with help becoming less likely as the number of bystanders increases.
central-route processing	type of information processing that involves attending to the content of the message itself.
cognitive dissonance	sense of discomfort or distress that occurs when a person's behavior does not correspond to that person's attitudes.
companionate love	type of love proposed by Robert Sternberg consisting of intimacy and commitment.
compliance	changing one's behavior as a result of other people directing or asking for the change.
conformity	changing one's own behavior to match that of other people.
consumer psychology	branch of psychology that studies people's buying habits in the marketplace.
cult	any group of people with a particular religious or philosophical set of beliefs and identity.

diffusion of responsibility	occurring when a person fails to take responsibility for actions or for inaction because of the presence of other people who are seen to share the responsibility.
discrimination	treating people differently because of prejudice toward the social group to which they belong.
dispositional cause	cause of behavior attributed to internal factors such as personality or character.
door-in-the-face technique	asking for a large commitment and being refused, and then asking for a smaller commitment.
elaboration likelihood model	model of persuasion stating that people will either elaborate on the persuasive message or fail to elaborate on it, and that the future actions of those who do elaborate are more predictable than those who do not.
equal status contact	contact between groups in which the groups have equal status, with neither group having power over the other.
foot-in-the-door technique	asking for a small commitment and, after gaining compliance, asking for a bigger commitment.
Fritz Heider	1896-1988. German social psychologist known for the development of attribution theory.
fundamental attribution error	the tendency to overestimate the influence of internal factors in determining behavior while underestimating situational factors.
groupthink	kind of thinking that occurs when people place more importance on maintaining group cohesiveness than on assessing the facts of the problem with which the group is concerned
implicit personality theories	sets of assumptions about how different types of people, personality traits, and actions are related to each other.
impression formation	the forming of the first knowledge that a person has concerning another person.
in-groups	social groups with whom a person identifies; "us."
interpersonal attraction	liking or having the desire for a relationship with another person.
jigsaw classroom	educational technique in which each individual is given only part of the information needed to solve a problem, causing the separate individuals to be forced to work together to find the solution.
lowball technique	getting a commitment from a person and then raising the cost of that commitment.
norm of reciprocity	assumption that if someone does something for a person, that person should do something for the other in return.
obedience	changing one's behavior at the command of an authority figure.
out-groups	social groups with whom a person does not identify; "them."
peripheral-route processing	type of information processing that involves attending to factors not involved in the message, such as the appearance of the source of the message, the length of the message, and other noncontent factors.
persuasion	the process by which one person tries to change the belief, opinion, position, or course of action of another person through argument, pleading, or explanation.
prejudice	negative attitude held by a person about the members of a particular social group.
prosocial behavior	socially desirable behavior that benefits others.
proximity	physical or geographical nearness. Greater proximity increases the likelihood of forming a relationship.
realistic conflict theory	theory stating that prejudice and discrimination will be increased between groups that are in conflict.

reciprocity of liking	tendency of people to like other people who like them in return.
romantic love	type of love proposed by Robert Sternberg consisting of intimacy and passion.
scapegoat	an individual who is punished for the mistakes of someone else.
self-fulfilling prophecy	the tendency of one's expectations to affect one's behavior in such a way as to make the expectation more likely to be occur.
situational cause	cause of behavior attributed to external factors, such as delays, the action of others, or some other aspect of the situation.
social categorization	the assignment of a newly met person to a category based on characteristics the new person has in common with other people with whom the person doing the assigning has had experience in the past.
social cognition	deals with the ways people think about other people and includes attitudes, impressions, and attributions.
social comparison	the comparison of oneself to others in ways that raise one's self-esteem.
social facilitation	the tendency for the presence of other people to have a positive impact on the performance of an easy task.
social identification	the part of the self-concept including one's view of self as a member of a particular social category.
social identity theory	theory in which the formation of a person's identity within a particular social group is explained by social categorization, social identity, and social comparison.
social influence	the process through which the real or implied presence of others can directly or indirectly influence the thoughts, feelings, and behavior of an individual
social interaction	the relationship between people.
social loafing	the tendency for people to put less effort into a simple task when working with others on that task.
social psychology	the scientific study of how a person's thoughts, feelings, and behavior are influenced by the real, imagined, or implied presence of others
social role	the pattern of behavior that is expected of a person who is in a particular social position.
Solomon Asch	1907-1996. Pioneer in the field of social psychologist well known for his experiments on conformity.
Stanley Milgram	1933-1984. Social psychologist at Yale University famous for his experiments on obedience to authority.
stereotype threat	the feeling of anxiety that a person's knowledge of someone else's stereotyped opinion can have on that person's behavior.
stereotype vulnerability	the effect that people's awareness of the stereotypes associated with their social group affect their behavior.
stereotypes	a set of characteristics that people believe are shared by all members of a particular social category.
that's-not-all technique	the persuader makes an offer and then adds something extra to make the offer look better before the target person can make a decision.

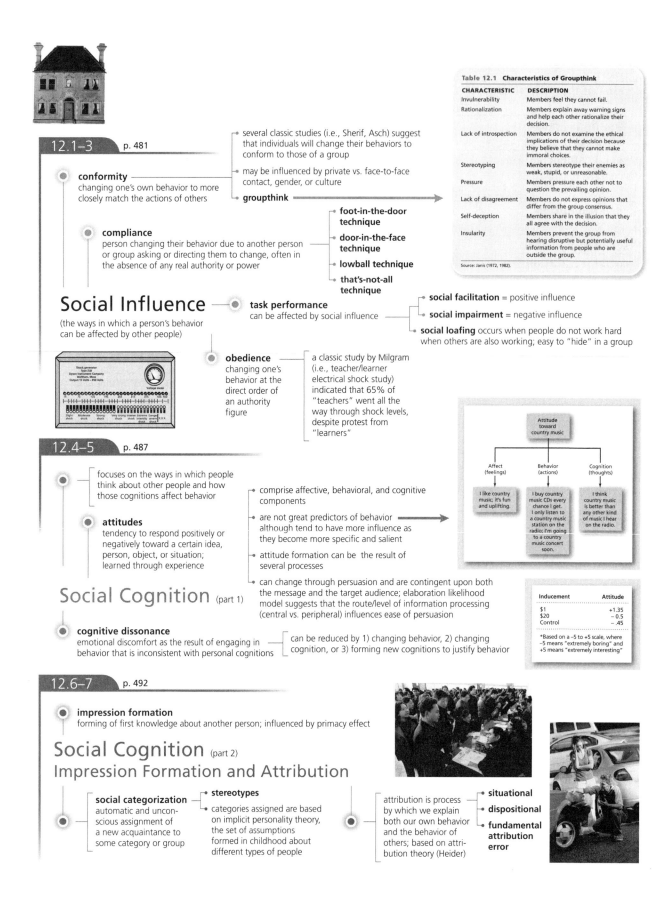

Table 12.1 Characteristics of Groupthink

CHARACTERISTIC	DESCRIPTION
Invulnerability	Members feel they cannot fail.
Rationalization	Members explain away warning signs and help each other rationalize their decision.
Lack of introspection	Members do not examine the ethical implications of their decision because they believe that they cannot make immoral choices.
Stereotyping	Members stereotype their enemies as weak, stupid, or unreasonable.
Pressure	Members pressure each other not to question the prevailing opinion.
Lack of disagreement	Members do not express opinions that differ from the group consensus.
Self-deception	Members share in the illusion that they all agree with the decision.
Insularity	Members prevent the group from hearing disruptive but potentially useful information from people who are outside the group.

Source: Janis (1972, 1982).

12.1–3 p. 481

conformity
changing one's own behavior to more closely match the actions of others

- several classic studies (i.e., Sherif, Asch) suggest that individuals will change their behaviors to conform to those of a group
- may be influenced by private vs. face-to-face contact, gender, or culture

groupthink

compliance
person changing their behavior due to another person or group asking or directing them to change, often in the absence of any real authority or power

- foot-in-the-door technique
- door-in-the-face technique
- lowball technique
- that's-not-all technique

Social Influence
(the ways in which a person's behavior can be affected by other people)

task performance
can be affected by social influence

- **social facilitation** = positive influence
- **social impairment** = negative influence
- **social loafing** occurs when people do not work hard when others are also working; easy to "hide" in a group

obedience
changing one's behavior at the direct order of an authority figure

a classic study by Milgram (i.e., teacher/learner electrical shock study) indicated that 65% of "teachers" went all the way through shock levels, despite protest from "learners"

12.4–5 p. 487

focuses on the ways in which people think about other people and how those cognitions affect behavior

attitudes
tendency to respond positively or negatively toward a certain idea, person, object, or situation; learned through experience

- comprise affective, behavioral, and cognitive components
- are not great predictors of behavior although tend to have more influence as they become more specific and salient
- attitude formation can be the result of several processes
- can change through persuasion and are contingent upon both the message and the target audience; elaboration likelihood model suggests that the route/level of information processing (central vs. peripheral) influences ease of persuasion

Social Cognition (part 1)

cognitive dissonance
emotional discomfort as the result of engaging in behavior that is inconsistent with personal cognitions

can be reduced by 1) changing behavior, 2) changing cognition, or 3) forming new cognitions to justify behavior

Inducement	Attitude
$1	+1.35
$20	− 0.5
Control	− .45

*Based on a –5 to +5 scale, where –5 means "extremely boring" and +5 means "extremely interesting"

12.6–7 p. 492

impression formation
forming of first knowledge about another person; influenced by primacy effect

Social Cognition (part 2)
Impression Formation and Attribution

social categorization
automatic and unconscious assignment of a new acquaintance to some category or group

- **stereotypes**
- categories assigned are based on implicit personality theory, the set of assumptions formed in childhood about different types of people

attribution is process by which we explain both our own behavior and the behavior of others; based on attribution theory (Heider)

- situational
- dispositional
- fundamental attribution error

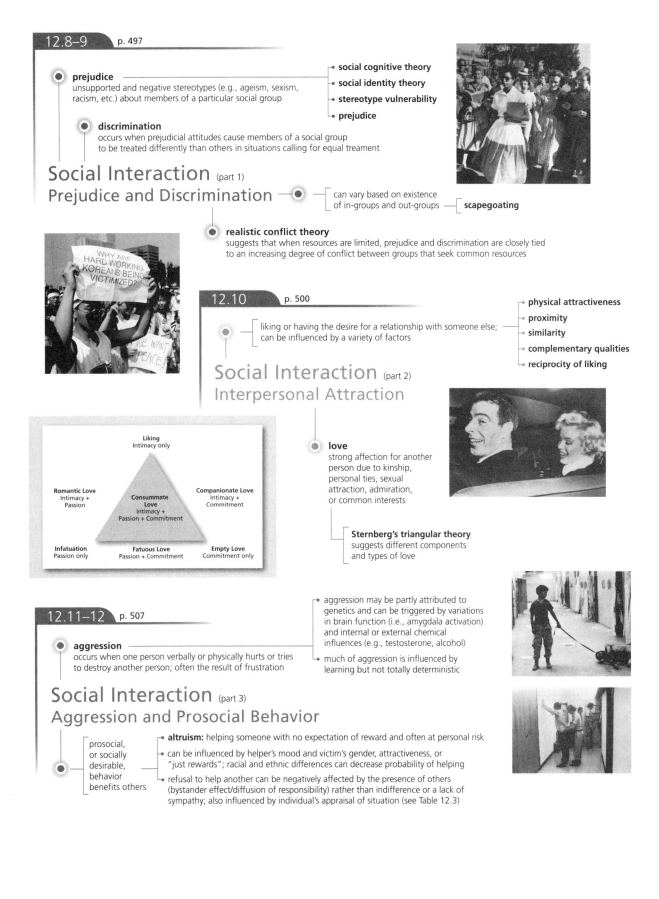

● **prejudice** —————— unsupported and negative stereotypes (e.g., ageism, sexism, racism, etc.) about members of a particular social group

- ► **social cognitive theory**
- ► **social identity theory**
- ► **stereotype vulnerability**
- ► **prejudice**

● **discrimination**
occurs when prejudicial attitudes cause members of a social group to be treated differently than others in situations calling for equal treament

Social Interaction (part 1)
Prejudice and Discrimination ——●——
┌ can vary based on existence
└ of in-groups and out-groups —— **scapegoating**

● **realistic conflict theory**
suggests that when resources are limited, prejudice and discrimination are closely tied to an increasing degree of conflict between groups that seek common resources

WHY ARE HARD WORKING KOREANS BEING VICTIMIZED?

WE WANT PEACE!

● ┌ liking or having the desire for a relationship with someone else;
   └ can be influenced by a variety of factors

- ► **physical attractiveness**
- ► **proximity**
- ► **similarity**
- ► **complementary qualities**
- ► **reciprocity of liking**

Social Interaction (part 2)
Interpersonal Attraction

```
                    Liking
                 Intimacy only

Romantic Love                      Companionate Love
 Intimacy +        Consummate         Intimacy +
  Passion             Love            Commitment
                   Intimacy +
                Passion + Commitment

Infatuation       Fatuous Love        Empty Love
Passion only   Passion + Commitment  Commitment only
```

● **love**
strong affection for another person due to kinship, personal ties, sexual attraction, admiration, or common interests

┌ **Sternberg's triangular theory**
│ suggests different components
└ and types of love

┌ aggression may be partly attributed to genetics and can be triggered by variations in brain function (i.e., amygdala activation) and internal or external chemical influences (e.g., testosterone, alcohol)

└ much of aggression is influenced by learning but not totally deterministic

● **aggression** —————— occurs when one person verbally or physically hurts or tries to destroy another person; often the result of frustration

Social Interaction (part 3)
Aggression and Prosocial Behavior

● ┌ prosocial, or socially desirable, behavior benefits others

- ► **altruism:** helping someone with no expectation of reward and often at personal risk
- ► can be influenced by helper's mood and victim's gender, attractiveness, or "just rewards"; racial and ethnic differences can decrease probability of helping
- ► refusal to help another can be negatively affected by the presence of others (bystander effect/diffusion of responsibility) rather than indifference or a lack of sympathy; also influenced by individual's appraisal of situation (see Table 12.3)

Figure 12.1 **Stimuli Used in Asch's Study**

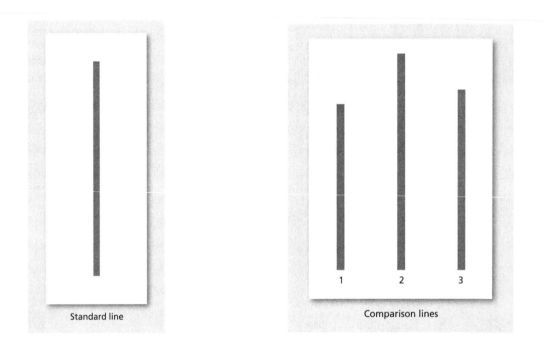

Standard line

Comparison lines

Table 12.1 **Characteristics of Groupthink**

Table 12.1	**Characteristics of Groupthink**
CHARACTERISTIC	**DESCRIPTION**
Invulnerability	Members feel they cannot fail.
Rationalization	Members explain away warning signs and help each other rationalize their decision.
Lack of introspection	Members do not examine the ethical implications of their decision because they believe that they cannot make immoral choices.
Stereotyping	Members stereotype their enemies as weak, stupid, or unreasonable.
Pressure	Members pressure each other not to question the prevailing opinion.
Lack of disagreement	Members do not express opinions that differ from the group consensus.
Self-deception	Members share in the illusion that they all agree with the decision.
Insularity	Members prevent the group from hearing disruptive but potentially useful information from people who are outside the group.

Source: Janis (1972, 1982).

Figure 12.2 **Control Panel in Milgram's Experiment**

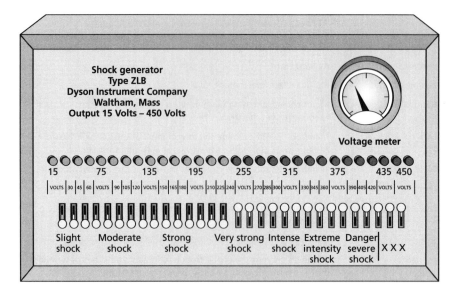

Table 12.2 **Sample Script Items from Milgram's Classic Experiment**

Table 12.2 **Sample Script Items from Milgram's Classic Experiment**

VOLTAGE OF "SHOCK"	LEARNER'S SCRIPT
150	"Ugh!! Experimenter! That's all. Get me out of here. I told you I had heart trouble. My heart's starting to bother me now. Get me out of here, please. My heart's starting to bother me. I refuse to go on. Let me out."
210	"Ugh!! Experimenter! Get me out of here. I've had enough. I *won't* be in this experiment any more."
300	(*Agonized scream*) "I absolutely refuse to answer any more. Get me out of here. You can't hold me here. Get me out. Get me out of here."
330	(*Intense and prolonged agonized scream*) "Let me out of here. Let me out of here. My heart's bothering me. Let me out, I tell you. (*Hysterically*) Let me out of here. Let me out of here. You have no right to hold me here. Let me out! Let me out! Let me out of here! Let me out! Let me out!"

Source: Milgram (1964a, 1974).

_____
_____
_____
_____
_____
_____
_____
_____
_____
_____
_____
_____
_____
_____
_____
_____
_____
_____
_____
_____
_____
_____
_____
_____
_____
_____
_____
_____

_____
_____
_____
_____
_____
_____
_____
_____
_____
_____
_____

Figure 12.3 **Three Components of an Attitude**

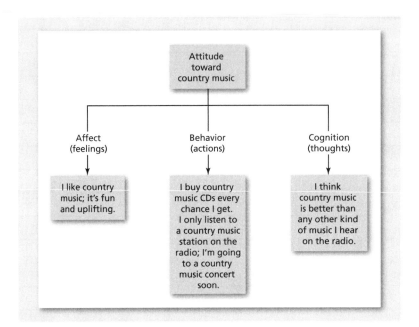

_____
_____
_____
_____
_____
_____
_____
_____
_____
_____
_____

Figure 12.4 **Cognitive Dissonance: Attitude Toward a Task**

Inducement	Attitude
$1	+1.35
$20	− 0.5
Control	− .45

*Based on a −5 to +5 scale, where −5 means "extremely boring" and +5 means "extremely interesting"

12.8–12.10 Social Interaction: Prejudice, Love, and Aggression

Figure 12.5 **Sternberg's Triangular Theory of Love**

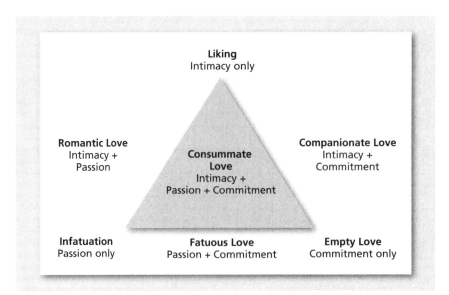

12.11 Aggression

_____
_____
_____
_____
_____
_____
_____
_____
_____
_____
_____

Figure 12.6 **Elements Involved in Bystander Response**

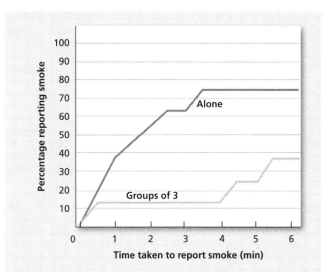

_____
_____
_____
_____
_____
_____
_____
_____
_____
_____
_____
_____

Table 12.3 **Help or Don't Help: Five Decision Points**

Table 12.3   **Help or Don't Help: Five Decision Points**

DECISION POINT	DESCRIPTION	FACTORS INFLUENCING DECISION
Noticing	Realizing that there is a situation that might be an emergency.	Hearing a loud crash or a cry for help.
Defining an Emergency	Interpreting the cues as signaling an emergency.	Loud crash is associated with a car accident, people are obviously hurt.
Taking Responsibility	Personally assuming the responsibility to act.	A single bystander is much more likely to act than when others are present (Latané & Darley, 1969).
Planning a Course of Action	Deciding how to help and what skills might be needed.	People who feel they have the necessary skills to help are more likely to help.
Taking Action	Actually helping.	Costs of helping (e.g., danger to self) must not outweigh the rewards of helping.

12.13   Cults

YOU KNOW YOU ARE READY FOR THE TEST IF YOU ARE ABLE TO...

- Define personality according to the various perspectives in psychology.
- Discuss Freud's psychoanalytical perspective on personality including the division of the mind, components of personality, stages of development, and modifications of his theory by the neo-Freudians.
- Describe the behaviorists' perspective on personality and the social cognitive theory including Albert Bandura's model.
- Introduce the humanistic perspective of personality including Carl Rogers view of the self and concept of unconditional positive regard.
- Discuss trait theory with regard to the description of personality.
- Explain what is known about the role of biology and heredity in personality development
- Describe major methods of personality assessment including interviews, projective tests, behavioral assessment, and personality inventories.

RAPID REVIEW

Personality is the unique way in which each individual thinks, acts, and feels throughout life. Two components of personality are **character**, which refers to value judgments made about a person's morals or ethical behavior and **temperament**, or the enduring characteristics a person is born with. There are at least four different perspectives regarding personality including the psychoanalytic, behaviorist, humanistic, and trait perspectives.

The **psychoanalytic perspective** originated with the theories of Sigmund Freud and focuses on the role of unconscious thoughts and desires in the development of personality. It is important to take into account the sexually repressed Victorian era in which Freud grew up when evaluating his theory or personality. Freud believed the mind was divided into three parts: the **conscious** mind contains all of the things a person is aware of at any given moment, the **preconscious** mind contains all the memories and facts that can be recalled with only minimal effort, and the **unconscious** mind is the part of our mind which remains hidden at all times. Freud believed the unconscious mind was the most important factor in directing behavior and personality. In addition to the divisions of the mind, Freud also believed that personality could be divided into three components: the id, ego, and superego. The **id** resides completely in the unconscious mind and represents the most primitive part of the personality containing all of the basic biological drives such as hunger, thirst, and sex. According to Freud, the id operates on **the pleasure principle**, which attempts to seek immediate gratification of needs with no regard for consequences. Freud referred to the psychological tension created by a person's unconscious desires as the libido. The **ego** represents the mostly conscious and rational aspect of personality, which operates on the **reality principle**, attempting to satisfy the desires of the id in a way that will minimize negative consequences. The **superego** is the last part of the personality to develop according to Freud's theory and represents the moral center of personality. The superego contains the **conscience**, or the part of personality that makes a person feel good or bad depending on whether they do the right or wrong thing. According to Freud, the id demands immediate satisfaction, while the superego places restrictions on which behaviors are morally acceptable, and the ego is left in the middle to come up with a compromise.

For Freud, the three components of personality develop in a series of **psychosexual stages** with each stage focused on a different erogenous zone, or area of the body that produces pleasurable feelings. Unresolved conflicts at any of the stages of development can lead to **fixation** and subsequent emotional or psychological problems as an adult. The first stage is called the **oral stage** because the erogenous zone is the mouth. Fixation can occur in this stage if the baby is weaned from the mother's breast too soon or too late. The second stage in Freud's theory is the **anal stage**, during which time period the anus serves as the erogenous zone and the conflict centers around toilet training. Fixation resulting from openly rebelling against the toilet training results in adults who are characteristically messy and are referred to as

anal expulsive personalities. Fixation resulting from overly strict toilet training results in adults who are stingy, stubborn, and excessively neat and would be referred to as **anal retentive personalities**. The third stage is the **phallic stage** and focuses on the child's own genitals. During this stage the child develops a sexual attraction to the opposite-sex parent, becomes jealous of the same-sex parent, develops anxiety due to the attraction and the jealousy, and resolves the anxiety through sexual repression and identification with the same-sex parent. Freud referred to this process in boys as the **Oedipus complex** and suggested that girls go through a similar process with their fathers as the target of their affection. The process of **identification** leads to the development of the superego so that by the end of Freud's third stage of development, all three components of personality are in place. The fourth stage, known as the **latency stage**, consists of repressed sexual feelings during which children focus on intellectual, physical, and social development but not sexual development. The final stage occurs around the start of puberty when sexual feelings can no longer be repressed and is referred to as the **genital stage**.

A number of psychologists, referred to as **neo-Freudians**, agreed with parts of Freud's theories but not all aspects. Carl Gustav Jung believed that there were two parts of the unconscious, a **personal unconscious** similar to the unconscious described by Freud and a **collective unconscious** which contained universal human memories that Jung called **archetypes**. Alfred Adler felt that the motivating factor of behavior was not the pleasure-seeking drive of the libido suggested by Freud, but rather the seeking of superiority through defense mechanisms such as compensation. Karen Horney disagreed with Freud's emphasis on sexuality and thought personalities were shaped more by a child's sense of **basic anxiety**, which if unattended to could lead to the development of **neurotic personalities**. Erik Erikson developed eight psychosocial stages of development which focused on the role of social relationships in the development of personality.

Although Freud's theory has had a significant impact on the culture of modern Western societies, his theory has been criticized on the scientific grounds due to the fact that it was not developed based on scientific experiments but rather on Freud's personal observations in his private practice as a psychiatrist, and that Freud's personal observations were limited to a specific group of wealthy Austrian women living in the sexually repressed Victorian era.

According to the behaviorists' perspective, personality consists of a set of learned responses or **habits**. A variation on the behaviorist perspective is that of the **social cognitive learning theorists**, who emphasize the role of conditioning along with an individual's thought processes in the development of personality. A strong proponent of the **social cognitive view**, Albert Bandura, suggested that the environment, behavior, and personal/cognitive factors all act together to determine an individual's actions in a process Bandura referred to as **reciprocal determinism**. An important component of the cognitive factors is the person's sense of **self-efficacy**, or perception of how effective a behavior will be in a particular context. Julian Rotter proposed that individuals develop a relatively set way of responding and this behavior represented "personality." An important determinant of the individual's response was his or her sense of **locus of control**. According to Rotter, the individual's **expectancy** and the response's reinforcement value were the two key factors that determined how an individual would react.

The **humanistic perspective** of personality focuses more on qualities that are considered uniquely human such as free will and subjective emotions. Carl Rogers proposed that humans are always striving to fulfill their innate capacities in a process known as the **self-actualizing tendency**. Rogers defined **positive regard** as warmth, affection, love, and respect that comes from significant others. In order for an individual to work towards self-actualization, they need to be exposed to a certain level of **unconditional positive regard** from the significant others in their lives. Rogers felt that **conditional positive regard** would restrict a person's ability to become a fully functioning person. Rogers believed an individual's image of oneself, or **self-concept**, also played a role in becoming **fully functional**. The self-concept was based on what an individual is told by others and also his or her own sense of **self**. According to Rogers, self-concept could be divided into a **real self** and an **ideal self**. If the real self and ideal self concept were too far apart, anxiety and neurotic behavior would result.

Trait theories of personality have focused on describing personality and predicting behavior based on that description. A **trait** is a consistent, enduring way of thinking, feeling, or behaving. Gordon Allport identified approximately 200 traits in the English language that he felt were "wired" into each person's nervous system. Raymond Cattell narrowed the number of traits down further by dividing traits into **surface traits**, such as the 200 traits described by Allport and **source traits**, or the more basic traits that underlie the surface traits and form the core of personality. **Introversion** is an example of a source trait. Cattell believed that there were 16 basic, or source traits. Later researchers narrowed this list to five source traits and developed the personality model known as the **five-factor model**, or the Big Five. The five trait dimensions are **openness**, **conscientiousness**, **extraversion**, **agreeableness**, and **neuroticism**. Critics of the five-factor model have argued that the situation plays a more significant role in determining an individual's behavior than is suggested by trait theory and have proposed a theory that includes a **trait-situation interaction**.

The field of **behavioral genetics** studies the role of inherited traits in personality. Twin studies have found that identical twins are more similar than fraternal twins or unrelated people in certain aspects of personality such as intelligence, leadership, tendency to follow rules, assertiveness, and aggressiveness. Adoption studies have supported some of these findings and have suggested a biological basis for shyness and aggressiveness.

In an attempt to describe "national personalities," Geert Hofstede conducted a cross-cultural study for IBM which resulted in a description of each country along four basic dimensions. The dimensions Hofstede observed were individualism/collectivism, power distance, masculinity/femininity, and uncertainty avoidance.

Methods for assessing personality have been developed based on specific theories of personality as well as the various goals of classification, self-insight, and the diagnosis of psychological disorders. An **interview** is a method of personality assessment in which the professional asks questions of the client and allows the client to answer in either a structured or unstructured manner. Interviews are limited by the fact that clients can lie, intentionally or unintentionally, and the interviewers can bring their own biases into their interpretations including the **halo effect**, which is the tendency of a person's first impression to influence later assessments. Psychoanalysts have developed **projective tests** in an attempt to assess a person's unconscious conflicts or desires by having them **projected** onto an ambiguous visual stimulus. Two of the most commonly used projective tests are the **Rorschach inkblot test** and the **Thematic Apperception Test or TAT**. Projective tests are highly **subjective** and have been found to have very low reliability and validity. A behaviorist would be more likely to measure personality by directly observing an individual's actions. In **direct observation**, the psychologist would observe an individual in a specific setting and record his or her behaviors through the use of a **rating scale** or a **frequency count**. Critics of this approach have pointed out the possibility for both the observer effect and observer bias. Trait theorists would be most likely to use a **personality inventory**, which consists of a questionnaire that has a standard list of questions that require specific answers such as "yes" or "no." Examples of commonly used personality inventories include Cattell's 16 PF, the Neuroticism/Extraversion/Openness Personality Inventory (NEO-PI), the Myers-Briggs Type Indicator (MPTI) and the Minnesota Multiphasic Personality Inventory, Version II (MMPI-2). The advantage of personality inventories is that they are scored objectively, which eliminates the possibility of observer bias, and they have been found to have very high reliability and validity scores. However, the inventories are still based on self-report.

A large number of personality tests are accessible over the Internet; however, the results of such tests should be interpreted with an appropriate level of skepticism.

STUDY HINTS

1. Students often confuse the levels of awareness suggested by Freud with his three components of personality. The next two exercises should help you keep them straight. To start with let's think about your levels of awareness. For each of the levels listed, list at least three examples of the information or memories that would be found there. Start with the conscious level.

My <u>conscious</u> level of awareness might contain the following:

My <u>preconscious</u> level of awareness might contain the following:

_____

_____

My <u>unconscious</u> level of awareness might contain the following:

_____

_____

2. Now think about the three components that Freud suggested make up an individual's personality; the id, the ego, and the superego. For each of the situations listed below, describe how a person's id, ego, and superego might respond. The first example has been completed for you. Notice how the ego always represents the compromise between the two extremes.

Situation	Id	Ego	Superego

Your roommate just made a batch of chocolate chip cookies and said he is going to take most of them to work with him tomorrow.			
You just finished watching two hours of TV and still have a lot of homework to do for tomorrow but you don't feel like doing it.			

LEARNING OBJECTIVES

13.1   What is personality, and how do the various perspectives in psychology view personality?

13.2   How did Freud's historical view of the mind and personality form a basis for psychodynamic theory?

13.3   How did Jung, Adler, Horney, and Erikson modify Freud's theory?

13.4   How does modern psychoanalytic theory differ from that of Freud?

13.5   How do behaviorist and social cognitive theorists explain personality?

13.6   How do humanists such as Carl Rogers explain personality?

13.7   What are the history and current views of the trait perspective?

13.8   What part do biology, heredity, and culture play in personality?

13.9   What are the advantages and disadvantages of the following measures of personality: interviews, projective tests, behavioral, personality inventories, and online personality tests?

PRACTICE EXAM

For the following multiple choice questions, select the answer you feel best answers the question.

1.   The unique way in which each individual thinks, acts, and feels throughout life is called _____.
  a)   character
  b)   personality
  c)   temperament
  d)   the unconscious

2.   One limitation of the trait perspective compared to the other perspectives is there is not much
  a)   description.
  b)   research.
  c)   material.
  d)   explanation.

3. Many have compared Freud's idea of the mind to an iceberg. If that were the case and you were standing on the deck of a ship in Alaska, what part of the mind would you see above the water?
    a) ego
    b) superego
    c) id
    d) preconscious

4. Information that cannot be recalled even when a person makes a determined effort to retrieve it would be said by Freud to be residing in the
    a) conscious.
    b) preconscious.
    c) unconscious.
    d) superego.

5. In Sigmund Freud's theory, the _____ operates according to the pleasure principle.
    a) id
    b) ego
    c) thanatos
    d) superego

6. According to Freud, the last component of an individual's personality to develop is the
    a) ego.
    b) superego.
    c) id.
    d) libido.

7. What is Freud's term for the executive of the personality that has a realistic plan for obtaining gratification of an individual's desires?
    a) id
    b) ego
    c) superego
    d) preconscious

8. Freud called the developmental stage in which the Oedipus complex occurs the
    a) oral stage.
    b) anal stage.
    c) phallic stage.
    d) latency stage.

9. Freud believed that the personality characteristics of overeating, gum chewing, being too dependent or overly optimistic developed due to fixation during the
    a) oral stage.
    b) anal stage.
    c) phallic stage.
    d) latency stage.

10. Which neo-Freudian viewed personality disturbances as resulting from the feelings of inferiority all people share?
    a) Carl Jung
    b) Alfred Adler
    c) Carl Rogers
    d) Karen Horney

11. Karen Horney disagreed with Freud about the unconscious force that influences behavior. She believed the force was not sexual desire, but rather
    a) feelings of inferiority.
    b) basic anxiety.
    c) the collective unconscious.
    d) self-regard.

12. Which of the following is NOT a current criticism of Freud's psychoanalytic theory?
    a) the significant impact it has had on culture
    b) the lack of empirical evidence
    c) observations based on Freud's personal clients
    d) role of women in Freud's theory

13. Albert Bandura's notion that people are affected by their environment but can also influence that environment is known as
    a) self-efficacy.
    b) locus of control.
    c) phenomenology.
    d) reciprocal determinism.

14. A baseball player's son is quite talented; he has received lots of awards over the years. When he gets up to bat he expects to get a hit, and when he is in the field he expects to make every catch. According to Bandura, what characteristic does this young man seem to have?
    a) self-regard
    b) self-centeredness
    c) self-efficacy
    d) self-actualization

15. _____ theory is called the third force in personality theory.
    a) Psychoanalytic.
    b) Behaviorist
    c) Cognitive
    d) Humanistic

16. In Carl Rogers's theory, our perception of our abilities, behaviors, and characteristics is known as _____.
    a) personality
    b) self-regard
    c) self-esteem
    d) self-concept

17. Which of the following represents an example of unconditional positive regard?
    a) a mother telling her son that she hopes he becomes an engineer like his father
    b) a father telling his daughter that he will really only be proud of her if she gets all As like she did last semester
    c) an owner only pays attention to her dog when he is well-behaved
    d) a parent telling his son he loves him even though he just wrecked the family car

18. What did Gordon Allport think about traits?
    a) He thought they were like stages.
    b) He thought they were wired into the nervous system.
    c) He thought they were learned.
    d) He thought they were the result of cognitive modeling.

19. How many source traits did Raymond Cattell discover through the process of factor analysis?
    a) 5
    b) 16
    c) 200
    d) 4,500

20. What psychoanalytic theorist most notably influenced the Big Five theory of personality?
    a) Freud
    b) Jung
    c) Erikson
    d) Horney

21. The fact that an outgoing extravert might be very talkative at a party but very quiet at a funeral is an example of
    a) trait-situation interaction.
    b) cross-cultural similarities.
    c) source trait reliability.
    d) neuroticism.

22. What major conclusion about personality traits emerged from the Minnesota twin study?
    a) Identical twins are more similar than any other type of sibling.
    b) Siblings reared apart were much more similar than identical twins.
    c) Fraternal twins reared together were much more similar than identical twins.
    d) Personality scores for twins were not related in either case.

23. Which of the following countries would NOT be considered a collectivist country according to the studies by Geert Hofstede?
    a) Japan
    b) United States
    c) Mexico
    d) Korea

24. Which of the following terms describes the cultural personality of the United States according to Hofstede's dimensions of cultural personality?
    a) individualistic
    b) high in power distance
    c) low in individualism
    d) high in uncertainty avoidance

25. Which of the following is NOT considered a disadvantage in the use of interviews for personality assessment?
    a) halo effect
    b) answers are based on self-report
    c) bias of the interviewer
    d) natural flow of the questions

26. Which personality test relies on the interpretation of inkblots to understand personality?
    a) MMPI
    b) 16PF
    c) TAT
    d) Rorschach

27. Which of the following is NOT a criticism of projective tests?
    a) They are a projection of the person's unconscious concern.
    b) They are low in reliability.
    c) Their interpretation is more an art than a science.
    d) They lack validity.

28. Direct observation is most like
    a) case studies.
    b) naturalistic observation.
    c) experimental methods.
    d) correlation.

29. The most commonly used personality inventory is the
    a) MMPI-2.
    b) MBTI.
    c) TAT.
    d) CPI.

30. Which of the following is an advantage to using personality inventories?
    a) observer bias
    b) They are standardized.
    c) biases of interpretation
    d) They rely on self-report.

31. A personality test that results in statements that are so general that they could apply to just about anyone is a good example of
    a) high validity.
    b) the Barnum Effect.
    c) observer bias.
    d) inter-rater reliability.

PRACTICE EXAM ANSWERS

1. b   Temperament and character are both part of personality. Character refers to value judgments made about a person's morals, and temperament refers to the enduring characteristics that a person is born with.
2. a   Trait theories are descriptive and deal with the actual end result of personality.
3. a   The ego is the part of the mind that is conscious and in view.
4. c   Freud thought that information sometimes seeped out of the unconscious through our dreams or slips of the tongue, but for the most part, the information was not readily available to our conscious awareness.
5. a   According to Freud, the id represents the most basic part of the personality and operates on the pleasure principle. The ego operates on the reality principle.
6. b   Freud's theory states that the superego develops during the phallic stage or when an individual is around 5-6 years old.

7.   b   The ego is in charge of reality and decisions and the superego is there for moral judgments, but the ego makes the decisions.

8.   c   The Oedipus complex leads to the development of the superego and occurs during the phallic stage.

9.   a   Freud described those personality traits as resulting from fixation during the oral stage of development.

10.   b   Adler viewed personality disturbances as resulting from the feelings of inferiority all people share. Jung focused on archetypes in the collective unconscious.

11.   b   Horney believed that basic anxiety was the unconscious driving force behind many of the behaviors people exhibited.

12.   a   The impact of Freud's theory on culture is not considered a criticism.

13.   d   Self-efficacy refers to one's perception of how effective a behavior will be in any particular circumstance, whereas reciprocal determinism is Bandura's notion that people are affected by their environment but can also influence that environment.

14.   c   Self-efficacy refers to one's perception of how effective a behavior will be in any particular circumstance. Self-actualization has to do with self-fulfillment and reaching one's full potential.

15.   d   Humanistic theory is called the third force in personality theory; the first two are psychoanalytic theory and behaviorist theory.

16.   d   Self-esteem has more to do with one's sense of worth.

17.   d   Rogers defined unconditional positive regard as being love, affection, and respect with no strings attached.

18.   b   Allport thought traits were not learned, but rather were wired into the nervous system.

19.   b   Cattell proposed that there were 16 source traits of personality.

20.   b   Freud's views are not involved in trait theory, but Jung's theory mentioned extroversion, which is one of the Big Five traits.

21.   a   The trait-situation interaction focuses on the interaction of source traits with the specific environment or situation that a person is in.

22.   a   Identical twins, who share the same genes, are more similar in personality than are any other type of siblings.

23.   b   The Hofstede study found that the United States could be described as more of an individualistic culture.

24.   a   Americans expect power to be well distributed rather than held by an elite few; democracies are typically low in power distance.

25.   d   The natural flow of the interview process is one of the advantages of this method.

26.   d   The Rorschach is a projective test that relies on the use of inkblot interpretation.

27.   a   The reason a psychologist would use a projective test is in order to get a "projection" of that individual's unconscious concerns.

28.   b   In naturalistic observation, one directly observes behavior in a relatively natural environment. Doing case studies involves gathering information through interviews rather than through actually observing the individual in a natural setting.

29.   a   The MMPI-2 is used more than any other inventory.

30.   b   The fact that personality inventories are standardized represents one of the greatest advantages to using this assessment technique.

31.   b   The Barnum Effect can also be seen in daily horoscope readings.

CHAPTER GLOSSARY

agreeableness	the emotional style of a person which may range from easy-going, friendly, and likeable to grumpy, crabby, and unpleasant.
Albert Bandura	born 1925. Bandura developed the theory of reciprocal determinism to explain personality development.

Alfred Adler	1870–1937. One of the Neo-Freudians who continued the pursuit of the unconscious. Adler focused on the need for power as a driving force in an individual's life.
anal expulsive personalities	a person fixated in the anal stage who is messy, destructive, and hostile.
anal retentive personalities	a person fixated in the anal stage who is neat, fussy, stingy, and stubborn.
anal stage	second stage occurring from about 1 to 3 years of age, in which the anus is the erogenous zone and toilet training is the source of conflict.
archetypes	Jung's collective, universal human memories.
basic anxiety	type of anxiety proposed by Karen Horney that is created when a child is born into the bigger and more powerful world of older children and adults.
behavioral genetics	field of study devoted to discovering the genetic bases for personality characteristics.
Carl Jung	1875–1961. Swiss psychiatrist who was a pioneer in the psychoanalytic school of thought and was heavily influenced by Freud.
Carl Rogers	1902–1987. Humanist psychologist who focused on the role of the self-concept and positive regard on personality development.
character	value judgments of a person's moral and ethical behavior.
collective unconscious	Jung's name for the memories shared by all members of the human species.
conditional positive regard	positive regard that is given only when the person is doing what the providers of positive regard wish.
conscience	a person's sense of morality, or sense of right and wrong.
conscientiousness	the care a person gives to organization and thoughtfulness of others, dependability.
conscious mind	level of the mind which is aware of immediate surroundings and perceptions.
direct observation	assessment in which the professional observes the client engaged in ordinary, day-to-day behavior in either a clinical or natural setting.
ego	part of the personality that develops out of a need to deal with reality, mostly conscious, rational and logical.
Erik Erikson	1902–1994. Developmental psychologist who believed that personality developed through a series of psychosocial crises.
erogenous zone	an area of the body especially sensitive to sexual stimulation.
expectancy	a person's subjective feeling that a particular behavior will lead to a reinforcing consequence.
extraversion	dimension of personality referring to one's need to be with other people.
five-factor model	also known as the Big Five, model of personality traits that describes five basic trait dimensions.
fixation	disorder in which the person does not fully resolve the conflict in a particular psychosexual stage, resulting in personality traits and behavior associated with that earlier stage.
frequency count	assessment in which the frequency of a particular behavior is counted.
fully functioning person	a term proposed by Carl Rogers to describe a person who is in touch with and trusting of their own innermost urges and feelings.
genital stage	fifth stage of Freud's theory occurring from adolescence on; sexual energy is focused on sexual activity with others.
habits	in behaviorism, sets of well-learned responses that have become automatic.
halo effect	tendency of an interviewer to allow positive characteristics of a client to influence the assessments of the client's behavior and statements.

humanistic perspective	the "third force" in psychology that focuses on those aspects of personality that make people uniquely human, such as subjective feelings and freedom of choice.
id	part of the personality present at birth and completely unconscious.
ideal self	one's perception of who one should be or would like to be.
identification	defense mechanism in which a person tries to become like someone else to deal with anxiety.
interview	method of personality assessment in which the professional asks questions of the client and allows the client to answer, either in a structured or unstructured fashion.
introversion	dimension of personality in which people tend to withdraw from excessive stimulation.
Karen Horney	1885–1952. A neo-Freudian who focused on more equal representation of men and women in psychoanalytic theory and also the role of basic anxiety as a motivating force.
latency stage	fourth stage occurring during the school years, in which the sexual feelings of the child are repressed while the child develops in other ways.
libido	the instinctual energy that may come into conflict with the demands of a society's standards for behavior.
locus of control	the tendency for people to assume that they either have control or do not have control over events and consequences in their lives.
neo-Freudians	followers of Freud who developed their own, competing theories of psychoanalysis.
neurotic personalities	personality type proposed by Karen Horney in which the individual is characterized by maladaptive ways of dealing with relationships.
neuroticism	degree of emotional instability or stability.
Oedipus complex	situation occurring in the phallic stage in which a child develops a sexual attraction to the opposite-sex parent and jealousy of the same sex-parent.
openness	one of the five factors, willingness to try new things and be open to new experiences.
oral stage	first stage occurring in the first year of life, and in which the mouth is the erogenous zone and weaning is the primary conflict.
personal unconscious	Jung's name for the unconscious mind as described by Freud.
personality	the unique and relatively stable ways in which people think, feel, and behave.
personality inventory	paper and pencil or computerized test that consists of statements that require a specific, standardized response from the person taking the test.
phallic stage	third stage occurring from about 3 to 6 years of age, in which the child discovers sexual feelings.
pleasure principle	principle by which the id functions; the immediate satisfaction of needs without regard for the consequences.
positive regard	warmth, affection, love, and respect that come from significant others in one's life.
preconscious mind	level of the mind in which information is available, but not currently conscious.
projection	defense mechanism involving placing, or "projecting" one's own unacceptable thoughts onto others, as if the thoughts actually belonged to those others and not to oneself.
projective tests	personality assessments that present ambiguous visual stimuli to the client and ask the client to respond with whatever comes to mind.

psychoanalytic perspective	Freud's term for both the theory of personality and the therapy based upon it.
psychosexual stages	five stages of personality development proposed by Freud and tied to the sexual development of the child.
rating scale	assessment in which a numerical value is assigned to specific behavior that is listed in the scale.
real self	one's perception of actual characteristics, traits, and abilities.
reality principle	principle by which the ego functions; the satisfaction of the demands of the id only when negative consequences will not result.
reciprocal determinism	Bandura's explanation of how the factors of environment, personal characteristics, and behavior can interact to determine future behavior.
Rorschach inkblot test	projective test that uses 10 inkblots as the ambiguous stimuli.
self	an individual's awareness of his or her own identity.
self-actualizing tendency	the striving to fulfill one's innate capacities and capabilities.
self-concept	the image of oneself that develops from interactions with important, significant people in one's life.
self-efficacy	individual's perception of how effective a behavior will be in any particular circumstance.
Sigmund Freud	1856-1939. Founder of the psychoanalytic school of thought which focuses on the role of the unconscious on behavior.
social cognitive learning theorists	theorists who emphasize the importance of both the influences of other people's behavior and of a person's own expectancies on learning.
social cognitive view	learning theory that includes cognitive processes such as anticipating, judging, memory, and imitation of models.
source traits	the more basic traits that underlie the surface traits, forming the core of personality.
subjective	referring to concepts and impressions that are only valid within a particular person's perception and may be influenced by biases, prejudice, and personal experiences.
superego	part of the personality that acts as a moral center.
surface traits	aspects of personality that can easily be seen by other people in the outward actions of a person.
temperament	the enduring characteristics with which each person is born.
Thematic Apperception Test (TAT)	projective test that uses twenty pictures of people in ambiguous situations as the visual stimuli.
trait	a consistent, enduring way of thinking, feeling, or behaving.
trait theories	theories that endeavor to describe the characteristics that make up human personality in an effort to predict future behavior.
trait-situation interaction	the assumption that the particular circumstances of any given situation will influence the way in which a trait is expressed.
unconditional positive regard	positive regard that is given without conditions or strings attached.
unconscious mind	level of the mind in which thoughts, feelings, memories, and other information is kept that is not easily or voluntarily brought into consciousness.

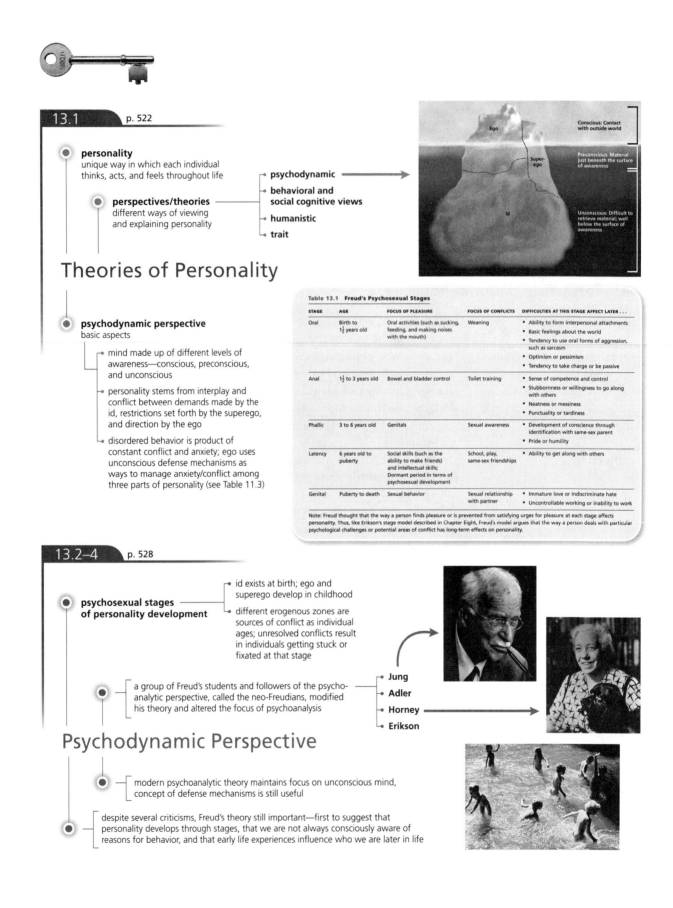

personality
unique way in which each individual thinks, acts, and feels throughout life

→ **psychodynamic**

→ **behavioral and social cognitive views**

→ **humanistic**

→ **trait**

perspectives/theories
different ways of viewing and explaining personality

Conscious: Contact with outside world

Preconscious: Material just beneath the surface of awareness

Unconscious: Difficult to retrieve material; well below the surface of awareness

Ego

Super-ego

Id

Theories of Personality

psychodynamic perspective
basic aspects

→ mind made up of different levels of awareness—conscious, preconscious, and unconscious

→ personality stems from interplay and conflict between demands made by the id, restrictions set forth by the superego, and direction by the ego

→ disordered behavior is product of constant conflict and anxiety; ego uses unconscious defense mechanisms as ways to manage anxiety/conflict among three parts of personality (see Table 11.3)

Table 13.1 Freud's Psychosexual Stages

STAGE	AGE	FOCUS OF PLEASURE	FOCUS OF CONFLICTS	DIFFICULTIES AT THIS STAGE AFFECT LATER . . .
Oral	Birth to 1½ years old	Oral activities (such as sucking, feeding, and making noises with the mouth)	Weaning	• Ability to form interpersonal attachments • Basic feelings about the world • Tendency to use oral forms of aggression, such as sarcasm • Optimism or pessimism • Tendency to take charge or be passive
Anal	1½ to 3 years old	Bowel and bladder control	Toilet training	• Sense of competence and control • Stubbornness or willingness to go along with others • Neatness or messiness • Punctuality or tardiness
Phallic	3 to 6 years old	Genitals	Sexual awareness	• Development of conscience through identification with same-sex parent • Pride or humility
Latency	6 years old to puberty	Social skills (such as the ability to make friends) and intellectual skills; Dormant period in terms of psychosexual development	School, play, same-sex friendships	• Ability to get along with others
Genital	Puberty to death	Sexual behavior	Sexual relationship with partner	• Immature love or indiscriminate hate • Uncontrollable working or inability to work

Note: Freud thought that the way a person finds pleasure or is prevented from satisfying urges for pleasure at each stage affects personality. Thus, like Erikson's stage model described in Chapter Eight, Freud's model argues that the way a person deals with particular psychological challenges or potential areas of conflict has long-term effects on personality.

psychosexual stages of personality development

→ id exists at birth; ego and superego develop in childhood

→ different erogenous zones are sources of conflict as individual ages; unresolved conflicts result in individuals getting stuck or fixated at that stage

a group of Freud's students and followers of the psycho-analytic perspective, called the neo-Freudians, modified his theory and altered the focus of psychoanalysis

→ **Jung**
→ **Adler**
→ **Horney**
→ **Erikson**

Psychodynamic Perspective

modern psychoanalytic theory maintains focus on unconscious mind, concept of defense mechanisms is still useful

despite several criticisms, Freud's theory still important—first to suggest that personality develops through stages, that we are not always consciously aware of reasons for behavior, and that early life experiences influence who we are later in life

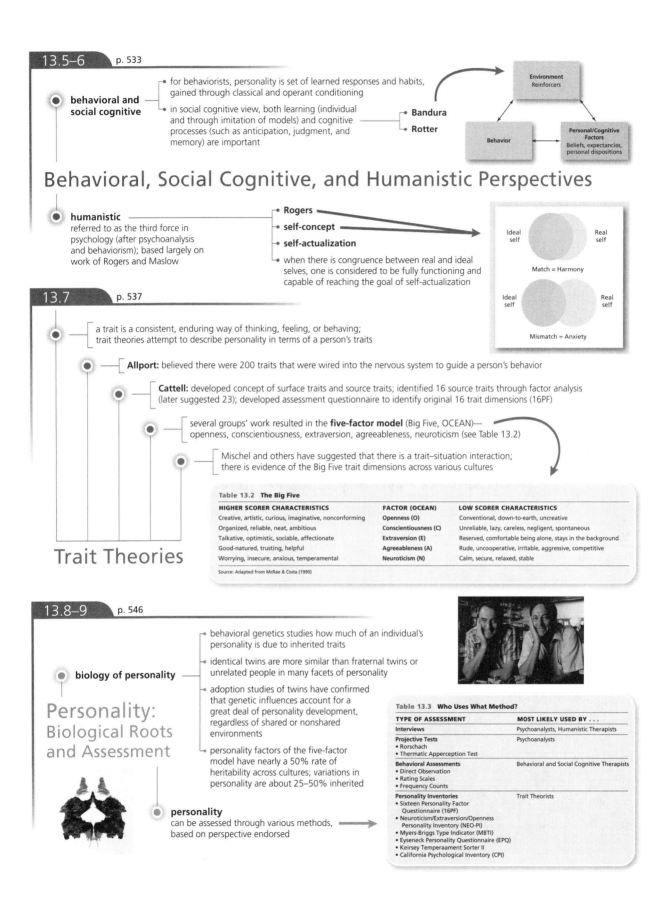

p. 533

13.5–6

behavioral and social cognitive

- for behaviorists, personality is set of learned responses and habits, gained through classical and operant conditioning
- in social cognitive view, both learning (individual and through imitation of models) and cognitive processes (such as anticipation, judgment, and memory) are important

- Bandura
- Rotter

Environment
Reinforcers

Behavior

Personal/Cognitive Factors
Beliefs, expectancies, personal dispositions

Behavioral, Social Cognitive, and Humanistic Perspectives

humanistic
referred to as the third force in psychology (after psychoanalysis and behaviorism); based largely on work of Rogers and Maslow

- Rogers
- self-concept
- self-actualization
- when there is congruence between real and ideal selves, one is considered to be fully functioning and capable of reaching the goal of self-actualization

Ideal self   Real self

Match = Harmony

Ideal self   Real self

Mismatch = Anxiety

p. 537

13.7

- a trait is a consistent, enduring way of thinking, feeling, or behaving; trait theories attempt to describe personality in terms of a person's traits

Allport: believed there were 200 traits that were wired into the nervous system to guide a person's behavior

Cattell: developed concept of surface traits and source traits; identified 16 source traits through factor analysis (later suggested 23); developed assessment questionnaire to identify original 16 trait dimensions (16PF)

several groups' work resulted in the **five-factor model** (Big Five, OCEAN)—openness, conscientiousness, extraversion, agreeableness, neuroticism (see Table 13.2)

Mischel and others have suggested that there is a trait–situation interaction; there is evidence of the Big Five trait dimensions across various cultures

Trait Theories

Table 13.2 The Big Five

HIGHER SCORER CHARACTERISTICS	FACTOR (OCEAN)	LOW SCORER CHARACTERISTICS
Creative, artistic, curious, imaginative, nonconforming	Openness (O)	Conventional, down-to-earth, uncreative
Organized, reliable, neat, ambitious	Conscientiousness (C)	Unreliable, lazy, careless, negligent, spontaneous
Talkative, optimistic, sociable, affectionate	Extraversion (E)	Reserved, comfortable being alone, stays in the background
Good-natured, trusting, helpful	Agreeableness (A)	Rude, uncooperative, irritable, aggressive, competitive
Worrying, insecure, anxious, temperamental	Neuroticism (N)	Calm, secure, relaxed, stable

Source: Adapted from McRae & Costa (1990)

p. 546

13.8–9

biology of personality

- behavioral genetics studies how much of an individual's personality is due to inherited traits
- identical twins are more similar than fraternal twins or unrelated people in many facets of personality
- adoption studies of twins have confirmed that genetic influences account for a great deal of personality development, regardless of shared or nonshared environments
- personality factors of the five-factor model have nearly a 50% rate of heritability across cultures; variations in personality are about 25–50% inherited

Personality: Biological Roots and Assessment

personality
can be assessed through various methods, based on perspective endorsed

Table 13.3 Who Uses What Method?

TYPE OF ASSESSMENT	MOST LIKELY USED BY . . .
Interviews	Psychoanalysts, Humanistic Therapists
Projective Tests • Rorschach • Thematic Apperception Test	Psychoanalysts
Behavioral Assessments • Direct Observation • Rating Scales • Frequency Counts	Behavioral and Social Cognitive Therapists
Personality Inventories • Sixteen Personality Factor Questionnaire (16PF) • Neuroticism/Extraversion/Openness Personality Inventory (NEO-PI) • Myers-Briggs Type Indicator (MBTI) • Eyseneck Personality Questionnaire (EPQ) • Keirsey Temperament Sorter II • California Psychological Inventory (CPI)	Trait Theorists

Figure 13.1 **Freud's Conception of the Personality**

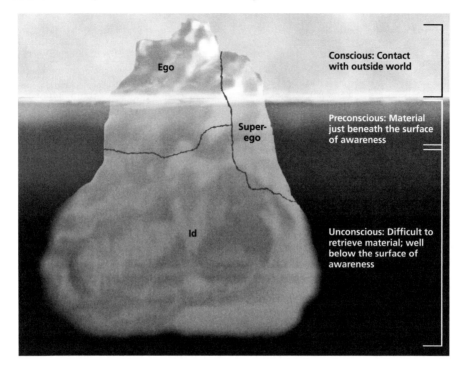

Table 13.1 **Freud's Psychosexual Stages**

Table 13.1   **Freud's Psychosexual Stages**

STAGE	AGE	FOCUS OF PLEASURE	FOCUS OF CONFLICTS	DIFFICULTIES AT THIS STAGE AFFECT LATER . . .
Oral	Birth to 1½ years old	Oral activities (such as sucking, feeding, and making noises with the mouth)	Weaning	• Ability to form interpersonal attachments • Basic feelings about the world • Tendency to use oral forms of aggression, such as sarcasm • Optimism or pessimism • Tendency to take charge or be passive
Anal	1½ to 3 years old	Bowel and bladder control	Toilet training	• Sense of competence and control • Stubbornness or willingness to go along with others • Neatness or messiness • Punctuality or tardiness
Phallic	3 to 6 years old	Genitals	Sexual awareness	• Development of conscience through identification with same-sex parent • Pride or humility
Latency	6 years old to puberty	Social skills (such as the ability to make friends) and intellectual skills; Dormant period in terms of psychosexual development	School, play, same-sex friendships	• Ability to get along with others
Genital	Puberty to death	Sexual behavior	Sexual relationship with partner	• Immature love or indiscriminate hate • Uncontrollable working or inability to work

Note: Freud thought that the way a person finds pleasure or is prevented from satisfying urges for pleasure at each stage affects personality. Thus, like Erikson's stage model described in Chapter Eight, Freud's model argues that the way a person deals with particular psychological challenges or potential areas of conflict has long-term effects on personality.

13.3–13.4 Neofreudians and Current Thoughts

_____

_____

_____

_____

_____

_____

_____

_____

_____

_____

_____

Figure 13.2 **Reciprocal Determinism**

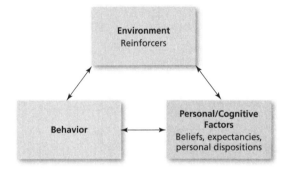

_____

_____

_____

_____

_____

_____

_____

_____

_____

_____

Figure 13.3 **Real and Ideal Selves**

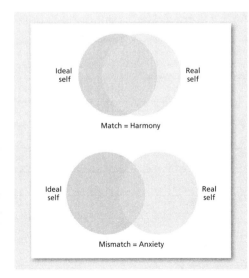

_____

_____

_____

_____

_____

_____

_____

_____

_____

_____

Figure 13.4 **Cattell's Self-Report Inventory**

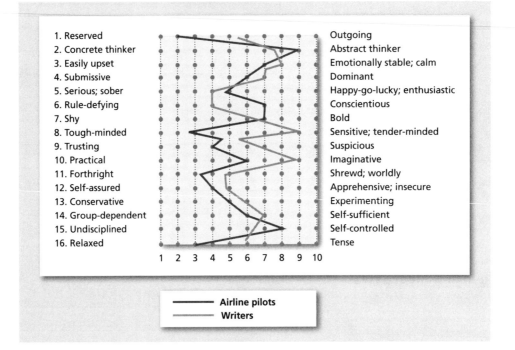

1. Reserved	Outgoing
2. Concrete thinker	Abstract thinker
3. Easily upset	Emotionally stable; calm
4. Submissive	Dominant
5. Serious; sober	Happy-go-lucky; enthusiastic
6. Rule-defying	Conscientious
7. Shy	Bold
8. Tough-minded	Sensitive; tender-minded
9. Trusting	Suspicious
10. Practical	Imaginative
11. Forthright	Shrewd; worldly
12. Self-assured	Apprehensive; insecure
13. Conservative	Experimenting
14. Group-dependent	Self-sufficient
15. Undisciplined	Self-controlled
16. Relaxed	Tense

1 2 3 4 5 6 7 8 9 10

—— Airline pilots
—— Writers

Table 13.2 **The Big Five**

Table 13.2   **The Big Five**

HIGH SCORER CHARACTERISTICS	FACTOR (OCEAN)	LOW SCORER CHARACTERISTICS
Creative, artistic, curious, imaginative, nonconforming	Openness (O)	Conventional, down-to-earth, uncreative
Organized, reliable, neat, ambitious	Conscientiousness (C)	Unreliable, lazy, careless, negligent, spontaneous
Talkative, optimistic, sociable, affectionate	Extraversion (E)	Reserved, comfortable being alone, stays in the background
Good-natured, trusting, helpful	Agreeableness (A)	Rude, uncooperative, irritable, aggressive, competitive
Worrying, insecure, anxious, temperamental	Neuroticism (N)	Calm, secure, relaxed, stable

Source: Adapted from McRae & Costa (1990).

_____
_____
_____
_____
_____
_____
_____
_____
_____
_____
_____
_____
_____
_____

13.8   Biology, Heredity, and Culture

_____
_____
_____
_____
_____
_____
_____
_____
_____
_____
_____

Figure 13.5 **Personalities of Identical and Fraternal Twins**

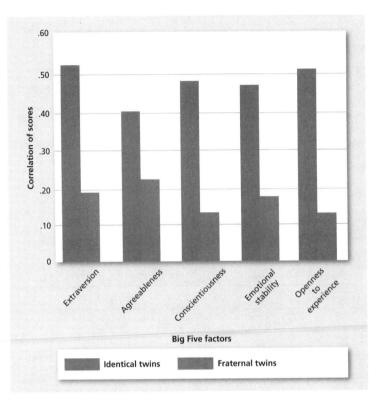

_____

_____

_____

_____

_____

_____

_____

_____

_____

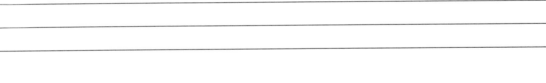

13.9 Assessment of Personality

_____

_____

_____

_____

_____

_____

_____

_____

_____

_____

_____

_____

Table 13.2 **Who Uses What Method?**

Table 13.3 Who Uses What Method?

TYPE OF ASSESSMENT	MOST LIKELY USED BY . . .
Interviews	Psychoanalysts, Humanistic Therapists

Projective Tests
  Rorschach
  Thematic Apperception Test
	Psychoanalysts

Behavioral Assessments
  Direct Observation
  Rating Scales
  Frequency Counts
	Behavioral and Social Cognitive Therapists

Personality Inventories
  Sixteen Personality Factor Questionnaire (16PF)
  Neuroticism/Extraversion/Openness Personality Inventory (NEO-PI)
  Myers-Briggs Type Indicator (MBTI)
  Eysenck Personality Questionnaire (EPQ)
  Keirsey Temperament Sorter II
  California Psychological Inventory (CPI)
	Trait Theorists

_____
_____
_____
_____
_____
_____
_____
_____
_____
_____
_____

Figure 13.6 **Rorschach Inkblot Example**

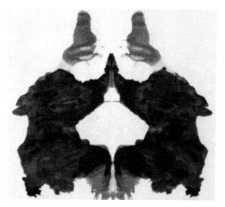

_____
_____
_____
_____
_____
_____
_____
_____
_____
_____

Figure 13.7 **Thematic Apperception
Test Example**

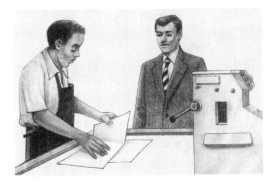

NOTES

CHAPTER 14 – PSYCHOLOGICAL DISORDERS

YOU KNOW YOU ARE READY FOR THE TEST IF YOU ARE ABLE TO...

- Define abnormality and briefly discuss the historical and cultural impact on defining psychological disorders.
- Present the biological and psychological models of psychopathology.
- Discuss the diagnosis and prevalence rates of psychological disorders in the U.S.
- Describe specific categories of psychological disorders including anxiety, somatoform, dissociative, mood, schizophrenia, and personality disorders.
- Understand the diagnosis of seasonal affective disorder and its treatment.

RAPID REVIEW

The study of abnormal behavior, or **psychopathology**, can be traced to at least as early as 3000 B.C. from evidence of trepanning, or drilling some holes in the skull. Today abnormal behavior is considered to be any behavior that is rare, deviates from the social norm within the **situational context**, causes **subjective discomfort**, or is **maladaptive**. **Psychological disorders** are defined as a pattern of behavior that causes people significant distress, causes them to harm themselves or others, or interferes with their ability to function in daily life. The **sociocultural perspective** of abnormality takes into account the effect of culture on behavior and suggests that psychological disorders should be assessed within the realm of **cultural relativity**. **Culture-bound syndromes** are certain psychological disorders that are only found in particular cultures. The **biological model** of psychopathology proposes that psychological disorders arise from a physical or biological cause. The **psychoanalytical model** suggests that disorders are the result of repressed thoughts in the unconscious mind, while the **behaviorist model** explains disorders as a set of learned behaviors. **Cognitive psychologists** have proposed the **cognitive model** which describes psychological disorders as resulting from faulty thinking patterns. The **biopsychosocial model** proposes that abnormal behavior is the result of biological, psychological, social, and cultural influences.

Currently in the United States, psychological disorders are assessed by referring to the *Diagnostics and Statistical Manual of Mental Disorders, Version 4, Text Revision* (**DSM-IV-TR**) which provides information about 250 different disorders including common symptoms, prevalence rates, and criteria for diagnosis. The individual is assessed in five different categories, or axes. Axis 1 contains all the psychological disorders except personality disorders. Axis II includes personality disorders and mental retardation. Axis III includes an assessment of any physical disorders that affect a person psychologically. Axis IV consists of problems in a person's environment that may be affecting his or her psychological functioning, and Axis V is an assessment of a person's overall (or global) level of functioning ranging from 0 to 100. In a given year, about 22 percent of adults in the United States could be diagnosed with a mental disorder.

Anxiety disorders include all disorders characterized by excessive or unrealistic anxiety. **Free-floating anxiety** is the term given to anxiety that seems to be unrelated to any realistic, known factor. **Phobias** are a specific form of anxiety disorder defined as an irrational and persistent fear of something and includes **social phobias**; **specific phobias** such as **claustrophobia**; and **acrophobia**; and **agoraphobia**, or fear of being in a place that would be difficult to escape from if something happened to go wrong. **Obsessive-compulsive disorder** involves a reoccurring thought (or obsession) that causes extreme anxiety and leads to some repetitive or ritualistic behavior (or compulsion). **Panic disorder** is characterized by frequent occurrences of **panic attacks** or sudden onsets of extreme panic. If a fear of having panic attacks prevents an individual from going to public places it is called **panic disorder with agoraphobia**. Individuals diagnosed with **generalized anxiety disorder** display excessive anxiety and worries with no real source that can be pinpointed as leading to the anxiety. The psychoanalytical model states that anxiety disorders are caused by repressed urges or conflicts that are threatening to surface, while the behaviorist model sees anxious behavior as learned or conditioned responses. Cognitive psychologists believe that anxiety disorders are caused by illogical thinking including maladaptive thinking process such as **magnification**, **all-or-nothing thinking**, **overgeneralization**, and **minimization**. Evidence also supports biological factors, such as an imbalance in neurotransmitter levels, as playing a role in anxiety disorders.

Disorders in which people believe they are sick when they are not are called **somatoform disorders**. These disorders are different from **psychosomatic** or **psychophysiological disorders** in which an individual experiences an actual physical illness that is believed to be caused by psychological stress. Somatoform disorders include **hypochondrias**, a disorder in which a person worries excessively about becoming ill; **somatization disorder**, in which the person complains about a specific physical symptom for which there is no real physical cause; and **conversion disorder**, which includes the lost of motor and/or sensory function. Freud believed somatoform disorders were caused by the repression of unacceptable thoughts; behaviorists believe the disorders are learned through both positive and negative reinforcement; and cognitive psychologists point to faulty thinking such as magnification and false beliefs as the cause.

Dissociative disorders involve a break, or dissociation, in a person's sense of identity.   In **dissociative amnesia**, an individual cannot remember information contained in long-term memory such as her own name or where she lives. A **dissociative fugue** occurs when a person suddenly travels away from his home and afterwards cannot remember the trip or even his own identity. In **dissociative identity disorder**, formerly referred to as multiple personality disorder, a person seems to experience at least two or more distinct personalities. According to the psychoanalytical model, dissociation is a defense mechanism and is associated with emotional or physical trauma.   Behaviorists believe that "not thinking" about certain events can be negatively reinforced by reducing anxiety and unpleasant feelings, while cognitive psychologists focus on the feelings of guilt, shame, or anxiety that may be avoided through "thought avoidance." Biological explanations for dissociative disorders also exist. Researchers have found that individuals with **depersonalization disorder** also have lower brain activity in areas of the brain responsible for our sense of body awareness.

Mood disorders, also referred to as **affective** disorders, represent a disturbance in emotion. Two mild forms of mood disorders include **dysthymia**, a chronic depression that lasts for at least two years or more and **cyclothymia**, a cycle of sadness and happiness that also persists for two or more years. The most common mood disorder is **major depression**, which is characterized by prolonged feelings of extreme sadness. **Bipolar disorder** involves all the symptoms of major depression in addition to brief periods of extreme **mania**, or excessive excitement, energy, and feelings of happiness. Psychoanalyts explain depression as anger turned inward on the person, while many learning theorists attribute depression to learned helplessness. Biological explanations have focused on the role of brain chemicals such as serotonin, norepiniphrine, and dopamine.

Schizophrenia is a severe **psychotic** disorder in which the person is not able to distinguish fantasy from reality and experiences disturbances in thinking, emotions, behavior, and perception. Many people with schizophrenia experience **delusions** (false beliefs about the world), **hallucinations** (seeing or hearing things that are not really there), and **flat affect** (the display of little or no emotion).   If an individual experiences delusions alone they would more likely be diagnosed with a type of **delusional disorder**. Schizophrenia can be divided into five basic categories: **disorganized**, characterized by confused speech along with frequent and vivid hallucinations; **catatonic**, in which the individual may sit without moving for hours or may move about wildly; **paranoid**, identified by hallucinations and delusions; underdifferentiated, in which the individual does not fit in one of the three categories already mentioned; and residual, in which a person is in a state of recovery from the symptoms of schizophrenia. Schizophrenia can also be classified according to the kind of symptoms displayed. **Positive symptoms** reflect an excess or distortion of normal functions, such as hallucinations, whereas **negative symptoms** reflect a decrease of normal functions. Medication appears to be more effective in treating the positive symptoms of schizophrenia. The causes of schizophrenia have been attempted to be explained with the biological model. Increased levels of dopamine and brain structural defects are currently the two explanations with the strongest support. In addition, the **stress-vulnerability model** proposes that individuals may have a biological sensitivity which is then made worse by environmental stress.

Disorders which affect a person's entire life adjustment are referred to as **personality disorders**. The DSM-IV-TR recognizes ten different personality disorders. An individual with **antisocial personality disorder** typically feel no remorse and often behave in an impulsive manner with no regard for the consequences. **Borderline personality disorder** is defined by moody, unstable behaviors in which the individual lacks a clear sense of identity. Psychoanalytic theorists point to an incomplete resolution of the Oedipus complex as explanation for personality disorders, while cognitive and learning theorists focus on how the specific behaviors are learned and reinforced over time.

      Seasonal affective disorder (SAD) is a mood disorder that is caused by the body's reaction to low levels of light, especially during the winter months. One of the most effective treatments for SAD is **phototherapy** which involves daily exposure to bright light, typically from an artificial source such as a lamp.

STUDY HINTS

1. Six different categories of psychological disorders are presented in this chapter. In order to help organize the new terms try creating a table of the different disorders including a general description of each category and the specific disorders within the category. The first category has been completed for you as an example.

Disorder Type	General Description	Specific Examples
Anxiety disorders	*a psychological disorder in which the main symptom is an intense fear or anxiety*	*social phobias, specific phobias, agoraphobia, obsessive-compulsive disorder generalized anxiety disorder, panic disorder*
Somatoform disorders		
Dissociative disorders		
Mood disorders		
Schizophrenia		

Personality disorders		

2. In addition to understanding the disorders themselves, it is important to understand the different theories as to the causes of each disorder. Your textbook discusses five models of explanation for each disorder. The models are the biological, psychoanalytical, behavioral, cognitive, and biopsychosocial. In order to enhance your understanding of these models, briefly describe how each of them would explain the disorders listed below.

Model	Depression	Schizophrenia	Dissociative Identity Disorder
Psychoanalytic			
Behavioral			
Cognitive			
Biological			
Biopsychosocial			

Model	Depression	Schizophrenia	Dissociative Identity Disorder
Psychoanalytic	*anger turned inwards and then repressed*	*severe breakdown of the ego and regression back to child-like state*	*motivated forgetting*
Behavioral	*learned helplessness*	*bizarre behavior that has been shaped through reinforcement*	*behavior shaped through positive reinforcement such as attention from others*
Cognitive	*negative and self-defeating thoughts*	*severe form of illogical thinking*	*thought avoidance*
Biological	*brain chemical imbalance (in neurotransmitters such as serotonin and dopamine)*	*chemical imbalance and brain structure abnormalities*	*variation in brain activity between different "personalities"*
Biopsychosocial	*genetic susceptibility made worse by a stressful environment*	*unstable family environment triggers biological sensitivity*	*traumatic childhood event causes changes in neural activity*

LEARNING OBJECTIVES

14.1   How has mental illness been explained in the past, how is abnormal behavior defined today, and what is the impact of cultural differences in defining abnormality?

14.2   How can psychological disorders be explained within the biological and psychological models?

14.3   What are the different types of psychological disorders, and how common are they?

14.4   What are the different types of anxiety disorders, their symptoms, and causes?

14.5   What are the different kinds of somatoform disorders and their causes?

14.6   How do various dissociative disorders differ, and how do they develop?

14.7   What are the different types of mood disorders and their causes?

14.8   What are the main symptoms, types, and causes of schizophrenia?

14.9   How do the various personality disorders differ, and what is thought to be the cause of personality disorders?

14.10   What is seasonal affective disorder, and how can it be treated?

PRACTICE EXAM

For the following multiple choice questions, select the answer you feel best answers the question.

1.   It is probably accurate to assume that in ancient times signs of mental illness were believed to be caused by_____.
   a)   imbalance of body fluids
   b)   demons
   c)   improper diet
   d)   social forces

2. What is the primary difficulty with applying the criterion of "social norm deviance" to define abnormal behavior?
    a) Norms are difficult to enumerate.
    b) Cultures accept and view all behaviors as normal.
    c) Behavior that is considered disordered in one culture may be acceptable in another.
    d) Norms do not guide behavior except in rare instances.

3. Which of the following is NOT a criterion used to decide if a pattern of behavior should be considered to be a psychological disorder?
    a) The behavior is physically exhausting.
    b) The behavior causes subjective distress.
    c) The behavior goes against the norms of the society.
    d) The behavior is maladaptive.

4. The biological model views psychological disorders as resulting from_____.
    a) distorted thought patterns
    b) repressed memories
    c) underlying behavioral issues
    d) physiological causes

5. The psychoanalytic model holds that abnormal behavior is the result of _____.
    a) learning
    b) repressed thoughts
    c) biology
    d) biochemical imbalances

6. Alan went to see a psychologist to get some help overcoming his anxiety in public. The psychologist spent a lot of time discussing the specific thoughts Alan has when he is in public and trying to help him change those thought patterns. The psychologist could be best described as adhering to the _____.
    a) cognitive perspective
    b) behaviorist model
    c) psychoanalytical perspective
    d) biological model

7. Disorders such as koro, susto, and amok are considered _____.
    a) restricted syndromes
    b) naturalistic syndromes
    c) sociocultural disorders
    d) culture-bound syndromes

8. _____is used to help psychological professionals diagnose psychological disorders.
    a) The *Diagnostic and Statistical Manual of Mental Disorders*
    b) The *Physician's Desk Reference*
    c) The *Textbook of Psychological Disorders*
    d) The *Textbook of Physiological Disorders*

9. When a psychologist or psychiatrist is using the DSM-IV-TR as a guide to evaluating a client, he or she would assess the client on each of five _____.
   a) axes
   b) stages
   c) phases
   d) steps

10. In any given year in the United States, approximately how many adults over age 18 experience a mental disorder?
    a) 5 percent
    b) 22 percent
    c) 52 percent
    d) 76 percent

11. Which of the following statements is true about anxiety?
    a) It is never considered realistic or normal.
    b) Some anxiety is realistic when its source is obvious and understandable.
    c) It always manifests itself as a disorder.
    d) It is unusual for a mentally healthy person to experience anxiety.

12. Over the past few years, Sam has become extremely fearful of going to any public place such as a restaurant, concert, or even the grocery store. There are many days when Sam does not even leave his house for fear that he might be caught somewhere that would not be easy to escape from. Which anxiety disorder would Sam most likely be diagnosed with?
    a) a specific phobia
    b) obsessive-compulsive disorder
    c) generalized anxiety disorder
    d) agoraphobia

13. Liza has an anxiety disorder. She is currently seeing a therapist who believes that anxiety disorders are a result of illogical, irrational thought processes. Liza is probably seeking treatment from a
    a) behaviorial psychologist.
    b) cognitive psychologist.
    c) psychoanalyst.
    d) psychologist with a biological perspective.

14. The cognitive process of magnification could be most accurately described as
    a) interpreting a single negative event as a never-ending pattern of defeat.
    b) making mountains out of molehills.
    c) giving little or no emphasis to one's successes or positive events.
    d) throwing the baby out with the bath water.

15. A person who is preoccupied with every sensation of her body, worries excessively about getting ill, and continuously goes to doctors who never find anything physically wrong with her is likely to be diagnosed with
    a) hypochondriasis.
    b) conversion disorder.
    c) somatization disorder.
    d) psychophysiological disorder.

16. Disorders that take the form of a physical illness that has no real physical cause are referred to as
    a) dissociate disorders.
    b) schizophrenia.
    c) somatoform disorders.
    d) mood disorders.

17. What did Freud believe about somatoform disorders?.
    a) They are caused by the repression of disturbing thoughts, conflicts, or memories.
    b) They result from magnifying symptoms and allowing false beliefs to dominate one's thinking.
    c) They are the result of positive and negative reinforcement.
    d) They are due to an imbalance of the neurotransmitters GABA and serotonin.

18. Disorders in which there is a break in conscious awareness, memory, the sense of identity, or some combination are called _____.
    a) paraphilias
    b) anxiety disorders
    c) somatoform disorders
    d) dissociative disorders

19. Dissociative identity disorder is a psychological disorder more commonly known as
    a) amnesia
    b) fugue or flight disorder
    c) schizophrenia
    d) multiple personality disorder

20. Which of the following perspectives claims that shaping may play a big role in the development of some cases of dissociative identity disorder?
    a) behavioral
    b) humanistic
    c) biological
    d) psychoanalytic

21. Spanos conducted studies to determine the validity of dissociative identity disorder. He found that ordinary college students, under hypnosis, showed signs of a second personality. Based on his studies, what did he conclude about the disorder?
    a) Many of the diagnoses were incorrect, as professionals had been fooled by the clients' tendency to play the role of a multiple personality.
    b) Many cases had clearly been caused by childhood trauma.
    c) Many cases were a misdiagnosis of other psychological disorders.
    d) Very few cases had been misdiagnosed.

22. Disorders characterized by disturbances in emotion are known as _____ disorders.
    a) conversion
    b) somatoform
    c) mood
    d) dissociative

23. An individual diagnosed with dysthymia would most likely exhibit which of the following symptoms?
    a) cycles of being sad then happy then sad
    b) mild depression over a period of several years
    c) severe depression that appears very rapidly without any apparent reason
    d) periods of excessive excitement followed by days or weeks of severe depression

24. Which of the following is the biological explanation for mood disorders?
    a) They are a result of learned helplessness.
    b) They are a result of anger turned inward on oneself.
    c) They are a result of distortions in thinking.
    d) They are a result of an imbalance of brain chemicals.

25. A person suffering from disordered thinking, bizarre behavior, and hallucinations, who is unable to distinguish between fantasy and reality, is likely suffering from
    a) schizophrenia.
    b) bipolar disorder.
    c) a dissociative disorder.
    d) passive-aggressive personality.

26. The condition in which a person shows little or no emotion is referred to as _____.
    a) flat affect
    b) hallucinations
    c) delusions
    d) disorganization

27. The primary feature of _____ schizophrenia is severe disturbance of motor behavior.
    a) disorganized
    b) catatonic
    c) residual
    d) paranoid

28. Which of the following symptoms would NOT be considered a negative symptom of schizophrenia?
    a) lack of affect
    b) poor attention
    c) social withdrawal
    d) hallucinations

29. Sal has decreased levels of the neurotransmitter dopamine in his prefrontal cortex. Which disorder might he be at risk of experiencing?
    a) antisocial personality disorder
    b) agoraphobia
    c) schizophrenia
    d) dissociative fugue

30. Disorders that affect the entire life adjustment of a person are referred to as
    a) somatoform disorders
    b) dissociative disorders
    c) mood disorders
    d) personality disorders

31. A person with antisocial personality disorder would be likely to engage in which of the following behaviors?
   a) lying to other people without worrying about the consequences
   b) display excessive and inappropriate emotions
   c) report hallucinations
   d) completely withdraw from society

32. Which of the following statements represents the biological view of personality disorders?
   a) They are due to an inadequate resolution of the Oedipus complex.
   b) They are a type of learned behavior.
   c) They have physiological causes.
   d) They are due to disturbances in family relationships.

33. _____ is a mood disorder that is caused by the body's reaction to low levels of light present in the winter months.
   a) Panic disorder
   b) Bipolar disorder
   c) Dysthymic disorder
   d) Seasonal affective disorder

PRACTICE EXAM ANSWERS

1. b   B is the correct choice because people of ancient times perceived signs of mental illness as caused by demons. Hippocrates, a Greek physician, viewed the imbalance of body fluids as the cause of mental illness, but Hippocrates' time period is not considered "ancient times."
2. b   B is the correct answer, since behavior that is considered disordered in one culture may be acceptable in another. D is incorrect because most people do allow social norms to guide much of their behavior.
3. a   The three main criteria for a behavior to be considered a psychological disorder are that it deviates from social norms, is maladaptive, and causes the individual personal distress or discomfort.
4. d   The biological model emphasizes physiological or physical causes for psychological disorders. The other three choices represent the psychological models of cognitive, psychoanalytical, and behavioral for a, b, and c, respectively.
5. b   Originating with the theories of Freud, psychoanalysts view disorder behavior as resulting from thoughts that are below the level of conscious awareness.
6. a   Cognitive psychologists tend to treat disorders by attempting to change the person's thought patterns.
7. d   Koro, susto, and amok are considered culture-bound disorders because they occur only in particular cultures.
8. a   The DSM helps psychological professionals diagnose psychological disorders, while the *Physician's Desk Reference* is used by medical professionals to diagnose physiological problems.
9. a   The DSM-IV-TR uses a system of five different axes for evaluations.
10. b   According to recent studies, approximately 22 percent of the U.S. adult population experiences a mental disorder in a given year.
11. b   This statement is true because some types of anxiety are normal.
12. d   Agoraphobia is an anxiety disorder characterized by an extreme fear of going in public places that would be difficult to escape from if necessary.
13. b   Cognitive psychologists view anxiety disorders as a result of distorted thought processes, while behaviorists view anxiety disorders as a result of learning.

14. b   Magnification is the tendency to interpret a situation as being far more harmful, dangerous, or embarrassing than it actually is, or in other words, making a big deal out of something that is actually very small.

15. a   Someone with hypochondriasis is excessively worried about getting ill and frequently goes to see doctors. People with somatization disorder do not worry so much about every aspect of theirhealth; they complain in dramatic terms about one particular symptom.

16. c   The term "somatic" literally means bodily.

17. a   Freud viewed somatoform disorders as the physical symptoms of repressed thoughts, conflicts, or memories. Cognitive psychologists believe somatoform disorders result from faulty thought processes, such as magnifying symptoms and allowing false beliefs to dominate thinking.

18. d   Dissociative disorders are characterized by a break in conscious awareness, memory, the sense of identity, or some combination.

19. d   Multiple personality disorder is no longer used by psychologists but is still very common in the general public.

20. a   Behavioral psychologists emphasize shaping through positive and negative reinforcement as a factor in the development of some cases of dissociate identity disorder.

21. a   Spanos found that many supposed cases of dissociative identity disorder had been misdiagnosed.

22. c   Mood disorders are characterized by disturbances in emotion, while somatoform disorders take the form of bodily ailments that have no physical cause

23. b   Dysthymia can be thought of as a mild version of depression, while cyclothymia more closely resembles a mild version of bipolar disorder.

24. a   The biological explanation emphasizes an imbalance of brain chemicals.

25. a   Disordered thinking, bizarre behavior, hallucinations, and inability to distinguish between fantasy and reality are all symptoms of schizophrenia. Bipolar disorder is characterized by mood swings between depression and mania and does not involve hallucinations or inability to distinguish between fantasy and reality.

26. a   The word "affect" is used to mean emotion or mood.

27. b   Severe motor disturbance is a feature of catatonic schizophrenia. Symptoms of residual schizophrenia include negative beliefs, poor language skills, unusual ideas and perceptions.

28. d   Negative symptoms of schizophrenia reflect a decrease in normal function (such as lack of social interactions or displays of emotions). Hallucinations represent an excess or addition in normal function and would be classified as a positive symptom of schizophrenia.

29. c   Schizophrenia is associated with an imbalance of dopamine.

30. d   Personality disorders do not just affect a single aspect of a person's life but rather affect the person's entire life adjustment.

31. a   Antisocial personality disorder is characterized by an individual who acts "against society." For example, an individual might commit a crime without feeling any remorse.

32. c   The biological perspective focuses on physiological causes for psychological disorders, and cognitive-learning theorists do believe that the behavior displayed by people with personality disorders is learned through reinforcement, shaping, and modeling.

33.   d   Seasonal affective disorder occurs primarily during the winter months. Dysthymic
            disorder consists of similar symptoms but is not seasonal in nature.

CHAPTER GLOSSARY

acrophobia	fear of heights.
affect	in psychology, a term indicating emotion or mood.
agoraphobia	fear of being in a place or situation from which escape is difficult or impossible.
all-or-nothing thinking	the tendency to believe that one's performance must be perfect or the result will be a total failure.
antisocial personality disorder	disorder in which a person has no morals or conscience and often behaves in an impulsive manner without regard for the consequences of that behavior.
anxiety disorders	disorders in which the main symptom is excessive or unrealistic anxiety and fearfulness.
behaviorist model	explanation of disorder behavior as being learned just like normal behavior.
biological model	model of explaining behavior as caused by biological changes in the chemical, structural, or genetic systems of the body.
biopsychosocial model	perspective in which abnormal behavior is seen as the result of the combined and interacting forces of biological, psychological, social, and cultural influences.
bipolar disorder	severe mood swings between major depressive episodes and manic episodes.
borderline personality disorder	maladaptive personality pattern in which the person is moody, unstable, lacks a clear sense of identity, and often clings to others.
catatonic	type of schizophrenia in which the person experiences periods of statue-like immobility mixed with occasional bursts of energetic, frantic movement and talking.
claustrophobia	fear of being in a small enclosed space.
cognitive model	model which explains abnormal behavior as resulting from illogical thinking patterns.
conversion disorder	somatoform disorder in which the person experiences a specific symptom in the somatic nervous system's functioning, such as paralysis, numbness, or blindness, for which there is no physical cause.
cultural relativity	the need to consider the unique characteristics of the culture in which behavior takes place.
culture-bound syndromes	disorders found only in particular cultures.
cyclothymia	disorder that consists of mood swings from moderate depression to hypomania and lasts two years or more.
delusional disorder	a psychotic disorder in which the primary symptom is one or more delusions.
delusions	false beliefs held by a person who refuses to accept evidence of their falseness.
depersonalization disorder	dissociative disorder in which individuals feel detached and disconnected from themselves, their bodies, and their surroundings.

disorganized	type of schizophrenia in which behavior is bizarre and childish and thinking, speech, and motor actions are very disordered.
dissociative amnesia	loss of memory for personal information, either partial or complete.
dissociative disorders	disorders in which there is a break in conscious awareness, memory, the sense of identity, or some combination.
dissociative fugue	traveling away from familiar surroundings with amnesia for the trip and possible amnesia for personal information.
dissociative identity disorder	disorder occurring when a person seems to have two or more distinct personalities within one body.
DSM-IV-TR	*Diagnostic and Statistical Manual of Mental Disorders, Version Four, Text Revision.* Manual written and used primarily by psychologists and psychiatrists as a guide in diagnosing and assessing psychological disorders.
dysthymia	a moderate depression that lasts for two years or more and is typically a reaction to some external stressor.
flat affect	a lack of emotional responsiveness.
free-floating anxiety	anxiety that is unrelated to any realistic, known source.
generalized anxiety disorder	disorder in which a person has feelings of dread and impending doom along with physical symptoms of stress, and which lasts six months or more.
hallucinations	false sensory perceptions, such as hearing voices that do not really exist.
hypochondrias	somatoform disorder in which the person is terrified of being sick and worries constantly, going to doctors repeatedly, and becoming preoccupied with every sensation of the body.
magnification	the tendency to interpret situations as far more dangerous, harmful, or important than they actually are.
major depression	severe depression that comes on suddenly and seems to have no external cause.
maladaptive	anything that does not allow a person to function within or adapt to the stresses and everyday demands on life.
manic	having the quality of excessive excitement, energy, and elation or irritability.
minimization	the tendency to give little or no importance to one's successes or positive events and traits.
mood disorders	disorders in which mood is severely disturbed.
negative symptoms	symptoms of schizophrenia that are less than normal behavior or an absence of normal behavior; poor attention, flat affect, and poor speech production.
obsessive-compulsive disorder	disorder in which intruding, recurring thoughts or obsessions create anxiety that is relieved by performing a repetitive, ritualistic behavior (compulsion).
overgeneralization	the tendency to interpret a single negative event as a never-ending pattern of defeat and failure.
panic attack	sudden onset of intense panic in which multiple physical symptoms of stress occur, often with feelings that one is dying.
panic disorder	disorder in which panic attacks occur frequently enough to cause the person difficulty in adjusting to daily life.

panic disorder with agoraphobia	fear of leaving one's familiar surroundings because one might have a panic attack in public.
paranoid	type of schizophrenia in which the person suffers from delusions of persecution, grandeur, and jealousy, together with hallucinations.
personality disorders	disorders in which a person adopts a persistent, rigid, and maladaptive pattern of behavior that interferes with normal social interactions.
phobias	an irrational, persistent fear of an object, situation, or social activity.
phototherapy	the use of lights to treat seasonal affective disorder or other disorders.
positive symptoms	symptoms of schizophrenia that are excesses of behavior or occur in addition to normal behavior; hallucinations, delusions, and distorted thinking.
postpartum depression	depression occurring within a year after giving birth in about 10 percent of women and that includes intense worry about the baby, thoughts of suicide, and fears of harming the baby.
postpartum psychosis	a rare and severe form of depression that occurs in women just after giving birth and includes delusional thinking and hallucinations.
psychoanalytical model	model based on the work of Freud and his followers. Typically explains disorder behavior as the result of repressing thoughts and memories in the unconscious mind.
psychological disorders	any pattern of behavior that causes people significant distress, causes them to harm others, or harms their ability to function in daily life.
psychopathology	the study of abnormal behavior.
psychophysiological disorder	modern term for psychosomatic disorder.
psychosomatic disorder	disorder in which psychological stress causes a real physical disorder or illness.
psychotic	term applied to a person who is no longer able to distinguish between fantasy and reality.
residual	type of schizophrenia in which there are no delusions and hallucinations, but the person still experiences negative thoughts, poor language skills, and odd behavior.
schizophrenia	severe disorder in which the person suffers from disordered thinking, bizarre behavior, hallucinations, and is unable to distinguish between fantasy and reality.
seasonal affective disorder (SAD)	a mood disorder caused by the body's reaction to low levels of sunlight in the winter months.
situational context	the social or environmental setting of a person's behavior.
social phobias	fear of interacting with others or being in social situations that might lead to a negative evaluation.
sociocultural perspective	perspective in which behavior is seen as the product of the learning within the context of the family, social group, and culture to which the individual belongs.
somatization disorder	somatoform disorder in which the person dramatically complains of a specific symptom such as nausea, difficulty swallowing, or pain for which there is no real physical cause.
somatoform disorders	disorders that take the form of bodily illnesses and symptoms, but for which there are no real physical disorders.
specific phobias	fear of objects or specific situations or events.
stress-vulnerability model	explanation of disorder proposing that environmental stress can trigger the development of a disorder in an individual with a biological sensitivity.

subjective discomfort	emotional distress or emotional pain.
undifferentiated	type of schizophrenia in which the person shows no particular pattern, shifts from one pattern to another, and cannot be neatly classified as disorganized, paranoid, or catatonic.

14.1–2   p. 561

psychopathology is the study of abnormal behavior; mental illness has been defined in various ways throughout history (e.g., possession, evil spirits, bodily imbalances)

current definitions of abnormality are based on several factors

disorders vary according to culture; cultural sensitivity and relativity are necessary in diagnosing and treating psychological disorders

overall, psychological disorders are any pattern of behavior that causes significant distress, causes them to harm themselves or others, or harms their ability to function in daily life

what is abnormality?

Psychological Disorders

models of abnormality
explanations for disordered behavior depend on theoretical model used to explain personality in general

- biological model
- psychological models
- biopsychosocial perspective

14.3–4   p. 570

DSM first published in 1952, current version (*DSM–IV–TR*) published in 2000

currently describes approximately 250 different psychological disorders and includes diagnostic criteria along five different categories, or axes (see Tables 14.1 and 14.2)

in general, approximately 22% of adults over age 18 in the United States suffer from a mental disorder

Diagnostic and Statistical Manual of Mental Disorders, Fourth Edition, Text Revision (DSM–IV–TR)

Table 14.1 The Axes of the *DSM-IV-TR*

AXIS	TYPE OF INFORMATION	DESCRIPTION
Axis I	Clinical Disorders and Other Conditions That May Be a Focus of Clinical Attention	Psychological disorders that impair functioning and are stressful and factors that are not disorders but that may affect functioning, such as academic or social problems
Axis II	Personality Disorders and Mental Retardation	Rigid, enduring, maladaptive personality patterns and mental retardation
Axis III	General Medical Conditions	Chronic and acute illnesses and medical conditions that may have an impact on mental health
Axis IV	Psychosocial and Environmental Problems	Problems in the physical surroundings of the person that may have an impact on diagnosis, treatment, and outcome
Axis V	Global Assessment of Functioning	Overall judgment of current functioning, including mental, social, and occupational

Adapted from the American Psychiatric Association, *DSM-IV-TR* (2000).

Psychological Disorders

anxiety disorders
most dominant symptom is excessive or unrealistic anxiety

anxiety can be free-floating (nonspecific, anxious in general) or more specific, as in the case of phobias

- **panic disorder**
- **obsessive compulsive disorder (OCD)**
- **generalized anxiety disorder**
- causes
  - **behaviorists**
  - **cognitive psychologists**
  - **biological**
  - **culture**

Table 14.2 Axis I Disorders of the *DSM-IV-TR*

DISORDER	EXAMPLES
Disorders usually first diagnosed in infancy, childhood, or adolescence	Learning disabilities, ADHD, bed-wetting, speech disorders
Delirium, dementia, amnesia, and other cognitive disorders	Alzheimer's, Parkinson's, amnesia due to physical causes
Psychological disorders due to a general medical condition	Personality change because of a brain tumor
Substance-related disorders	Alcoholism, drug addictions
Schizophrenia and other psychotic disorders	Schizophrenia, delusional disorders, paranoid psychosis
Mood disorders	Depression, mania, bipolar disorders
Anxiety disorders	Panic disorder, phobias, stress disorders
Somatoform disorders	Hypochondria, conversion disorder
Factitious disorders	Pathological lying, Munchausen syndrome
Dissociative disorders	Dissociative identity disorder (formerly multiple personality), amnesia not due to physical causes
Sexual and gender identity disorders	Sexual desire disorders, paraphilias
Eating disorders	Anorexia, bulimia
Sleep disorders	Insomnia, sleep terror disorder, sleepwalking, narcolepsy
Impulse-control disorders not classified elsewhere	Kleptomania, pathological gambling, pyromania
Adjustment disorders	Mixed anxiety, conduct disturbances

Adapted from the American Psychiatric Association, *DSM-IV-TR* (2000).

14.5–6   p. 577

somatoform disorders
include disorders in which individuals believe they are sick and may experience physical symptoms but there is no physical illness or problem

- **hypochondriasis**
- **somatization disorder**
- **conversion disorder**
- causes
  - **psychodynamic**
  - **cognitive**

Somatoform and Dissociative Disorders

dissociative disorders
involve a dissociation in consciousness, memory, or sense of identity, often associated with extreme stress or trauma

- **dissociative amnesia**
- **dissociative fugue**
- **dissociative identity disorder**
- causes
  - **psychodynamic**
  - **cognitive and behavioral**
  - **biological**

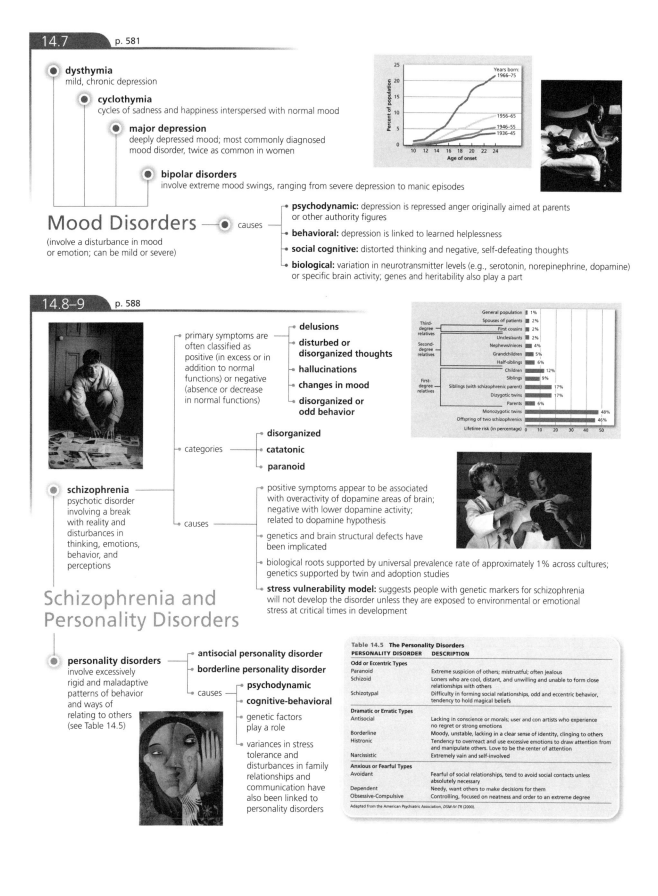

dysthymia
mild, chronic depression

cyclothymia
cycles of sadness and happiness interspersed with normal mood

major depression
deeply depressed mood; most commonly diagnosed mood disorder, twice as common in women

bipolar disorders
involve extreme mood swings, ranging from severe depression to manic episodes

Mood Disorders
(involve a disturbance in mood or emotion; can be mild or severe)

causes

- **psychodynamic:** depression is repressed anger originally aimed at parents or other authority figures
- **behavioral:** depression is linked to learned helplessness
- **social cognitive:** distorted thinking and negative, self-defeating thoughts
- **biological:** variation in neurotransmitter levels (e.g., serotonin, norepinephrine, dopamine) or specific brain activity; genes and heritability also play a part

Graph: Percent of population vs. Age of onset, with lines for Years born: 1966–75, 1956–65, 1946–55, 1936–45.

schizophrenia
psychotic disorder involving a break with reality and disturbances in thinking, emotions, behavior, and perceptions

primary symptoms are often classified as positive (in excess or in addition to normal functions) or negative (absence or decrease in normal functions)

- **delusions**
- **disturbed or disorganized thoughts**
- **hallucinations**
- **changes in mood**
- **disorganized or odd behavior**

categories

- **disorganized**
- **catatonic**
- **paranoid**

causes

- positive symptoms appear to be associated with overactivity of dopamine areas of brain; negative with lower dopamine activity; related to dopamine hypothesis
- genetics and brain structural defects have been implicated
- biological roots supported by universal prevalence rate of approximately 1% across cultures; genetics supported by twin and adoption studies
- **stress vulnerability model:** suggests people with genetic markers for schizophrenia will not develop the disorder unless they are exposed to environmental or emotional stress at critical times in development

Chart: Lifetime risk (in percentage) of schizophrenia by relationship —
Third-degree relatives: General population 1%, Spouses of patients 2%, First cousins 2%
Second-degree relatives: Uncles/aunts 2%, Nephews/nieces 4%, Grandchildren 5%, Half-siblings 6%
First-degree relatives: Children 12%, Siblings 9%, Siblings (with schizophrenic parent) 17%, Dizygotic twins 17%, Parents 6%, Monozygotic twins 48%, Offspring of two schizophrenics 46%

Schizophrenia and Personality Disorders

personality disorders
involve excessively rigid and maladaptive patterns of behavior and ways of relating to others (see Table 14.5)

- **antisocial personality disorder**
- **borderline personality disorder**

causes

- **psychodynamic**
- **cognitive-behavioral**
- genetic factors play a role
- variances in stress tolerance and disturbances in family relationships and communication have also been linked to personality disorders

Table 14.5 The Personality Disorders

PERSONALITY DISORDER	DESCRIPTION
Odd or Eccentric Types	
Paranoid	Extreme suspicion of others; mistrustful; often jealous
Schizoid	Loners who are cool, distant, and unwilling and unable to form close relationships with others
Schizotypal	Difficulty in forming social relationships, odd and eccentric behavior, tendency to hold magical beliefs
Dramatic or Erratic Types	
Antisocial	Lacking in conscience or morals; user and con artists who experience no regret or strong emotions
Borderline	Moody, unstable, lacking in a clear sense of identity, clinging to others
Histrionic	Tendency to overreact and use excessive emotions to draw attention from and manipulate others. Love to be the center of attention
Narcissistic	Extremely vain and self-involved
Anxious or Fearful Types	
Avoidant	Fearful of social relationships, tend to avoid social contacts unless absolutely necessary
Dependent	Needy, want others to make decisions for them
Obsessive-Compulsive	Controlling, focused on neatness and order to an extreme degree

Adapted from the American Psychiatric Association, *DSM-IV-TR* (2000).

14.1–14.2 Definition and Models of Abnormality

14.3 DSM-IV-TR

Table 14.1 **The Axes of the *DSM-IV-TR***

Table 14.1   The Axes of the *DSM-IV-TR*

AXIS	TYPE OF INFORMATION	DESCRIPTION IN BRIEF
Axis I	Clinical Disorders and Other Conditions That May Be a Focus of Clinical Attention	Psychological disorders that impair functioning and are stressful and factors that are not disorders but that may affect functioning, such as academic or social problems
Axis II	Personality Disorders and Mental Retardation	Rigid, enduring, maladaptive personality patterns and mental retardation
Axis III	General Medical Conditions	Chronic and acute illnesses and medical conditions that may have an impact on mental health
Axis IV	Psychosocial and Environmental Problems	Problems in the physical surroundings of the person that may have an impact on diagnosis, treatment, and outcome
Axis V	Global Assessment of Functioning	Overall judgment of current functioning, including mental, social, and occupational

Adapted from the American Psychiatric Association, *DSM-IV-TR* (2000).

Table 14.2 **Axis I Disorders of the *DSM-IV-TR***

Table 14.2   Axis I Disorders of the *DSM-IV-TR*

DISORDER	EXAMPLES
Disorders usually first diagnosed in infancy, childhood, or adolescence	Learning disabilities, ADHD, bed-wetting, speech disorders
Delirium, dementia, amnesia, and other cognitive disorders	Alzheimer's, Parkinson's, amnesia due to physical causes
Psychological disorders due to a general medical condition	Personality change because of a brain tumor
Substance-related disorders	Alcoholism, drug addictions
Schizophrenia and other psychotic disorders	Schizophrenia, delusional disorders, paranoid psychosis
Mood disorders	Depression, mania, bipolar disorders
Anxiety disorders	Panic disorder, phobias, stress disorders
Somatoform disorders	Hypochondria, conversion disorder
Factitious disorders	Pathological lying, Munchausen syndrome
Dissociative disorders	Dissociative identity disorder (formerly multiple personality), amnesia not due to physical causes
Sexual and gender identity disorders	Sexual desire disorders, paraphilias
Eating disorders	Anorexia, bulimia
Sleep disorders	Insomnia, sleep terror disorder, sleepwalking, narcolepsy
Impulse-control disorders not classified elsewhere	Kleptomania, pathological gambling, pyromania
Adjustment disorders	Mixed anxiety, conduct disturbances

Adapted from the American Psychiatric Association, *DSM-IV-TR* (2000).

Table 14.3 Occurrence of Psychological Disorders in the United States

Table 14.3 Occurrence of Psychological Disorders in the United States

CATEGORY OF DISORDER	SPECIFIC DISORDER	PERCENTAGE/NUMBER*
Depressive disorders	Major depressive disorder	5%/9.9 million
	Dysthymic disorder	5.4%/10.9 million
	Bipolar disorder	1.2%/2.3 million
Schizophrenia	All types	1.1%/2.2 million
Anxiety disorders	Panic disorder	1.7%/2.4 million
	Obsessive-compulsive disorder	2.3%/3.3 million
	Post-traumatic stress disorder	3.6%/5.2 million
	Generalized anxiety disorder	2.8%/4.0 million
	Social phobia	3.7%/5.3 million
	Agoraphobia	2.2%/3.2 million
	Specific phobia	4.4%/6.3 million

*Percentage of adults over age 18 affected annually/actual number within the population where available, in the United States.
Adapted from NIMH (2001).

14.4 **Anxiety Disorders**

Table 14.4 **Common Phobias and Their Scientific Names**

Table 14.4   **Common Phobias and Their Scientific Names**

FEAR OF	SCIENTIFIC NAME
Washing and bathing	Ablutophobia
Spiders	Arachnophobia
Lightning	Ceraunophobia
Dirt, germs	Mysophobia
Snakes	Ophidiophobia
Darkness	Nyctophobia
Fire	Pyrophobia
Foreigners, strangers	Xenophobia
Animals	Zoophobia

Source: Adapted from Culbertson (2003).

_____
_____
_____
_____
_____
_____
_____
_____
_____
_____

14.5   Somatoform Disorders

_____
_____
_____
_____
_____
_____
_____
_____
_____
_____

Figure 14.1 **Glove Anesthesia**

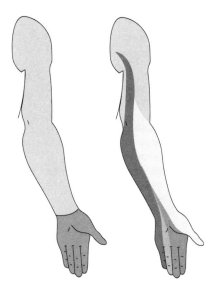

14.6 Dissociative Disorders

14.7 Mood Disorders

Figure 14.2 **The Range of Emotions**

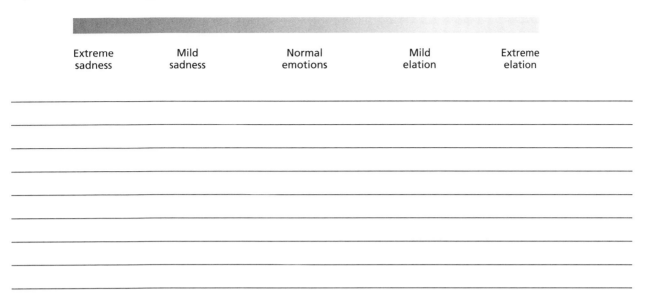

| Extreme sadness | Mild sadness | Normal emotions | Mild elation | Extreme elation |

_____
_____
_____
_____
_____
_____
_____
_____
_____

Figure 14.3 **Prevalence of Major Depression**

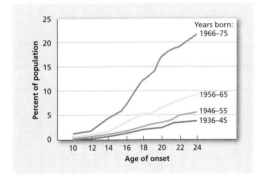

_____
_____
_____
_____
_____
_____
_____
_____
_____

14.8 Schizophrenia

_____
_____
_____
_____
_____
_____
_____
_____
_____
_____
_____
_____

Figure 14.4 **Genetics and Schizophrenia**

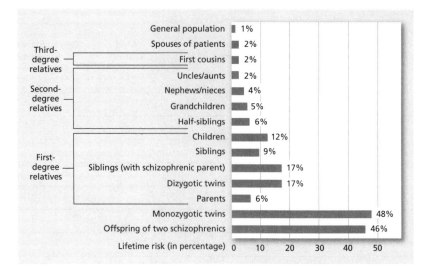

14.9 Personality Disorders

Table 14.5 **The Personality Disorders**

Table 14.5 **The Personality Disorders**

PERSONALITY DISORDER	DESCRIPTION
Odd or Eccentric Types	
Paranoid	Extreme suspicion of others; mistrustful, often jealous
Schizoid	Loners who are cool, distant, and unwilling and unable to form close relationships with others
Schizotypal	Difficulty in forming social relationships, odd and eccentric behavior, tendency to hold magical beliefs
Dramatic or Erratic Types	
Antisocial	Lacking in conscience or morals; users and con artists who experience no regret or strong emotions
Borderline	Moody, unstable, lacking in a clear sense of identity, clinging to others
Histrionic	Tendency to overreact and use excessive emotions to draw attention from and manipulate others. Love to be the center of attention
Narcissistic	Extremely vain and self-involved
Anxious or Fearful Types	
Avoidant	Fearful of social relationships, tend to avoid social contacts unless absolutely necessary
Dependent	Needy, want others to make decisions for them
Obsessive-Compulsive	Controlling, focused on neatness and order to an extreme degree

Adapted from the American Psychiatric Association, *DSM-IV-TR* (2000).

14.10 Seasonal Affective Disorder

Figure 14.5 **Prevalence of SAD in the United States**

MORE THAN .90
.70 TO .89
.50 TO .69
.20 TO .49
LESS THAN .19

* SAMPLE SIZE TOO SMALL
TO BE STATISTICALLY RELIABLE

NOTES

YOU KNOW YOU ARE READY FOR THE TEST IF YOU ARE ABLE TO...

- Define two main types of theory and briefly discuss the history of treatment of the mentally ill.
- Introduce the major types of psychotherapy including psychoanalysis, humanistic, behavior, cognitive, and group therapy.
- Discuss the assessment and effectiveness of the psychotherapy treatments.
- Describe the biomedical approaches of treating psychological disorders including the use of drugs, electroconvulsive therapy and psychosurgery.
- Understand the controversy surrounding the treatment of youth with antidepressant drugs.

RAPID REVIEW

Therapy for psychological disorders consists of treatment methods aimed at making people feel better and function more effectively. The two main types of therapy are **psychotherapy**, which consists of talking things out with a professional and **biomedical therapy**, which consists of using biological methods such as medication to treat a psychological disorder. Psychotherapy techniques can be roughly divided into **insight therapies**, which have the goal of self-understanding and **action therapies**, which focus on changing an individual's behaviors. Biomedical therapies consist mainly of the use of drugs, surgical techniques, or electroconvulsive therapy. Early treatment of the mentally ill often consisted of fatal attempts to "rid" the individual of the physical impurities causing the abnormal behavior. It was not until 1793 that Philippe Pinel began the movement of humane treatment of the mentally ill.

Psychoanalysis is an insight therapy developed by Sigmund Freud with the goal of revealing the unconscious conflicts, urges, and desires that Freud assumed were the cause of the psychological disorder. Freud utilized a number of techniques in his attempt to reveal the unconscious. **Dream interpretation** involved an analysis of the actual or **manifest content** of a dream as well as the hidden or **latent content**. Freud felt the latent content of dreams could reveal unconscious conflict. In addition, Freud used **free association**, or allowing the patients to freely say whatever came to their mind, to uncover the repressed material; **resistance**, in which the patient became unwilling to discuss a topic any further; and **transference**, in which the therapist became a symbol of a parental authority figure. Today, psychoanalytic therapy is often referred to as **psychodynamic therapy** and is **directive**, places more emphasis on transference, and is usually much shorter than traditional psychoanalysis. Individuals with anxiety, somatoform, or dissociative disorders are more likely to benefit from psychodynamic therapy than individuals with other types of disorders.

Humanistic therapy is also an insight therapy, but unlike psychoanalysis, humanistic therapy focuses on conscious experiences of emotion and an individual's sense of self. The two most common humanistic therapies are person-centered therapy and Gestalt therapy. Carl Rogers developed **person-centered therapy** which has the goal of helping an individual get their real and ideal selves to more closely match up. According to Rogers, the role of the therapist is to provide the unconditional positive regard that was missing in the individual's life. He felt the therapy should be **nondirective** with the individual doing most of the work and believed the four key elements of **reflection**, **unconditional positive regard**, **empathy** and **authenticity** were crucial for a successful person-therapist relationship. Fritz Perls believed that people's problems arose from hiding important parts of their feelings from themselves and developed another humanistic therapy called **Gestalt therapy**, a directive form of insight therapy. Gestalt therapy focuses on the client's feelings and subjective experiences and uses leading questions and planned experiences such as role-playing to help the person reveal the feelings they may be hiding from themselves. Humanistic therapies have been found to be more successful with individuals who are able to express their thoughts and feelings in a logical manner and are not necessarily the best choice for individuals with more severe psychological disorders.

Behavior therapies use action-based therapy to change behavior based on basic principles of classical and operant conditioning. The abnormal behavior is not seen as a symptom, but rather seen as the problem itself. **Behavior modification or applied behavior analysis** refers to the use of conditioning techniques to modify behavior. Behavior therapies that rely on classical conditioning include systematic desensitization, aversion therapy, and flooding. **Systematic desensitization** consists of a three-step process which utilizes counter-conditioning in order to reduce fear and anxiety. First the client learns deep muscle relaxation techniques, then the client creates a list of anxiety-producing events called a hierarchy of fear, and finally the client confronts the anxiety-producing event while remaining in a relaxed state. **Aversion therapy** uses classical conditioning to decrease a behavior by pairing an aversive (unpleasant) stimulus with the stimulus that normally produces the unwanted behavior. For example, the drub Antabuse produces severe nausea when paired with alcohol so that the individual learns to associate drinking alcohol with getting sick, so that the CS (alcohol) is now paired with an undesirable UCS (nausea) instead of the desirable UCS (drunkenness). **Flooding** involves rapid and intense exposure to an anxiety-producing object in order to produce extinction of the conditioned fear response. Behavior therapies that utilize operant conditioning include participant modeling, token economies, contingency contracts, and extinction techniques such as the use of a time-out. **Participant modeling** has been used to successfully treat phobias and obsessive-compulsive disorders by having the client watch and mimic a **model** demonstrating the desired behaviors. In a **token economy**, clients are **reinforced** with tokens for behaving correctly and can later exchange the tokens for things they want such as food, candy, or special privileges. A **contingency contract** is a written statement of specific required behaviors, contingent penalties, and subsequent rewards. **Extinction techniques** such as **time-outs** work by removing the reinforcement for a behavior. In adults, simply refusing to acknowledge a person's behavior is often successful in reducing the frequency of that behavior. Behavior therapies have been effective in the treatment of disorders including overeating, drug addictions, and phobias.

Cognitive therapy is an action therapy that focuses on helping people change the distorted thinking and unrealistic beliefs that lead to maladaptive behaviors. Common distortions in thought include **arbitrary inference** (or "jumping to conclusions"), **selective thinking**, **overgeneralization**, **magnification and minimization**, and **personalization**. **Cognitive behavioral therapy (CBT)** is a type of cognitive therapy in which the goal is to help clients overcome problems by learning to think more rationally and logically. Albert Ellis developed a version of CBT called **rational-emotive behavioral therapy** in which clients are taught to replace their own irrational beliefs with more rational, helpful statements. Cognitive therapies have considerable success in treating disorders such as depression, stress disorders, anxiety disorders, and some types of schizophrenia.

An alternative to individual therapy is **group therapy**, in which a group of clients with similar problems gather together and discuss their problems under the guidance of a single therapist. Types of group therapies include **family counseling** and **self-help (or support) groups**. The advantages of group therapy are the lower cost, exposure to the ways other people handle the same kinds of problems, the opportunity for the therapist to see how that person interacts with others, and the social and emotional support from the people in the group. The disadvantages are that the person may not feel as free to reveal embarrassing or personal information, the therapist's time must be shared during the session, a shy person may have difficulty speaking up in the group setting, and people with severe disorders such as schizophrenia may not tolerate a group setting. Group therapy seems to be most successful as a long-term treatment intended to promote the development of skilled social interactions.

Francine Shapiro developed a therapy technique called **eye-movement desensitization reprocessing (EMDR)** in which clients attempt to decrease their fears, anxieties, and disturbing thoughts by moving their eyes rapidly back and forth. Although EMDR has been a popular treatment for post-traumatic stress disorder, the effectiveness of the treatment has yet to be firmly established and has not been found to be any more effective than other more traditional techniques such as simple muscle relaxation or exposure therapy.

The effectiveness of the various psychotherapy techniques is difficult to determine due to various timeframes required for the different therapies, alternate explanations of "effectiveness," the lack of adequate control groups, experimenter bias, and the inaccuracies of self-report information. Most psychological professionals today take an **eclectic approach** to psychotherapy which involves using a combination of methods to fit the particular client's needs. The most important aspect of successful psychotherapy appears to be the relationship between the client and the therapist, also referred to as the **therapeutic alliance**. Differences in culture between the therapist and the client can make it difficult for the therapist to understand the exact nature of the client's problems. Several studies have found that members of minority racial or ethnic groups drop out of therapy at significantly higher rates than the majority group clients. Barriers to effective psychotherapy include difference in language, cultural values, social class, and nonverbal communication. A new form of therapy that is delivered via the Internet, called **cybertherapy**, is now available.

Biomedical therapies directly affect the biological function of the body and include the three categories of drug therapy, shock therapy, and surgical treatments. **Psychopharmacology** refers to the use of drugs to control or relieve the symptoms of a psychological disorder and is often combined with psychotherapy for a more effective outcome. Psychopharmacological drugs can be divided according to the disorders they treat including drugs for psychotic disorders, anxiety disorders, manic symptoms of mood disorders, and depression. Drugs used to treat psychotic symptoms such as hallucinations, delusions, and bizarre behaviors are called **antipsychotic drugs** and include typical neuroleptics, atypical neuroleptics, and partial dopamine agonists. In general, these drugs work to decrease dopamine levels in the brain. The newer drugs tend to have fewer negative side effects than the older typical neuroleptics. The two kinds of drugs currently used to treat anxiety disorders include the traditional **antianxiety drugs** such as the minor tranquilizers, or benzodiazepines, including Xanax, Ativan, and Valium and **antidepressant drugs** to be discussed in more detail shortly. The most common treatment for the manic symptoms of bipolar disorder is the antimanic drug of lithium. The exact mechanism of lithium is still not clearly understood. Antidepressant drugs can be divided into three separate categories: the monamine oxidase inhibitors (MAOIs) such as Marplan and Nardil, tricyclic antidepressants such as Tofranil and Elavil, and the selective serotonin reuptake inhibitors (SSRIs) such as Prozac and Zoloft. **Electroconvulsive therapy (ECT)**, also known as shock therapy, is still in use today to treat severe cases of depression, schizophrenia, and mania. The treatment involves delivery of an electric shock to one (**unilateral ECT**) or both sides (**bilateral ECT**) of a person's head, causing a release of neurotransmitters and almost immediate improvement in the individual's mood. One of the main side effects of ECT is at least a short-term loss of memory. **Psychosurgery** involves operating on an individual's brain to remove or destroy brain tissue for the purpose of relieving symptoms of psychological disorders. One of the earliest psychosurgery techniques is the **prefrontal lobotomy**, which is no longer performed today. The main psychosurgery technique in use today is the **bilateral cingulotomy** which destroys the cingulated gyrus and has been shown to be effective in about one-third of cases of depression, bipolar disorder, and obsessive-compulsive disorder. This procedure is only performed with the patient's full and informed consent after all other treatment options have been exhausted.

A recent controversy involves the use of antidepressant drugs for the treatment of depression and anxiety in adolescents. It is not clear whether or not these drugs may lead to an increased risk of suicide in the adolescent patient. Currently the Food and Drug Administration requires a "black box" warning on these drugs urging close monitoring of a child or adolescent taking the medication.

STUDY HINTS

1. An important task in this chapter is to understand the differences among the multiple types of therapy. Listed below are several of the psychotherapies discussed in the chapter. For each therapy, indicate the type of therapy (insight or action), the role of the therapist (directive or nondirective), the school of thought most likely to use this technique, and the overall goal of the therapy. The first psychotherapy has been filled in as an example.

Therapy	Type of therapy	Role of therapist	School of thought	Goal of therapy
Traditional psychoanalysis	*Insight*	*Nondirective*	*Psychoanalysis*	*Uncover unconscious conflicts*
Person-centered therapy				
Gestalt therapy				
Rational-emotive behavioral therapy (REBT)				
Systematic desensitization				

suggested answers

Therapy	Type of therapy	Role of therapist	School of thought	Goal of therapy
Traditional Psychoanalysis	*Insight*	*Nondirective*	*Psychoanalysis*	*Uncover unconscious conflicts*

Person-centered therapy	*Insight*	*Nondirective*	*Humanistic*	*Bring ideal self and real self into congruence*
Gestalt therapy	*Insight*	*Directive*	*Humanistic*	*Increase self awareness*
Rational-emotive behavioral therapy (REBT)	*Action*	*Directive*	*Cognitive-Behavioral*	*Replace irrational beliefs with more rational, helpful statements*
Systematic Desensitization	*Action*	*Directive*	*Behaviorist*	*Reduce fear and anxiety*

Which of the therapies listed above would you find most helpful? _____

Why? _____

_____

_____

2. Rational-emotive behavioral therapy is commonly used for individuals with depression and anxiety. The therapy is based on the idea that an individual has adopted irrational beliefs that have in turn led to their condition of anxiety and depression. The goal of the therapy is to identify the irrational beliefs and teach the individual how to respond with more rational thought processes. In order to better understand the process, assume you are a therapist using the REBT technique and your client makes the following irrational statements. List a suggestion for a rational belief the client could adopt instead. The first one has already been completed.

Irrational Belief	Rational Belief
1. I must be loved, or at least liked, and approved by every significant person I meet.	*I want to be loved or liked by some of the people in my life, and I know I may feel disappointed or lonely when that doesn't happen, but I can cope with those feelings.*
2. I must be completely competent, make no mistakes, and achieve in every possible way if I am to be worthwhile.	
3. It is dreadful, nearly the end of the world, when things aren't how I would like them to be.	
4. Human unhappiness, including mine, is caused by factors outside of my control, so little can be done about it.	
5. If something might be dangerous, unpleasant, or frightening, I should worry about it a great deal.	
6. My problem(s) were caused by event(s) in my past, and that's why I have my problem(s) now.	
7. I should be very upset by other people's problems and difficulties	

LEARNING OBJECTIVES

15.1 *What are the two modern ways in which psychological disorders can be treated, and how have they been treated in the past?*

15.2 *What were the basic elements of Freud's psychoanalysis, and how does psychoanalysis differ today?*

15.7 *What are the various types of group therapies and the advantages and disadvantages of group therapy?*

15.8 *How effective is psychotherapy, and how is the effectiveness of psychotherapy influenced by cultural, ethnic, and gender differences?*

15.3 What are the basic elements of the humanistic therapies known as person-centered therapy and Gestalt therapy?

15.4 How do behavior therapists use classical and operant conditioning to treat disordered behavior?

15.5 How successful are behavior therapies?

15.6 What are the goals and basic elements of cognitive therapies such as cognitive-behavioral therapy and rational-emotive behavioral therapy?

15.9 What are the various types of drugs used to treat psychological disorders?

15.10 How are electroconvulsive therapy and psychosurgery used to treat psychological disorders today?

15.11 What are the dangers of treating children and adolescents with antidepressant drugs?

PRACTICE EXAM

For the following multiple choice questions, select the answer you feel best answers the question.

1. Therapies directed at changing disordered behavior are referred to as _____.
   a) action therapies
   b) insight therapies
   c) biomedical therapies
   d) relationship therapies

2. Which of the following is the best example of biomedical therapy?
   a) use of antidepressants to treat depression
   b) use of insight therapy for social phobia
   c) psychoanalysis to help treat an anxiety disorder
   d) flooding treatment for an individual with obsessive-compulsive disorder

3. Approximately how long ago were the first efforts made to treat the mentally ill with kindness, rather than subjecting them to harsh physical treatment?
   a) 20 years ago
   b) 100 years ago
   c) 200 years ago
   d) 500 years ago

4. Psychoanalysis was a therapy technique designed by
   a) Alfred Adler.
   b) Carl Rogers.
   c) Fritz Perls.
   d) Sigmund Freud.

5. Freud believed one of the indications that he was close to discovering an unconscious conflict was when a patient became unwilling to talk about a topic. He referred to this response in the patient as
   a) transference.
   b) latent content.
   c) dream analysis.
   d) resistance.

6. Which of the following individuals would be least likely to benefit from psychoanalysis?
    a) Mary, who has a somatoform disorder
    b) Kaleem, who suffers from a severe psychotic disorder
    c) Pasha, who has panic attacks
    d) Lou, who suffers from anxiety

7. The modern psychoanalyst provides more guidance to the patient, asks questions, suggests helpful behaviors, and gives opinions and interpretations. This type of role for the therapist is described as a _____ approach.
    a) free association
    b) directive
    c) biomedical
    d) nondirective

8. What did Carl Rogers view as a cause of most personal problems and unhappiness?
    a) reinforcement of maladaptive behavior patterns
    b) unrealistic modes of thought employed by many people
    c) mismatch between an individual's ideal self and real self
    d) unresolved unconscious conflicts occur between the id and superego

9. Which of the following was NOT one of the four key elements Rogers viewed as necessary for a successful person-therapist relationship?
    a) reflection
    b) unconditional positive regard
    c) authenticity
    d) resistance

10. What is a major goal of the Gestalt therapist?
    a) to facilitate transference
    b) to eliminate the client's undesirable behaviors
    c) to provide unconditional positive regard
    d) to help clients become more aware of their own feelings

11. Which of the following is a limitation of humanistic therapy?
    a) Clients do not need to be verbal.
    b) There is not enough empirical research to support its basic ideas.
    c) It cannot be used in a variety of contexts.
    d) The therapist runs the risk of having his or her words misinterpreted by the client.

12. In the aversion therapy technique known as rapid smoking the client takes a puff on a cigarette every five or six seconds so that the nicotine now produces unpleasant responses such as nausea and dizziness, so that eventually the cigarette itself produces a sensation of nausea in the client. In the terms of classical conditioning, the cigarette functions as the _____ and the nicotine is the
    _____.
    a) UCS; CS
    b) CS; UCS
    c) CR; UCS
    d) CS; UCR

13. Which method of treating phobias involves progressive relaxation and exposure to the feared object?
    a) extinction
    b) punishment
    c) token economy
    d) systematic desensitization

14. In a token economy, what role does the token play in shaping behavior?
    a) The tokens are used as punishment to decrease the maladaptive behavior.
    b) The tokens are used to reinforce the desired behavior.
    c) The token is the actual behavior itself.
    d) The token represents the written contract between the client and therapist.

15. What is an advantage of using operant conditioning in treating undesirable behaviors?
    a) The results are usually quickly obtained.
    b) Clients can get an understanding of the underlying cause of the problem.
    c) Unconscious urges are revealed.
    d) Clients can change distorted thought patterns that affect behavior.

16. Which of the following is one of the criticisms of behavior therapy?
    a) It focuses on the underlying cause of behavior and not the symptoms.
    b) Therapy typically lasts for several years and is very expensive.
    c) It focuses too much on the past.
    d) It only relieves some symptoms of schizophrenia but does not treat the overall disorder.

17. What is the goal of cognitive therapy?
    a) to help clients gain insight into their unconscious
    b) to help people change their ways of thinking
    c) to change a person's behavior through shaping and reinforcement
    d) to provide unconditional positive regard for the client

18. Which of these clients is the most likely candidate for Aaron Beck's form of cognitive therapy?
    a) Albert, who suffers from mania
    b) Barbara, who suffers from depression
    c) Robert, who suffers from schizophrenia
    d) Virginia, who has been diagnosed with dissociative identity disorder

19. Which approach assumes that disorders come from illogical, irrational cognitions and that changing the thinking patterns to more rational, logical ones will relieve the symptoms of the disorder?
    a) cognitive-behavioral
    b) person-centered
    c) psychoanalytic
    d) Gestalt

20. According to Albert Ellis, we become unhappy and depressed about events because of _____.
    a) our behaviors
    b) our irrational beliefs
    c) the events that happen to us
    d) other people's irrational beliefs

21. Which of the following is the best example of an irrational belief that a therapist using rational-emotive behavioral therapy would challenge you to change?
    a) It is disappointing when things don't go my way.
    b) If I fail this test, it will hurt my grade in this class but I will try to make it up on the next exam.
    c) There must be something wrong with Bob since he turned down my invitation for a date.
    d) Everyone should love and approve of me and if they don't, there must be something wrong with me.

22. Which of the following is an advantage of cognitive and cognitive-behavioral therapies?
    a) Clients do not need to be verbal.
    b) They treat the underlying cause of the problem.
    c) They are less expensive and short-term than typical insight therapies
    d) The therapist decides which of the client's beliefs are rational and which are irrational.

23. An advantage to group therapy is that groups
    a) are a source of social support.
    b) allow countertransference to occur.
    c) provide unconditional approval to the group members.
    d) allow an extremely shy person to feel more comfortable speaking up.

24. In family therapy, the therapist would most likely
    a) focus on one individual who has been identified as the source of the problem.
    b) have each family member come in for therapy individually.
    c) provide unconditional approval to all the family members.
    d) focus on the entire family system to understand the problem.

25. Which of the following is NOT true about self-help support groups?
    a) Self-help groups do not have leaders.
    b) Currently there are only a limited number of self-help groups operating in the United States.
    c) Self-help groups are typically not directed by a licensed therapist.
    d) Self-help groups are usually free to attend.

26. An advantage of group therapy is that it
    a) can provide help to individuals who may be unable to afford individual psychotherapy.
    b) can be helpful to individuals who are uncomfortable in social situations.
    c) can only be used alone and not in combination with any other form of therapy.
    d) can be helpful to those who have difficulty speaking in public.

27. _____ is a controversial form of therapy in which the client is directed to move the eyes rapidly back and forth while thinking of a disturbing memory.
    a) Eye-movement desensitization reprocessing
    b) Systematic desensitization
    c) Eye-memory therapy
    d) Eye therapy

28. Most psychological professionals today take a(n) _____ view of psychotherapy.
    a) group treatment
    b) humanistic
    c) eclectic
    d) behavioral

29. The most important aspect of a successful psychotherapy treatment is
    a) the length of the session.
    b) the specific approach of the therapist.
    c) the relationship between the client and the therapist.
    d) the severity of the disorder.

30. Studies that have examined cultural and ethnic factors in the therapeutic relationship have found that
    a) members of minority racial or ethnic groups are more likely to continue treatment until the problem has been resolved.
    b) members of the majority racial or ethnic group usually have lower prevalence rates of disorders.
    c) members of minority racial or ethnic groups drop out of therapy at a higher rate than members of the majority group.
    d) members of minority racial or ethnic groups rarely or never seek therapy.

31. Which of the following has NOT been found to be a barrier to effective psychotherapy when the cultural background of client and therapist is different?
    a) language differences
    b) differing cultural values
    c) nonverbal communication
    d) severity of the disorder

32. Antipsychotic drugs treat symptoms such as
    a) hopelessness, sadness, and suicide ideations.
    b) excessive worry, repetitive thoughts, and compulsive behavior.
    c) hallucinations, delusions, and bizarre behavior.
    d) manipulation, lying, and cheating.

33. In what way is the new class of antidepressants known as the SSRIs an improvement over the older types of antidepressants?
    a) They work faster.
    b) They are more effective.
    c) They target a larger number of different neurotransmitters.
    d) They have fewer side effects.

34. For which disorder was electroconvulsive therapy originally developed as a treatment?
    a) panic
    b) schizophrenia
    c) bipolar disorder
    d) cyclothymia

35. Which of the following is the appropriate definition of psychosurgery?
   a) information given to a patient about a surgical procedure before the surgery in order to prevent anxiety
   b) surgery that is performed on brain tissue to relieve or control severe psychological disorders.
   c) surgery that severs the spinal cord of the patient
   d) a procedure in which a brief current of electricity is used to trigger a seizure that typically lasts one minute, causing the body to convulse

36. Psychosurgery is no longer performed in the United States.
   a) True, long-term studies highlighting the serious negative side effects of lobotomies led to the discontinuation of all psychosurgery techniques in the United States.
   b) False, although frontal lobotomies are no longer performed, bilateral cingulotomies are still carried out on patients that have not been helped by any other treatment.
   c) False, frontal lobotomies are still performed on a small number of patients in the United States today.
   d) True, all forms of psychosurgery have been banned in the United States.

37. Which of the following statements about antidepressants taken by children and adolescents is true?
   a) They are known to be very effective.
   b) They are not very effective.
   c) Their effects are clearly understood.
   d) Their effects are not clearly understood.

PRACTICE EXAM ANSWERS

1. a   Action therapy emphasizes changing behavior, whereas insight therapy emphasizes understanding one's motives and actions.
2. a   Any medical treatment that is directed at changing the physiological functioning of an individual is classified as a biomedical therapy. All of the remaining choices are examples of types of psychotherapy treatments.
3. c   In 1793 Philippe Pinel unchained the mentally ill inmates at an asylum in Paris, France, and began the movement of humane treatment for the mentally ill.
4. d   Freud was the founder of psychoanalysis, while Rogers developed person-centered therapy.
5. d   Resistance occurred when a patient became unwilling to discuss a concept. In transference the patient would transfer positive and negative feelings for an authority figure in their past onto the therapist.
6. b   People with severe psychotic disorders are less likely to benefit from psychoanalysis than are people who suffer from somatoform or anxiety disorders.
7. b   A directive approach involves asking questions and suggesting behaviors. The more traditional psychoanalyst typically takes a more nondirective approach in which the therapist remains neutral and does not interpret or take direct actions with regard to the client.
8. c   Rogers believed the closer the match between a person's ideal and real selves, the happier the person. It was Freud, not Rogers, who viewed unresolved unconscious conflicts between the id and superego as the cause of personal problems.
9. d   Rogers felt a therapist must provide the four elements of reflection, unconditional positive regard, empathy, and authenticity in order for successful treatment.
10. d   The major goal of Gestalt therapists is to help clients become more aware of their feelings. Providing unconditional positive regard is the primary goal of person-centered therapy, not Gestalt.

11. b The humanistic therapist does not run the risk of having his or her words misinterpreted by the client because the therapist uses reflection as the main means of communication. However, unfortunately at this point there is not enough empirical evidence to support or refute the basic ideas of humanistic therapy.

12. b Both the cigarette and nicotine are stimuli, so choices c and d can be immediately eliminated. In rapid smoking, the cigarette serves as the conditioned stimulus and the nicotine serves as the unconditioned stimulus.

13. d Systematic desensitization involves progressive relaxation and exposure to the feared object, while extinction involves the removal of a reinforcer to reduce the frequency of a particular response.

14. b In a token economy, the tokens are the reinforcers used to shape and strengthen the desired behaviors.

15. a Operant conditioning is not concerned with the cause of the problems, rather it is concerned with changing behavior. However, operant conditioning does provide rapid change in behavior in comparison to other therapies.

16. d Behavior therapy may help relieve some symptoms but does not treat the overall disorder of schizophrenia.

17. b Cognitive therapy focuses on changing an individual's <u>cognitions</u> or thought processes.

18. b Beck's cognitive therapy is especially effective in treating distortions related to depression.

19. a Cognitive behavioral therapists are concerned with helping clients change their irrational thoughts to more rational and positive thoughts. A person-centered therapist believes disorders come from a mismatch between the ideal self and the real self and a lack of unconditional positive regard.

20. b Ellis believes irrational beliefs cause dissatisfaction and depression.

21. d Irrational beliefs typically have one thing in common; they are all-or-none types of statements.

22. c Cognitive and cognitive-behavioral therapies are relatively inexpensive and are short-term.

23. a Group therapy provides social support for people who have similar problems. However, an extremely shy person is not likely to do as well in group therapy.

24. d Family therapy focuses on the entire family as a part of the problem.

25. b Currently there are an extremely large number of self-help groups in the United States.

26. a Group therapy can provide help to those who may be unable to afford individual psychotherapy.

27. a EMDR is a form of therapy in which the client is directed to move the eyes rapidly back and forth while thinking of a disturbing memory. Systematic desensitization gradually exposes the client to the feared object while using relaxation techniques to reduce anxiety.

28. c An eclectic view is one that combines a number of different approaches to best fit the needs of the client.

29. c A number of studies have found that the client-therapist relationship (also called the therapeutic alliance) is the best predictor of successful treatment.

30. c Members of minority groups are much more likely to drop out of therapy when compared to members of majority racial and ethnic groups.

31. d The severity of the disorder has not been found to be a cultural barrier for treatment.

32. c Hallucinations, delusions, and bizarre behaviors are defined as psychotic behaviors and are treated with antipsychotic drugs. Antidepressant drugs, not antipsychotic drugs, treat feelings of hopelessness, sadness, and suicide ideations.

33. d   The speed of action and effectiveness is similar among the three classes of antidepressants but the main difference is the number of negative side effects. The SSRIs actually target only one neurotransmitter: serotonin.
34. b   ECT was originally designed to induce seizures in schizophrenics.
35. b   Severing the spinal cord would lead to the very negative side effect of paralysis of the body. Psychosurgery is performed on brain tissue.
36. b   Frontal lobotomies are no longer performed; however, bilateral cingulotomies are still performed on severe cases in which no other treatments have been found to be effective.
37. d   Currently the effects of antidepressants in children are not clearly understood.

CHAPTER GLOSSARY

action therapies	therapies in which the main goal is to change disordered or inappropriate behavior directly.
antianxiety drugs	drugs used to treat and calm anxiety reactions, typically minor tranquilizers.
antidepressant drugs	drugs used to treat depression and anxiety.
antipsychotic drugs	drugs used to treat psychotic symptoms such as delusions, hallucinations, and other bizarre behavior.
arbitrary inference	distortion of thinking in which a person draws a conclusion that is not based on any evidence.
authenticity	the genuine, open, and honest response of the therapist to the client.
aversion therapy	form of behavioral therapy in which an undesirable behavior is paired with an aversive stimulus to reduce the frequency of the behavior.
behavior modification or applied behavior analysis	the use of learning techniques to modify or change undesirable behavior and increase desirable behavior.
behavior therapies	action therapies based on the principles of classical and operant conditioning and aimed at changing disordered behavior without concern for the original causes of such behavior.
bilateral cingulotomy	surgical technique that destroys part of the cingulate gyrus. Used to treat obsessive-compulsive disorder, depression, and chronic pain.
bilateral ECT	electroconvulsive therapy where the electrodes are placed on both sides of the head and forehead.
biomedical therapy	therapy for mental disorders in which a person with a problem is treated with biological or medical methods to relieve symptoms.
Carl Rogers	1902-1987. Humanist psychologist who focused on the role of the self-concept and positive regard on personality development.
cognitive behavioral therapy (CBT)	action therapy in which the goal is to help clients overcome problems by learning to think more rationally and logically.
cognitive therapy	therapy in which the focus is on helping clients recognize distortions in their thinking and replace distorted, unrealistic beliefs with more realistic, helpful thoughts.
contingency contract	a formal, written agreement between the therapist and client (or teacher and student; parent and child) in which goals for behavioral change, reinforcements, and penalties are clearly stated.
counter-conditioning	replacing an old conditioned response with a new one by changing the unconditioned stimulus.

cybertherapy	psychotherapy that is offered on the Internet. Also called online, Internet, or Web therapy or counseling.
directive	therapy in which the therapist actively gives interpretations of a client's statements and may suggest certain behavior or actions.
dream interpretation	the analysis of the elements within a patient's reported dream as a means of revealing unconscious conflicts and desires.
eclectic therapies	therapy style that results from combining elements of several different therapy techniques.
electroconvulsive therapy (ECT)	form of biomedical therapy to treat severe depression in which electrodes are placed on either one or both sides of a person's head and running an electric current through the electrodes that is strong enough to cause a seizure or convulsion.
empathy	the ability of the therapist to understand the feelings of the client.
extinction techniques	the removal of a reinforcer to reduce the frequency of a behavior.
eye-movement desensitization reprocessing (EMDR)	controversial form of therapy for post-traumatic stress disorder and similar anxiety problems in which the client is directed to move the eyes rapidly back and forth while thinking of a disturbing memory.
family counseling	a form of group therapy in which family members meet together with a counselor or therapist to resolve problems that affect the entire family.
flooding	technique for treating phobias and other stress disorders in which the person is rapidly and intensely exposed to the fear-provoking situation or object and prevented from making the usual avoidance or escape response.
free association	Freudian technique in which a patient was encouraged to talk about anything that came to mind without fear of negative evaluations.
Fritz Perls	1893-1970. Developed and popularized Gestalt therapy.
Gestalt therapy	form of directive insight therapy in which the therapist helps the client to accept all parts of his or her feelings and subjective experiences, using leading questions and planned experiences such as role-playing.
group therapy	type of therapy in which a group of clients meet together with a therapist.
humanistic therapy	psychotherapy focused on conscious, subjective experiences of emotion and people's sense of self.
insight therapies	therapies in which the main goal is helping people to gain insight with respect to their behavior, thoughts, and feelings.
latent content	the symbolic or hidden meaning of dreams.
magnification and minimization	distortions of thinking in which a person blows a negative event out of proportion to its importance (magnification) while ignoring relevant positive events (minimization).
manifest content	the actual content of one's dream.
modeling	learning through the observation and imitation of others.
nondirective	therapy in which the therapist remains relatively neutral and does not interpret or take direct actions with regard to the client, instead remaining a calm, nonjudging listener while the client talks.
overgeneralization	distortion of thinking in which a person draws sweeping conclusions based on only one incident or event and applies those conclusions to events that are unrelated to the original.
participant modeling	technique in which a model demonstrates the desired behavior in a step-by-step, gradual process while the client is encouraged to imitate the model.

personalization	distortion of thinking in which a person takes responsibility or blame for events that are unconnected to the person.
person-centered therapy	a nondirective insight therapy based on the work of Carl Rogers in which the client does all the talking and the therapist listens.
prefrontal lobotomy	psychosurgery in which the connections of the prefrontal lobes of the brain to the rear portions are severed.
psychoanalysis	an insight therapy based on the theory of Freud, emphasizing the revealing of unconscious conflicts.
psychodynamic therapy	a newer and more general term for therapies based on psychoanalysis, with an emphasis on transference, shorter treatment times and a more direct therapeutic approach.
psychopharmacology	the use of drugs to control or relieve the symptoms of psychological disorders.
psychosurgery	surgery performed on brain tissue to relieve or control severe psychological disorders.
psychotherapy	therapy for mental disorders in which a person with a problem talks with a psychological professional.
rational-emotive behavioral therapy (REBT)	cognitive-behavioral therapy in which clients are directly challenged in their irrational beliefs and helped to restructure their thinking into more rational belief statements.
reflection	therapy technique in which the therapist restates what the client says rather than interpreting those statements.
reinforcement	the strengthening of a response by following it with a pleasurable consequence or the removal of an unpleasant stimulus.
resistance	occurring when a patient becomes reluctant to talk about a certain topic, either changing the subject or becoming silent.
selective thinking	distortion of thinking in which a person focuses on only one aspect of a situation while ignoring all other relevant aspects.
self-help groups (support groups)	a group composed of people who have similar problems and who meet together without a therapist or counselor for the purpose of discussion, problem solving, and social and emotional support.
Sigmund Freud	1856–1939. Founder of the psychoanalytic school of thought which focuses on the role of the unconscious on behavior.
systematic desensitization	behavior technique used to treat phobias, in which a client is asked to make a list of ordered fears and taught to relax while concentrating on those fears.
therapeutic alliance	the relationship between therapist and client that develops as a warm, caring, accepting relationship characterized by empathy, mutual respect, and understanding.
therapy	treatment methods aimed at making people feel better and function more effectively.
time-out	an extinction process in which a person is removed from the situation that provides reinforcement for undesirable behavior, usually by being placed in a quiet corner or room away from possible attention and reinforcement opportunities.
token economy	the use of objects called tokens to reinforce behavior in which the tokens can be accumulated and exchanged for desired items or privileges.

transference	in psychoanalysis, the tendency for a patient or client to project positive or negative feelings for important people from the past onto the therapist.
unconditional positive regard	referring to the warmth, respect, and accepting atmosphere created by the therapist for the client in client-centered therapy.
unilateral ECT	electroconvulsive therapy where the electrodes are placed on only one side of the head and the forehead.

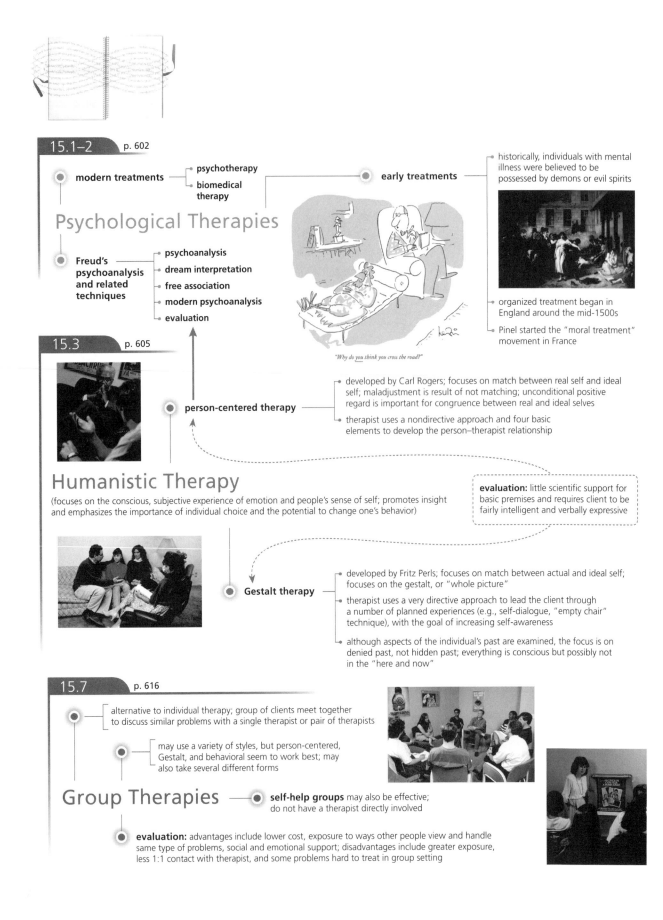

15.1–2   p. 602

modern treatments — psychotherapy
— biomedical therapy

early treatments — historically, individuals with mental illness were believed to be possessed by demons or evil spirits

Psychological Therapies

Freud's psychoanalysis and related techniques
→ psychoanalysis
→ dream interpretation
→ free association
→ modern psychoanalysis
→ evaluation

- organized treatment began in England around the mid-1500s
- Pinel started the "moral treatment" movement in France

"Why do you think you cross the road?"

15.3   p. 605

person-centered therapy
- developed by Carl Rogers; focuses on match between real self and ideal self; maladjustment is result of not matching; unconditional positive regard is important for congruence between real and ideal selves
- therapist uses a nondirective approach and four basic elements to develop the person–therapist relationship

Humanistic Therapy

(focuses on the conscious, subjective experience of emotion and people's sense of self; promotes insight and emphasizes the importance of individual choice and the potential to change one's behavior)

evaluation: little scientific support for basic premises and requires client to be fairly intelligent and verbally expressive

Gestalt therapy
- developed by Fritz Perls; focuses on match between actual and ideal self; focuses on the gestalt, or "whole picture"
- therapist uses a very directive approach to lead the client through a number of planned experiences (e.g., self-dialogue, "empty chair" technique), with the goal of increasing self-awareness
- although aspects of the individual's past are examined, the focus is on denied past, not hidden past; everything is conscious but possibly not in the "here and now"

15.7   p. 616

- alternative to individual therapy; group of clients meet together to discuss similar problems with a single therapist or pair of therapists
- may use a variety of styles, but person-centered, Gestalt, and behavioral seem to work best; may also take several different forms

Group Therapies
— **self-help groups** may also be effective; do not have a therapist directly involved

- **evaluation:** advantages include lower cost, exposure to ways other people view and handle same type of problems, social and emotional support; disadvantages include greater exposure, less 1:1 contact with therapist, and some problems hard to treat in group setting

behavior therapies
action-based therapies operating on the premise that all behaviors, both normal and abnormal, are learned; applied behavior analysis involves functional analysis and learning techniques to increase desirable behaviors and decrease undesirable behaviors

- techniques based on classical conditioning—pairing of stimuli; work of Watson and Jones
- techniques based on operant conditioning—reinforcement, extinction, shaping, and modeling; work of Skinner and Bandura
- **evaluation:** more effective than others for specific behavioral problems (e.g., bed-wetting, overeating, drug addictions, phobic reactions)

THE SEVEN DWARFS AFTER THERAPY

Action Therapies

cognitive therapies
action-based therapies that focus on helping people change their ways of thinking; emphasis on identifying distorted and unrealistic beliefs that lead to maladaptive behavior and problem emotions and then replacing them with more positive, helpful thoughts

- **Beck's cognitive therapy**
- **cognitive–behavioral therapy (CBT)**
- **rational–emotive behavior therapy (REBT)**
- **evaluation:** typically shorter and less expensive than insight therapies; treating the symptom, not the cause, is both a feature and a criticism; especially effective for many disorders, including depression, anxiety disorders, and personality disorders

Table 15.1   **Characteristics of Psychotherapies**

TYPE OF THERAPY	GOAL	KEY PEOPLE
Psychodynamic therapy	Insight	Freud
Person-centered therapy	Insight	Rogers
Gestalt therapy	Insight	Perls
Behavior therapy	Action	Watson, Jones, Skinner, Bandura
Cognitive therapy	Action	Beck
CBT	Action	Various professionals
REBT	Action	Ellis

- effectiveness is not easy to study due to different theories, techniques, time frames for success, etc.; tendency of some therapists to be eclectic (using variety of techniques) is also a challenge

Does Psychotherapy Work?

- where effective, greater success is often tied to the relationship between the therapist and client (therapeutic alliance), a sense of safety, and longer time in therapy

- cultural, ethnic, and gender concerns should also be examined; these factors can affect not only the therapeutic alliance but problem identification and treatment options as well

Table 15.2   **Types of Drugs Used in Psychopharmacology**

CLASSIFICATION	TREATMENT AREAS	SIDE EFFECTS	EXAMPLES
Antipsychotic: Typical Neuroleptic	Positive (excessive) symptoms	Motor problems, tardive dyskinesia	Chlorpromazine, Droperidol, Haloperidol
Antipsychotic: Atypical Neuroleptic	Positive and some negative symptoms of psychoses	Fewer than typical neuroleptics; clozapine may cause serious blood disorder	Risperidone, Clozapine, Aripiprazole
Antianxiety: Minor Tranquilizers	Symptoms of anxiety and phobic reactions	Slight sedative effect; potential for physical dependence	Xanax, Ativan, Valium
Antimanic	Manic behavior	Potential for toxic buildup	Lithium, anticonvulsant drugs
Antidepressants: MAOIs	Depression	Weight gain, constipation, dry mouth, dizziness, headache, drowsiness, insomnia, some sexual arousal disorders	Iproniazid, Isocarboxazid, Phenelzine sulfite, Tranylcypromine sulfate
Antidepressants: Tricyclics	Depression	Skin rashes, blurred vision, lowered blood pressure, weight loss	Imipramine, Desipramine, Amitriptyline, Doxepin
Antidepressants: SSRIs	Depression	Nausea, nervousness, insomnia, diarrhea, rash, agitation, some sexual arousal problems	Fluoxetine, Sertraline, Paroxetine

psychopharmacology
the use of drugs to control or relieve the symptoms of a psychological disorder; may be used alone or in combination with other therapies (see Table 15.2)

Biomedical Therapies

electroconvulsive therapy

- still used to treat severe depression and a few other disorders that have not responded to other forms of treatment
- involves the application of an electric shock and resulting seizure that appears to normalize the balance of neurotransmitters within the brain
- traditional side effects (extreme memory loss, broken bones) have been minimized by lower levels of current and the use of both muscle relaxers and anesthesia

psychosurgery

- used as a last resort, involves cutting into the brain to remove or destroy brain tissues associated with symptoms of a mental disorder
- prefrontal lobotomies were widely used in the mid-1900s up until the development of antipsychotic drugs
- at present, bilateral cingulotomy (involves selective areas of cingulate gyrus) is used, primarily for obsessive-compulsive disorder; has also been used with depression and bipolar disorder

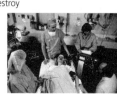

_____

_____

_____

_____

_____

_____

_____

_____

_____

Table 15.1 **Characteristics of Psychotherapies**

Table 15.1   Characteristics of Psychotherapies

TYPE OF THERAPY	GOAL	KEY PEOPLE
Psychodynamic therapy	Insight	Freud
Person-centered therapy	Insight	Rogers
Gestalt therapy	Insight	Perls
Behavior therapy	Action	Watson, Jones, Skinner, Bandura
Cognitive therapy	Action	Beck
CBT	Action	Various professionals
REBT	Action	Ellis

_____

_____

_____

_____

_____

_____

_____

_____

_____

_____

_____

_____

15.2   Freud and Psychoanalysis

15.3   Humanistic Therapy

15.4–15.5   Behavior Therapy

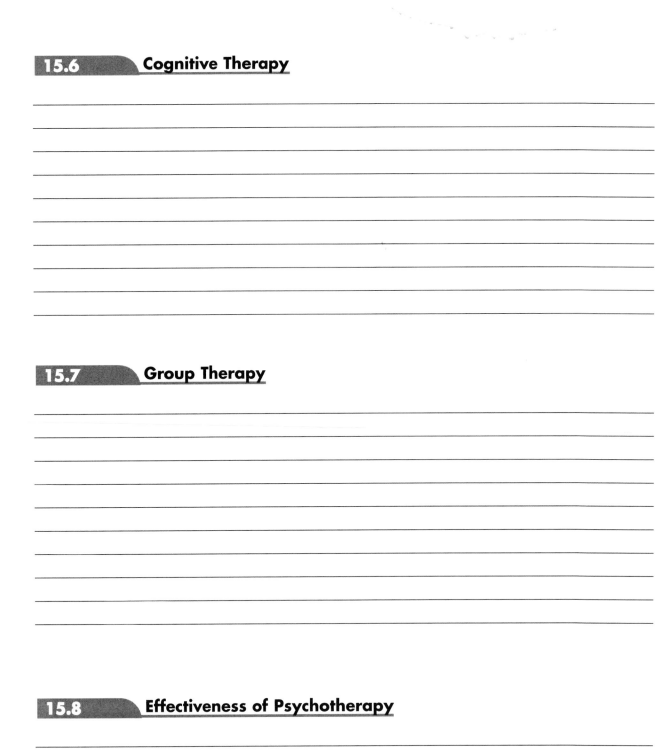

15.6   Cognitive Therapy

15.7   Group Therapy

15.8   Effectiveness of Psychotherapy

_____

_____

_____

_____

_____

_____

_____

_____

_____

_____

Table 15.2 **Types of Drugs Used in Psychopharmacology**

Table 15.2   **Types of Drugs Used in Psychopharmacology**

CLASSIFICATION	TREATMENT AREAS	SIDE EFFECTS	EXAMPLES
Antipsychotic: Typical Neuroleptic	Positive (excessive) symptoms such as delusions or hallucinations	Motor problems, tardive dyskinesia	Chlorpromazine, Droperidol, Haloperidol
Antipsychotic: Atypical Neuroleptic	Positive and some negative symptoms of psychoses	Fewer than typical neuroleptics; clozapine may cause serious blood disorder	Risperidone, Clozapine, Aripiprazole
Antianxiety: Minor Tranquilizers	Symptoms of anxiety and phobic reactions	Slight sedative effect; potential for physical dependence	Xanax, Ativan, Valium
Antimanic	Manic behavior	Potential for toxic buildup	Lithium, anticonvulsant drugs
Antidepressants: MAOIs	Depression	Weight gain, constipation, dry mouth, dizziness, headache, drowsiness, insomnia, some sexual arousal disorders	Iproniazid, Isocarboxazid, Phenelzine sulfite, Tranylcypromine sulfate
Antidepressants: Tricyclics	Depression	Skin rashes, blurred vision, lowered blood pressure, weight loss	Imipramine, Desipramine, Amitriptyline, Doxepin
Antidepressants: SSRIs	Depression	Nausea, nervousness, insomnia, diarrhea, rash, agitation, some sexual arousal problems	Fluoxetine, Sertraline, Paroxetine

_____

_____

_____

_____

_____

_____

_____

_____

_____

NOTES